MW00996263

# Substance Abuse Prevention

## The Intersection of Science and Practice

**Julie A. Hogan**

**Kristen Reed Gabrielsen**

**Nora Luna**

**Denise Grothaus**

*University of Nevada, Reno*

Boston   New York   San Francisco
Mexico City   Montreal   Toronto   London   Madrid   Munich   Paris
Hong Kong   Singapore   Tokyo   Cape Town   Sydney

**Executive editor:**  *Virginia Lanigan*
**Editorial assistant:**  *Rob Champagne*
**Marketing manager:**  *Taryn Wahlquist*
**Manufacturing buyer:**  *JoAnne Sweeney*
**Cover designer:**  *hannusdesign.com*
**Production coordinator:**  *Pat Torelli Publishing Services*
**Editorial-production service:**  *Stratford Publishing Services*
**Electronic composition:**  *Stratford Publishing Services*

For related titles and support materials, visit our online catalog at www.ablongman.com.

Between the time Website information is gathered and then published, it is not unusual for some sites to have closed. Also, the transcription of URLs can result in unintended typographical errors. The publisher would appreciate notification where these errors occur so that they may be corrected in subsequent editions.

**Library of Congress Cataloging-in-Publication Data**

Substance abuse prevention : the intersection of science and practice / Julie Hogan . . . [ et al.].
    p.  cm.
    Includes bibliographical references and index.
    ISBN 0-205-34162-4
    1. Substance abuse--United States--Prevention. 2. Drug abuse--United
States--Prevention. I. Hogan, Julie

HV4999.2 .S82 2003
362.29'17'0973--dc21                                                2002071698

Printed in the United States of America

10   9   8   7   6   5   4                    06   05

*This textbook is dedicated to all the substance abuse prevention specialists who have spent their lives trying to make a drug-free healthy lifestyle a reality for all youth. Additionally, this textbook is dedicated to children and youth who have made the choice to engage life to its fullest extent without the use of tobacco, alcohol, and other drugs.*

# C O N T E N T S

# PREFACE

*Substance Abuse Prevention: The Intersection of Science and Practice* represents our desire to share the wealth of information we have acquired during this exciting time in the field of substance abuse prevention. Never before has such a strong body of knowledge existed regarding "what works" in prevention.

However, even with all the existing knowledge, much of what we know works in substance abuse prevention is not being applied. Furthermore, what we know does *not* work is still being implemented in communities across the nation. Consequently, we felt strongly that a book needed to be written to educate future and current prevention professionals about the field of substance abuse prevention.

Information about what works and what does not work has not been gained from the efforts of researchers alone. Much of what researchers know comes only after numerous trials in the field. Grassroots prevention professionals from communities all across the nation performed the trials. They struggled to acquire knowledge in a newly emerging field where little existed previously. They created action plans based on bits of theory and research that they acquired. Then they measured their results to determine their effectiveness and continued to improve their programs even when it meant letting go of beloved strategies and activities that weren't leading to the desired effect—reducing substance abuse within their communities.

Because the state-of-the-art information contained in this book stems from the wisdom of both researchers and those practicing prevention, the information can easily be applied when working in communities. Those who aspire to foster the development of healthy communities can discover within this book "shortcuts" for making prevention a powerful and effective component of their community public health approaches.

We believe the substance abuse prevention information in this book fits within the context of many disciplines. These include social work, criminal justice, nursing, psychology, sociology, education, public health, recreation, human and community sciences, and others. Specific topics within the book include the evolution of prevention, prevention research findings, comprehensive prevention program planning, facts about drugs, the cultural context and ethics of prevention, incorporating human development theory into prevention, the role of media in prevention, evaluating prevention efforts, communication strategies, and grant writing.

Throughout the book, suggestions for discussion topics and application exercises stimulate thoughtful consideration. They help readers begin the process of applying new information to the work they will begin in their communities. Finally, the book offers a concluding chapter that will help readers to track their own evolution through the process of learning about both the science and the art of prevention.

This book will ultimately help to professionalize the field of prevention. Professionalizing the field of prevention will help to ensure that prevention professionals will engage in effective, comprehensive strategies that are grounded in proven theories. Additionally, professionals will be better able to provide culturally competent services to individuals, families, and communities. They will rigorously test what they are doing to guide the improvement of their programs and to ensure their effectiveness.

While this book offers a significant amount of information regarding substance abuse prevention, readers are encouraged to remain inquisitive about emerging research. Because the field is new, much valuable information can be obtained from many resources. The Internet is one valuable source of prevention information that enables readers to remain freshly informed.

We hope that this book will provide aspiring and current prevention professionals with the information and skills needed to begin their work in the substance abuse prevention field. With the skills and information about what works and what does not work in prevention, these professionals will enhance their effectiveness in creating healthy communities across our nation.

## Acknowledgments

We gratefully acknowledge the love and support of our friends and families during this endeavor. Special thanks are extended to John Dell and Anna Hogan Dell, Eric Gabrielsen, Luis and Agueda Luna, and Tom and Elise Grothaus, who provided much emotional support and patience during the development and writing of this book.

We are appreciative of Steve Rock for inspiring the dream that became this book. Also, we thank Gary Fisher for his guidance and support throughout the writing and editing process.

We wish to thank the following individuals for their reviews, suggestions, and technical assistance: Diane Arnold, Teresa Carrera, Gretchen Casey, Don Coyhis, Susan Doctor, William Gallegos, Jackie Hogan, Elda Luna, Ali Makley, Janet Myers, Mary O'Malia, Jennifer Rasmussen, Margie Reed, Nancy Roget, Garry Rubinstein, Ken Smith, and Liz Wilhelm. Our appreciation also goes to Carl Hanson, Montana State University-Billings; Michael Langer, prevention professional; and Jill Parker, Bear River Health Department for their insightful review and comments on the manuscript, and to Virginia Lanigan, executive editor, Allyn and Bacon.

We would also like to thank Beth Green for allowing us to build upon her wonderful ideas for the Logic Model and Evaluation chapter of the textbook. Furthermore, CSAP's National CAPT Steering Committee graciously allowed us to publish their valuable lessons-learned paper as an appendix to this textbook. We are also thankful for the work done by Colorado preventionists who pioneered the way in providing prevention education through their Prevention Generalist Training curriculum.

# ABOUT THE AUTHORS

JULIE A. HOGAN, PH.D.
KRISTEN REED GABRIELSEN, M.P.H., C.P.S.
NORA LUNA, B.S., C.P.S.
DENISE GROTHAUS, B.S., C.P.S.

Currently, all four authors work as administrative faculty members at the University of Nevada, Reno's Center for the Application of Substance Abuse Technologies. Collectively, they have over thirty-eight years of substance abuse prevention experience, including work at the community, county, statewide, and national levels. All the authors provide technical assistance to state agencies and community groups on science-based prevention practice; three authors have obtained certification in substance abuse prevention; and one author conducted an evaluation of a substance abuse prevention program for her doctoral dissertation. As faculty members, several of the authors have taught a number of college courses in substance abuse prevention, both at the undergraduate and graduate level. They have also conducted trainings and workshops on science-based substance abuse prevention for national, state, and local audiences. The authors are committed to bridging the gap between substance abuse prevention research and practice.

To contact the authors, please write to:

Center for the Application of Substance Abuse Technologies
University of Nevada, Reno
Mail Stop 279
Reno, Nevada 89557-0258

# 1

# Introduction

The profession of substance abuse prevention, like many professions, is in the evolutionary process of development. Training, university courses, textbook development, and certification are processes that occur as disciplines develop. This chapter explains the evolutionary processes of professions, defines some key concepts unique to the field of substance abuse, discusses the importance of theory when implementing actual substance abuse prevention programs, and presents a short history of United States drug policy development.

The field of substance abuse prevention is currently evolving into a more professionalized field. Substance abuse prevention professionals are being introduced to credentialing requirements through their state government. However, before taking the credentialing examination, students are in need of education and training in substance abuse prevention. This textbook provides an overview of some of the crucial learnings required before taking certification examinations in prevention. As in any field, learning key concepts allows prevention professionals to share ideas and information. Several of these key concepts, including use, misuse, abuse, and addiction, are explored in this chapter to foster a deeper understanding of the stages of substance use and abuse worked with in prevention. Theory, in the field of substance abuse prevention and in all disciplines, provides a common framework of understanding for people to implement successful programming. This chapter introduces a discussion on the cycle of theoretical development that occurs in all disciplines, including the field of substance abuse prevention. Finally, an understanding of United States prevention policy and programming orients the reader to past successes and failures.

This chapter concludes with a conceptual discussion of each of the subsequent chapters in this textbook. This chapter overview is provided to orient readers to the layout of the book for successful navigation and learning. Each chapter proceeds in a specific order and builds on the information introduced in prior chapters.

## Evolution and Training of the Prevention Discipline

Hundreds of years ago, barbers who used techniques such as "bloodletting" practiced medicine, according to Fisher and Harrison (2000). Fifty years ago, school counseling was conducted by teachers or athletic coaches who had no formal training in counseling or human behavior. Twenty years ago, in the alcohol and other drug field, many treatment providers were alcoholics and addicts in recovery who used only their own recovery experience to help others. Today, physicians now undergo years of academic training and extensive internships. Nearly all school counselors complete graduate-training programs specifically designed for their field. Finally, more and more universities have undergraduate and graduate courses of study in addiction counseling.

Professions often evolve in this manner. For purposes of this discussion, a **profession** is defined as a vocation or occupation requiring advanced education and training, and involving intellectual skills, such as medicine, law, or teaching. As the public comes to understand the value or need of a discipline, there is often an effort to develop standards for training and practice of the profession. Frequently, states develop certification and/or licensure requirements and universities develop programs to train people to work in the profession. There is logic behind this sequence. In medicine, barbers were not very effective in curing illnesses and diseases. Teachers and coaches were ill equipped to deal with the complex problems of youth in the 1960s. Recovering individuals did not know how to treat poly-drug abusers, culturally and ethnically diverse clients, women and their children, addicts involved with the criminal justice system, clients with co-occurring disorders, and so on. Therefore, the stimulus to develop standards of training and practice for a profession is often the lack of expertise of practitioners to handle the complexity of the discipline.

The **ATOD** (alcohol, tobacco, and other drug) prevention field is currently in the beginning stages of this evolution. Society's need to address the ATOD problems of this country combined with a growing body of knowledge of "what works" is stimulating an effort to increase the professionalism of prevention professionals. In addition, the prevention field has had the burden of explaining why some highly publicized, widespread prevention programs have failed to demonstrate an impact on the ATOD use patterns of youth. Consequently, there are state and national efforts to develop certification standards for prevention professionals. Universities are developing courses and internships in prevention. In addition, government entities that distribute prevention dollars are insisting that prevention programs use "scientifically defensible" prevention strategies and programs and use established practices to evaluate the outcomes of funded programs. A well-trained staff is necessary to meet these requirements.

This textbook is designed to be part of the effort to professionalize the prevention field. We know that there are numerous individuals working in prevention programs in this country who want to increase their effectiveness and are eager to find out "what works." Furthermore, there are many college students who are interested in working in prevention and need training and experience to develop entry-level competence. This textbook offers a general overview of the prevention field and serves as a stimulus for further learning.

## Attitudes about Alcohol, Tobacco, and Other Drugs (ATOD)

Close your eyes and visualize an alcoholic. Now visualize a crack addict. What were your visualizations like? What was the ethnic background of your alcoholic? What sex was your crack addict? Did you see a seedy, down-and-out person going through garbage cans? Did you visualize a well-known comedian or a professional athlete? If a 15-year-old is caught with a marijuana joint, does that person have a problem? What about the same teenager with a bottle of beer? (Fisher & Harrison, 2000).

It is essential for professionals who work in the ATOD prevention field to examine their attitudes about ATOD. Obviously, knowledge is important and can affect some attitudes. However, sometimes people are not aware how firmly their attitudes are entrenched. For example, most people know that addiction to alcohol and other drugs is not a function of sex, ethnicity, or socioeconomic class. However, when visualizing an alcoholic and a crack addict, there may have been some stereotypes that occurred during the visualization process. That is normal and is not harmful as long as it's understood that these stereotypes do not reflect reality. For example, when working in a prevention program that has a largely white clientele, it would be erroneous to assume that crack is not used in the community. A 15-year-old with a joint or a beer may or may not have a problem. Only a chemical dependency assessment can determine this. However, in this case, the drug of choice is not related to a conclusion as to whether a problem exists or not (Fisher & Harrison, 2000).

Prevention providers are encouraged to examine their attitudes about ATOD and to learn as much about substances as possible. The information found in Chapter 4, "Facts about Drugs," is only a start. While prevention professionals certainly do not need to be experts on pharmacology, they do need to understand basic information about the categories of drugs and their effects. This information should be based on science and not on scare tactics (Fisher & Harrison, 2000).

## Definitions of Use, Misuse, Abuse, and Dependence/Addiction

For most helping professionals without extensive training in the field of alcohol and other drugs, it is somewhat difficult to determine whether a client's substance use is problematic. They may rely on personal experience and information (or misinformation) that they pick up. For example, a high school counselor gets a call from a parent of one of the students. The young man is 17 years old, came home from a party on Saturday night smelling of alcohol, and admitted to drinking at the party. His parents belong to a religious group that prohibits the use of alcohol, so neither has any experience with alcohol or other drug use. They want to know if their son has a problem. The high school counselor did her share of experimentation in adolescence but is a moderate user as an adult. She assures the parents that nearly all adolescents experiment and they have nothing to worry about. Is she right (Fisher & Harrison, 2000)?

A simple conceptualization of the distinction between different levels of use can be helpful to the health professional in determining the type of intervention that is appropriate for a client. Yet, these definitions are not appropriate for diagnosis. They are simply a guide for recommending the appropriate course of action for a client. The following definitions are offered to frame the discussion of alcohol and other drug abuse progression. It should be understood that multiple definitions of use, abuse, and misuse exist. However, for purposes of this discussion, these definitions are offered for consideration (Fisher & Harrison, 2000). Please note that a more complete discussion will occur on the theories of addiction in Chapter 4.

Nearly everyone uses alcohol or other drugs (including caffeine and tobacco) at some point in their life. We define "**substance use**" as the ingestion of alcohol or other drugs without the experience of any negative consequences. If our high school student imbibed a beer at the party and his parents had not found out, one could say that he had used alcohol. Any drug can be "used," according to this definition. However, the type of drug taken and the characteristics of the individual contribute to the probability of experiencing negative consequences. For example, it is illegal for minors to drink alcohol. Therefore, the probability that our high school student will experience negative consequences from drinking alcohol may be far greater than the probability is for an adult. The chances that an adult will experience negative consequences from shooting heroin are greater than are negative consequences from drinking alcohol (Fisher & Harrison, 2000).

When a person experiences negative consequences from the use of alcohol or other drugs, or the use of these substances is illegal, it is defined as "**substance misuse**." Again, a large percentage of the population misuses alcohol or other drugs at some point. Our high school student misused alcohol because his parents found out he had been drinking at a party and because it is illegal for him to drink. Many people overuse alcohol at some point, become ill, and experience the symptoms of a hangover. This is misuse. However, misuse does not imply that the negative consequences are minor. Let us say that an adult uses alcohol on an infrequent basis. It is her 30th birthday, and her friends throw a surprise party. She drinks more than usual and, on the way home, is arrested for driving under the influence of alcohol or other drugs (DUI). She really does not have any problems with alcohol, but, in this instance, the consequence is not minor (Fisher & Harrison, 2000).

One may be wondering about the heavy user of alcohol or other drugs who does not appear to experience negative consequences. First of all, remember that these definitions are meant to provide the helping professional with a simple conceptualization as a guide. Second, the probability of experiencing negative consequences is directly related to the frequency and level of use. If a person uses alcohol or other drugs on an occasional basis, the probability of negative consequences is far less than if one uses them on a daily basis. However, since we are talking about probability, it is possible that a person could be a daily, heavy user and not experience negative consequences that are obvious to others. We say "obvious" because people may be damaging their health without anyone being aware of this for a long period of time.

"**Substance abuse**" is defined as the continued use of alcohol or other drugs in spite of negative consequences. Our high school student is grounded for two weeks by his parents. Right after his grounding is completed, he goes to a party and drinks again. He continues to drink in spite of the consequences he experienced. Now, he might become sneakier and escape detection. However, as discussed previously, the probability of detection increases the more he uses and, if he does have a problem with alcohol, it is likely that his use will be discovered. As another example, let us go back to the DUI the woman got after her birthday party. For people who do not have an alcohol or other drug problem, getting a DUI would be so disturbing that they would avoid alcohol altogether or only use at home. If, a month after the DUI, the woman was at another party or a bar drinking when she would later be driving, this would be considered abuse (Fisher & Harrison, 2000).

**Addiction/dependence** is the "compulsive" use of alcohol or other drugs regardless of the consequences. Hypothetically, assume that a substance abuse professional worked with a man who had received three DUIs in one year. He was on probation and would be sentenced to one year in prison if he were caught drinking and driving. Yet he continued to drink. The man was clearly addicted to alcohol, as the negative consequences did not affect his use (Fisher & Harrison, 2000).

## Justification for Theory

As disciplines develop, one of the core commonalities they achieve is a body of theories, which drive both research and application. A **theory** is a "formulation of apparent relationships or underlying principles of certain observed phenomena which has been verified to some degree" (Guralnik, 1984, p. 1475). This textbook advances the current theories used in substance abuse prevention, which include the perspectives of risk and protective factors, resiliency, and the developmental assets model. Some theories and related research have reached high levels of **scientific rigor**, which means that they have been tested and have shown some consistent correlations or outcomes. All disciplines support certain theories that attempt to explain why a certain condition exists. In substance abuse prevention, for example, risk and protective factor theory predicts that the greater the number of risk factors, the greater the likelihood that youth will abuse substances at some point in their development. Also, the greater the number of protective factors, the less likely that substance abuse will occur. This is important because protective factors do not decrease substance abuse that already exists.

The ultimate goal of this textbook is to move the field of substance abuse prevention to "praxis." **Praxis** means the combination of both theory and practice. The practice of substance abuse prevention should be enlightened and informed by theory. One of the challenges faced in prevention is understanding theory and the findings from research to the degree that they can be applied to substance abuse prevention programs. When this goal is achieved, "prevention praxis" has occurred. If the prevention field did not have a theoretical base, prevention programs would be conducted based on what people thought or felt were the right ideas. In this case, prevention professionals would try to glean progress from only their own observations and would not consider what had been tried, tested, changed, and tested again. Theory enhances the overall understanding of how to prevent substance abuse by answering questions about why some youths use substances and others do not.

The textbook presents, in depth, the three most dominant theoretical perspectives today. This does not mean that other theories do not exist or that these are the three best theories available. Theories change and go through a dynamic process, as do most things in life. Thomas Kuhn (1970) identified four stages or changes through which theories cycle, including normal science, anomalies, crisis, and revolution. Normal science, the first stage, is when theory is accepted as the dominant view in the field. Researchers experiment with new applications of the established theory, extend and refine it, and accumulate knowledge. The second stage is the anomalies stage. During this stage, people question why the theory does not fit the social problem they are trying to solve. Things happen in the social world and the theory cannot explain why these things are occurring. The third stage is crisis. During this step questions abound, people severely critique the theory, and new theories emerge that propose alternative ways of looking at the social problem. Anomalies to the original theory mount and accumulate as people begin formally attacking the perspective. The fourth stage is called "revolution." During revolution a new theory establishes itself as the reigning paradigm. The old theory is overthrown and the new theory establishes itself as the dominant perspective.

The point in explaining this evolutionary process is that the theories of today may not be the theories of tomorrow. If this is true, why even consider any theory at all if it will go through this process eventually? The answer is that all theories help people understand the larger social context of substance abuse prevention. Without theories to guide us, we simply employ old techniques that may "feel" as though they work, but in fact may be harmful. Theories, like research knowledge, change over time. This is normal, expected, and a valid part of a developing discipline.

A history of substance abuse prevention in the United States is offered in Box 1.1.

---

**BOX  1.1**

## United States History of Substance Abuse Prevention

Alcoholic beverages have been a part of the Nation's past since the landing of the Pilgrims. According to "Alcohol and Public Policy: Beyond the Shadow of Prohibition," a publication commissioned by the National Institute on Alcohol Abuse and Alcoholism (**NIAAA**) and prepared by the National Academy of Sciences, the colonists brought with them from Europe a high regard for alcoholic beverages, which were considered an important part of their diet. Drinking was pervasive because alcohol was regarded primarily as a healthy substance with preventive and curative powers, not as an intoxicant. Alcohol was also believed to be conducive to social as well as personal health. It played an essential role in rituals of conviviality and collective activity, such as barn raisings. While drunkenness was condemned and punished, it was viewed only as an abuse of a God-given gift.

The first temperance movement began in the early 1800s in response to dramatic increases in production and consumption of alcoholic beverages, which also coincided with rapid demographic changes. Agitation against ardent spirits and the public disorder they spawned gradually increased during the 1820s. In addition, inspired by the writings of Benjamin Rush, the concept that alcohol was addicting and that this addiction was capable of corrupting the mind and the body took hold. The American Society of Temperance, created in 1826 by clergymen, spread the anti-drinking gospel. By 1835, out of a total population of 13 million citizens, 1.5 million had taken the pledge to refrain from distilled spirits. The first wave of the temperance movement (1825 to 1855) resulted in dramatic reductions in the consumption of distilled spirits, although beer drinking increased sharply after 1850.

The second wave of the temperance movement occurred in the late 1800s with the emergence of the Women's Christian Temperance Movement that, unlike the first wave, embraced the concept of prohibition. It was marked both by the recruitment of women into the movement and the mobilization of crusades to close down saloons. The movement set out to remove the destructive substance, and the industries that promoted its use, from the country. The movement held that while some drinkers may escape problems of alcohol use, even moderate drinkers flirted with danger.

The culmination of this second wave was the passage of the 18th Amendment and the Volstead Act, which took effect in 1920. While Prohibition was successful in reducing per capita consumption and some problems related to drinking, its social turmoil resulted in its repeal in 1933.

Since the repeal of Prohibition, the dominant view of alcohol problems has been that alcoholism is the principle problem. With its focus on treatment, the rise of the alcoholism movement depoliticized alcohol problems as the object of attention, as the alcoholic was considered a deviant from the predominant styles of life of either abstinence or "normal" drinking. The alcoholism movement is based on the belief that chronic or addictive drinking is limited to a few, highly susceptible individuals suffering from the disease of alcoholism. The disease concept of alcoholism focuses on individual vulnerability, be it genetic, biochemical, psychological or social/cultural in nature. Under this view, if the collective problems of each alcoholic are solved, it follows that society's alcohol problem will be solved.

Nevertheless, the pre-Prohibition view of alcohol as a special commodity has persisted in American society and is an accepted legacy of alcohol control policies. Following the repeal of Prohibition, all States restricted the sale of alcoholic beverages in one way or another in order to prevent or reduce certain alcohol problems. In general, however, alcohol control policies disappeared from the public agenda as both the alcoholism movement and the alcoholic beverage industry embraced the view that the problem existed with the people and not the beverage.

This view of alcoholism problems has also been the dominant force in contemporary alcohol abuse prevention. Until recently, the principal prevention strategies focused on education and early treatment. Within this view, education is intended to inform society about the disease and to teach people about the early warning signs so that they can initiate treatment as soon as possible. Efforts focus on "high-risk" populations and attempt to correct a suspect process or flaw in the individual, such as low self-esteem or lack of social skills. The belief is that the success of education and treatment efforts in solving each alcoholic's problem will solve society's alcohol problem as well. Contemporary alcohol abuse prevention began in the 1970s as new information on the nature, magnitude and incidence of alcohol problems raised public awareness that alcohol can be problematic when used by any drinker, depending upon the situation. There was a renewed emphasis on the diverse consequences of alcohol use—particularly trauma associated with drinking and driving, fires and violence, as well as long-term health consequences.

The history of nonmedical drug use, other than alcohol, and the development of policies in response to drug use, also extends back to the early settlement of the country. Like alcohol, the classification of certain drugs as legal or illegal has changed over time. These changes sometimes had racial and class overtones. According to Mosher and Yanagisako (1993), for example, Prohibition was in part a response to the drinking practices of European immigrants, who became the new lower class. Cocaine and opium were legal during the 19th century and were favored drugs among the middle and upper classes. Cocaine became illegal after it became associated with African Americans following Reconstruction. Opium was first restricted in California in 1875 when it became associated with Chinese immigrant workers. Marijuana was legal until the 1930s, when it became associated with Mexicans. LSD, legal in the 1950s, became illegal in 1967 when it became associated with the counterculture.

By the end of the 19th century, concern had grown over the indiscriminate use of these drugs, especially the addicting patent medicines. Cocaine, opium and morphine were common ingredients in various potions sold over the counter. Until 1903, cocaine was an ingredient of Coca-Cola®. Heroin, which was isolated in 1868, was hailed as a non-addicting treatment for morphine addiction and alcoholism. As time progressed, States began to enact control and prescription laws, and in 1906 Congress passed the Pure Food and Drug Act. It was designed to control opiate addiction by requiring labels on the amount of drugs contained in products, including opium, morphine and heroin. It also required accurate labeling of products containing alcohol, marijuana and cocaine. The Harrison Act of 1914 imposed a system of taxes on opium and coca products with registration and record-keeping requirements in an effort to control their sale or distribution. However, it did not prohibit the legal supply of certain drugs, especially opiates.

Current drug laws are rooted in the 1970 Controlled Substances Act. Under this Act, drugs are classified according to their medical use, their potential for abuse, and their likelihood of

*(continued)*

BOX  **1.1**    **Continued**

producing dependence. The act contains provisions for adding drugs to the schedule and rescheduling drugs. It also establishes maximum penalties for the criminal manufacture or distribution of scheduled drugs.

Increases in per capita alcohol consumption as well as increased use of illegal drugs during the 1960s raised public concern regarding alcohol and other drug problems. Prevention issues gained prominence on the national level with the creation of the National Institute on Alcohol Abuse and Alcoholism (NIAAA) in 1971 and the National Institute on Drug Abuse (**NIDA**) in 1974. In addition to mandates for research and the management of national programs for treatment, both Institutes included prevention components.

To further prevention initiatives at the federal level, the Anti-Drug Abuse Act of 1986 created the United States Office for Substance Abuse Prevention (OSAP), which consolidated alcohol and other drug prevention activities under the Alcohol, Drug Abuse and Mental Health Administration (ADAMHA). The ADAMHA block grant mandate called for states to set aside 20 percent of the alcohol and drug funds for prevention while 80 percent remained for treatment services. In a 1992 reorganization, OSAP was changed to the Center for Substance Abuse Prevention (**CSAP**), part of the new Substance Abuse and Mental Health Services Administration (**SAMHSA**), retaining its major program areas, while the research institutes of NIAAA and NIDA transferred to the National Institutes of Health (NIH).

The Office of National Drug Control Policy (**ONDCP**) was established by the Anti-Drug Abuse Act of 1988. Its primary objective was to develop a drug control policy that included roles for the public and private sectors to "restore order and security to American neighborhoods, to dismantle drug trafficking organizations, to help people break the habit of drug use, and to prevent those who have never used illegal drugs from starting." In early 1991, underage alcohol use was included among the drugs to be addressed by ONDCP.

*Source: The Prevention Primer,* Center for Substance Abuse Prevention, 1993, pp. 68–71.

In the 1990s, despite the best efforts of the federal, state, and local governments, drug abuse continued to pose serious threats to the health, social, and economic stability of American communities. However, a hopeful trend began. The knowledge gained through prevention research (e.g., the results of demonstration projects and program evaluations) has led to the development of formal theories, "**promising approaches**," "**best practices**," and "**model programs**." Promising approaches are defined as programs for which the level of certainty from available evidence is too low to support generalized conclusions, but for which there is some empirical basis for predicting that further research could support such conclusions. Best practices are defined as prevention strategies, activities, or approaches, which have been shown through research and evaluation to be effective in the prevention and/or delay of substance use or abuse. Finally, model programs are defined as prevention programs that have been rigorously evaluated and have repeatedly demonstrated positive outcomes.

In the late 1990s, policies, laws, and norms changed to influence the incidence and prevalence of drug use. Tobacco companies were forced to stop unethical advertising campaigns geared toward teenagers. In addition, many communities increased the price of alcohol and tobacco through excise taxes and passed ordinances prohibiting billboard advertisements by the alcohol industry.

Table 1.1 depicts a snapshot view of the preceding discussion. For the purposes of this textbook, however, only the past 50 years of drug prevention perspectives, strategies, and activities are presented in the table.

**TABLE 1.1    A Timeline of Prevention**

| Time | National Perspective | Strategy | Activities |
|------|---------------------|----------|------------|
| 1950s | Drugs are a problem of the ghetto, used to escape pain and to avoid reality. | Scare tactics. | Films and speakers. |
| Early 1960s | Drugs are used to escape pain and to avoid reality, but they're more than just a problem of the ghetto. | Scare tactics. | Films and speakers. |
| Late 1960s | Drugs are used to intensify life, to have psychedelic experiences. Drug use is considered a national epidemic. | Information. | Films and speakers. |
| Early 1970s | A variety of drugs are used for a variety of reasons: to speed up experiences, to intensify experiences, to escape, to expand perceptions, to relieve boredom, and to conform to peers. | Drug education. | Curricula based on factual information. |
| Mid- to late 1970s | Users become more sophisticated and society develops an increasing tolerance of drug use. | Affective education and alternatives to drug use. | Curricula based on communication, decision making, values clarification, and self-esteem. |
| Late 1970s to early 1980s | Parents begin to form organizations that combat the incidence of drug abuse. | Affective education, alternatives to drug use and training. | Blaming and cooperation. |
| Late 1980s to mid-1990s | Drug use is highly complex. | Partnerships. | Research-based curricula, linkages, and peer programs. |
| Mid-1990s to 2000 | The gap between research and application is gradually being bridged. | Replication of research-based models and application of research-based approaches. | Environmental approaches, comprehensive programs targeting many domains and strategies, evaluation of prevention programs, media campaigns, and culturally sensitive programs. |

*Source:* Adapted with permission from the Rocky Mountain Center for Health Promotion and Education, *Prevention Generalist Training.* Copyright © 1991, Alcohol and Drug Abuse Division, Colorado Department of Health and Human Services.

# Building Blocks for the Prevention Profession

This textbook is designed to provide some crucial building blocks of knowledge for the seasoned prevention professional and to "jump-start" the learning process for new professionals in the field. It contains science-based information, orients the professional to current issues in prevention, and provides many essential competencies one needs when working in prevention programs or coalitions.

As with any developing profession, key building blocks or essential facts need to be presented and explored to train new members in the field. This textbook has many chapters that are important to understand before implementing prevention programming. Just as the discipline of medicine began by advancing fundamental courses needed for all future doctors, this textbook contains fundamental information for all prevention professionals. This textbook, as mentioned earlier, is to be viewed as the "first step" to gaining knowledge about the field of substance abuse prevention.

The textbook is divided into 11 chapters. Each chapter functions as an independent building block that orients new professionals to the field of prevention. It offers core knowledge that begins the lifelong process of educating the student about substance abuse prevention. The following building blocks of successful prevention programs will be carefully explored in this textbook:

- The program is based on sound theory and uses practices grounded in research.
- The program is systematically planned and assessed.
- Knowledgeable and competent staff facilitates the program.
- The program addresses participants from a variety of backgrounds and cultures, and it uses a code of ethics.
- The program is developmentally appropriate.
- The program incorporates the media.
- The program is evaluated.

It is very important for prevention professionals to understand each of these building blocks and to apply them in their daily prevention work. Without this knowledge and skill, prevention professionals will continue to make the same mistakes made historically. Each textbook chapter, then, has been developed to teach these building blocks or skills to students who may choose to work as prevention professionals in the future.

**Chapter 2, Prevention Research**, is an in-depth chapter on current prevention research. This module gives in-depth information on science-based prevention research findings, Center for Substance Abuse Prevention (CSAP) strategies, and best practices. Tips are given on how to design an effective prevention program. Three dominant theoretical orientations are thoroughly reviewed in this chapter, including risk and protective factor theory, resiliency, and developmental assets.

**Chapter 3, Prevention Program Planning**, contains information on planning, assessment, and evaluation and highlights the seven steps for building a successful prevention program. All the information contained in this section is science based and is designed to encourage a careful prevention planning process. This chapter also contains information on the Institute of Medicine's (**IOM**) classification scheme for prevention: universal, selective, and indicated.

**Chapter 4, Facts about Drugs**, provides an elementary orientation to pharmacology and to the various models of addiction. It is important for all prevention professionals to understand some basic facts about tobacco, alcohol, and other drugs. Although an extensive understanding of drugs is not necessary for prevention work, understanding the effects of tobacco, alcohol, and other drugs is helpful.

**Chapter 5, The Cultural Context and Ethics of Prevention**, presents prevention information on culture and ethics. Culture is an important attribute to consider when planning and implementing prevention programs. Discussion in this chapter centers on defining culture, elements of culture, characteristics of culture, and how to adapt prevention programs to specific cultural populations. Identifying a code of ethics for the prevention field is also introduced here. This is important because ethics guide professionals on what behavior is appropriate when encountering a variety of situations.

**Chapter 6, Incorporating Human Development Theory into Prevention**, contains information on human development models. It is important for prevention professionals to understand human development needs and desires before working with a prevention population. Erik Erikson's classical developmental stages are presented as one approach to understanding human development. This chapter is not meant to be an exhaustive overview of the multiple theories and perspectives in human development, but is intended to engage the prevention professional in thinking about developmental stages when designing a prevention program and working with people.

**Chapter 7, The Media and Prevention**, provides a special discussion on how the media influences prevention. Social marketing, which is a relatively new development in the field of prevention, is discussed. This provides positive "social norming" to media messages about alcohol, tobacco, and other drugs. An overview of media advocacy is provided with information on the skills needed to advocate for prevention policies. Additionally, media literacy, which is the ability to analyze messages critically, is discussed.

**Chapter 8, The Logic Model and Evaluation**, provides information on scientific methods that measure programmatic impact. This chapter discusses the logic model, defines key concepts used in the science of evaluation, and teaches the reader how to use evaluation to enhance and improve prevention services.

**Chapter 9, Communication Strategies**, provides information for prevention professionals on the basics of communication skills. This chapter includes a discussion on a classical communication model, tips for speaking in public, successful facilitation skills, and leadership styles. Numerous examples that demonstrate why good communication skills are necessary for prevention professionals are provided.

**Chapter 10, Grant Writing**, provides some pragmatic suggestions for writing, and winning, successful grants. A discussion is provided on the differences between approaching government agencies and foundations to fund substance abuse prevention programs. Additionally, some resources are suggested to help prevention professionals gain knowledge in this area.

**Chapter 11, Bringing It All Together**, summarizes all of the chapters and challenges readers to begin applying the knowledge they have learned. Some sample grant applications are provided that prompt students' skills and get them thinking about how to apply the core building blocks to actual grant applications. Additionally, a case study is provided in the appendix, which allows students to read about the lessons learned from the Center for Substance Abuse Prevention's National Centers for the Application of Prevention Technologies.

This is an exciting time in the evolution of prevention. Today, more knowledge exists about what works in substance abuse prevention programming than existed in the past. At the same time, new cohorts of substance abuse prevention professionals are demonstrating interest in the field. College campuses are offering courses in substance abuse prevention and students can earn degrees in this field. This curriculum captures some of the fundamental building blocks that all students and prevention professionals need to incorporate into their practice to help advance effective and efficient substance abuse prevention programming at the national, state, county, and community levels.

## Summary

This chapter has provided an overview of a number of important considerations when implementing substance abuse prevention programs and working within the substance abuse prevention field. The first is that the profession of prevention is evolving. Part of that evolving process is learning about the field, exploring dominant theories within the field, knowing the history of the field, and engaging concepts and definitions that derive from the work of prevention. The building blocks for prevention, which are found in subsequent chapters in this book, help the prevention professional better understand the science behind successful prevention programming.

## KEY TERMS

addiction/dependence
ATOD (alcohol, tobacco, and
   other drugs)
best practices
CSAP (Center for Substance
   Abuse Prevention)
IOM (Institute of
   Medicine)
model programs

NIAAA (National Institute on
   Alcohol Abuse and
   Alcoholism)
NIDA (National Institute on
   Drug Abuse)
ONDCP (Office of National
   Drug Control Policy)
praxis
profession

promising approaches
SAMHSA (Substance Abuse
   and Mental Health Services
   Administration)
scientific rigor
substance abuse
substance misuse
substance use
theory

## DISCUSSION QUESTIONS

1. What lessons, if any, have been learned from the history of prevention? Explain and defend your answer.

2. What strengths and limitations exist from defining key concepts used in substance abuse prevention, such as use, misuse, abuse, and addiction/dependence? Is there any controversy behind these definitions? If so, what are they?

3. Why is it important to understand theory and theoretical processes when implementing prevention programs?

4. How can attitudes about tobacco, alcohol, and other drug use influence actual work in prevention?

## APPLICATION EXERCISES

1. Which philosophies of prevention have been dominant in our history? Why do you think we have not seemed to learn from our mistakes? How have attitudes toward different cultures affected alcohol and drug policies?

2. What elements define a discipline? How does this apply to the field of substance abuse prevention?

## SUGGESTED READINGS

Center for Substance Abuse Prevention. (1993). *Prevention primer: An encyclopedia of alcohol, tobacco, and other drug prevention terms.* (DHHS Publication No. SMA 2060). Rockville, MD: National Clearinghouse for Alcohol and Drug Information. This publication can also be accessed on the following Website: *http://www.health.org*
Kuhn, T. (1970). *The structure of scientific revolutions* (2nd ed.). Chicago: University of Chicago Press.

## REFERENCES

Center for Substance Abuse Prevention. (1993). *Prevention primer: An encyclopedia of alcohol, tobacco, and other drug prevention terms.* (DHHS Publication No. SMA 2060). Rockville, MD: National Clearinghouse for Alcohol and Drug Information.
Fisher, G. L., & Harrison, T. C. (2000). *Substance abuse: Information for school counselors, social workers, therapists and counselors* (2nd ed.). Boston: Allyn and Bacon.
Guralnik, D. B. (Ed.). 1984. *Webster's new world dictionary of the American language.* New York: Simon and Schuster.
Kuhn, T. (1970). *The structure of scientific revolutions* (2nd ed.). Chicago: University of Chicago Press.
Rocky Mountain Center for Health Promotion and Education. (1986). *Prevention generalist training.* Alcohol and Drug Abuse Division, Colorado Department of Health and Human Services.

# 2 Prevention Research

The field of substance abuse prevention, like any other complex field, cannot be fully contained within a single, simple theory. Multiple theoretical approaches can be helpful in providing useful perspectives on particular aspects of prevention. According to Bellack (1990), a theory makes numerous contributions to our understanding of the social world, and in this case, the work of substance abuse prevention. A good theory should provide a number of contributions to prevention work:

1. The theory should identify the factors that predict substance abuse.
2. The theory should explain the mechanisms through which the tenets operate.
3. The theory should identify the internal and external variables that influence these mechanisms, including cultural factors.
4. The theory should predict points to interrupt the course leading to substance abuse.
5. The theory should specify the interventions to prevent onset of substance abuse.

These five theoretical principles frame our understanding of substance abuse and guide the practitioner to design prevention programs accordingly.

Currently, the field of substance abuse prevention is predominately informed by three theoretical perspectives: the risk and protective factor theory, the resiliency approach, and the developmental assets model. All three major perspectives will be explored in this chapter but only one approach, risk and protective factor theory, has been shown to be predictive. A **predictive theory** is one that empirically states that if certain conditions are present, a probable outcome may result. In other words, a prediction can be made that people may use tobacco, alcohol, and other drugs if certain factors or conditions exist. At this time, the developmental assets approach and the resiliency approach are considered promising approaches because of to the fact that limited research has been done showing that implementation of the approaches leads to the future reduction or prevention of substance abuse. Before going any further, let us turn our attention to the careful exploration of each of the three major theoretical perspectives in the field of substance abuse prevention.

# The Risk and Protective Factors Theory

Risk and protective factor-focused prevention is based on a simple premise: to prevent a problem from happening, one needs to identify the factors that increase the risk of that problem developing and then find ways to reduce the risk. At the same time, we must also identify those factors that buffer individuals from the risk factors present in their environments and then find ways to increase the protection. **Risk factors** are factors shown to increase the likelihood of adolescent substance abuse, teenage pregnancy, school drop-out, youth violence, and delinquency. **Protective factors** counter risk factors and the more protective factors that are present, the less the risk. Protective factors fall into three basic categories: individual characteristics, bonding, and healthy beliefs and clear standards. The risk and protective factors approach is similar to the medical model for heart disease, which contends that there are several factors that put adults at risk of heart disease, such as eating fatty foods and smoking. Additionally, several protective factors exist that have been shown to shield adults from acquiring heart disease, such as eating diets low in fat and getting plenty of exercise. The same model works in understanding substance abuse prevention. There are some factors that put youth at risk of using substances and some factors that protect or shield youth from using substances. It is this theoretical approach that we will explore first. The information offered in Box 2.1 outlines risk and protective factor theory in detail.

---

BOX **2.1**

## Risk and Protective Factors Overview

Risk and protective factor-focused prevention is based on the work of J. David Hawkins, Ph.D., Richard F. Catalano, Ph.D., and a team of researchers at the University of Washington in Seattle. In the early 1980s, they conducted a review of 30 years of youth substance abuse and delinquency research and identified risk factors for adolescent substance abuse and delinquency. They have continually updated this review. Other researchers, including Joy Dryfoos, Robert Slavin and Richard Jessor, have reviewed the literature on behavior problems, such as school dropout, teen pregnancy, violence and the identified risk factors of these problems. Young people who are seriously involved in either juvenile delinquency, substance abuse, school dropout, teenage pregnancy or violence are more likely to engage in one or more of the other problem behaviors. Furthermore, all of these teen problems share many common risk factors. [It is important to note that this theory has been tested with the following populations: Hispanic/Latinos, Native Americans, African Americans, Asian Americans and Pacific Islanders, and Caucasians.] Before looking at the risk factors and the problems they predict, it is important to establish a working definition of the terms "**delinquency**" and "**violence**." For our purposes, delinquency is defined as crimes committed by juveniles under 18. Violence is defined as acts against a person that involve physical harm or the threat of physical harm.

*(continued)*

BOX **2.1**    **Continued**

TABLE 2.1    **Risk Factor Checklist**

| RISK FACTORS | Adolescent Problem Behaviors | | | | |
|---|---|---|---|---|---|
| | Substance Abuse | Delinquency | Teen Pregnancy | School Drop-Out | Violence |
| **Community** | | | | | |
| Availability of Drugs | ✓ | | | | ✓ |
| Availability of Firearms | | ✓ | | | ✓ |
| Community Laws and Norms Favorable Toward Drug Use, Firearms and Crime | ✓ | ✓ | | | ✓ |
| Media Portrayals of Violence | | | | | ✓ |
| Transitions and Mobility | ✓ | ✓ | | ✓ | |
| Low Neighborhood Attachment and Community Disorganization | ✓ | ✓ | | | ✓ |
| Extreme Economic Deprivation | ✓ | ✓ | ✓ | ✓ | ✓ |
| **Family** | | | | | |
| Family History of the Problem Behavior | ✓ | ✓ | ✓ | ✓ | ✓ |
| Family Management Problems | ✓ | ✓ | ✓ | ✓ | ✓ |
| Family Conflict | ✓ | ✓ | ✓ | ✓ | ✓ |

**TABLE 2.1   Continued**

|  | **Adolescent Problem Behaviors** | | | | |
|---|---|---|---|---|---|
| **RISK FACTORS** | *Substance Abuse* | *Delinquency* | *Teen Pregnancy* | *School Drop-Out* | *Violence* |
| **Family (continued)** | | | | | |
| Favorable Parental Attitudes and Involvement in the Problem Behavior | ✓ | ✓ | | | ✓ |
| **School** | | | | | |
| Early and Persistent Antisocial Behavior | ✓ | ✓ | ✓ | ✓ | ✓ |
| Academic Failure Beginning in Late Elementary School | ✓ | ✓ | ✓ | ✓ | ✓ |
| Lack of Commitment to School | ✓ | ✓ | ✓ | ✓ | ✓ |
| **Individual/Peer** | | | | | |
| Alienation and Rebelliousness | ✓ | ✓ | | ✓ | |
| Friends Who Engage in the Problem Behavior | ✓ | ✓ | ✓ | ✓ | ✓ |
| Favorable Attitudes Toward the Problem Behavior | ✓ | ✓ | ✓ | ✓ | |
| Early Initiation of the Problem Behavior | ✓ | ✓ | ✓ | ✓ | ✓ |
| Constitutional Factors | ✓ | ✓ | | | ✓ |

*(continued)*

B O X   **2.1**    **Continued**

The primary focus of substance abuse prevention programs is reducing or preventing substance abuse; however, since problem behaviors, including substance abuse, violence, delinquency, teenage pregnancy and school dropout, share many common risk factors, reducing common risk factors is likely to reduce multiple problem behaviors. [The Risk Factor Checklist Table on pages 16–17 provides a list of risk factors within each domain and has a checkmark for each problem behavior it predicts.]

[The following section is a summary of the research-based risk factors and the problem behaviors they predict (given in parentheses). Please note that the research is divided into four domains: community, family, school, and individual/peer risk factors.]

**Community Risk Factors**

*Availability of Drugs (Substance Abuse and Violence).* The more available drugs are in a community, the higher the risk that young people will abuse drugs in the community. Perceived availability of drugs is also associated with risk. In schools where children just think that drugs are more available, a higher rate of use occurs. [For example, a condition may exist in a community where children think that drugs are easily available, maybe more so then they really are. It makes sense that if kids think they can get drugs easily, more drug use will occur. This perceived availability, regardless of the fact that drugs are not that easily available, can become a risk factor because it supports a social norm that drugs are easy to get and okay to use.]

*Community Laws and Norms Favorable toward Drug Use, Firearms and Crime (Substance Abuse, Delinquency and Violence).* **Community norms**—the attitudes and policies a community holds about substance use and crime—are communicated in a variety of ways: through laws and written policies, through informal social practices and through the expectations parents and other members of the community have of young people. One example of a community law affecting drug use is the taxation of alcoholic beverages. Higher rates of taxation decrease the rate of alcohol use at every level of use. When laws, tax rates and community standards are favorable toward substance use or crime, or even if they are just unclear, children are at higher risk.

Another concern is conflicting messages about alcohol / other drugs from key social institutions. An example of conflicting messages about substance abuse can be found in the acceptance of alcohol use as a social activity within the community. The "Beer Gardens," popular at street fairs and community festivals frequented by young people, are in contrast to the "Just Say No" messages that schools and parents may be promoting. These conflicting messages make it difficult for children to decide which norms to follow.

Laws regulating the sale of firearms have had small effects on violent crime and those effects usually diminish after the law has been in effect for multiple years. In addition, laws regulating the penalties for violating licensing laws or using a firearm in the commission of a crime have also been related to reduction in the amount of violent crime, especially involving firearms. A number of studies suggest the small and diminishing effect is due to two factors: the availability of firearms from other jurisdictions without legal prohibitions on sales or illegal access and community norms that include lack of proactive monitoring or enforcement of the laws.

*Transitions and Mobility (Substance Abuse, Delinquency, School Drop-out).* Even normal school transitions can predict increases in problem behaviors. When children move from elementary school to middle school or from middle school to high school, significant increases in the rate of drug use, school misbehavior, and anti-social behavior may occur.

Communities with high rates of mobility appear to be linked to an increased risk of drug and crime problems. The more often people in a community move, the greater the risk of both criminal behavior and drug-related problems in families. While some people find buffers against the negative effects of mobility by making connections in new communities, others are less likely to have the resources to deal with the effects of frequent moves and are more likely to have problems.

*Low Neighborhood Attachment and Community Disorganization (Substance Abuse, Delinquency, and Violence).* Higher rates of drug problems, delinquency and violence and higher rates of drug trafficking occur in communities or neighborhoods where people have little attachment to the community, where the rates of vandalism are high and where there is low surveillance of public places. These conditions are not limited to low-income neighborhoods; they can also be found in more well to do neighborhoods.

The less homogenous a community is in terms of race, class, and religion, the less connected its residents may feel to the overall community, and the more difficult it is to establish clear community goals and identity. The challenge of creating neighborhood attachment and organization is greater in these neighborhoods.

Perhaps the most significant issue affecting community attachment is whether residents feel they can make a difference in their lives. If the key players in the neighborhood—such as merchants, teachers, police, human and social services personnel—live outside the neighborhood, residents' sense of commitment will be less. Lower rates of voter participation and parental involvement in school also reflect attitudes about community attachment. [Neighborhood disorganization makes it more difficult for schools, churches, and families to promote prosocial values and norms.]

*Extreme Economic Deprivation (Substance Abuse, Delinquency, Violence, Teen Pregnancy and School Dropout).* Children who live in deteriorating and crime-ridden neighborhoods characterized by extreme poverty are more likely to develop problems with delinquency, teen pregnancy, school dropout and violence. Children who live in these areas—and have behavior and adjustment problems early in life—are also more likely to have problems with drugs later on. [However, "only when poverty is extreme and occurs in conjunction with childhood behavior problems has it been shown to increase risk for later alcoholism and drug problems" (Hawkins et al. 1992, p. 81).]

**Family Risk Factors**
[Note: The family domain can include traditional and non-traditional, nuclear and extended, or other forms of family we find in contemporary society.]

*Family History of the Problem Behavior (Substance Abuse, Delinquency, Violence, Teen Pregnancy and School Dropout).* If children are raised in a family with a history of addiction to alcohol or other drugs, the risk of having alcohol and other drug problems themselves increases. If children are born or raised in a family with a history of criminal activity, the risk of juvenile delinquency increases. Similarly, children who are raised by a teenage mother are more likely to be teen parents, and children of dropouts are more likely to drop out of school themselves. [The point here is that familiar patterns of addiction predispose children to addiction themselves.]

*Family Management Problems (Substance Abuse, Delinquency, Violence, Teen Pregnancy and School Dropout).* This risk factor has been shown to increase the risk of substance abuse,

*(continued)*

delinquency, teen pregnancy, school dropout and violence. Poor family management practices include lack of clear expectations for behavior, failure of parents to monitor their children (knowing where they are and whom they are with) and excessively severe or inconsistent punishment. [Examples of harsh and inconsistent discipline include situations where in one instance there is no consequence for an action and in other instances the consequence is severe. This situation puts youth at risk for developing problem behaviors because they do not know which behaviors are desirable or undesirable over time. They receive unclear communication from their parents and end up confused.]

***Family Conflict (Substance Abuse, Delinquency, Violence, Teen Pregnancy and School Dropout).*** Persistent, serious conflict between primary caregivers or between caregivers and children appears to enhance risk for children raised in these families. Conflict between family members appears to be more important than family structure. Whether the family is headed by two biological parents, a single parent or some other primary caregiver heads the family, children raised in families high in conflict appear to be at risk for all of the problem behaviors. For example, domestic violence in a family increases the likelihood that young people will engage in delinquent behaviors and substance abuse, as well as become pregnant or drop out of school.

***Parental Attitudes and Involvement in Drug Use, Crime and Violence (Substance Abuse, Delinquency and Violence).*** Parental attitudes and behavior toward drugs, crime and violence influence the attitudes and behavior of their children. Parental approval of young people's moderate drinking, even under parental supervision, increases the risk of the young person using marijuana. Similarly, children of parents who excuse their children for breaking the law are more likely to develop problems with juvenile delinquency. In families where parents display violent behavior towards those outside the family, there is an increase in the risk that a child will become violent. Further, in families where parents involve children in their own drug or alcohol behavior— for example, asking the child to light the parent's cigarette or get the parent a beer from the refrigerator—there is an increased likelihood that their children will become substance abusers in adolescence.

**School Risk Factors**

***Early and Persistent Antisocial Behavior (Substance Abuse, Delinquency, Violence, Teen Pregnancy and School Dropout).*** Boys who are aggressive in grades K–3 are at higher risk of substance abuse and juvenile delinquency. However, aggressive behavior very early in childhood does not appear to increase risk. When a boy's aggressive behavior in the early grades is combined with isolation or withdrawal, there is an even greater risk of problems in adolescence. This increased risk also applies to aggressive behavior combined with hyperactivity or attention deficit disorder.

This risk factor also includes persistent antisocial behavior in early adolescence, like misbehaving in school, skipping school and getting into fights with other children. Young people, both girls and boys, who engage in these behaviors during early adolescence, are at increased risk for substance abuse, juvenile delinquency, violence, school dropout and teen pregnancy.

***Academic Failure Beginning in Elementary School (Substance Abuse, Delinquency, Violence, Teen Pregnancy and School Dropout).*** Beginning in the late elementary grades [grades 4–6], academic failure increases the risk of substance abuse, delinquency, violence, pregnancy and school dropout. Children fail for many reasons. It appears that *the experience of failure*—not necessarily ability—increases the risk of problem behaviors. This is particularly troubling because, in many school districts, African American, Native American and Hispanic students have disproportionately higher rates of academic failure compared to white students. Consequently, school improvement and reducing academic failure are particularly important prevention strategies for communities of color.

***Lack of Commitment to School (Substance Abuse, Delinquency, Violence, Teen Pregnancy and School Dropout).*** Low commitment to school means the young person has ceased to see the role of student as a viable one. Young people who have lost this commitment to school are at higher risk for substance abuse, delinquency, teen pregnancy and school dropout. In many communities of color, education is seen as a "way out," similar to the way early immigrants viewed education. Other subgroups in the same community may view education and school as a form of negative acculturation. In essence, if you get an education, you have "sold out" to the majority culture. Young people who adopt this view are likely to be at higher risk for health and problem behaviors.

### Individual/Peer Risk Factors

***Alienation/Rebelliousness (Substance Abuse, Delinquency and School Dropout).*** Young people who feel they are not part of society, are not bound by rules, do not believe in trying to be successful or responsible, or who take an active rebellious stance toward society, are at higher risk of substance abuse, delinquency and school dropout. Alienation and rebelliousness may be an especially significant risk for young people of color. Children who are consistently discriminated against may respond by removing themselves from the dominant culture and rebelling against it. On the other hand, many communities of color are experiencing significant cultural change due to integration. The conflicting emotions about family and friends working, socializing or marrying outside of the culture may well interfere with a young person's development of a clear and positive racial identity.

***Friends Who Engage in the Problem Behavior (Substance Abuse, Delinquency, Violence, Teen Pregnancy and School Dropout).*** Young people who associate with peers who engage in problem behavior—delinquency, substance abuse, violent activity, sexual activity or school dropout—are much more likely to engage in the same problem behavior. This is one of the most consistent predictors that research has identified. Even when young people come from well-managed families and do not experience other risk factors, just hanging out with friends who engage in the problem behavior greatly increases the child's risk of that problem. However, young people who experience a low number of risk factors are less likely to associate with friends who are involved in the problem behavior.

***Favorable Attitudes Toward the Problem Behavior (Substance Abuse, Delinquency, Teen Pregnancy and School Dropout).*** During the elementary school years, children usually express anti-drug, anti-crime and pro-social attitudes. They have difficulty imagining why people use drugs, commit crimes and drop out of school. However, in middle school, as others they know participate in such activities, their attitudes often shift toward greater acceptance of these behaviors. This acceptance places them at higher risk due to the fact that a shift in attitudes precedes a shift in behavior. [Some examples include kids wearing tee shirts with alcohol advertisements on them, kids hanging liquor posters in their bedrooms, or other behaviors, which demonstrate favorable attitudes toward substance use.]

*(continued)*

BOX  **2.1**    **Continued**

*Early Initiation of the Problem Behavior (Substance Abuse, Delinquency, Violence, Teen Pregnancy and School Dropout).* The earlier young people begin using drugs, committing crimes, engaging in violent activity, dropping out of school and becoming sexually active, the greater the likelihood that they will have problems with these behaviors later on. For example, research shows that young people who initiate drug use before the age of 15 are at twice the risk of having drug problems as those who wait until after the age of 19.

*Constitutional Factors (Substance Abuse, Delinquency and Violence).* Constitutional factors are factors that may have a biological or physiological basis. These factors are often seen in young people with behaviors such as high sensation-seeking, low harm-avoidance and lack of impulse control. These factors appear to increase the risk of young people abusing drugs, engaging in delinquent behavior and/or committing violent acts.

**Generalizations about Risks**
[There are a number of generalizations that can be made about the risk factors presented in this theoretical perspective.] First, risk factors exist in all areas of life. [In other words, risk factors exist across all four categories including community, family, school, and individual/peer.] If a single risk factor is addressed in a single area, problem behaviors may not be significantly reduced. Communities should focus on reducing risks across several areas or domains.

Second, the more risk factors, the greater the risk. While exposure to one risk factor does not condemn a child to problems later in life, exposure to a greater number of risk factors increases a young person's risk exponentially. Even if a community cannot eliminate all the risk factors that are present, reducing or eliminating even a few risk factors may significantly decrease problem behaviors for [the] young.

Third, common risk factors predict diverse problem behaviors. Since many individual risk factors predict multiple problems, the reduction of risk factors is likely to affect a number of different problems in the community. [The same is true for the heart disease model. When a person reduces a single risk factor, such as smoking, the risk decreases for lung, throat, and mouth cancers as well as heart disease.]

Fourth, risk factors show much consistency in effects across different races and cultures. While levels of risk may vary in different racial or cultural groups, the way in which these risk factors work does not appear to vary. One implication for community prevention is to prioritize prevention efforts for groups with higher levels of risk exposure.

Fifth, protective factors may buffer exposure to risk. Protective factors are conditions that buffer young people from the negative consequences of exposure to risks by either reducing the impact of the risk or changing the way a person responds to the risk. Consequently, enhancing protective factors can reduce the likelihood of problem behaviors arising.

## Protective Factors

Protective factors have an important role to play in the lives of young people. Protective factors are conditions that protect youth from the negative consequences of exposure to risks, either by reducing the impact of the risk or by changing the way a person responds to the risk. Some youth who have multiple risk factors in their lives do not become substance abusers, juvenile delinquents, school dropouts, or teen parents. The importance of protective factors cannot be overstated because they promote positive behavior, health, well-being, and personal success (Development Research and Programs, 1997, p. 60). Research has identified protective factors that fall into three basic categories: individual characteristics, bonding, and healthy beliefs and clear standards. These categories are described in depth in Box 2.2.

---

BOX **2.2**

## Protective Factors

### Individual Characteristics

Research has identified four individual characteristics as protective factors. These are characteristics children are born with and are difficult to change including: gender, a resilient temperament, a positive social orientation and intelligence. Intelligence, however, does not protect against substance abuse [although it does offer protection from the other problem behaviors such as school drop out, violence, delinquency, and teen pregnancy.]

### Bonding

Positive bonding makes up for many other disadvantages caused by other risk factors or environmental characteristics. Children who are attached to positive families, friends, school and community and who are committed to achieving the goals valued by these groups are less likely to develop problems in adolescence. Studies of successful children who live in high-risk neighborhoods or situations indicate that strong bonds with a caregiver can keep children from getting into trouble.

To build bonding, three conditions are necessary: opportunities, skills and recognition. First, children must be provided with opportunities to contribute to their community, family, peers and school. The challenge is to provide children with meaningful opportunities that help them feel responsible and significant. Second, children must be taught the skills necessary to effectively take advantage of the opportunity they are provided. If they don't have the necessary skills to be successful, they experience frustration and/or failure. And third, children must also be recognized and acknowledged for their efforts. This gives them the incentive to contribute and reinforces their skillful performance. When opportunities, skills, and recognition are all in place, bonding is likely to occur.

### Healthy Beliefs and Clear Standards

The people to whom youth are bonded need to have clear, positive standards for behavior. The content of these standards is what protects young people. When parents, teachers and communities set clear standards for children's behavior, when they are widely and consistently supported, and

*(continued)*

when the consequences for not following the standards are consistent, young people are more likely to follow the standards.

Figure 2.1 visually demonstrates the social development strategy. This strategy describes how protective factors work together to buffer youth from risks. If you start at the bottom of the diagram and work your way to the top, you will see how individual characteristics, bonding, and healthy beliefs and clear standards help young people develop healthy behaviors.]

**Actively Creating Healthy Communities**
The research [on risk and protective factors] supports the importance of a community focus. Risk and protective factors are found in all aspects of the community: schools, families, individuals and the community. Community efforts can affect the entire local environment, including community norms, values and policies. Because substance abuse is a phenomenon influenced by multiple risk factors, its prevention may be most effectively accomplished with a combination of interventions. A community-wide approach promotes the development of strong bonds to family, school and community. Because community approaches are likely to involve a wide spectrum of individuals, groups and organizations, they create a base of support for behavior change. The firm support of community leaders and their involvement in a prevention effort are likely to lead to long-term

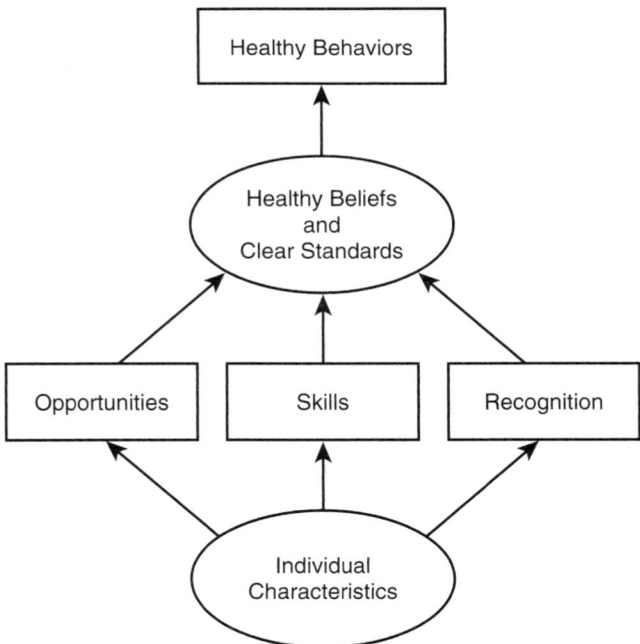

**FIGURE 2.1   Social Development Strategy Model**

*Source:* Copyright © 2001 Channing L. Bete Co., Inc. All rights reserved.
Reproduced with permission of the publisher.

behavior change. This reallocation of resources to reduce risk factors and enhance protective factors becomes feasible with support from community leaders.

Programs and strategies gradually become integrated into the regular services and activities of local organizations and institutions. The community-wide focus creates a synergy; the whole is more powerful than the sum of its parts. Because many attempts to change families, schools and other institutions have operated in isolation, they have had limited success. For meaningful change to occur, multiple interconnected forces of the community must share a common vision and agenda.

*Source:* Developmental Research and Programs, detailed in a publication from the Western Center for the Application of Prevention Technologies. Copyright © 2001 Channing L. Bete Co., Inc. All rights reserved. Reproduced with permission of the publisher.

## The Resiliency Approach

The resiliency approach stems from research on young people from troubled backgrounds who have learned to bounce back when the odds are stacked against them. For purposes of this discussion, **resiliency factors** are factors that protect or buffer people against social problems or risk factors. Emmy Werner is one such researcher. From studying children born on Kauai, Hawaii, in 1955, Werner (1986) identified several environmental factors that foster resilience in kids, including the following:

- The age of the parent of the opposite sex (younger mothers for resilient boys, older fathers for resilient girls).
- The number of children in the family (four or fewer).
- Spacing between children (two years or more was best).
- The number and type of people available to help the mother rear the children (such as grandparents, aunts, or uncles).
- Steady employment for the mother, especially if she was a single mother.
- The availability of a sibling as a caretaker in childhood.
- The presence of a multigenerational network of friends, teachers, and relatives during adolescence.
- Church attendance.

Werner (1986) conducted a 35-year longitudinal study of 505 children born on Kauai, Hawaii. Her research explored how children remained resilient despite the role that existing risk factors played in their lives. Although no simple, single list of risk or protective factors was included in Werner's study, several themes emerged. The risk factor themes included poverty, parental psychopathology, caregiving deficits, delinquencies, and teenage parenthood. The protective or resiliency factors included the following three clusters. First, average intelligence and positive disposition attributes such as robustness, vigor, and active and social temperament were cited as providing resiliency for children. Second, affectionate ties with parental substitutes, such as teachers or other mentors helped develop trust, autonomy, and initiative in children. Finally, the third cluster of protective factors included external support systems, such as churches, youth group, and schools, which rewarded competence and provided coherence for the youth.

Other researchers have come to different conclusions but most agree that much more needs to be studied, especially across cultures. Werner and others have also concluded that youths who overcome adversity better than others tend not to seek out formal professional or institutional help. Instead, they turn to people they have grown to trust because they see them regularly; this includes teachers, school counselors, ministers, grandparents, and friends.

Werner has several suggestions for schools to foster resilient children:

- Establish better relations with local companies and community groups to encourage college students and grown-ups to work as mentors.
- Avoid cutting art, music, or athletic programs.
- Establish school schedules that allow students to have the same teachers for at least two years.
- Decrease class sizes.

Currently, the resiliency approach is considered a promising approach only because most research has not yet conclusively shown that increasing resiliency leads to a reduction in the prevention of substance abuse (Bushweller, 1995). It is important to note that the list of risk and protective factors developed in the resiliency perspective are different from the list identified by Hawkins and Catalano. Although these factors can be argued to overlap in some areas, the thrust of the perspectives is unique.

## The Developmental Assets Approach

Since 1989, Search Institute has been conducting research—grounded in the vast literature on resilience, prevention, and adolescent development—that has illuminated the positive relationships, opportunities, competencies, values, and self-perceptions that youth need to succeed. The institute's framework of "developmental assets" grows out of that research, which has involved more than one million 6th- to 12th-grade youth in communities across the country. Developmental assets are the building blocks that all youth need to be healthy, caring, principled, and productive (Scales & Leffert, 1999).

The developmental assets approach—or framework, since it merely suggests approaches—introduces a variety of strategies that build assets for young people. Some of these strategies call for establishing caring relationships between adults and young people. Other strategies call for providing an environment—in schools, in homes, in communities—that are conducive to building assets. And still other strategies call for programs and practices, found in formal structures that help build assets for young people. All the strategies rely on an understanding of the assets framework, an assessment of the assets for each person, an inventory of which resources are available to build the assets, and finally, on an implementation and continuance of the strategies.

Table 2.2 shows a list of the 40 developmental assets. They are divided into "external" assets and "internal" assets. **External assets** are factors that surround young people with the support, empowerment, boundaries, expectations, and opportunities that guide them to behave in healthy ways and to make wise choices. **Internal assets** are the commitments, values, competencies, and self-perceptions that must be nurtured within young people to provide them with "internal compasses" to guide their behaviors and choices (Leffert, Bensen, & Roehlkepartain, 1997, p. 16). Each of these categories is, in turn, divided into types of assets or domains: support, empowerment, boundaries and expectations, and constructive use of time comprise the external assets; and commitment to learning, positive values, social competencies, and positive identity comprise the internal assets (Leffert et al., 1997).

The four external assets domains need further exploration. When referring to the assets within the "support" domain, we are referring to the ways children are loved, affirmed, and accepted. The "empowerment" domain focuses on community perceptions of children and the opportunities available to them to contribute to society in a meaningful way. "Boundaries and expectations" is the domain for healthy development that maintains that clear and consistent boundaries be coupled with support and empowerment. Finally, the "constructive use of time" domain is comprised of assets that contain a rich array of constructive, positive opportunities in which children can engage.

The four internal assets domains describe those attributes that are internal to the children. These include the values, competencies, and identity needed to guide and create a sense of "centeredness" in children. The "commitment to learning" domain consists of assets that speak to the learning and educational process for children. These include achievement motivation and school bonding. The "positive values" domain includes assets on family values such as honesty, responsibility, and integrity. The "social competencies" domain is made up of assets on conflict resolution and interpersonal interactions. Finally, the "positive identity" domain addresses the assets of self-esteem, sense of purpose, and other self-actualizing behaviors (Leffert et al., 1997, pp. 18–25).

The developmental assets framework emphasizes the strengths, not limitations, in people. Schools and communities that have adopted this framework consider young people as resources, not as problems. This approach contends that by building on strengths and increasing the assets that have been found to be associated with healthy, caring, responsible people, young people will choose not to use drugs. The framework is considered a promising approach because, although data indicate an association between the presence of assets and the absence of substance abuse, research has not yet conclusively shown that increasing assets reduces or delays substance abuse.

In conclusion, theoretical understanding is important for the applied prevention professional because it provides valuable tools for prevention program development. All three frameworks presented in this chapter aid the prevention professional in understanding the delicate relationship between risks, assets, resiliency, protective factors, and other social problems. Without theoretical underpinnings, prevention professionals might plan and implement programs that may have "felt" like they worked but in fact caused harm. In addition to theoretical insights, the Center for Substance Abuse Prevention (CSAP) has developed six strategies that classify the work of prevention. It is now time to turn our attention to these strategies and explore what research tells us works in each category.

**TABLE 2.2   Forty Developmental Assets**

| Category | Asset Name and Definition |
| --- | --- |
| **External Assets** | |
| Support | 1. Family support—Family life provides high levels of love and support. |
| | 2. Positive family communication—Young person and her or his parent(s) communicate positively and young person is willing to seek advice and counsel from parent(s). |
| | 3. Other adult relationships—Young person receives support from three or more nonparent adults. |
| | 4. Caring neighborhood—Young person experiences caring neighbors. |
| | 5. Caring school climate—School provides a caring, encouraging environment. |
| | 6. Parent involvement in schooling—Parent(s) are actively involved in helping young person succeed in school. |
| Empowerment | 7. Community values youth—Young person perceives that adults in the community value youth. |
| | 8. Youth as resources—Young people are given useful roles in the community. |
| | 9. Service to others—Young person serves in the community one hour or more per week. |
| | 10. Safety—Young person feels safe at home, at school, and in the neighborhood. |
| Boundaries and Expectations | 11. Family boundaries—Family has clear rules and consequences, and monitors the young person's whereabouts. |
| | 12. School boundaries—School provides clear rules and consequences. |
| | 13. Neighborhood boundaries—Neighbors take responsibility for monitoring young people's behavior. |
| | 14. Adult role models—Parent(s) and other adults model positive, responsible behavior. |
| | 15. Positive peer influence—Young person's best friends model responsible behavior. |
| | 16. High expectations—Both parent(s) and teachers encourage the young person to do well. |
| Constructive Use of Time | 17. Creative activities—Young person spends three or more hours per week in lessons or practice in music, theater or other arts. |
| | 18. Youth programs—Young person spends three or more hours per week in sports, clubs, or organizations at school and/or in the community. |
| | 19. Religious community—Young person spends one or more hours per week in activities in a religious institution. |
| | 20. Time at home—Young person is out with friends "with nothing special to do" two or fewer nights per week. |

| Category | Asset Name and Definition |
|----------|---------------------------|
| **Internal Assets** | |
| Commitment to Learning | **21.** Achievement motivation—Young person is motivated to do well in school. |
| | **22.** School engagement—Young person is actively engaged in learning. |
| | **23.** Homework—Young person reports doing at least one hour of homework every school day. |
| | **24.** Bonding to school—Young person cares about her or his school. |
| | **25.** Reading for pleasure—Young person reads for pleasure three or more hours per week. |
| Positive Values | **26.** Caring—Young person places high value on helping other people. |
| | **27.** Equality and social justice—Young person places high value on promoting equality and reducing hunger and poverty. |
| | **28.** Integrity—Young person acts on convictions and stands up for her or his beliefs. |
| | **29.** Honesty—Young person "tells the truth even when it is not easy." |
| | **30.** Responsibility—Young person accepts and takes personal responsibility. |
| | **31.** Restraint—Young person believes it is important not to be sexually active or to use alcohol or other drugs. |
| Social Competencies | **32.** Planning and decision making—Young person knows how to plan ahead and make choices. |
| | **33.** Interpersonal competence—Young person has empathy, sensitivity, and friendship skills. |
| | **34.** Cultural competence—Young person has knowledge of and comfort with people of different cultural/racial/ethnic backgrounds. |
| | **35.** Resistance skills—Young person can resist negative peer pressure and dangerous situations. |
| | **36.** Peaceful conflict resolution—Young person seeks to resolve conflict nonviolently. |
| Positive Identity | **37.** Personal power—Young person feels he or she has control over "things that happen to me." |
| | **38.** Self-esteem—Young person reports having a high self-esteem. |
| | **39.** Sense of purpose—Young person reports that "my life has a purpose." |
| | **40.** Positive view of personal future—Young person is optimistic about her or his personal future. |

*Source*: Reprinted with permission from Search Institute, Minneapolis, MN: www.search-institute.org.

# The Six CSAP Strategies

The Center for Substance Abuse Prevention (CSAP) has created six strategies that can form a comprehensive prevention program. Integration of theories and strategies are an important consideration when implementing substance abuse prevention programs. All six strategies will be explored, followed by a discussion of the research-based findings for each strategy.

## Information Dissemination

This strategy includes providing information about the nature and extent of drug use, abuse, and addiction and the effects on individuals, families, and communities. It also provides information of available prevention programs and services. The dissemination of information is characterized by one-way communication from the source to the audience, with limited contact between the two. Examples of methods used for this strategy include the following: clearinghouses and other information resource centers, resource directories, media campaigns, brochures, radio and television public service announcements, speaking engagements, and health fairs.

## Prevention Education

This strategy involves two-way communication and is distinguished from merely disseminating information by the fact that it is based on an interaction between the educator and the participants. Activities under this strategy aim to affect critical life and social skills, including decision making, refusal, and critical analysis skills. Examples of methods used for this strategy include the following: classroom and small group sessions, parenting and family management classes, peer leader and peer helper programs, education programs for youth groups, and groups for children of substance abusers.

## Alternative Activities

The goal of this strategy is to have target populations participate in activities that are alcohol-, tobacco-, and other drug-free. The assumption is that because "constructive and healthy activities offset the attraction to drugs, or otherwise meet the needs usually filled by drugs" (CSAP, 1993, p. 100), then the population would avoid using drugs. Examples of methods used for this strategy include the following: drug-free social and recreational activities, drug-free dances and parties, youth and adult leadership activities, community drop-in centers, community service activities, and mentoring programs.

## Community-Based Processes

This strategy aims to enhance the ability of the community to provide more effective prevention and treatment services for substance abuse disorders. Activities in this strategy include the following: "organizing, planning, enhancing efficiency and effectiveness of services implementation, interagency collaboration, coalition building, and networking"

(CSAP, 1993, p. 100). Examples of methods used for this strategy include community and volunteer training (e.g., neighborhood action training, training of key people in the system); planning; multiagency coordination and collaboration; accessing service and funding; and community team building.

## Environmental Approaches

This strategy seeks to establish or change community standards, codes, and attitudes, thereby influencing the incidence and prevalence of substance abuse in the general population. Examples of methods used for this strategy include the establishment and review of drug policies in schools, technical assistance to communities to maximize local enforcement procedures governing the availability and distribution of drugs, the review and modification of alcohol and tobacco advertising practices, and product pricing strategies.

## Problem Identification and Referral

This strategy aims to identify those who have indulged in the illegal use of drugs in order to determine whether their behavior can be reversed through education or whether they need a referral for a chemical dependency assessment. It should be noted, however, that this strategy does not include any activity designed to determine whether an individual is in need of treatment. Examples of methods used for this strategy include the following: driving-while-intoxicated education programs, employee assistance programs, and student assistance programs.

## Research Findings and CSAP Strategies

The Center for Substance Abuse Prevention (CSAP) has identified a number of research-based findings for each strategy. This is important knowledge for the field of substance abuse prevention because each CSAP strategy can be used effectively or ineffectively. Remember that the goal is to have a positive impact on all youth and families involved in a prevention program. In other words, the ultimate goal of any substance abuse prevention program is to keep the participants from ever using alcohol, tobacco, and other drugs. Some programs, although their intentions are good, do not reach that goal. The following is a list of CSAP's research-based principles, by Brounstein, Zweig, and Gardner (1998, pp. 57–65), that should be followed by prevention professionals when developing, expanding, or changing existing programming. One final thought: Research has shown that the most effective prevention programs present a comprehensive approach that includes all or many of the CSAP strategies.

### Information Dissemination
- Educational programming regarding alcohol, tobacco, and other drugs can increase knowledge regarding the hazards of substance use, and aid in the development of negative attitudes toward these substances.
- Workplace programs for drug-free workplace policies can increase community awareness of substance abuse issues.

- Information dissemination campaigns should be viewed as complementary to more intensive and interactive prevention approaches. Effective use of the media is primarily demonstrated when the intervention is combined with other prevention strategies (e.g., education, enforcement of existing laws).
- Effective use of media to change substance-related knowledge, behavior, and attitudes relies on creating messages that appeal to youth's motives for using substances or perceptions of substance use (e.g., the perception of risk associated with a particular substance).
- Effective use of the mass media requires paying for television and radio spots in choice air times, when youth are more likely to be viewing or listening. Public service announcements can enhance any media campaign, but by themselves are unlikely to have an impact on youth if they air at times when few youth are tuning in.
- Media campaigns should use radio and television appropriately, allowing for the different viewing habits of younger and older adolescents. Effective use of media must also recognize that the interests of youth vary, depending on age and sex, so that the images and sounds should resonate with the target audience.
- Youth-oriented mass media campaigns are more effective if they avoid the use of authority figures and exhortations. Focus group research indicates that overbearing messages are likely to lose the target audience.

### Prevention Education

- Traditional education about harms and risks associated with substance use and abuse cannot, by itself, produce measurable and long-lasting changes in substance abuse-related behavior and attitudes. Educational approaches that combine the conveyance of information about the harms of substance abuse with the fostering of skills (e.g., problem solving, communication) and the promotion of protective factors have been shown to be more effective.
- Didactic approaches are among the least effective educational strategies. Research suggests that interactive approaches engaging the target audience are more effective. These approaches include cooperative learning, role playing, and group exercises.
- Educational interventions for youth that are led by peers or include peer-led components are more effective. However, peer-led programs tend to require extensive prior instruction for peer educators.
- Intensively implemented educational programs with youth appear to be effective. These types of programs usually last one academic year or longer and may involve booster sessions one to several years after the original intervention.
- Social skills training programs target many risk factors across many domains (e.g., individual, family, peer, school). Programs of this nature have demonstrated reductions in the onset of substance abuse.
- Programs that involve booster sessions help youth maintain skills over longer periods of time. Comprehensive programs designed to last over longer periods of time can result in broader and longer gains.
- Programs that involve interactive teaching where students can actually practice newly acquired skills (e.g., role playing) are beneficial. These programs can take

place in any environment. For instance, social skills can be taught via in-school curricula, individual therapy, and after-school mentoring.

- Research shows that educational approaches targeting the family and school-based approaches involving parents or complementing student-focused curricula can be effective in preventing adolescent substance use.
    — Parent and family skills training has had positive effects on measures related to knowledge, parenting skills, communication skills, problem-solving skills, child-management skills, parenting satisfaction, and coping skills. Also, these programs have been shown to decrease parental stress, family conflict, and substance abuse; improve parent-child bonding and cohesion; and increase attitudes toward and acceptance of children. For children and youth, positive outcomes have included increases in prosocial behavior and decreases in hyperactivity, social withdrawal, aggression, and delinquency.
    — Programs with two sets of workshops that work to improve parent skills along with adolescent skills have positive outcomes for both parents and youth.
    — Programs that involve sessions where parents and youth learn and practice skills both separately and together are also beneficial.
    — Videotaped training and education can be effective and cost efficient.
    — Providing meals, child care (for nontarget children), and transportation encourages family participation.

### Alternative Activities

- Alternatives should be part of a comprehensive prevention plan that includes other strategies with proven effectiveness. Environmental strategies that reduce the availability of alcohol, tobacco, and other drugs appear to be among the more effective strategies.
- The appropriateness and effectiveness of alternatives depends in part on the target group. Some research indicates that alternatives are more likely to be effective with high-risk youth who may not have adequate adult supervision or access to a variety of activities and who have few opportunities to develop the kinds of personal skills needed to avoid behavioral problems.
- The effectiveness of alternative approaches depends on the nature of the alternatives offered. Clearly, if the alternative activity offered is not attractive or appropriate to the target group, it would not garner participation. Recently, prevention professionals have involved youth in the development of alternatives programs.
    — Community service has been related to an increased sense of well-being and positive attitudes toward people, the future, and the community, while allowing youth to "give back" to their community.
    — Mentoring programs provide youth with structured time with adults; they are related to reduction in substance use, increased school attendance, and increased positive attitudes toward others, the future, and school.
    — The more highly involved the mentor, the greater the positive results.
    — These programs have positive effects on others besides the youth because they involve other community members (e.g., the elderly).
    — Provision of organized recreation and cultural activities by community agencies

can decrease substance use and delinquency by providing drug-free alternatives, monitoring, and supervision of children.

- More intensive programs that include a variety of approaches seem to be most effective. Not surprisingly, meta-analyses, as well as individual evaluations, find that programs that provide intensive interventions, including many hours of involvement in the program and related services, are most effective.
- Alternatives provide a natural and effective way of providing prevention services to high-risk youth. Youth who may already be disengaged from school (and therefore do not respond to school-based prevention programs) may make use of alternatives programs (e.g., drop-in centers). The enjoyable activities may provide the incentive for involvement and provide the opportunity for more structured intervention in drug use or other high-risk behavior.
- Alternatives can be part of a comprehensive prevention effort in a community, serving to establish strong community norms against misuse of alcohol and use of illicit drugs. While one-shot community events may not, in themselves, change the behavior of participants, these events can serve as strong community statements that support and celebrate a no-use norm. These events also draw public and media attention to drug issues and therefore increase awareness and support for other important prevention efforts. For these alternative activities to be truly effective, however, they must be viewed not as ends in themselves, but rather as a component of an integrated, comprehensive prevention strategy.

### Community-based Processes
- Community partnerships can be effective in eliciting change both at the systems level and at the individual behavior level. Characteristics of successful partnerships include:
  - A vision of the partnership's objectives.
  - Committed partnership members.
  - Participation of groups from all parts of the community.
  - Extensive prevention activities that reach a large number of individuals.
- Multiagency activities can increase coordination of efforts between public and private agencies, and between law enforcement and service providers:
  - Groups can work together to secure funding for substance use prevention programming efforts.
  - Interagency coordination can increase access to and quality of prevention and treatment services.
  - Active, mobilized communities have shown clear decreases in alcohol, tobacco, and other drug use and changes in perceived norms about substance use. In addition, these communities have improved perceptions of neighborhood quality as a result of environmental changes such as closing crack houses and removing billboards for alcohol and tobacco.
  - Provision of constructive activities for youth can reduce or prevent substance use and delinquency and increase cultural pride and coping skills.
- Community-based coalitions should begin with a clear understanding of their purpose. Prevention-oriented coalitions can aim to improve the nature and delivery of services to a community (comprehensive service coordination), generate community

activism to address substance-related problems (community mobilization), or both (community linkage). Clarity of purpose will facilitate coalition development and, ultimately, coalition success.

■ Coalition membership must be appropriate to the shared purpose and plan for action. If comprehensive service coordination is the task, organization leaders need to be involved, especially if an organization is expected to be a key contributor to a particular intervention. If community mobilization is the task, grassroots activists and community citizens must be involved. Community linkage coalition models require a mix of both types of community members. This results in diverse expectations and operating assumptions for the coalition that must be resolved in order to avoid conflict and role confusion.

■ Active membership participation depends on meeting the needs of members. Community leaders and professionals seek accomplishments related to their organizational interests and receive rewards through the organizational aspects of the coalition and through the distribution of resources. Citizen activists and members seek a useful application of their time and receive rewards from participation in program activities and not in activities related to organizational maintenance.

■ Appropriate organizations can facilitate collective action. Coalition-based community interventions tend to devote a lot of energy, at least initially, on developing organizational structure and procedures (committees, task forces, roles, responsibilities). Experience indicates that elaborate committee structures are not productive and sometimes are counterproductive. Committees or task forces with specific purposes or responsibility for specified programmatic activity sustain higher membership.

■ Leadership is essential, and can take different forms. Effective leadership may reside with a dynamic or visionary individual. But one problem associated with this type of leadership is that it is not transferable. Well-functioning coalitions often create opportunities for satisfying and effective participation of members resulting in a "leadership of ideas" demonstrated in a well-articulated plan of action.

■ Planning is critical and should be adapted to the coalition's purpose, organization, and membership. A coalition must begin with a clear understanding of the substance-related problems it seeks to change. Information about these problems should be validated through available empirical evidence. Coalition-generated needs assessments are often difficult to conduct or, due to an absence of resources or skills, poorly implemented. Once outcome-based objectives are set, specific action plans can be developed.

■ Voluntary coalitions should implement proven effective strategies. Community-based approaches are rooted, in part, on a deep appreciation for local involvement and authority, in choosing and carrying out collective action. This philosophy is embodied by the concept of "empowerment," and although this "paradigm shift" in prevention is important, it should not result in barriers to effective coalition action. Research has identified effective prevention approaches; this knowledge must be used.

■ Facilitating community-based collective action requires appropriate roles for paid staff. Paid coalition staff operate more effectively as resource providers and facilitators rather than as direct community organizers. They can fill essential clerical, coordination, and communications functions that provide the glue to hold diverse coalitions together. Paid staff can also provide leadership through expertise in strategies and programmatic activities that will further the coalition goals.

■ Coalition-based community processes must approach their strategies and programmatic actions from an outcome-based perspective and must be ready to make adjustments to the plan of action in order to meet these outcome-based goals. The effectiveness of community-based processes is not a reflection of a coalition's organizational structure or design. It is a function of strategies and activity. If the intervention appears to be ineffective, changes and adjustments in the coalition's action plan—not its organizational structure—are required.

■ Clear purpose, appropriate planning, and commitment to results will produce effective collective action. Community-based processes will break the traditional bounds of organizational inertia and pathology only if the primacy of purpose is recognized and an action strategy is shaped by research-based findings on effective interventions.

***Environmental Approaches.***    The limitations of individualized approaches have led to increased emphasis on the shared environment, the world in which children face and cope with health threats. The shared environment can be a neighborhood, town, city, state, or the nation as a whole. Properly designed and managed, the shared environment can support healthy behavior and thwart risky behavior for all children, regardless of how well prepared they may be by their individualized environments (Klitzner, 1998).

Environmental strategies have been found to be more efficient because they affect every member of a target population. Training store clerks to check IDs reduces the availability of tobacco and alcohol for all neighborhood youth, regardless of whether some youth are unaware that these strategies are being implemented. They also produce more rapid results. Enforcement of the minimum alcohol purchase age can produce more or less immediate reductions in youth alcohol use. Environmental strategies can also enhance the prevention efforts of many communities that already have a number of programs aimed at the individualized environment (Klitzner, 1998). The following are environmental strategies that have been evaluated and found to be effective (Brounstein, Zweig, & Gardner, 1998, pp. 65–70).

### *Price interventions*

■ Increasing the price of alcohol and tobacco through excise taxes is an effective strategy for reducing consumption—both the prevalence of use and the amount consumed. It can also reduce various alcohol-related problems, including motor vehicle fatalities, driving while intoxicated, rapes, robberies, cirrhosis mortality, suicide, and cancer death rates. However, some efforts—source-country crop destruction, interdiction, and disruption of distribution networks—have been relatively ineffective in reducing drug sales.

### *Minimum-purchase-age interventions*

■ Increasing the minimum purchase age for alcohol to age 21 has been effective in decreasing alcohol use among youth, particularly beer consumption. It is associated with reductions in other alcohol-related problems, including alcohol-related traffic crashes, suicides, and deaths resulting from pedestrian injuries, other unintentional injuries, youth homicide, and vandalism. Outcomes related to minimum-purchase-age laws for tobacco are not known because such laws have only recently begun to be enforced.

■ Enforcement of minimum-purchase-age laws against selling alcohol and tobacco to minors using undercover buying operations (also known as "decoy" or "sting" operations) can substantially increase the proportion of retailers who comply with such laws. Undercover buying operations conducted by community groups that provide positive and negative feedback to merchants are also effective in increasing retailer compliance, as are more frequent enforcement operations.

■ "Use and lose" laws, which allow for the suspension of the driver's license of a person under 21 years of age following a conviction of any alcohol or other drug violation (e.g., use, possession or attempt to purchase with or without false identification), are an effective means for increasing compliance with minimum-purchase-age laws among youth. Penalties should be swift, certain, and meaningful. Penalties should not be too harsh, however, since severity is not related to their effectiveness and, if too severe, law enforcement and judicial officers may refuse to apply them.

■ Community awareness and media efforts can be effective tools for increasing perceptions regarding the likelihood of apprehension and punishment and can increase retailer compliance. They also offer a means for changing social norms to be less tolerant of sales to and use by minors and for decreasing the costs of law enforcement operations.

### Deterrence interventions

■ Deterrence laws and policies for impaired driving have been effective in reducing the number of alcohol-related traffic crashes and fatalities among the general population, particularly among youth. Reducing the legal blood alcohol content (BAC) limit to .08 or lower has been shown to reduce the level of impaired driving and alcohol-related crashes.

■ Enforcement of impaired-driving laws is important to deterrence because it serves to increase the public's perceptions of the risks of being caught and punished for driving under the influence of alcohol.

■ Administrative license revocation, which allows for confiscation of the driver's license by the arresting officer if a person is arrested with an illegal BAC or if the driver refuses to be tested, has been shown to reduce the number of fatal traffic crashes and recidivism among driving under the influence (DUI) offenders. Actions against vehicles and license tags have been applied mostly to multiple offenders, with some preliminary evidence that they can lead to significant decreases in recidivism and overall impaired driving.

■ Impaired-driving policies targeting underage drivers (particularly zero tolerance laws setting BAC limits at .00 to .02 percent for youth) and graduated driving privileges, in which a variety of driving restrictions are gradually lifted as the driver gains experience (and maturity), have been shown to reduce significantly traffic deaths among young people.

### Interventions addressing location and density of retail outlets

■ Limitations on the location and density of retail outlets may help contribute to reductions in alcohol consumption, traffic crashes, and certain other alcohol-related problems, including cirrhosis mortality, suicide, and assaults. With respect to illicit drugs, neighborhood anti-drug strategies, such as citizen surveillance and the use of civil remedies—particularly nuisance abatement programs—can be effective in dislocating dealers and reducing the number and density of retail drug markets and possibly other crimes and signs of physical disorder within small geographical areas.

### Restrictions on use

- Restrictions on use in public places and private workplaces (also known as "clean indoor air laws") have been shown to be effective in curtailing cigarette sales and tobacco use among adults and youth. Additional benefits of clean indoor air laws are that they reduce nonsmokers' exposure to cigarette smoke and help to alter norms regarding the social acceptability of smoking. The effects of restrictions on alcohol use have not been systematically evaluated.

### Server-oriented interventions

- With respect to alcohol, server-training programs have been found to affect beliefs and knowledge, with mixed findings of impacts on server practices and traffic safety measures. Retailer education for tobacco merchants has led to relatively small, short-term reductions in sales to minors.
- When server training is combined with the enforcement of laws (e.g., laws against service to intoxicated patrons, against sales to minors), training programs are much more effective in producing changes in both selling and serving practices.
- Education and training programs are important to teach servers about laws, the penalties for violation, recognition of signs of intoxication and false identification, and ways to refuse sales, but they generally are not sufficient when used alone to produce substantial and sustained shifts in compliance with laws.

### Counteradvertising

- Counteradvertising campaigns that disseminate information about the hazards of a product or the industry that promotes it may help reduce cigarette sales and tobacco consumption. The limited research on alcohol warning labels suggests that they may affect awareness, attitudes, and intentions regarding drinking but do not appear to have had a major influence on behavior. Studies have suggested that more conspicuous labels would have a greater effect on awareness and behavior.

**Problem Identification and Referral.**    The following offers research-based information regarding problem identification and referral (Brounstein, Zweig, & Gardner, 1998, pp. 62–63).

- Before implementing this type of strategy, planners should obtain accurate estimates of the numbers of youth whose substance abuse patterns justify intervention services. These estimates must begin with an acknowledgment of the multidimensional nature of youth substance abuse patterns—patterns that include experimental use not progressing to abuse or problem behavior. Ultimately, these estimates are needed to answer basic questions concerning the relative emphasis that should be placed on problem identification versus other prevention approaches.

- Incorporating problem identification and referral into prevention programs ensures that youth who may already be using at the time of the prevention effort will receive the appropriate treatment to meet their needs.
  — Providing transportation to appropriate treatment programs (e.g., Alcoholics Anonymous) encourages youth to participate.
- Problem identification and referral programs should not ignore the relationship between substance use and a variety of other adolescent health problems, such as mental health problems, family problems, early and unwanted pregnancies, sexually transmitted diseases, school failure, and delinquency. This clustering of problems will greatly shape the identification of desired program effects.
- Program planners should be aware that early identification programs could pose risks to the youth involved. Early identification programs target specific individuals for participation and are more intensive in nature than prevention efforts directed to the general adolescent population. The labeling associated with this prevention strategy may increase the probability of future deviance. Another risk may result from exposing youth whose patterns of use may be only experimental to youth with more problematic substance abuse and other deviant behaviors.
- Rigorous research on the effectiveness of this prevention strategy limits the degree to which additional implementation guidance can be offered. Research on brief interventions with the general population in healthcare settings (e.g., tobacco cessation and reducing-problem-drinking programs delivered in dental and primary care practices) has produced positive results in randomized controlled studies. The application of brief interventions to children and adolescents appears promising.
  — Family therapy has been shown to be an effective resource for improving family functioning, increasing parenting skills, and decreasing recidivism of juvenile offenders.
  — Family therapy can serve as one part of a multicomponent prevention effort.
  — It is not clear if family clinical therapy is as effective with young children as it is with adolescents. Younger children have less severe behavioral problems than do adolescents and much of the research on family therapy has focused on juvenile offenders.

## Summary

The theories, principles, and strategies based on prevention research clearly indicate that many considerations and steps must be taken to build, maintain, evaluate, and improve prevention programs. Historically, many substance abuse prevention programs have been developed and implemented based on the "good intentions" of prevention professionals. Many of those efforts have worked, but more have been found to be less than effective. It makes good sense to implement programs that work so that greater numbers of program participants choose to abstain from substance use. This chapter on prevention research has presented the latest science-based findings to guide prevention professionals when working in prevention programs. The three predominant substance abuse prevention theoretical perspectives—risk and protective factors, resiliency, and developmental assets—have also been explored in this chapter. Additionally, discussion ensued on the six CSAP strategies and the research-based learning associated with each category. The work of substance abuse prevention is informed by scientific research-based knowledge. It is imperative that substance abuse prevention professionals understand theory and related research-based findings to implement programs that work.

## KEY TERMS

community norms

delinquency

external assets

internal assets

predictive theory

protective factors

risk factors

resiliency factors

violence

## DISCUSSION QUESTIONS

1. What are the strengths and limitations to each of the three theoretical perspectives? Defend your answer.

2. Compare and contrast each theory. Where do the perspectives intersect, or seem similar? What differences exist?

3. How can the six CSAP strategies be useful in designing and implementing prevention programs?

4. List two research-based principles for each of the six CSAP strategies. Describe each.

5. Why is a comprehensive approach in prevention important? Defend your answer.

## APPLICATION EXERCISES

1. Get copies of the case studies from your instructor, read them, and prepare to answer the following questions.

   a. Identify the risk and protective factors at work in your case study.

   b. How did you determine which factors to identify, and why did you identify them?

   c. Was it easy to identify the factors? If not, what was confusing?

   d. Pick one prevention theory and apply it to a local prevention program. How does the theory fit? If it does not fit, why not?

## SUGGESTED READINGS

Hawkins, J. D., Catalano, R. F., & Miller, J. Y. (1992). Risk and protective factors for alcohol and other drug problems in adolescence and early adulthood: Implications for substance abuse prevention. *Psychological Bulletin, 112*, 64–105.

Scales, P., & Leffert, N. (1999). *Developmental assets: A synthesis of the scientific research on adolescent development.* Minneapolis, MN: Search Institute.
Werner, E. E., & Smith, R. S. (1992). *Overcoming the odds: High-risk children from birth to adulthood.* New York: Cornell University Press.

# REFERENCES

Bellack, A., Hersen, M., & Kazdin, A. (Eds.). (1990). *International handbook of modification and therapy.* New York: Plenum Press.
Brounstein, P., Zweig, J., & Gardner, S. (1998, December). *Science-based practices in substance abuse prevention: A guide.* Rockville, MD: Center for Substance Abuse Prevention, Division of Knowledge Development and Evaluation.
Bushweller, K. (1995, May). The resilient child. *The American School Board Journal,* 18–23.
Center for Substance Abuse Prevention. (1993). *Prevention primer: An encyclopedia of alcohol, tobacco, and other drug prevention terms.* (DHHS Publication No. SMA 2060). Rockville, MD: National Clearinghouse for Alcohol and Drug Information.
Developmental Research and Programs. (1997). *Communities that care: Risk assessment for preventing adolescent problem behaviors.* Seattle, WA: Developmental Research and Programs.
Hawkins, J. D., Catalano, R. F., & Miller, J. Y. (1992). Risk and protective factors for alcohol and other drug problems in adolescence and early adulthood: Implications for substance abuse prevention. *Psychological Bulletin, 112,* 64–105.
Klitzner, M. (1998). *Integrating environmental change theory into prevention practice.* Vienna, VA: Klitzner and Associates.
Leffert, N., Benson, P., & Roehlkepartain, J. (1997). *Starting out right: Developmental assets for children.* Minneapolis, MN: Search Institute.
Scales, P., & Leffert, N. (1999). *Developmental assets: A synthesis of the scientific research on adolescent development.* Minneapolis, MN: Search Institute.
Werner, E. E. (1986). Resilient offspring of alcoholics: A longitudinal study from birth to age 18. *Journal of Studies on Alcohol, 47,* 34–40.
Werner, E. E., & Smith, R. S. (1992). *Overcoming the odds: High-risk children from birth to adulthood.* New York: Cornell University Press.
Western Center for the Application of Prevention Technologies. (n.d.). *Developing healthy communities: A risk and protective factor approach to preventing alcohol and other drug abuse* [Brochure]. Reno, NV: Author.

# CHAPTER

# 3

# Prevention Program Planning

In this chapter we explore how to plan an effective prevention program. Although various theories and models exist for prevention program planning, the one presented in this chapter is based on the scientifically defensible risk and protective factor theory, as described by Hawkins, Catalano, and Miller (1992). In order for prevention efforts to be effective, a comprehensive plan involving multiple and diverse segments of the community (e.g., school, family, religious institutions, grassroots neighborhood organizations, and businesses) is crucial. The steps discussed in this chapter can assist prevention professionals in completing this planning process.

The seven steps of program planning are:

1. Assess the readiness of the community and mobilize the community to take action.
2. Assess the levels of risk factors and protective factors in the community.
3. Translate the risk and protective factor data into priorities.
4. Examine the resources in the community that are reducing the priority risk factors and increasing protective factors.
5. Select a target population.
6. Apply "best practices" and "guiding principles."
7. Evaluate the prevention program or strategy implemented.

It is crucial that prevention professionals implement each step in order to ensure the greatest success possible. If only a few steps are implemented, then the likelihood for success decreases. For example, if a prevention professional has completed Steps 2 through 7 but did not address the denial present in his or her community (Step 1), then all the good planning could be for naught. Many good prevention programs have been known to fail simply due to the lack of readiness of communities for prevention. Therefore, it is essential that prevention professionals complete all seven steps of the planning process.

Before any of the steps are undertaken, however, prevention professionals must define what they mean by "community." Is their community a school, a neighborhood, a city block, or a county? Once "community" is defined, then the program planning steps should be completed with those boundaries in mind.

# Step 1: Assess the Readiness of the Community and Mobilize for Action

The first step in planning a prevention program is assessing **community readiness** for prevention and mobilizing the community to take action. The National Institute on Drug Abuse (NIDA) (1997a) offers these guidelines:

1. Community readiness is the extent to which a community is adequately prepared to implement a drug abuse prevention program.
2. A community must have the support and commitment of its members and the needed resources to implement an effective prevention effort.
3. Because community readiness is a process, factors associated with it can be objectively assessed and systematically enhanced.

Consequently, it is essential that prevention professionals begin their program planning by reviewing their communities' level of readiness.

Edwards, Jumper-Thurman, Plested, Oetting, and Swanson (2000) identified nine stages of community readiness that are found in communities. They found that prevention efforts are more likely to succeed in communities that have achieved a higher stage of readiness. Therefore, to increase a community's readiness for prevention programming, it is important to give careful consideration to the nine stages of community readiness, starting with an objective needs assessment to gauge the level at which a community stands.

In many communities, a high level of denial exists around the effects of alcohol, tobacco, and other drug abuse. Community members do not believe that substance abuse exists in their community. Instead, they view drugs as being abused only in other communities. If a prevention professional attempts to implement a program, no matter how good the program is, the likelihood that the program will be successful is very limited. However, when communities are in a state of readiness (they believe a problem exists in their community and they are ready to take action), the likelihood for success is greatly enhanced. Consequently, prevention specialists must know the stages of readiness and how to increase a community's readiness for prevention.

The following are the nine stages of community readiness, as identified by NIDA (1997a) and Edwards et al. (2000). After the description of each stage, suggested strategies are described that can assist in moving communities to the next, greater level of readiness.

## Stage 1: Community Tolerance/No Knowledge

In the first stage of readiness, "community norms actively tolerate or encourage the problem behavior, although the behavior may be expected of one group and not another (e.g., by sex, race, social class, or age). The behavior, when occurring in the appropriate social context, is viewed as acceptable or as part of the community norm" (NIDA, 1997a, p. 13). For example, in a community that has "tolerance" for alcohol abuse, a middle-aged man at a county fair's popular "beer garden" could become intoxicated and not reap any repercussions for doing so. Furthermore, "those who do not engage in the behavior may be tolerated, but might be viewed as somewhat deviant" (p. 13). For example, if another middle-aged man at that fair is hanging around with his buddies at the beer garden but is not drinking alcohol, he may be viewed as an outcast or abnormal.

***Strategies to Move to the Next Stage.***    Several strategies exist that can help move communities out of Stage 1. One strategy includes holding "small-group and one-on-one discussions with community leaders to identify the perceived benefits of substance abuse and how norms reinforce use" (NIDA, 1997a, p. 29). In the example above, this strategy could involve meeting with the chairperson of the fair to discuss the perceived benefits of public intoxication at the fair's beer garden. Another strategy is to hold small-group and one-on-one discussions with community leaders on the health, psychological, and social costs of substance abuse (NIDA, 1997a). This can aid in changing the perceptions of those who are most likely to be part of the group that begins prevention program development (NIDA, 1997a).

## Stage 2: Denial

If a community is in Stage 2 of readiness, the problem behavior is usually recognized as such (NIDA, 1997a): "Community norms usually would not approve of the behavior, but there is little or no recognition that this might be a local problem" (NIDA, 1997a, p. 13). For example, community members may view that teenagers using drugs is not acceptable; however, they think that very few, if any, kids in their community use drugs. "If there is some idea that it is a problem, there is a feeling that nothing needs to be done about this locally, or that nothing can be done about it" (p. 13).

***Strategies to Move to the Next Stage.***    One strategy to increase readiness from Stage 2 is to provide educational outreach to community leaders and community groups interested in sponsoring local programs focusing on the health, psychological, and social costs of substance abuse (NIDA, 1997a). Another strategy is to use local incidents in one-on-one discussions and educational outreach programs in order to illustrate harmful consequences of substance abuse (NIDA, 1997a). Many communities have used this approach, transforming some very tragic situations (e.g., alcohol poisoning of a local high school student, or the death of a family at the hands of a person who had been driving under the influence of alcohol) into opportunities to educate the community on the harmful effects of substance abuse.

## Stage 3: Vague Awareness

Communities in Stage 3 have a "general belief that there is a local problem and that something ought to be done about it" (NIDA, 1997a, p. 13). However, "knowledge about local problems tends to be stereotypical and vague, or linked only to a specific incident or two. There is no immediate motivation to do anything. No identifiable leadership exists, or if it does, the leadership lacks energy or motivation" (p. 13).

***Strategies to Move to the Next Stage.***    A strategy to move communities out of "vague awareness" is to conduct educational outreach programs on the national and state prevalence rates of substance abuse, prevalence rates in communities with similar characteristics, and local incidents that illustrate harmful consequences of substance abuse (NIDA, 1997a). For example, a prevention professional could use statistics on alcohol use from Monitoring the Future, a national survey, and compare them with data from a state and local survey, such as the Youth Risk Behavior Survey. Then they could illustrate the effects that alcohol has had on youth in their community, such as drinking-and-driving injuries and/or deaths and overdoses. Another strategy is to produce local media campaigns that emphasize the consequences of substance abuse (NIDA, 1997a). Many national media campaigns exist that can provide tools and materials for local initiatives.

## Stage 4: Preplanning

A clear recognition that a local problem exists and that something should be done about it is evident in communities in Stage 4 (NIDA, 1997a). "There are identifiable leaders, and there may be a committee, but no real planning is occurring. There is general information about local problems, but ideas about etiology or risk factors tend to be stereotyped" (NIDA, 1997a, p. 14). For example, while there is a belief a problem exists in the community, the belief of the cause of substance abuse may be "gut" feelings or guesses. Often people who are passionate about starting prevention programs in a community have been affected personally by substance abuse, such as the parent of a child who was killed by alcohol poisoning. Consequently, they may generalize their situation to all situations in the community. Solutions in these situations often are not science-based or effective. One solution often heard is, "If only kids had something to do, they would not drink." The result of this etiology is often drug-free dances and youth centers. However, research has shown that just keeping youth busy is not an effective strategy. Therefore, the lack of knowledge of the etiology or risk factors can be the sign of a lower level of readiness.

***Strategies to Move to the Next Stage.***    One strategy to increase readiness from Stage 4 is to provide educational outreach programs to community leaders and sponsorship groups (NIDA, 1997a). These outreach programs can highlight prevalence rates, as well as the correlates or causes of substance abuse (NIDA, 1997a). For example, a training on risk and protective factors for community leaders and sponsorship groups can be useful. Another strategy is to conduct educational outreach programs that introduce the concept of prevention and illustrate specific prevention programs adopted by communities with similar profiles (NIDA, 1997a). Finally, "local media campaigns emphasizing the consequences of substance abuse and ways of reducing demand for illicit substances through prevention programming" (NIDA, 1997a, p. 30) can help move a community out of Stage 4. As mentioned above, prevention professionals can use materials and information from several national media campaigns to assist them in creating and implementing local campaigns.

## Stage 5: Preparation

Stage 5 communities are planning and focusing on practical details of implementing prevention programs (NIDA, 1997a). "There is general information about local problems and about the pros and cons of prevention programs, but planning may not be based on formally collected data" (NIDA, 1997a, p. 13). In this stage, leaders are active and energetic. One or more prevention programs "may have started on a trial basis and funding is being actively sought or has been committed" (p. 13).

***Strategies to Move to the Next Stage.***    One way to assist a community in moving out of Stage 5 is to implement educational outreach programs for the "general public on specific types of prevention programs, their goals, and how they can be implemented" (NIDA, 1997a, p. 30). Another method is to enact "educational outreach programs for community leaders and local sponsorship groups on prevention programs, goals, staff requirements, and other startup aspects of programming" (p. 30). Finally, "a local media campaign describing the benefits of prevention programs for reducing consequences of substance abuse" (p. 30) could be performed.

## Stage 6: Initiation

At the stage of initiation, "enough information is available to justify a prevention program, but knowledge of risk factors is likely to be stereotyped" (NIDA, 1997a, p. 14). At Stage 6, a prevention program is being implemented, but it is still on trial. Staff members are receiving training or are just finished with training. This can be a time of "great enthusiasm because limitations and problems have not yet been experienced" (p. 14).

***Strategies to Move to the Next Stage.***    Examples of strategies to increase readiness from Stage 6 include the following. First, "an in-service educational training for program staff (paid and volunteer) can be held on the consequences, correlates, and causes of substance abuse and the nature of the problem in the local community" (NIDA, 1997a, p. 30). This could be training covering the topics listed in Chapter 2, such as the risk and protective factor theory. Second, "publicity efforts associated with the kickoff of the program" (p. 30) can aid communities to move beyond Stage 6. Finally, holding a meeting with community leaders and local sponsorship groups to provide an update and review of initial program activities can be a useful strategy (NIDA, 1997a). This can be a good time to share initial evaluation information, such as number of individuals served, types of individuals served (age, race/ethnicity, gender, etc.), and activities completed. (See "Step 7: Evaluation" below, as well as Chapter 8, for more information on evaluation.)

## Stage 7: Institutionalization/Stabilization

In Stage 7, one or two prevention programs are being implemented that are supported by the administration and are accepted as a routine and valuable activity (NIDA, 1997a). The prevention program staff are now trained and experienced. At this point, no need for change or expansion exists (NIDA, 1997a). "Limitations may be known, but there is not much sense that the limitations suggest a need for change" (NIDA, 1997a, p. 14). A system has been established to track prevalence data (NIDA, 1997a). In this stage, "There is not necessarily permanent funding, but there is established funding that allows the program the opportunity to implement its action plan" (p. 14).

*Strategies to Move to the Next Stage.*   One strategy to increase readiness from Stage 7 is "in-service educational programs on the evaluation process, new trends in substance abuse and new initiatives in prevention programming" (NIDA, 1997a, p. 31). This can be done with trainers brought in from the outside or staff can be sent to trainings sponsored by others (NIDA, 1997a). Another method for increasing readiness is to have "periodic review meetings and special recognition events for local supporters of prevention programs" (1997a, p. 31). Local publicity efforts providing information about meetings and recognition events can also be useful in moving communities out of Stage 7 (1997a).

## Stage 8: Confirmation/Expansion

In Stage 8 "standard programs are viewed as valuable and authorities support expanding or improving programs" (NIDA, 1997a, p. 14). Some focus has been shifted to creating and/or trying new prevention programs in order to reach more people, such as those thought to be more at risk or different demographic groups (NIDA, 1997a). For example, the community may have been supporting a school-based curriculum in two middle schools in the past. At this stage, the curriculum is being expanded to other middle schools in the community and a curriculum is initiated in the elementary schools. In communities in Stage 8 efforts are also focused on obtaining funds for new programs (p. 14). Furthermore, "data are obtained regularly on the extent of local problems, and efforts are made to assess risk factors and causes of the problem" (p. 14).

*Strategies to Move to the Next Stage.*   To assist in moving a community from Stage 8, in-service educational programs on conducting local needs assessments to target specific groups in the community for prevention programming can be either held with trainers brought in from the outside, or staff can be sent to trainings sponsored by others (NIDA, 1997a). "Periodic review meetings and special recognition events for local supporters of the prevention program" (1997a, p. 31) can also be held. Finally, "results of research and evaluation activities of the prevention program can be presented to the public through local media and public meetings" (p. 31).

## Stage 9: Professionalization

"Detailed and sophisticated knowledge of the prevalence, risk factors, and etiology exists" (NIDA, 1997a, p. 15) in Stage 9 communities. Prevention programs being implemented "may be aimed at general populations, while others are targeted at specific risk factors or groups at risk" (p. 15). Staff are now highly trained, authorities are supportive, and community involvement is high (1997a). Strong evaluation designs and plans are being used to assess and modify programs (1997a).

*Strategies to Maintain Stage.*   In order to maintain readiness, several strategies can be employed. First, continued training of staff is important, particularly when new staff members are hired. Next, "continued assessment of new drug-related problems and reassessment of targeted groups" (NIDA, 1997a, p. 31) within the community is useful. Also, ongoing evaluation of the program is essential (NIDA, 1997a). This is important because most funders will require evidence of effectiveness of prevention programs in order to continue to fund the programs. Finally, "update[s] on program activities and results should be released for the benefit of community leaders and local sponsorship groups" (1997a, p. 31). This can occur through stories and reports disseminated through local media and public meetings. The combination of evaluation results and anecdotal evidence can be very powerful in these situations.

## Community Readiness Assessment Tools

Some tools exist to help prevention professionals assess community readiness. One key informant survey is found in Appendix A. This tool can be used to assist prevention professionals in identifying how ready a community is for substance abuse prevention. The prevention professional or community coalition members can interview key informants using the survey, or the survey can be sent by mail to the key informants. In-person interviews can increase the response rate; however, they take more time to implement. While mailing surveys can save time, one must expect lower response rates. Regardless of which tool or method is used, it is essential that prevention program planning begin with the identification of a community's level of readiness and action to improve that community's readiness.

## Community Mobilization

The second part to Step 1 is mobilizing the community to take action. This can be done hand-in-hand with assessing and addressing community readiness. The following is an explanation of the benefits of community mobilization, as well as tips on forming a coalition.

***Benefits of Community Mobilization.***    Several benefits emerge through the community mobilization process as identified by the National Highway Traffic Safety Administration (NHTSA) (2001). First, the number of people involved enhances credibility by creating a broad-based, grassroots coalition. NHTSA (2001) further explains,

> One saying is especially appropriate for coalitions: "It is easy to cut one blade of grass, but if you bind many blades together into a sheaf, they are very difficult to cut through." The more widespread support a project can demonstrate, the more seriously the effort is perceived. When the project demonstrates both widespread support and active involvement, opinion leaders, the media and the public begin to take the effort seriously and pay attention. ("Advantages of a Coalition" section, para. 1)

Next, mobilizing community coalitions is useful because it pulls in diverse participants with diverse skills. Also, it provides access to important target populations such as youth, parents, policy makers, law enforcement, the media, prevention programs, and businesses. NHTSA (2001) further explains,

> Each coalition member or member organization can contribute their particular expertise or resources to facilitate activities by other members or by the coalition as a whole. They

can . . . assist with training, recruit new members or volunteers, hand out flyers, or conduct a market survey. By working together, members often find they solve mutual problems. . . . By pooling resources, coalition members multiply opportunities. ("Advantages of a Coalition" section, para. 2)

Yet another benefit to community coalitions is the opportunity for networking to occur. The coalition provides a great opportunity for networking because of the varied individuals participating in it. In fact, this may be the reason why many individuals are willing to participate. Networking also provides the opportunity to do effective problem solving because of the wide range of knowledge and skills that the participants possess. "Effective networking also means coalition members can identify organizations that can fill a specific need, answer a question, facilitate an introduction, or help to secure funds" (NHTSA, 2001, "Advantages of a Coalition" section, para. 3).

Next, the creation of a community coalition can aid in ensuring that new ideas and energy are infused over time. As NHTSA (2001) points out,

Any program can get stale and die out if it isn't re-energized with new people and new energy. A fresh perspective on the project's issue may be just what is needed to get things moving again. Substance abuse prevention organizations, for instance, may require the shot in the arm that a broad-based program to prevent underage drinking can provide. ("Advantages of a Coalition" section, para. 4)

Another benefit is that coalitions are a good source of information regarding community attitudes and norms on substance abuse. This is essential when assessing and improving community readiness for prevention. A wide variety of individuals on the coalition ensures a wider perspective on the attitudes and beliefs in different sectors of the community. NHTSA (2001) states,

One person, or even a small staff, cannot know everything that is relevant to their issue, including information about related programs and potential funding. A grassroots coalition can be the eyes and ears and provide important intelligence information. A wise coalition coordinator will solicit and coalesce the information available from individual members. ("Advantages of a Coalition" section, para. 5)

When a coalition consists of a large variety of constituents, it can assist in creating publicity and marketing for the program. As ambassadors for the program, coalition members can increase awareness across the community about the coalition and its prevention programs and activities. This can be important in ensuring participation in the programs. It is also useful when the coalition needs to find funds to continue and/or expand its programs and activities. If the coalition can provide sample articles, press releases, and other marketing materials to its members, then there is a greater likelihood that it will be successful in marketing the coalition.

Finally, a community coalition can assist in distributing materials in the community. Due to a lack of staff and funding often present in community coalitions, the ability to have coalition members assist in distributing public information and media campaigns materials can be hugely beneficial. As NHTSA (2001) described, "Materials may be beautifully produced, but if they are unseen, they are valueless. Through their jobs and neighborhood connections, coalition members can serve as an effective network for dissemination" ("Advantages of a Coalition" section, para. 8). Distribution can be done through employers on the coalition who can establish and implement company policies in support of a program. Employers can also distribute campaign materials to its employees through posters at the job site, materials in wellness programs, paycheck stuffers, e-mails, and presentations. Furthermore, members of the community coalition who also participate in civic associations, service clubs (such as Rotary, Elks, Kiwanis, Jaycees, and Junior League), and chambers of commerce can help disseminate campaign materials in their newsletters, presentations, and distribution of materials. Therefore, using coalition members to assist in the implementation of public information and media campaigns can augment the coalition's opportunity for success.

***Tips on Forming a Community Coalition.***    Forming a coalition requires strong, proactive planning to increase the likelihood of success. Many prevention professionals are charged with the task of creating a community coalition, but often do not have the proper tools and knowledge to be successful. Consequently, the following steps from NHTSA (2001), explored in detail below, can assist in helping to build the knowledge and skills to create an effective community coalition:

1. Determine whether a new coalition is needed.
2. Brainstorm ideas about potential members of the coalition.
3. Determine staffing, budget, and resources.
4. Invite people to join.
5. Clarify expectations.
6. Create a mission statement.
7. Define goals and objectives.

The first step is to determine whether a new coalition is needed in the community (NHTSA, 2001). It is very possible that an existing coalition or coalitions in the community focus(es) on problem behaviors similar to substance abuse prevention. For example, a community may have a youth violence prevention coalition, a teenage pregnancy prevention coalition, and/or a school dropout prevention coalition. As was discussed in Chapter 2, because youth violence, teenage pregnancy, school drop-out and substance abuse have many of the same risk and protective factors, coalitions for each would likely have similar missions, goals, and objectives. Similarly, a community may have several coalitions already focused on substance abuse, such as Mothers Against Drunk Drivers or Driving Under the Influence (DUI) task forces. It is highly likely that if the community does have one or more coalitions addressing substance abuse or similar problem behaviors, the individuals that a prevention professional wants on the coalition may be the same ones.

However, disadvantages may be present when considering becoming a part of an existing community coalition. For example, it is possible that the substance abuse prevention issue would not be addressed by the community coalition because it is mandated to address a singular issue. Alternately, the existing coalition leaders and/or members may not be interested in expanding the scope of the coalition. Consequently, prevention professionals should proceed cautiously before simply joining an existing coalition.

The second step to forming a community coalition is to brainstorm in order to compile a list of potential members of the coalition (NHTSA, 2001). Prevention professionals should identify three or four individuals who are likely key stakeholders for the coalition to assist them in this process. The stakeholders could be affiliated with the organization looking to create the coalition, well-connected individuals from the community, or "champions" to the cause. One such champion "may be a judge, political leader, businessperson, civic leader or member of the faith community, but they should be someone who is well respected and able to generate support for the new entity" (NHTSA, 2001, "How to Form a Coalition" section, para. 4). The goal is to create a list of individuals who will be contacted to participate in the coalition. Several questions should be answered during this process, as identified by NHTSA (2001), including: "Who are the community's key leaders? Who are the obvious stakeholders in the issue? Whose participation will be critical to the success of the effort? Are diverse populations of the community represented?" ("How to Form a Coalition" section, para. 3).

Step three in forming a community coalition is to determine staffing, budget, and resources (NHTSA, 2001). One of the key determinants of success for a community coalition is a paid staff person. Without that staff person, it can be difficult to administer programs as designed and to complete all the paperwork that seems inevitable in prevention programs (e.g., reports for the funding agency). If having a paid staff person is not a possibility, it is essential that the coalition decide early in the process how coalition members will complete tasks. In summary, NHTSA (2001) identified the following questions that a coalition should answer to determine staffing needs:

> Will the project director or other manager be paid? Where will those funds come from and how much money will be needed? How much time will the project coordinator be required to dedicate to the program? Will that person have other responsibilities? Who will supervise the coordinator? ("How to Form a Coalition" section, para. 6)

Beyond staffing costs, coalitions need funding to cover office space, furniture, equipment, postage, printing, and refreshments for meetings (NHTSA, 2001). Consequently, coalition members must ensure that either funding or donations are in place to cover these costs.

The fourth step to forming a coalition is inviting people to join (NHTSA, 2001). This can be done through personal contact or a letter. It is important to gauge whether the potential coalition members will react most positively to personal contact or a formal letter of invitation. If a champion is on board with the coalition, it is useful to have this person sign the letter of invitation and/or assist with the personal contacts.

Once coalition members are on board, the fifth step to building a coalition is to clarify expectations (NHTSA, 2001). It is essential that coalition members understand their roles and responsibilities. This includes "the number of times the group can expect to meet throughout the year, the time of the meetings, what is expected of the group, and what individuals may be expected to contribute" (NHTSA, 2001, "How to Form a Coalition" section, para. 9). Finally, it is essential to create written guidelines or policies regarding membership (NHTSA, 2001).

The final two steps to forming a coalition include creating a mission statement and defining goals and objectives (NHTSA, 2001). It is essential to complete these steps because the diverse groups represented on the coalition may have differing ideas of the purpose of the coalition. The process of creating a mission statement, goals, and objectives creates consensus among coalition members, ensuring that the coalition is starting from a solid base.

Once a coalition is formed, it is time to turn attention to assessing the levels of risk and protective factors in the community. Coalition members are important players in completing this and other tasks in the program planning and evaluation process. They can assist in the collection and analysis of data, as well as the implementation and analysis of the evaluation.

# Step 2: Assess the Levels of Risk Factors and Protective Factors in the Community

After assessing and improving community readiness for prevention and mobilizing the community, it is important to complete a **needs assessment**. Traditionally, needs assessments identify the current conditions of a situation. For example, a needs assessment for substance abuse treatment involves identifying how many people in a community are currently needing treatment services. However, when conducting a needs assessment for prevention, we need to know how many youth will abuse drugs *in the future*. In other words, "assessing the need for prevention services requires methods for assessing the probability of future drug abuse within populations that are not currently using substances" (Arthur & Blitz, 2000). Fortunately, risk and protective factor theory provides a framework through which we can calculate the risk for future substance abuse in communities. Therefore, the identification of how prevalent risk and protective factors are in a community provides the ideal "needs" assessment for substance abuse prevention.

Several benefits exist when a needs assessment is completed. A needs assessment helps create an objective profile of the community, determine the geographic and demographic areas that are at greatest risk, indicate where time and money should be put in order to have the greatest impact, show policy makers the need for funding the prevention program, and identify research-based strategies to implement in the community (Western Center for the Application of Prevention Technologies, 2001).

The needs assessment is essential before moving into the implementation phase. Many communities have repeatedly made the mistake of jumping right into program implementation, ignoring the fact that the programs they implement often are not addressing the needs of the community. For example, an energetic prevention coalition attended a substance abuse prevention conference. They participated in a workshop where enthusiastic speakers presented a parenting education program that had been effectively implemented in another community. Very energized and sold on the program, the prevention coalition members returned to their community prepared to implement the parenting program. However, it turns out that this community had a very low prevalence of the "family management problems" and "favorable parental attitudes toward drug use" risk factors—the exact risk factors the parenting education program was designed to address. Consequently, the likelihood of seeing a significant impact on substance abuse in the community was minimal.

## Data Collection

Data collection is the first phase of conducting a needs assessment. Two kinds of data can be collected: (1) **archival data** (data that already exists), and (2) **survey data** (data that is created). The community coalition formed during the first step of the planning process can be very useful in the data collection process. Dividing the tasks to be completed among the coalition members can ensure a comprehensive and successful process.

In order to collect data, the following steps need to be taken. First, data currently available for each risk and protective factor needs to be identified, beginning with the list of archival indicators from the Social Development Research Group (n.d.). (See Appendix B for examples of archival indicator data.) Archival indicators are proxy data for the risk factors. These indicators are necessary because data sets do not exist currently for each risk factor. For example, one cannot go to the local health department and ask for the data on "family management problems." This data set does not exist. Consequently, other proxy data must be used to illuminate how prevalent each risk factor is in a community. For family management problems, the proxy data sets are "children living away from parents" and "children living in foster care." If a community is relatively high in these areas, then that means that the risk factor of family management problems is prevalent.

Note, however, that indicator data is to be used only as a method to identify which risk factors are prevalent in a community. Because they are proxy measures, they are not to be used while selecting a program/strategy to implement. For example, if a community finds the risk factor of family management problems is prevalent, they should *not* select strategies to reduce the number of children living away from parents. Instead, a program or strategy to increase family management skills would be in order.

After collecting the archival indicator data, it must be determined which factors need additional data. Then, a plan to collect the additional data that is needed must be developed. Finally, the additional data is to be collected.

## Data Analysis

Once the indicator data is collected, it is time to analyze the data. Data analysis assists in identifying which risk and protective factors need to be prioritized in a community action plan, and it provides justification for grant applications. It also supports existing policies and programs and assists in selecting new prevention programs to implement. In order to analyze data, the following questions from Developmental Research and Programs (1996) need to be answered.

1. What do the raw data tell you? At first glance, what do the data tell you? Do the raw numbers impress you as being low? Average? High? Are there any red flags?
2. How do the data compare to previous years? Is there a trend? By comparing numbers for previous years, a picture of how the data has been changing over time may

emerge. Is it increasing? Decreasing? Staying the same? How have trends changed in relation to population changes?

3. How do data compare with other similar data (national, state, county, etc.)? Are the trends similar? Are the rates about the same? Are they going up or down?

4. What can be interpreted from the data? After reviewing the raw data, the data trends, and the data comparisons, if available, what can be interpreted from the analysis? Why it is occurring? What could have caused the trend? What does the observed level or trend say about this risk or protective factor?

5. Are there relationships among risk factors that can be identified based on the data you have? Examine data across risk factors and across protective factors.

6. Finally, should this risk factor be prioritized? The more information obtained about the indicator data, the easier this question will be to answer. (Copyright © 2001 Channing L. Bete Co., Inc. All rights reserved. Reproduced with permission of the publisher.)

When communities and prevention professionals take the time to answer the above questions thoroughly, the next step, translating data into priorities, is much easier to complete. Consequently, some up-front work on data analysis will save time in the end.

## Step 3: Translate Data into Priorities

Once the collection and analysis of the data is complete, it is time to prioritize which risk and protective factors need to be addressed in the community. The following questions from Developmental Research and Programs (1996) will assist in identifying priorities.

First, looking across the data collected, are there risk factors or protective factors for which no data exists? If so, identify these factors, determine if and where the appropriate data can be collected and add this information to the data analysis to strengthen the overall assessment. Remember, the assessment is the foundation for a prevention action plan. The more thoroughly this step is completed, the more effective and accurate prevention programs can be designed and implemented.

Second, which risks are most prevalent in the community? Which of the protective factors is most lacking? Base this judgment on trends, comparisons with similar data (from national, state or other communities), comparisons across factors and interpretation of the data and possible explanations.

Third, at what developmental periods are children most at risk in the community?

Fourth, is there an identifiable "cluster" of risk factors that, addressed together, could provide a synergistic response? For example, if community laws and norms and favorable parental attitudes both are prevalent in a community, one prevention strategy may be able to address both risk factors, creating a synergistic response.

Finally, which two to five risk factors, identified as most prevalent in the community, should the community tackle first? Which protective factor should be tackled first? It is extremely important for community coalitions and prevention professionals to limit the number of risk and protective factors they wish to address at one time. Attempts by coalitions and professionals to address more than five risk and/or protective factors at one time often dilute their efforts so much that no one can see the effect of their efforts. By limiting the number of factors to be addressed, the likelihood increases that the risk and/or protective factors will be impacted by the efforts. (Copyright © 2001 Channing L. Bete Co., Inc. All rights reserved. Reproduced with permission of the publisher.)

## Step 4: Examine the Resources in the Community That Are Reducing Risk Factors and Increasing Protective Factors

Once the two to five priority risk and protective factors have been identified for the community, it is important to assess which community resources are already in place. A resource assessment answers the question, "What is going on in the community?" Resources are anything that can be used to reduce the likelihood that individuals in a community will begin or continue to abuse alcohol, tobacco, and other drugs.

A resource assessment can help accomplish many tasks, including identifying gaps where new services should be implemented and helping avoid duplication. The process of conducting a resource assessment helps build collaboration among service providers and identify existing resources to sponsor new programs. Furthermore, it indicates where time and money should be put to have the greatest impact. It can also show how existing programs can be modified to meet prevention needs. Ultimately, it assists in creating a comprehensive prevention strategy for the community, which in turn significantly affects the prioritized risk and protective factors.

It is important to conduct a resource assessment *after* the priority risk and/or protective factors are identified, because the resource assessment should only be done in the area of the priority risk and/or protective factors. When communities try to conduct a resource assessment covering all the risk and protective factors, the project becomes too enormous to complete. Therefore, the priority risk and/or protective factors help limit the scope of the resource assessment to a manageable size.

### Data Collection

The first step to conducting a resource assessment is to collect information on existing resources in the community that may be addressing the priority risk and protective factors identified through the needs assessment. To do this, the type of resources to be reviewed must be identified. For example, will only substance abuse prevention programs or generic prevention programs be included in the assessment? Will both direct and indirect services be included? Will only publicly funded programs be included? And will state, county, and local programs or only local programs be included? These questions must be answered before the data collection phase of the resource assessment begins.

Next, it must be determined how the potential resources will be assessed. For example, will a written survey be used or will key leaders be interviewed? Or do materials exist that contain the information needed? Once this has been decided, the data collection can begin. The following information should be collected for each resource being reviewed: risk and protective factor(s) addressed by the program; developmental appropriateness; target population; and evaluations conducted on the program.

## Data Analysis

Once the data has been collected on the resources available in the community that are addressing the priority risk and protective factors, the resources must be analyzed. The analysis should determine how effectively the resources are affecting the priority risk and protective factors. This will assist in identifying where the gaps in services are in the community.

To assist in the analysis, the following questions need to be asked of each resource that has been identified. First, does the program address known *risk factors*? If so, which ones? How does it reduce or eliminate the risk? It must be evident which risk factors are being addressed by the program/activity. Next, how does the program increase *protective factors*? Programs need to reduce risks in a way that builds bonds and strengthens clear standards for behavior. Specifically, the program should increase *opportunities* for youth to contribute, teach the *skills* to contribute, and *recognize* skillful or successful performance. To be effective, the program must do all three.

Next, does the program intervene early, at a developmentally appropriate time? Prevention programs need to address risk factors as they are becoming salient [e.g., before academic failure occurs], before the behavior stabilizes.

Fourth, is it likely the program reaches those individuals or groups at greatest risk? Prevention programs need to be implemented in places where there are a large proportion of youngsters who are facing multiple risk factors. One way to assess programs for this criterion is to look at the target populations being served by the program. How widespread is the program? Does it adequately cover the target population? A strategy may need to be implemented in more areas, or in different ways.

A fifth question to be asked of resources identified by the resource assessment is does the program work with the diverse racial, cultural, and economic groups in your community? The program needs to be delivered in a way the target population understands and accepts. Furthermore, the target population must see this strategy/program as a priority. The program must be appropriate to their needs and accessible to the group for whom it is designed.

Finally, it must be assessed whether the program has been evaluated. It is important to identify evidence of its effectiveness, if it exists. A program in the community may appear to be addressing the same priority risk and protective factor, but if no evidence exists that it is effective, another similar strategy with evidence of effectiveness may need to be implemented. If a program meets all other criteria and appears to be effective, but has not been evaluated, the program should be encouraged to do a formal evaluation.

After analyzing all of the resources using the above questions, one last set of questions must be addressed in the resource assessment. First, are the risk and protective factors identified as priorities through the needs assessment being adequately addressed by existing programs and services? If not, can existing programs and services be changed and/or modified to enhance their effectiveness? If so, how? Finally, do additional programs and/or services need to be selected and implemented to fill in gaps identified through the resource assessment? (Copyright © 2001 Channing L. Bete Co., Inc. All rights reserved. Reproduced with permission of the publisher.)

# Step 5: Select a Target Population

By this point in the planning process, the target of the program's time and funding (the priority risk and protective factors) has been identified, and the gaps that need to be filled are identified (results of the resource assessment). Consequently, it is time to identify what type of target population needs to be addressed: **universal**, **selective**, or **indicated**. The Institute of Medicine created these terms in order to facilitate a better understanding of the type of prevention program populations that need to be addressed.

## Universal

"Universal prevention strategies are designed to address an entire population (national, local community, school, neighborhood), with messages and programs aimed at preventing or delaying the abuse of alcohol, tobacco, and other drugs" (National Institute on Drug Abuse [NIDA], 1997b, p. 11). Consequently, participants for universal prevention strategies are not selected by level of risk, but simply because they belong to a population. For example, a universal population could be all elementary students in a town, the elderly, an ethnic community in a geographic area, or an entire city. The goal of universal prevention strategies is to prevent substance abuse by providing all individuals in a specified population with the information and skills necessary to prevent the problem. "All members of the population share the same general risk for substance abuse, although the risk may vary greatly among individuals" (NIDA, 1997b, p. 12).

An example of a universal prevention program is school-based curricula taught to all students in a grade or in a school. Some universal programs include Life Skills Training, Project Alert, and Project Toward No Tobacco Use. All of these programs are taught to all students within the appropriate grade. Specific students are not identified to participate in the curricula. This is what differentiates universal prevention strategies from selective or indicated ones. Other examples of universal prevention strategies include social marketing campaigns, parenting classes for all parents in a community, and laws and policies that discourage substance abuse.

## Selective

"Selective prevention strategies target subsets of the total population that are deemed to be at risk for substance abuse by virtue of their membership in a particular population segment—for example, children of adult alcoholics, dropouts, or students who are failing academically" (NIDA, 1997b, p. 11). In other words, participants in selective programs are *groups* at higher risk for substance abuse than the general population. Groups are determined to be at risk by the presence of risk factors. This includes those risk factors discussed in Chapter 2 that are found in the community, family, school, and individual/peer domains. It is important to note that "selective prevention targets the entire subgroup regardless of the degree of risk of any individual within the group. One individual in the subgroup may not be at personal risk for substance abuse, while another person in the same subgroup may be abusing substances" (NIDA, 1997b, p. 13).

One example of a selective strategy is a support group for children of alcoholics. In this case, children are selected to participate on the basis of living in an "at-risk" environment. However, they themselves may not have exhibited any at-risk behaviors. Another selective strategy is an after-school program for children living in a low-income housing unit. Again, living in a low-income situation places the children at greater risk. This results in a "selective" population for the prevention program.

## Indicated

Indicated prevention strategies are "designed to prevent the onset of substance abuse in individuals who do not meet DSM-IV criteria for addiction, but who are showing early danger signs, such as falling grades and consumption of alcohol, tobacco, marijuana, and/or inhalants" (NIDA, 1997b, p. 11). In other words, participants in indicated programs are *individuals* at higher risk for substance abuse than the general population. Therefore, the participants of indicated prevention programs may have used alcohol, tobacco, and other drugs, but would not be diagnosed as addicted. In the past, indicated prevention strategies were often referred to as "early intervention." The critical distinction between indicated prevention strategies and substance abuse treatment is that once a person is in need of an assessment for treatment, one has moved beyond prevention into the treatment realm. The goal of indicated prevention strategies is to "identify individuals who are exhibiting early signs of substance abuse and other problem behaviors associated with substance abuse and to target them with special programs" (NIDA, 1997b, p. 15).

An example of an indicated prevention activity is a parent education program for parents whose children are involved in the juvenile court system because of experimentation with drugs. Another example is family therapy for families whose children are displaying early signs of substance abuse. In both of these cases, the children have themselves exhibited problem behaviors, making them indicated populations.

## Determining Population

To determine what type of population a prevention program should reach, the following questions need to be answered. First, can priority risk factors, protective factors, and resource gaps be addressed at the universal level? Or would they be better addressed with selective or indicated populations? For example, if the priority risk factor is family management problems but the **resource assessment** showed that several local programs already offer parenting classes aimed at the general population, then a parenting program for selective or indicated populations may be needed.

Next, is there a need for a program or strategy that affects the broader community (e.g., a city), not just a particular segment of that community? If so, a universal program or strategy may be needed. If a program or strategy with greater intensity and duration for a specific population with identified risks is needed, then a selective or indicated program or strategy may need to be implemented. A final consideration is that if a selective or indicated program or strategy is being considered, adequate funding must be available. Selective and indicated programs and strategies often require more funds than do universal programs and strategies.

In summary, several questions must be answered before determining whether a universal, selective, or indicated population needs to be addressed. Once this has been completed, it is time to move to Step 6.

# Step 6: Apply "Guiding Principles" and "Best Practices"

After completing Steps 2 to 5 to identify the priority risk factors, identify gaps in the community, and select a target population, prevention planners must identify appropriate programs/strategies to implement. At this point, it is useful to review research about what has been shown through research to work, as well as what has shown not to be effective. If possible, it is important to implement programs and strategies that research has revealed to be effective practices.

## Guiding Principles

**Guiding principles** are findings, identified through research, about effective prevention programs. If a community already has a prevention program or strategy in place, guiding principles can be used to gauge the program's potential effectiveness. They can also be used to help market the importance of implementing prevention programs and strategies. Finally, guiding principles can be used to design an innovative program or strategy when none of the best practices (discussed below) are appropriate to the community's needs.

The following are guiding principles from the National Institute on Drug Abuse (1997c, p. i–ii):

- Prevention programs should be designed to enhance protective factors and move toward reversing or reducing known risk factors.
- Prevention programs should target all forms of substance abuse, including the use of tobacco, alcohol, marijuana, and inhalants.
- Prevention programs should include skills to resist drugs when offered, strengthen personal commitments against drug use, and increase social competency (e.g., in communications, peer relationships, self-efficacy, and assertiveness), in conjunction with reinforcement of attitudes against drug use.
- Prevention programs for adolescents should include interactive methods, such as peer discussion groups, rather than didactic teaching techniques alone.
- Prevention programs should include a parent or caregiver component that reinforces what the children are learning and that opens opportunities for family discussions about use of legal and illegal substances and family policies about their use.

- Prevention programs should be long-term, over the school career with repeat interventions to reinforce the original prevention goals. For example, school-based efforts directed at elementary and middle school students should include booster sessions to help with critical transitions from middle to high school.
- Family-focused prevention efforts have a greater impact than do strategies that focus on parents only or children only.
- Community programs that include media campaigns and policy changes, such as new regulations that restrict access to alcohol, tobacco, or other drugs, are more effective when school and family interventions accompany them.
- Community programs need to strengthen norms against drug use in all substance abuse prevention settings, including the family, the school, and the community.
- Schools offer opportunities to reach all populations and also serve as important settings for specific sub-populations at risk for substance abuse, such as children with behavior problems or learning disabilities and those who are potential dropouts.
- Prevention programming should be adapted to address the specific nature of the substance abuse problem in the local community.
- The higher the level of risk of the target population, the more intensive the prevention effort must be and the earlier it must begin.
- Prevention programs should be age-specific, developmentally appropriate, and culturally sensitive.
- Effective prevention programs are cost-effective. For every dollar spent on drug use prevention, communities can save four to five dollars in costs for substance abuse treatment and counseling.
- If a community opts to select a new program/strategy to implement, it is important to review new programs/strategies to ensure evidence of their effectiveness.

## Best Practices

Numerous programs and strategies have been identified through research as being effective at preventing substance abuse. It is important to match the program/strategy with the needs of a specific community. Consequently, if the risk factor of family management problems was identified as a priority, and a selective target population was selected, then The Incredible Years may be a program that a community reviews to see if it will be a good fit. This step of ensuring that programs/strategies are a good fit for the community is essential. If a **best practice** is implemented but it does not meet the needs of the community, then the practice will either be rejected or may prove to be ineffective at preventing substance abuse in that community. Furthermore, if a program is selected for implementation but then is not implemented as intended (e.g., only four of eight modules in a curriculum are implemented or it is implemented with the wrong target population), the likelihood for the program to be effective is extremely limited. In order to ensure effectiveness, best practices must be implemented with high fidelity.

It is also important for prevention professionals to remember that no single best practice will be successful at preventing substance abuse in a community. Multiple types of research-based programs and strategies addressing all areas of a community (family, school, individual, peer, community) need to be implemented. With comprehensive prevention programs in place that are reducing priority risk factors and enhancing protective factors, communities will begin to see the reduction of onset of substance abuse.

Three research-based prevention practices will be highlighted in this section: Tobacco-Free Environmental Policies, The Incredible Years, and Reconnecting Youth Program. These are simply examples of prevention programs and strategies that can be implemented in communities to reduce risk factors and enhance protective factors. Many other programs and strategies have been shown to be effective at preventing substance abuse.

***Tobacco-Free Environmental Policies.***  One universal prevention strategy that has been shown to be effective through research is "Tobacco-Free Environmental Policies." As described by the Center for Substance Abuse Prevention (1997),

> The primary goal of tobacco-free environmental policies is to create environments that do not expose youth to the use and possession of tobacco. Research demonstrates that tobacco use and exposure to secondhand tobacco smoke is a health threat. Policies restricting the use of tobacco in schools and other environments should reduce adolescents' exposure to secondhand tobacco smoke and limit places where they can use tobacco and thus reduce the health risks associated with tobacco use and secondhand smoke. (pp. 21–22)

Activities in this strategy can include reviewing existing laws and compliance with laws restricting tobacco use in certain settings; reviewing the effects of antismoking school policies on adolescent smoking; providing technical assistance and guidance on developing and implementing tobacco-free policies and environments; and educating and informing concerned parties about laws restricting tobacco use in certain settings.

This strategy has been shown to be effective at influencing the risk factor of community laws and norms favorable toward tobacco use. It also assists in enhancing the protective factor of healthy beliefs and clear standards. Research found that the establishment of smoking regulations could be accomplished through a variety of mechanisms, including state and local laws, and policies at businesses, schools, and child-care centers. These comprehensive policies can decrease prevalence rates, especially when their emphasis is on prevention and cessation.

Research also found that harsh penalties for the possession of tobacco products by minors, such as suspension from school, might be ineffective interventions for enhancing the enforcement of antismoking regulations or for preventing or decreasing adolescent tobacco use. Instead, programs that provide prevention or cessation services, such as tobacco education courses, tobacco cessation programs, or diversion alternatives, may be most effective.

***The Incredible Years: Parents, Teachers, and Children Training Series.***  The Incredible Years: Parents, Teachers, and Children Training Series was designed as selective prevention/intervention programs for parents and teachers of children ages 3 to 12. In particular, children with conduct problems are a target population for this program. Designers of the program used Bandura's modeling and self-efficacy theories to form the basis for the training (Incredible Years, n.d.). This included the use of principles of videotape modeling, rehearsal, self-management, and cognitive self-control.

The Incredible Years was designed to develop three sets of skills for parents: parenting skills, interpersonal skills, and academic skills. For the teachers, classroom management skills are the focus of the training. And for the children, the focus is on social skills, classroom management skills, and classroom behavior. These skills are developed through several training programs, including BASIC Parents Training Program (two versions, one for children ages 2 to 7 years and the other for children ages 5 to 12 years); Supporting Your Child's Education; Advanced Parent Training Program; Child Training Program, known as the "Dinosaur Social Skills and Problem-Solving Curriculum"; and the Teacher Training Program.

As described by Strengthening America's Families (1999):

The Incredible Years Training Programs have been researched and extensively field-tested in randomized trials over the past 18 years with over 1,000 families with young children who have aggressive behavior problems. The BASIC Parent Training Program has also been evaluated with over 700 high-risk Head Start families as a prevention program. The Teacher Training Program has been evaluated in two independent, randomized trials with head start teachers as well as in studies with teachers of students in grades kindergarten through grade three. Results indicate that parents and teachers were able to significantly reduce children's problem behaviors and increase their social competence and academic engagement. (The Incredible Years: Parent and Child Training Series section, para. 5)

Consequently, if a prevention professional is looking to implement a prevention program to reduce the risk factor of early antisocial behavior, this may be a useful program to have in place.

***Reconnecting Youth Program.*** As described by the National Institute on Drug Abuse (1997c), Reconnecting Youth is a school-based, indicated prevention program that targets young people in grades 9 through 12 who show signs of poor school achievement and have a potential for dropping out of school. They also may show signs of multiple problem behaviors (such as substance abuse, depression, and suicidal ideation). The program teaches skills to build resiliency with respect to risk factors and to moderate the early signs of substance abuse.

To enter the program, students must have fewer than the average number of credits earned for their grade level, have high absenteeism, and show a significant drop in grades. Alternatively, a youth may enter the program if he or she has a record of dropping out or has been referred as a significant dropout risk.

The program incorporates social support and life skills training with the following components:

- *Personal Growth Class:* a semester-long, daily class designed to enhance self-esteem, decision making, personal control, and interpersonal communication.
- *Social Activities and School Bonding:* to establish drug-free social activities and friendships, as well as improving a teenager's relationship to school.
- *School System Crisis Response Plan:* for addressing suicide prevention approaches.

This program has been shown to reduce the following risk factors: friends involved in problem behavior, academic failure, and persistent antisocial behavior. It has also been effective at increasing the protective factor of bonding, specifically bonding to school. More specifically, research showed that this program improves school performance; reduces drug involvement; decreases deviant peer bonding; increases self-esteem, personal control, school bonding, and social support; and decreases depression, anger, aggression, hopelessness, stress, and suicidal behaviors. It has also been shown that the support of Personal Growth Class teachers contributes to decrease in drug involvement and suicide risk behaviors.

## Unproven Programs

Over the past decade, several programs and strategies have been shown through research to be ineffective at preventing substance abuse. Incredibly, in some cases, the prevention field has implemented programs that have actually *increased* the rate of substance abuse. Consequently, it is important to review which programs and strategies are not supported by research. The following are examples of **unproven program strategies** that have been researched, and the results failed to support their effectiveness on preventing specific problem behaviors. However, it is important to note that they may be useful as one component of a comprehensive prevention program.

First, research has shown that alternative activities, when implemented alone, have not been effective at delaying the onset of substance abuse in youth (Center for Substance Abuse Prevention, 1996). Midnight basketball and drug-free dances are examples of alternative activities that have been popular in many communities. However, unless these activities are combined with other proven prevention strategies, they have not been shown to be effective at preventing substance abuse.

Next, the effectiveness of information dissemination strategies has not been supported by research (Office of Justice Programs and the University of Maryland, Department of Criminology and Criminal Justice, 1997). Information dissemination strategies include activities such as teaching youth about drugs and their effects, distributing brochures and posters, and conducting health fairs. For several years, prevention professionals thought that if young people just knew how horrible drugs were and what they did to their brains and bodies, then they would not use them. However, results of these efforts showed increased use and more educated drug users.

Similarly, "fear arousal" or "scare tactic" approaches emphasize the risks associated with tobacco, alcohol, or drug use (Office of Justice Programs and the University of Maryland, Department of Criminology and Criminal Justice, 1997). An example of this strategy is school assemblies where a recovering person or a person affected by substance abuse "scares" youth through tales of the devastating effect of substance abuse. Results have shown that while there may be a very short-term preventative effect, the effect dissipates quickly. Furthermore, if the recovering person is someone who has succeeded despite past abuse of alcohol, tobacco, or other drugs, youth can take home the message that it is acceptable to use drugs, because they will succeed in the long run. Consequently, this is a dangerous strategy to employ to prevent substance abuse. Similar to the fear arousal approach, long-term preventive effects have not been seen after implementation of "moral appeals" to youth (Office of Justice Programs and the University of Maryland, Department of Criminology and Criminal Justice, 1997). The "moral appeal" approach is one that teaches students about the evils of use.

"Affective education" programs that focus on building self-esteem are also *largely ineffective* for reducing substance use (Center for Substance Abuse Prevention, 1997). In fact, it is frequently seen in youth treatment programs, as well as adult treatment programs, that substance abusers often have a very high self-esteem. "Cocaine users in particular often exhibit unusually high levels of self-esteem before the onset of addiction" (Center for Substance Abuse Prevention, 1997, p. 11). Consequently, increased self-esteem should not be the goal of a substance abuse prevention program, nor should it be used as a measure of the effectiveness of a substance abuse prevention effort.

Finally, the effectiveness of the original Drug Abuse Resistance Education (DARE) program has not been supported through research (Office of Justice Programs and the University of Maryland, Department of Criminology and Criminal Justice, 1997; Lynam et al., 1999; Hansen et al., 1997; Rosenbaum et al., 1994; Ennett et al., 1994). "The program's content, teaching methods, and use of uniformed police officers rather than teachers might each explain its weak evaluations" (Office of Justice Programs and the University of Maryland, Department of Criminology and Criminal Justice, 1997, pp. 5–32). The short-term effects of the program on alcohol and other drug use were nonsignificant. Other prevention programs targeting the same age group as DARE have been shown to have more effect. Consequently, many school districts and communities have replaced DARE with other programs that have been shown to have a greater effect.

# Step 7: Evaluate

Evaluation is the systematic effort to collect and use program information for multiple purposes. Evaluation needs to be an integral part of every prevention program and strategy. It is necessary to determine whether the prevention efforts being implemented are accomplishing the goals set by the program. And, while evaluation is listed as the last step in the planning process, this does not mean that an evaluation plan should be developed and conducted after a program or strategy is implemented. Instead, an evaluation plan should be designed after the selection of which program/strategy will be implemented, but *before* the program/strategy is actually carried out.

There are many different ways to conduct evaluations. Professional evaluators tend to agree that there is no "one best way" to do any evaluation. Instead, good evaluation requires carefully thinking through the questions that need to be answered, the type of program being evaluated, and the ways in which the information generated will be used. A good evaluation provides useful information about program functioning that contributes to program improvement. Evaluation is covered in depth in Chapter 8.

# Summary

The purpose of the chapter was to introduce seven steps of prevention program planning. Used together, these steps will assist prevention professionals in creating comprehensive plans. First, a community's readiness for prevention must be assessed and improved, if needed, followed by mobilization of the community. Next, data for a community (needs) assessment must be collected and analyzed. In turn, this data must be used to prioritize which risk and protective factors need to be addressed in a community. At this point, a resource assessment must be completed to ensure that services are not duplicated in the community. Next, the target population (universal, selective, or indicated) must be identified. This is followed by the selection of an effective program or strategy to be implemented to reduce the prioritized risk factors and to enhance protective factors. Finally, an evaluation must be designed before the implementation of the program or strategy. By completing this comprehensive planning process, the likelihood of success in a community will be greatly enhanced.

## KEY TERMS

archival data
best practices
community readiness
guiding principles

indicated
needs assessment
resource assessment
selective

survey data
universal
unproven program strategies

## DISCUSSION QUESTIONS

1. Why is it important for prevention specialists to assess a community's readiness before attempting to implement a prevention program in a community?

2. Do you anticipate that it will be easy or difficult to complete all seven planning steps in a community? Why?

3. Which step do you think will be the hardest to implement? Which the easiest? Why?

4. Why is it important to complete Steps 1 through 5 before selecting a program or strategy to implement?

## APPLICATION EXERCISES

1. Contact a prevention professional in your community or a nearby community. Interview the person to identify which planning steps he or she has completed. Ask for information about what was difficult and what was easy in completing steps in the planning process.

2. Identify a prevention program or strategy your community has implemented. Conduct research to answer the resource assessment questions, as listed in Step 4, above.

## SUGGESTED READINGS

For more information on the Monitoring the Future Survey, visit NIDA's Website, http://www.nida.nih.gov/DrugPages/MTF.html.

For more information on community readiness, contact the Tri-Ethnic Center in Fort Collins, Colorado. Telephone: (800) 835–8091.

For more information on effective substance abuse prevention programs, visit CSAP's Model Program Website, http://www.samhsa.gov/centers/csap/modelprograms/ and the Western Center for the Application of Prevention Technologies' Website, http://www.open.org/~westcapt.

CSAP's Decision Support System provides a plethora of information on program planning and evaluation. http://www.preventiondss.org.

National Highway Traffic Safety Administration's *Community How To Guides* provide wonderful information on building community coalitions. Visit http://www.nhtsa.dot.gov/people/injury/alcohol/Community%20Guides%20HTML/Guides_index.html.

The following book from NIDA provides useful information on community readiness: National Institute on Drug Abuse. (1997a). *Community readiness for drug abuse prevention: Issues, tips and tools.* Rockville, MD: U.S. Department of Health and Human Services.

For more information on the theory behind prevention needs assessments and resource assessments, review: Arthur, M., & Blitz, C. (2000). Bridging the gap between science and practice in drug abuse prevention through needs assessment and strategic community planning. *Journal of Community Psychology, 28*(3), 241–255.

# REFERENCES

Arthur, M., & Blitz, C. (2000). Bridging the gap between science and practice in drug abuse prevention through needs assessment and strategic community planning. *Journal of Community Psychology, 28*(3), 241–255.

Center for Substance Abuse Prevention. (1996). *Selected findings in prevention: A decade of results from the Center for Substance Abuse Prevention.* Rockville, MD: U.S. Department of Health and Human Services.

Center for Substance Abuse Prevention. (1997). *Reducing tobacco use among youth: Community-based approaches.* Rockville, MD: U.S. Department of Health and Human Services.

Developmental Research and Programs. (1996). *Communities That Care planning kit.* Seattle: Author.

Edwards, R. W., Jumper-Thurman, P., Plested, B. A., Oetting, E. R., & Swanson, L. (2000). Community readiness: Research to practice. *Journal of Community Psychology, 28*(3), 291–307.

Ennett, S. T., Rosenbaum, D. P., Flewelling, R. L., et al. (1994). Long-term evaluation of Drug Abuse Resistance Education. *Addictive Behaviors, 19*(2), 113–125.

Hansen, W. B., & McNeal, R. B. (1997). How D.A.R.E. works: An examination of program effects on mediating variables. *Health Education and Behavior, 24*(2), 165–176.

Hawkins, J. D., Catalano, R. F., & Miller, J. Y. (1992). Risk and protective factors for alcohol and other drug problems in adolescence and early adulthood: Implications for substance abuse prevention. *Psychological Bulletin, 112*(1), 64–105.

The Incredible Years. (n.d.) Program history and theoretical assumptions. Seattle: Author. Retrieved April 10, 2001, from the World Wide Web: http://www.incredibleyears.com/research/history.htm.

Institute of Medicine. (1994). New directions in definitions. In P. J. Mrazek & R. J. Haggerty (Eds.). *Reducing risks for mental disorders: Frontiers for preventive intervention research.* Washington, DC: National Academy Press.

Lynam, D. R., Milich, R., Zimmerman, R., Novak, S. P., Logan, T. K., Martin, C., Leukefeld, C., & Clayton, R. (1999). Project DARE: No effects at 10-year follow-up. *Journal of Consulting and Clinical Psychology, 67*(4), 590–593.

National Highway Traffic Safety Administration. (2001, March). Community how to guide on . . . coalition building. *Community how to guides.* U.S. Department of Transportation. Retrieved July 8, 2001, from the World Wide Web: http://www.nhtsa.dot.gov/people/injury/alcohol/Community%20Guides%20HTML/Guides_index.html.

National Institute on Drug Abuse. (1997a). *Community readiness for drug abuse prevention: Issues, tips, and tools.* Rockville, MD: U.S. Department of Health and Human Services.

National Institute on Drug Abuse. (1997b). *Drug abuse prevention: What works.* Rockville, MD: U.S. Department of Health and Human Services.

National Institute on Drug Abuse. (1997c). *Preventing drug use among children and adolescents: A research-based guide.* Rockville, MD: U.S. Department of Health and Human Services.

Office of Justice Programs and the University of Maryland, Department of Criminology and Criminal Justice. (1997). *Preventing crime: What works, what doesn't, what's promising* (No. 165366). Washington DC: Department of Justice.

Rosenbaum, D. P., Flewelling, R., Bailey, S. L, et al. (1994). Cops in the classroom: A longitudinal evaluation of Drug Abuse Resistance Education (DARE). *Journal of Research in Crime and Delinquency, 31*(1), 3–31.

Social Development Research Group. (n.d.). *Validated archival indicators.* Unpublished document, University of Washington, Seattle.

Strengthening America's Families. (1999). 1999 model programs. Salt Lake City, UT: Department of Health Promotion and Education. Retrieved April 10, 2001, from the World Wide Web: http://www.strengtheningfamilies.org/html/model_programs.html.

Western Center for the Application of Prevention Technologies. (2001). Building a Successful Prevention Program. Reno: University of Nevada, Reno. Retrieved September 19, 2001, from the World Wide Web: http://www.open.org/~westcapt.

# 4 Facts about Drugs

The information in this chapter is intended for prevention professionals rather than those who provide treatment for alcohol, tobacco, and other drugs (ATOD). Therefore, the information provided will be fairly general. Although for the most part prevention professionals do treat chemically dependent individuals and may not deal directly with the effects of ATOD abuse, oftentimes they are asked questions about ATOD and their effects. It is not appropriate for prevention professionals to tell youth, parents, and community members that this is not their area of expertise. While it is appropriate to refer people to other sources, prevention professionals should be able to provide general information when asked about ATOD and their effects. Further, prevention professionals should understand the problems associated with ATOD that they are trying to prevent.

There are a variety of ways to classify drugs (Jacobs & Fehr, 1987). However, in this text they will be classified by their pharmacological similarities. Central nervous system depressants, opiates, central nervous system stimulants, hallucinogens, cannabinols, steroids, and inhalants will be covered. Psychotropic drugs, such as antidepressants, which are used to treat mental illness will not be discussed because although they can be abused, they generally are not. In general, the effects of the drugs within the category will be discussed, as well as the symptoms of overdose, withdrawal symptoms, tolerance, and short- and long-term effects of use. Please keep in mind that the information provided is based on research in controlled and specific settings. In the real world drugs may vary in potency and purity and the effects therefore may vary from the ones described here. Some of the street names or slang words for drugs will also be provided; however, these terms are different in various regions of the country and they are frequently outdated. For each category an example of why the information is relevant for prevention will be provided. An overview of the concept of gateway drugs will be offered in this chapter, as well as an overview of recent drug trends.

Before delving into the pharmacological information about drugs there is information about definitions, models of addiction, and routes of administration that may assist a prevention professional in understanding the complexities of substance use.

## Definitions

Terminology used in the alcohol, tobacco, and other drug field is not always clear. Sometimes a word is used one way by one author or prevention professional but it will have a different meaning to someone else. The following definitions from Fisher and Harrison (2000, pp. 15–16) will help you in understanding the terms used in this chapter.

> **Addiction**: Compulsion and a craving to use alcohol or other drugs regardless of negative or adverse consequences. Addiction is characterized by psychological dependence (see below) and often (depending on the drug or drugs) physical dependence (see below). Loss of control is also a characteristic of addiction.
>
> **Chemical dependency**: A term used to describe addiction to alcohol and/or other drugs and to differentiate this type of addiction from nonchemical addiction (e.g., gambling).
>
> **Dependence**: A recurrent or ongoing need to use alcohol, tobacco, or other drugs. Psychological dependence is the need to use alcohol, tobacco, or other drugs to think, feel, or function normally. Physical dependence exists when tissues of the body require the presence of alcohol, tobacco, or other drugs to function normally.
>
> **Intoxication**: State of being under the influence of alcohol, tobacco, or other drugs so that thinking, feeling, and/or behavior are affected ("high" is a slang word for intoxication).
>
> **Substance abuse**: The continued use of alcohol, tobacco, and/or other drugs in spite of adverse consequences in one or more areas of an individual's life.
>
> **Tolerance**: Requirement for increasing doses or quantities of alcohol, tobacco or other drugs in order to create the same effects as was obtained from the original dose. Tolerance results from physical or psychological adaptations of the individual. Cross tolerance refers to accompanying tolerance to other drugs from the same pharmacological group. For example, tolerance to alcohol results in tolerance to minor tranquilizers such as Xanax even when the individual has never used Xanax. Reverse tolerance refers to a condition in which smaller quantities of a drug produce the same effects as did previous large doses.
>
> **Withdrawal**: Physical and psychological effects that occur when drug-dependent individuals discontinue using alcohol, tobacco, or other drugs.

Examples and more detailed information of these definitions were described in Chapter 1; however they are restated here to refresh the readers' memories because these terms will be important in the following discussion.

# Models of Addiction

There are numerous models of addiction. Some attribute addiction to biological abnormalities, social learning, family pathology, sociocultural influences, psychological abnormalities, and personal choices. Although prevention professionals do not provide treatment to addicted persons, it is important to understand the general models of addiction because they have implications for prevention and intervention strategies. Most of the models that will be described have many variations and perspectives. However, for the purposes of this chapter only a general overview will be provided. Reid H. Hester and William R. Miller (1995) described the following historical perspectives of addiction.

## The Moral Model

The moral model emphasizes personal choice as the primary cause of addiction. From this perspective, addiction is viewed as a willful violation of society's rules, norms, or moral code of conduct. Addiction is considered a crime and a sin. The individual is thought to make a decision to use substances in a problematic manner and cause suffering for family members and is seen as capable of making different choices. Implicit in this model is that if people have willpower and moral determination then they will overcome the addiction. This model has been adopted by some religious groups and by the criminal justice system. From a religious viewpoint, the way to correct the behavior is through religious or spiritual intervention; from the criminal justice perspective, historically the way to correct the behavior has been through legal sanctions and punishments. For example, the U.S. Supreme Court has ruled that crimes committed by an alcoholic are not due to a disease but are a result of willful misconduct (Connors & Rychtarik, 1989). The individual is not believed to deserve care or help, but rather punishment is thought to correct past misdeeds and prevent further abuse. However, other models have been integrated in many jurisdictions. For example, drug courts have diverted "criminals" to treatment in many systems (G. Fisher, personal communication, July 11, 2001). One major disadvantage of this perspective is that, historically, punishment has been ineffective in reducing addictive behaviors. This model is almost always rejected by treatment professionals.

## The Temperance Model

The temperance model is based on the premise of a historical movement that alcohol is very dangerous and harmful. In the early years, the movement's view was that if alcohol was used, it should be used cautiously and moderately. As the temperance movement gained popularity, it evolved into Prohibition. Temperance advocates believed that alcohol could not be used by anyone safely and that it would eventually lead to alcoholism by anyone who used it. Abstinence was viewed as the only alternative. The main belief of the temperance advocates was that alcohol problems are caused by alcohol. This is similar to current beliefs about certain drugs, such as crack cocaine and heroin, which are believed to have such addictive properties that the problems associated with them are simply caused by the drug itself. Prevention strategies include temperance (or abstinence), and controlling the cost, availability, and promotion to the public.

## The Spiritual Model

The spiritual model was born after Prohibition was repealed and Alcoholics Anonymous (AA) came into being. Although individual AA members have many personal beliefs about addiction and AA endorses no particular theory, its writings demonstrate openness to various explanations. However, implicit in its writing is the central theme of a spiritual approach to recovery (Miller & Kurtz, 1994). Addiction is viewed as a condition that people are powerless to overcome, so they must turn their life over to a higher power and follow a spiritual path to recovery. Many religious organizations also consider drunkenness or addiction to be a sinful behavior reflecting a deviation from a spiritual path. Further, some believe addiction to be the result of demonic possession, although this belief is rare.

## The Education Model

The education model assumes that if people knew the effects of alcohol, tobacco, and other drugs, they would not use them. This model implies that people do not have accurate information about the impact and consequences of drug use and when they have correct information, they are less likely to use drugs and suffer the negative consequences of drugs. The education model also incorporates affective education, which seeks to instill motivation to avoid using alcohol, tobacco, and other drugs. Prevention strategies would include drug education programs and lectures from recovering addicts or by people who have experienced the negative consequences of substances.

## The Characterological/Personality Model

The characerological or personality model asserts that addiction is caused primarily by abnormalities of personality. Those who abuse substances are believed to have a predisposition or behavior trait that is an "addictive personality." Such behavior traits include "difficulty in impulse control; antisocial behaviors; low self-esteem; sex-role conflicts; difficulty in coping with stress; passive-dependent patterns of behavior; egocentricity with manipulative, demanding behaviors; and a drive for power and control by those who feel impotent and powerless" (Addiction Technology Transfer Center, 1997, section 4, p. 7). The view is that addicted persons have inadequate defense mechanisms stemming from a fixation of unresolved conflicts regarding dependence in early psychological development. Intervention strategies include psychotherapy to resolve the basic conflicts and to bring a person to mature functioning, improve self-image, and improve interpersonal skills. Prevention strategies include fostering normal psychological development.

## The Conditioning Model

During the early part of the 20th century psychologists began to consider that learning and conditioning processes explain how substance abuse problems develop. This view emphasizes that excessive drinking is a learned behavior, responding to the usual practices of behavior. Conditioning models are based on the assumption that if using substances leads to rewarding behaviors, then that behavior is likely to continue. Therefore, the two causal factors of problematic substance-taking behaviors are conditioned responses and reinforcement. Intervention strategies include aversion therapy and operant learning principles to help an individual stop problematic behavior and learn appropriate new behavior. Prevention strategies include removing positive associations with alcohol, tobacco, and other drugs such as advertisements and other factors that encourage using substances.

## The Sociocultural Model

The sociocultural model points to society's influence in shaping an individual's patterns of substance use. Included are the factors of culture, religious, family, and peers. This model proposes that substance use is higher among cultural groups that accept and tolerate that behavior and is low among cultural groups that disapprove of excessive use. For example, Jewish people in general do not disapprove of moderate drinking, but disapprove of excessive drinking. There is a low rate of alcoholism among Jews. However, children who grow up in religious groups that prohibit the use of alcohol completely and never observe moderate drinking are more likely to experience problem drinking if drinking is initiated at all. The risk factor associated with these influences include laws and norms favorable toward drug use. The use patterns and attitudes of family and peers that approve of using substances have been found to increase consumption among those around them. The risk factors described in Chapter 2 include parental attitudes favorable toward drug use, family history of drug use, parental involvement in drug use, family management problems, and friends who engage in the problem behavior. Prevention, from this perspective, includes limiting availability of substances and changing a person's relationship to her or his environment, such as changing one's friends and teaching parents skills to support a nonuse norm.

## The Social Learning Model

The theory of social learning indicates that using substances and other addictive behaviors are "bad habits" (Marlatt, 1985, p. 9) that are socially learned behavioral patterns involving cognitive processes and modeling influences. From this perspective, people observe others using drugs and learn: (1) how to do it, (2) under which circumstances the behavior is acceptable, and (3) the possible results. For example, it may be "acceptable" to use alcohol in social settings, but not alone. Smoking may be considered acceptable, but intravenous drug use may be considered unacceptable. Friends may encourage the behavior or give attention to it, which will increase the likelihood of the behavior reoccurring. The social learning perspective emphasizes the interactions between the person and the environment in shaping patterns of substance abuse. The psychological state of the individual is important, because it would elicit the craving to use the drug in the first place to handle problems, alter one's psychological state, or enhance interactions. As the individual used more and more, he or she would become dependent. Addiction, from this perspective, is based on psychological dependence. From this point of view, prevention and intervention would include changing the individual's relationship to the negative role models that foster problematic drug use and teaching coping skills to avoid relying on substances for coping.

## The Cognitive Model

The cognitive model stresses the importance of an individual's beliefs or expectancies about substances. From this perspective, positive expectancies will lead to increased use whereas negative expectancies will result in less or no use. This model asserts that using substances is mainly determined by the consequence an individual expects to receive as a result for using substances. Family, peers, culture, and the media can influence the expectancies that an individual has about using substances. According to this model, individuals do not drink because of a physiological mechanism that can be triggered by alcohol, but rather because of the individual's beliefs. Cognitive therapy is generally applied to cope with cravings and modify beliefs that promote problematic use.

## The Biological Model

The biological model places importance on heredity and physiological processes that may predispose individuals to addiction. Biological factors can include abnormal alcohol metabolism and unique brain chemistry. Strong evidence of higher rates of alcoholism among children of alcoholics supports this model (Inaba & Cohen, 2000). The prevention implications vary, but genetic counseling and education about cautious use, heredity, and risk factors for those at risk may be suggested (S. Doctor, personal communication, July 12, 2001). Others have proposed that the pharmacology of substances can be used to explain the escalation of use to addiction, which is a biological model. Proponents of the pharmacological impact of substance abuse propose low levels of consumption to avoid addiction and bodily harm.

## The Psychological Model

The primary emphasis of the psychological model is that addiction is secondary to another psychological problem, which causes emotional pain. From this perspective, alcohol, tobacco, and other drugs are taken in order to alleviate this pain. Advocates of the psychological model have attempted to identify an "addictive personality," which could explain why people with alcohol, tobacco, and other drug addictions also oftentimes have problems with gambling, shopping, food, sex, and other things. However, this theory of the "addictive personality" has largely been unsuccessful (Fisher & Harrison, 2000, p. 39). Intervention strategies include counseling and therapy to ensure that psychological issues are resolved. Prevention strategies include teaching life skills such as coping, communication, and stress management to instruct youth on how to deal with problems or where to seek assistance when confronted with stressful situations. Family and parenting classes can also be implemented to teach families how to communicate effectively and deal with discipline, and to address other family issues (G. Fisher, personal communication, July 15, 2001).

## The Dispositional Disease Model

The dispositional disease model, which is perhaps the most popular and controversial, is similar to the biological model (Jellinek, 1960). As with some of the other models, the disease model was first used to explain alcoholism but has been applied to other drugs. From this perspective, addiction is a disease and a condition that is different from normality. Addiction, rather than another condition, is viewed as the primary disease, unlike the biological/psychological model (Jellinek, 1952). People with the disease possess a condition that renders them incapable of controlling the amount of alcohol taken. The disease model, for example, explains alcoholism as being similar to an allergy. The most common symptoms in the early stages are tolerance to alcohol, sneaking drinks, blackouts, and feelings of guilt over drinking. In the middle stage the symptoms are loss of control over alcohol, the inability to stop drinking once started, loss of friends and jobs, and preoccupation with alcohol supply. The chronic phase is characterized by drinking in the morning, tremors, hallucinations, and violating personal ethics. These symptoms are what make addiction a disease as opposed to a bad habit or loss of willpower. The disease makes it impossible for affected individuals to drink responsibly. Therefore, the only way to control the disease is with complete abstinence. In this view, the disease is irreversible and incapable of being cured. The sequence of the stages are irreversible and are not affected by periods of sobriety. The implication of this model is that only those with the disease are at risk, and those without the disease are capable of drinking in moderation and without problems. Intervention strategies include identifying individuals with the disease and persuading them to abstain from alcohol for the rest of their lives. Prevention strategies include early identification of those with the condition and helping them to adjust to their disease.

## The General Systems Model

The general systems model views the individual problematic use of substances as an interactive part of a larger "dysfunctional" system. According to this model, systems are resistant to change, and an individual's behavior is functional to the system and may be a coping strategy within the malfunctioning system. The "system" in this model is most often the family. Some believe that addiction is a family problem and therefore, the entire family should be treated. If an individual is treated alone then the family system may be resistant to change. If the individual does change, the family may deteriorate or another family member may become dysfunctional. The abuse of substances is thought of as an effort to maintain balance in the family. If the individual family member stops using substances then the family is thrown off balance and family members may unconsciously sabotage the recovery process in an effort to restore stability. Addiction can provide stability (although not healthy stability) for families in several ways. For example, it can divert attention from marital problems. In essence, family members tolerate discomfort with substance abuse to avoid dealing with even more painful issues. From this perspective, family therapy can be used to work out the complex family problems that underlie addictions.

## The Public Health Model

The public health model is also used with other public health problems such as communicable diseases. This model integrates the agent, such as alcohol, tobacco, or other drugs; the host, the addicted person or drug user; and the environment, the social and physical context of use. Problems related to alcohol, tobacco, and other drugs are viewed as a result of the interaction and relationships between the agent, host, and environment. Hence, the public health model does not focus on one answer or factor but rather involves all three elements. From this view, the agent itself contains destructive components, the host may have individual differences or risk factors that affect susceptibility to addiction, and the environment may have factors that contribute to use, such as lenient policies and high availability. This model recognizes the dangerous aspects of substances, the significant individual differences, and mediation factors such as biological and psychological factors, and gives attention to the aspects in the environment that are believed to promote substance use. The models previously discussed have addressed one of these factors. For example, the temperance model emphasizes the destructive components of alcohol, the moral model emphasizes the host factors, and the social learning model emphasizes the environment.

Prevention strategies include health education, life skills, and self-efficacy training to youth and families through schools, social programs, workplaces, day cares, faith-based organizations, and other groups. Scare tactics have been used in the past to influence nonuse; however, as previously stated, they do not appear to be effective in deterring alcohol, tobacco, and other drug use. Prevention strategies aimed at the agent include warning labels on alcohol and tobacco products and spraying insecticides on marijuana fields. From the public health viewpoint, schools, families, neighborhoods, and communities are all part of the environment. Therefore, prevention strategies include legislation on severe and swift penalties for drug dealers, increased pricing of alcohol and tobacco products, and restricted advertising.

## The Biopsychosocial Model

The biopsychosocial model assumes that some people develop problems because of a genetic predisposition, psychological factors, physical factors, emotional pain, environmental factors, or any combination of these. According to Fisher and Harrison (2000), "In the biopsychosocial model of addiction the interactions of biological, psychological, cognitive, social development, and environmental variables are considered to 'explain' addiction" (p. 51). In essence, this model combines most of the other models into one and offers a comprehensive approach to treatment, as all variables are considered.

## Conclusion

Many models have been proposed to explain the etiology of addiction. The moral model discourages people from seeking treatment and is therefore not widely accepted by treatment professionals. Some models, such as the social learning and sociocultural models, place the explanation on the environment and in some way may remove responsibility of recovery from individuals. Other models are more conducive to seeking treatment. For example, the disease model removes the stigma associated with addiction, shifts the cause of addiction from the individual, removes the cause of the addiction from the individual, and provides a way to control the disease (G. Fisher, personal communication, July 11, 2001). The biopsychosocial model integrates all the relevant components and therefore may currently be the most useful.

The information about all the models may seem overwhelming to prevention professionals and in most cases it will be more important for prevention professionals to know the progression from use to misuse to abuse. These terms were discussed in Chapter 1. However, in summary, use is defined as the ingestion of ATOD without negative consequences, misuse is defined as the use of ATOD with negative consequences, and abuse is defined as the continued use of ATOD in spite of adverse consequences. These definitions are not concrete categories, as substance use/misuse/abuse/addiction can be viewed as a continuum (Fisher & Harrison, 2000). However, these definitions can assist prevention professionals in determining appropriate interventions or referrals for their service population.

## Routes of Administration

Drugs that enter the body eventually end up in the bloodstream, then are distributed to the rest of the body through the blood cells, in the plasma, or by the protein molecules. The drug then travels to every organ, tissue, and fluid in the body. Within seconds, the drug will cross the blood-brain barrier to reach the central nervous system, where it will have enormous effects on the brain and the spinal cord. The amount of blood in the body will determine how fast the drug travels through it. For example, a smaller person will have less blood to dilute the drug than a larger person, and therefore will feel the effects of a drug sooner. Other factors that influence the effects of a drug include the person's mood or attitude, emotions, nutrition, the setting, and other psychological and biological characteristics. Further, the method used to take the drug into the body determines how fast it will get to the brain and spinal cord. The methods used to administer drugs, in order of fastest to slowest, are inhaling, injecting, mucosal absorption, oral ingestion, and contact absorption (Inaba & Cohen, 2000).

Inhaling a drug takes 7–10 seconds to reach the brain and begin to have an effect. When a person smokes, the drug enters the lungs and is absorbed through the blood vessels, then the blood travels to the heart where it is pumped to the brain almost immediately. The person can control the amount of a drug taken with each puff. Drugs that are usually inhaled include tobacco cigarettes, marijuana, and freebase cocaine (Inaba & Cohen, 2000).

Injecting can be done intravenously into the bloodstream, which will take a drug about 15 to 30 seconds to be absorbed. It can also be done intramuscularly, into a muscle, which will take about three to five minutes to be absorbed; or subcutaneously, under the skin, which will also take about three to five minutes to be absorbed. Injecting a drug into the body is likely to cause a "rush" because so much of a drug is taken at one time. Because the drug user often does not know the purity of the drug, injecting it is more likely to cause an overdose. Injecting is also the most hazardous because it passes up the body's natural defense mechanisms, rendering the user vulnerable to many health problems such as hepatitis, abscesses, or HIV. Drugs that can be injected are cocaine, heroin, and methamphetamines (Inaba & Cohen, 2000).

Mucosal absorption can be done by snorting a drug, placing it under the tongue, chewing it, or placing it in the rectum or the vagina. Mucosal absorption passes the body's digestive system and therefore the effects are more intense and occur more rapidly than oral ingestion. Drugs that are usually absorbed are chewing tobacco, cocaine, and heroin (Inaba & Cohen, 2000).

When a drug is ingested orally the effects usually take between 20 to 30 minutes but can be less or more depending on contents of the stomach. The drug has to pass through the mouth enzymes, esophagus, and stomach acids. The drug enters the veins and the liver, where it is partially metabolized. Then it is pumped to the heart, then to the body. Some drugs—such as alcohol—are absorbed in the stomach and therefore take less time to reach the brain. Most psychoactive drugs move easily through the membranes. Alcohol, pills, and tablets are all taken orally (Inaba & Cohen, 2000).

Contact and transdermal absorption can be done through skin creams, ointments, eye drops, and adhesive patches. LSD in liquid form can be absorbed through eye drops or by placing it on moist parts of the body. Adhesive patches allow specific quantities of a drug to be absorbed into the body over a long period of time. This method can take up to two days (Inaba & Cohen, 2000).

The body is designed in such a way that toxins, viruses, and bacteria cannot cross the blood-brain barrier; however, certain drugs, such as stimulants, depressants, hallucinogens, steroids, and inhalants, do cross it and that is how they have an effect—by acting on the nerves of the central nervous system. The central nervous system, especially the brain, receives messages, analyzes them, and sends them to the appropriate part of the body. Drugs alter the messages sent to the brain, disrupt messages sent to the other parts of the body from the brain, and disrupt the capacity to think, reason, and interpret sensory input. Drugs can also affect other body parts directly as they pass through them. For example, cocaine harms the nasal passages. The way the drugs enter the body determines how fast they reach the central nervous system. Nonetheless, regardless of how a drug enters the body, it will reach the central nervous system (Inaba & Cohen, 2000).

# Central Nervous System Depressants

**Central nervous system (CNS) depressants** are referred to as "downers," sedatives, hypnotics, minor tranquilizers, anxiolytics, and antianxiety medications. Most depressants in the illicit market are diverted from legitimate pharmaceutical products. CNS depressants are usually taken to alleviate anxiety, induce sleep, or relieve stress. Alcohol is the most common and universally used CNS depressant. Sedative hypnotics are another popular form of CNS depressants.

The major effects of CNS depressants are muscle relaxation, disinhibition, reduced anxiety, impairment of judgment, and impairment of motor coordination. In addition, CNS depressants cause decreased reflexes, decreased pulse rate, decreased blood pressure, slurred speech, staggering, and sleepiness. CNS depressants have a synergistic or potentiation effect, meaning the ingestion of two or more CNS depressants can multiply their effects. For example, if a person takes a barbiturate (a CNS depressant) and drinks a beer (another CNS depressant), the combination of their effects will be more than just double.

Withdrawal from CNS depressants may vary but can include restlessness, anxiety, sleeping problems, agitation, tremors, low-grade fever, rapid heart rate, elevated blood pressure, hallucinations, vomiting, seizures, and death. Alcohol withdrawal seizures may occur 12 to 48 hours after the last drink; seizures from barbiturates usually occur within 72 hours after the last use. Withdrawal from long-acting benzodiazepines (minor tranquilizers) may not manifest for up to a month. Tolerance and cross-tolerance develops quickly with all CNS depressants and overdose of CNS depressants can be fatal because of respiratory depression.

## Alcohol

Alcohol is the oldest and most widely used psychoactive substance (any substance that directly alters the normal functioning of the central nervous system). The main alcoholic beverages are beer, wine, and distilled spirits. How quickly the effects of alcohol are felt is determined by the rates of absorption, which can be affected by body weight, body chemistry, emotional state, body fat, and overall health. Low doses of alcohol activate gastric juices, stimulate appetite, decrease pulse rate, increase self-confidence, and relax the body. High doses of alcohol cause low blood pressure, slowed motor reflexes, loss of body heat, diminished sexual performance, loss of balance, and mental confusion. Withdrawal symptoms can include sweating, tremors, altered perception, psychosis, fear, auditory hallucinations, and death.

Acute and chronic effects of alcohol can include memory loss, gastritis, esophagitis, ulcers, and pancreatitis. Further, cirrhosis of the liver, high blood pressure, and a weakened heart muscle can also occur with chronic alcohol use. Alcohol use during pregnancy can lead to Fetal Alcohol Syndrome or fetal alcohol effects, which is characterized by impaired growth, changes in facial structure, and CNS abnormalities. The toxic effect of alcohol on the fetus is called "Fetal Alcohol Syndrome" (Jones & Smith, 1973; Kleinfeld & Wescott, 1993).

Alcohol has other adverse social consequences. Alcohol can magnify existing traits and can trigger interpersonal and criminal violence. According to victim reports, alcohol use was involved in 27 percent of aggravated assaults, 37 percent of rapes and sexual assaults, 15 percent of robberies, and 50 percent of all homicides (U.S. Department of Justice, 1998; Roizen, 1997). In addition, alcohol contributes to motor vehicle crashes, serious and fatal injuries, suicide, loss of job productivity, and other social and family problems.

## Sedative Hypnotics

**Sedatives** calm and relax and **hypnotics** induce sleep. Sedative hypnotics are usually prescribed to relieve anxiety and panic attacks, to induce sleep, to relax muscles, and to control hypertension. Most sedative hypnotics are available as pills, tablets, or capsules. However, some forms are injected for more immediate results. The effects of sedative hypnotics are similar to the effects of alcohol. They can cause lower inhibitions, reduce physical depression, increase sedation, and increase muscle relaxation.

*Barbiturates.*    One form of sedative hypnotics is barbiturates. Some street names for barbiturates (Seconal, Nembutal, Fiorinal, and others) are reds, red devils, Mexican reds, yellow jackets, nebbies, rainbows, phenos, and blue heavens. Barbiturates produce a wide spectrum of effects, from mild sedation to coma, and have been used as anesthetics, sedatives, and anticonvulsants. They are usually used to induce sleep and lower inhibitions. Withdrawal effects include loss of appetite, nausea, vomiting, increased heart rate, excessive sweating, abdominal cramps, tremulousness, and death.

*Benzodiazepines.*    Another form of sedative hypnotics is benzodiazepines. Some street names for benzodiazepines (Valium, Librium, Xanax, and others) are vals and libs. Therapeutically, benzodiazepines are used to produce sedation, induce sleep, relieve anxiety and muscle spasms, and prevent seizures. These drugs are commonly prescribed, and, unfortunately, also frequently abused. The intoxication effects of benzodiazepines result in reduced inhibition and impaired judgment. Withdrawal effects are similar to that of alcohol, including the possibility of death, and generally last longer and are more unpleasant.

Rohypnol (Flunitrazepam) is also a benzodiazepine. Some street names for Rohypnol are roofies, rophies, roche, forget-me pill, circles, Mexican Valium, rib, roach 2, roopies, rope, ropies, ruffies, and roaches. Rohypnol has sedative-hypnotic effects, including muscle relaxation, amnesia, decreased blood pressure, drowsiness, visual disturbances, dizziness, confusion, gastrointestinal disturbances, and urinary retention. When mixed with alcohol, Rohypnol can incapacitate a victim and prevent her from resisting sexual assault. Also, Rohypnol may be lethal when mixed with alcohol and/or other depressants.

Users report an intoxication effect, yet no hangover. Rohypnol can produce physical and psychological dependence.

Rohypnol is popular in the "rave club" scene and nightclubs; therefore, it is referred to as a **club drug**. **Raves** are generally night-long dances, often held in warehouses. Many who attend rave events do not use drugs, but those who do may be attracted to the generally low cost, seemingly increased stamina, and intoxicating highs that are said to intensify the rave experience.

***GHB and GBL.***    Other sedative hypnotics are GHB (gamma hydroxybutyrate) and GBL (gamma butyl lactone), which are also popular in raves. Some street names for GHB are Liquid Ecstasy, Soap, and Grievous Bodily Harm. The effects of GHB include sedation, euphoria, and anabolic effects. Because of the amnestic effects, GHB has been used to lower women's defenses in rape cases. High doses of GHB can cause coma and seizures. Withdrawal effects of GHB include insomnia, anxiety, tremors, and sweating.

GBL is the active metabolite in GHB. It is sold under many trade names, including Blue Nitro, Revivarant, and Gamma G. GBL is an ingredient found in liquid paint stripper and is available through chemical suppliers. GBL increases the effects of alcohol, and can cause respiratory distress, seizures, coma, and death.

## CASE EXAMPLE

A prevention professional conducting parenting classes for parents referred by the court because of their child's alcohol use was asked, "What is the big deal about alcohol, anyway? At least my child is not out there injecting heroin or sniffing coke." The prevention professional was able to respond by discussing the effects of alcohol on the nervous system.

Another parent in the class proudly stated that she did understand the dangers of alcohol. Later in the class, she also said that she allows her daughters to attend rave clubs because her daughters tell her that alcohol is not provided there. Again, the prevention professional was able to explain to the parent that although alcohol is not always available at rave clubs, certain drugs are. She went on to explain the drugs and their dangers. The more-informed parent was then able to make better decisions about whether she would allow her daughters to continue to attend the raves.

# Opiates

Opiates and opioids such as heroin, morphine, codeine, hydrocodone (Vicodin), and methadone were developed for the treatment of acute pain, cough, diarrhea, and other illnesses. Opiates are naturally occurring in opium poppy extracts whereas opioids, also called narcotics, are synthetic. Opiates are taken for their euphoric effects, to avoid physical and emotional pain, and to avoid withdrawal symptoms. Opiates and opioids can be taken orally, injected, snorted, and smoked. The effects of opioid overdose include slow breathing rate, decreased blood pressure, decreased pulse rate, decreased temperature, decreased reflexes, drowsiness, nausea, vomiting, and even death.

Withdrawal effects from opioids are very rarely life threatening. However, the effects are extremely uncomfortable. Withdrawal effects include runny eyes and nose, restlessness, goose bumps, sweating, muscle cramps, nausea, vomiting, diarrhea, and drug craving. The fear of withdrawal is usually a greater trigger for continued use than the desire for the drug rush. Tolerance to opioids is related to frequency of use and amount of dosage.

## Heroin

Some street names for heroin are smack, horse, and tootsie roll. Heroin is the most abused and the most rapidly acting of the opiates. Although purer heroin is becoming more common, most street heroin is "cut" with other drugs or with substances such as sugar, starch, powdered milk, quinine, or other poisons. Heroin abusers do not know the actual strength of the drug or its true contents before they inject it; therefore, they are at risk of **overdose** or death. Heroin also poses special problems because of the transmission of HIV and other diseases that can occur from sharing needles or other injection equipment. Abusers typically report feeling a surge of pleasurable sensations, a "rush." Heroin is very addictive because of how fast the drug enters the brain (Inaba & Cohen, 2000). The short-term effects of heroin use are depressed respiration, clouded mental functioning, nausea and vomiting, suppression of pain, and, among pregnant women, spontaneous abortion. The long-term effects of heroin use are addiction, infectious diseases (for example, HIV/AIDS and hepatitis B and C), collapsed veins, bacterial infections, abscesses, infection of heart lining and valves, and arthritis and other rheumatologic problems.

## Morphine

Morphine is one of the most effective drugs for the relief of pain. It is processed from opium into tablets, suppositories, and liquid solutions. Because withdrawal symptoms are related to the amount taken, most short-term use of morphine will result in mild withdrawal symptoms. Physicians are sometimes reluctant to prescribe morphine because of the possibility of dependence and addiction and because of the possibility that it may mask clues to diagnosing cancer and other diseases (Inaba & Cohen, 2000).

## Codeine and Hydrocodone

Codeine is used primarily for the relief of moderate pain. It is also used in cough suppressants. Codeine is often mixed with aspirin or acetaminophen. Because codeine triggers nausea, hydrocodone is often prescribed instead of codeine. Hydrocodone has the same effects as codeine but produces less nausea. As with other opioids, respiratory depression and masking illness can be dangerous.

## Methadone

Methadone is a synthetic opioid used to treat heroin addiction. Methadone eliminates the withdrawal symptoms of heroin and alleviates the craving for the drug. It is administered orally at licensed clinics across the country. The effects of methadone typically last 24 to 36 hours.

A prevention professional working with a group of fifth-grade students on developing life skills was asked about heroin. The fifth-grade student told the prevention professional that he overheard his older brother talking about using heroin. Although the fifth-grader does not know what it is, he suspects that it is a dangerous drug. He does not know if the drug is "bad enough" that he should tell his parents. He does not want to get his older brother in trouble but he also does not want his brother to be harmed. The prevention professional was able to use knowledge about the effects of drugs to explain to the student that death and/or other seriously negative consequences are a possibility with heroin use.

# Central Nervous System Stimulants

Central nervous system (CNS) stimulants are referred to as "uppers." CNS stimulants are usually taken to alleviate fatigue and increase alertness and can cause a person to be more talkative, anxious, and exhilarated. Nicotine is the most common CNS stimulant. Other CNS stimulants include cocaine (including crack cocaine), amphetamines, nonamphetamine stimulants, ephedra, and caffeine.

The major effects of CNS stimulants are psychomotor stimulation, alertness, and elevation of mood. They are used for euphoric effects or to counteract the "down" feeling of alcohol and other depressants. In addition, CNS stimulants cause an increase in heart rate, increased blood pressure, and appetite suppression. Acute and chronic effects of CNS stimulants are heart attacks, strokes, seizures, respiratory depression, cardiovascular problems, perforation of the nasal septum, malnourishment, paranoid schizophrenia, and death.

Withdrawal symptoms of CNS stimulants can include intense drug craving, irritability, depression, anxiety, hallucinations, apathy, lethargy, and thoughts of and/or attempts at suicide. Unlike CNS depressants, the withdrawal from CNS stimulants is not life-threatening, but can be very uncomfortable.

## Nicotine

Nicotine is one of the most used CNS stimulants and has the highest potential for addiction, tolerance, and dependence. It is both a sedative and a stimulant to the central nervous system. Research has shown that stress and anxiety affect nicotine tolerance and dependence. Withdrawal symptoms can include increased anger, hostility, aggression, and loss of social cooperation. During periods of abstinence and/or craving, smokers have shown impairment across a wide range of psychomotor and cognitive functions, such as language comprehension.

## Cocaine

Some street names for cocaine (hydrochloride) are angie, barb, blow, toot, candy, coca, and coke. Cocaine is a powerfully addictive stimulant that directly affects the brain. It is made from the coca plant and causes a short-lived "high" with carefree feelings, euphoria, relaxation, and a feeling of being in control. However, that is followed immediately by the opposite: intense feelings of depression, edginess, and a craving for more of the drug. Cocaine may be used as a powder, converted to a liquid form for injection with a needle, or processed into a crystal form to be smoked. Cocaine generally is sold on the street as a fine, white, crystalline powder. Street dealers generally dilute it with such substances such as cornstarch, talcum powder, and/or sugar, or with active drugs such as procaine (a chemically related local anesthetic) or with other stimulants such as amphetamines.

## Crack Cocaine

Crack is the street name given to the freebase form of cocaine that has been processed from the powdered cocaine hydrochloride form to a smokable substance. Freebasing increases the potency and speed with which the drug reaches the brain, which increases the potential for addiction. The term "crack" refers to the crackling sound heard when the mixture is smoked. Crack cocaine is processed with ammonia or sodium bicarbonate (baking soda) and water, and heated to remove the hydrochloride. Because crack is smoked, the user experiences a high in less than 10 seconds. This rather immediate and euphoric effect is one of the reasons that crack became enormously popular in the mid-1980s. Another reason is that crack is inexpensive both to produce and to buy.

## Amphetamines

Amphetamines are also CNS stimulants. Amphetamines include Benzedrine (cross tops, and black beauties) and Methedrine (crank, meth, and crystal). Amphetamines generally are taken orally, smoked, or injected. Their effects are similar to cocaine, but the "high" onset is slower and duration is longer. Chronic abuse produces a psychosis similar to schizophrenia and characterized by paranoia, picking at the skin, preoccupation with one's own thoughts, and hallucinations.

Methedrine (methamphetamine) is a highly addictive drug. Over time, methamphetamine appears to cause reduced levels of dopamine, which can result in symptoms like those of Parkinson's disease. Methamphetamine is taken orally by snorting the powder, by intravenous injection, and by smoking. Immediately after smoking or intravenous injection, the user experiences an intense sensation, called a "rush" or "flash," which lasts only a few minutes and is described as extremely pleasurable. Oral or intranasal use produces euphoria. Methamphetamines are also popular at rave clubs.

## Nonamphetamine Stimulants

There are also nonamphetamine stimulants with similar properties as amphetamine stimulants, such as Ritalin (Methylphenidate) and Cylert. Ritalin may produce the same effects as cocaine and amphetamines. It is used medically to elevate moods, treat narcolepsy, and most often to treat children with Attention Deficit Disorder (ADA) and Attention Deficit Hyperactivity Disorder (ADHD). ADA and ADHD are characterized by inattentiveness and hyperactivity. Although it seems contradictory, low doses of stimulants often have the capability to focus attention and control hyperactivity. Even caffeine in low doses can help focus attention. Ritalin has not been produced clandestinely. However, abuse of this substance does exist.

Ephedra (ephedrine) is a mild stimulant that is used to treat asthma, narcolepsy, allergies, and low blood pressure. One common side effect of excessive use is drug-induced psychosis (Karch, 1996). Ephedra products have also been used for energy enhancement, but ephedra can lead to heart and blood vessel problems. Ephedra is used in many weight-loss products, is sold over the counter, and is often used as a precursor to methamphetamines. However, many states are beginning to ban ephedra-based products.

Caffeine is the most common stimulant in the world. Medically, it is used as a decongestant, an analgesic, an appetite suppressant, and for menstrual pain. It is also used as a mild stimulant. In low doses it can increase alertness, alleviate fatigue, and enhance thinking. However, excessive use can cause problems. At higher doses (350 milligrams or more per day) it can cause anxiety, insomnia, nervousness, gastric irritation, and high blood pressure. It can also lower fertility rates in women and effect fetuses in the womb. Long term and high doses of caffeine use can cause heart disease, heart attacks, intestinal ulcers, diabetes, and liver problems. Withdrawal effects include headaches, lethargy, fatigue, depression, decreased alertness, sleeping problems, and irritability.

## CASE EXAMPLE

A prevention professional working at a youth center sees a teenage girl taking a pill. The youth worker confronts the girl and she tells him that she is only taking a natural weight-loss supplement she purchased at the health food store. At first the prevention professional thinks nothing of it but then he reads the label and discovers it contains ephedra. The prevention professional explains the possible side effects and the girl promises to get rid of the pills and discontinue use.

# Hallucinogens

CNS stimulants excite the body and CNS depressants slow down the body. **Hallucinogens**, also called **psychedelics**, can do both by distorting perception, thought, and mood. Drugs in this category induce illusions and hallucinations. Many of the naturally occurring hallucinogens are found in plants and fungi. In recent years, synthetic hallucinogens have been produced. Some hallucinogens are PCP (phencyclidine), LSD (lysergic acid diethylamide), peyote (mescaline), psilocybin, MDMA (methylenedioxymethamphetamine), and ketamine.

The possible effects of hallucinogens are rapidly changing feelings, both immediately and long after use. Chronic use may cause persistent problems, such as depression, violent behavior, anxiety, and distorted perception of time. Large doses may cause convulsions, coma, heart/lung failure, ruptured blood vessels in the brain, hallucinations, illusions, dizziness, confusion, suspicion, anxiety, and loss of control. Delayed effects, also called "flashbacks," may occur long after use. When used with designer drugs, one use may cause irreversible brain damage (Julien, 1998). **Designer drugs** are similar to controlled substances that are formulated by street chemists. For example, MDMA is a designer amphetamine, which acts like a hallucinogen. Long-term effects may include longer, more intense "trip" episodes, psychosis, coma, and death. There are no known physical withdrawal symptoms. Tolerance and cross-tolerance occurs with some hallucinogens. With the exception of PCP, Ketamine, and a few plant hallucinogens, toxic overdose does not occur with hallucinogens.

## PCP

Some street names for PCP (phencyclidine) are angel dust, rocket fuel, and love boat. PCP is a white crystalline powder that is readily soluble in water or alcohol. It can be mixed easily with dyes and turns up on the illicit drug market in a variety of tablets, capsules, and colored powders. This drug normally is used in one of three ways: snorted, smoked, or eaten. Users report a feeling of strength, power, invulnerability, and numbness. In low doses, the effects of PCP include an increase in breathing rate and a rise in blood pressure and pulse rate. Respiration becomes shallow and flushing and profuse sweating occurs. Generalized numbness of the extremities and muscular incoordination also may occur. Psychological effects include distinct changes in body awareness. At high doses of PCP, there is a drop in blood pressure, pulse rate, and respiration. This may be accompanied by nausea, vomiting, blurred vision, flicking up and down of the eyes, drooling, loss of balance, and dizziness. High doses of PCP can also cause seizures, coma, and death (though death more often results from accidental injury or suicide during PCP intoxication). Psychological effects at high doses include illusions and hallucinations. Speech is often sparse and garbled. PCP is also popular at the rave clubs.

## LSD

Some street names for LSD (lysergic acid diethylamide) are acid and green/red dragon. LSD is the most potent hallucinogen; however, users are more likely to experience illusions. It is usually sold in the form of impregnated paper, tablets, or thin squares of gelatin. LSD causes an increase in heart rate and blood pressure, higher body temperature, dizziness, dilated pupils, and sweating. LSD overloads the senses and causes distortions in sounds, sight, hearing, or smelling. The user may suffer from impaired perceptional depth, time, movement, and touch. It also causes impaired concentration, altered moods, loss of motivation, and impaired communication skills. Users report intense sensations and emotions. After an LSD "trip" users may suffer from acute anxiety or depression. Flashbacks may occur days or even months after taking the last dose. LSD is also popular at rave clubs.

## Peyote

Peyote is a small cactus the principal ingredient of which is the hallucinogen mescaline. The plant has been used traditionally by natives in Mexico and the United States for religious purposes. The crowns of the peyote cactus are eaten fresh or dried and consumed as tea. The hallucinogen effects last about 12 hours. The effects of mescaline are similar to those of LSD, with an emphasis on colorful visions.

## Psilocybin

Psilocybin is the active chemical ingredient in magic mushrooms. The mushrooms have been used in native ritual ceremonies for centuries. The effects of the psilocybin last about six hours, causing nausea and other symptoms before the hallucinogenic effects occur. The effects include changes in sight, taste, hearing, and touch, along with altered states of consciousness.

## MDMA

Some street names for MDMA are ecstasy, XTC, E, X, Adam, and blue kisses. MDMA, a synthetic, **psychoactive** substance with stimulant and mild hallucinogenic properties, has physical symptoms that include muscle tension, involuntary teeth clenching, nausea, blurred vision, rapid eye movement, faintness, and chills or sweating. It reduces inhibitions, eliminates anxiety, causes extreme relaxation, and reduces the need to eat, drink, or sleep. (Users also report a calming effect and increased empathy toward others.) Psychological difficulties, including confusion, depression, sleep problems, drug craving, severe anxiety, and paranoia occur during use and sometimes weeks after taking MDMA. MDMA is usually found in tablet form and taken orally, with effects lasting from four to six hours. An MDMA overdose is usually characterized by a rapid heartbeat, high blood pressure, faintness, muscle cramping, panic attacks, and in severe cases, seizures or loss of consciousness. Hyperthermia or excessive body heat is the most critical, life-threatening response of MDMA. This drug is also popular in the rave club scene and is considered a designer drug.

## Ketamine

Some street names for Ketamine are K, Special K, and Cat Valium. Ketamine is a general anesthetic for human and veterinary use. It has sedative-hypnotic, analgesic (pain reliever), and hallucinogenic properties. It is abused as a date-rape drug. The use of the drug can cause delirium, amnesia, depression, long-term memory and cognitive difficulties, and fatal respiratory problems. Users experience a mild euphoria, illusions, and hallucinations lasting about six hours. Ketamine liquid can be injected, applied to smokable material, or consumed in drinks. A powdered form can be put into beverages, smoked, or injected. It is reportedly used as an alternative to cocaine and is generally snorted. Side effects are similar to those of PCP, including coma, convulsions, and belligerent behaviors. Ketamine is also popular in the rave clubs.

## CASE EXAMPLE

A group of high school students are gathered in the lunchroom cafeteria talking about their weekend party plans. One of the girls says that her boyfriend can get "magic mushrooms" for everyone. The other girls look at each other and say they have never used them but have heard they are "fun." One of the girls goes and talks to a school counselor about the plans. The school counselor, uncertain about what "magic mushrooms" are, contacts the school district prevention professional and explains the situation. The prevention professional, who is well versed in the knowledge of drugs and their effects, explains that "magic mushrooms" are a hallucinogenic drug containing psilocybin and have some serious effects (mystical thinking and conversations, hallucinations, and change in the appearance of the eyes). The school counselor, now armed with accurate information, realizes what the drug is and what its possible effects are. This information, coupled with science-based strategies on how best to address this problem, aids the counselor in developing a plan to intervene with the girls and prevent this event from occurring.

# Cannabinols

Cannabis is the hemp plant from which marijuana and hashish are produced. Marijuana is a tobacco-like substance and hashish consists of resinous secretions of the cannabis plant. "Hemp" is usually used to describe the cannabis plants that have a high fiber content, while marijuana is used to describe cannabis plants that are high in psychoactive components (Schultes & Hofmann, 1992; Stafford, 1992). Three drugs, **cannabinols**, that come from cannabis are marijuana, hashish, and hashish oil.

Possible effects of cannabis are euphoria followed by relaxation; increased appetite; impaired memory, concentration, and knowledge retention; loss of coordination; and more vivid sense of taste, sight, smell, and hearing. Stronger doses cause fluctuating emotions, fragmentary thoughts, disoriented behavior, irritation to the lung and respiratory system, increased pulse rate, increased blood pressure, bloodshot eyes, and dry mouth. It is unusual to overdose because the normal effects are not enhanced by larger doses. However, users report an intensification of emotional responses, mild hallucinations, and a feeling of being "out of control" (Julien, 1998) when using a larger amount. Withdrawal effects include insomnia, hyperactivity, decreased appetite, irritability, restlessness, chills, and increased body temperature. Long-term use may result in suppression of the immune system and decreased hormones.

## Marijuana

Some street terms for marijuana are weed, pot, herb, chronic, and grass. Marijuana can be both a stimulant and a depressant depending on how much of the chemical is absorbed, and depending on the personality of the user. The immediate effects of marijuana use include relaxation or sedation, increased appetite, loss of coordination, bloodshot eyes, coughing from lung irritation, loss of concentration, drowsiness, giddiness, and major distortions and perceptions of the senses. The main active chemical in marijuana is THC (delta-9 tetrahydrocannabinol). Because THC is stored in the fat cells, withdrawal effects do not appear until there is a period of abstinence. Nonetheless, withdrawal effects include irritability, aches, depression, loss of concentration, insomnia, decreased appetite, sweating, and craving for the drug.

Marijuana is usually smoked as a cigarette or in a pipe or bong. In recent years, marijuana has appeared in blunts, which are cigars that have been emptied of tobacco and refilled with marijuana, often in combination with another drug, such as crack. Some street names for these combinations include gremmies, cocoa puffs, and primos. Some users also mix marijuana into foods or use it to brew tea.

Studies regarding tolerance to marijuana vary. Some studies have shown that tolerance develops rapidly while others demonstrate that tolerance develops slowly and is mild (Palfai & Jankiewicz, 1997; Inaba, Cohen, & Holstein, 1997). High-dose users are able to tolerate much higher levels without the emotional and psychic effects of first-time users. Studies regarding physical dependence are controversial. However, there is a general acceptance that marijuana is psychologically addictive. Studies on the effects on memory are also controversial. Some studies suggest that marijuana has a negative effect on short-term and long-term memory. The major effects of marijuana last two to four hours; however, marijuana stays in the body for up to six months.

### Charas

Charas is the sticky resin on the cannabis plant that is the most potent. When charas is collected and pressed together into balls, cakes, or cookie-like sheets, it is called hashish. It is usually smoked or it can be added to marijuana cigarettes to enhance the potency. Hashish oil can be extracted from the plants and added to foods, be spread on paper or dripped into marijuana cigarettes to enhance the effects of marijuana. A drop or two of this liquid is equal to a single marijuana cigarette.

### CASE EXAMPLE

A prevention professional overhears a group of teenagers discussing marijuana. The teenagers believe that marijuana is not harmful and should be legal. They know they cannot die from a marijuana overdose and they do not think it has any negative effects. The prevention professional is able to dispel the myths by discussing with the teenagers exactly how harmful marijuana is and what the short- and long-term health effects are. Although just having the facts may not stop the teenagers from using this drug, it is important that teenagers understand that marijuana is harmful and will affect their health.

## Steroids

Anabolic **steroids** are used medically for testosterone replacement, treatment of muscle loss, blood anemia, and endometriosis. However, some athletes have used them to increase muscle mass and gain a competitive advantage. Some anabolic steroids are sold legally in the United States, including Depo-Testosterone, Durabolin, Danocrine, and Halotestin. The correct term for these compounds is "anabolic and androgenic" steroids, which means to build up muscle and strength. Some veterinary anabolic steroids are illegally sold to humans, including Finiject 30, Equipose, and Winstrol. The main reasons people abuse steroids are to improve their performance in sports, to increase their muscle size, and/or to reduce their body fat. Steroids have been abused primarily among competitive body builders. Among other athletes, the incidence of abuse probably varies depending on the specific sport.

The effects of anabolic steroids for males are reduced sperm production, shrinking of the testicles, acne, impotence, difficulty or pain during urination, baldness, and irreversible breast enlargement. The effects for females include development of more masculine characteristics, such as decreased body fat and breast size, deepening of the voice, excessive body hair growth, loss of scalp hair, and enlargement of the clitoris. In adolescents the effects include potentially fatal liver cysts and liver cancer, blood clotting, cholesterol changes, stunted growth, and hypertension.

There are no known symptoms of overdose. Possible symptoms of withdrawal include depression, fatigue, restlessness, insomnia, loss of appetite, decreased sex drive, headache, muscle pain, and a craving for the drug. Steroids are usually taken orally as capsules or tablets, by injection into muscles, or by ointment preparations rubbed into the skin. Doses taken by abusers can be up to 100 times the medical dosage. There is no evidence of tolerance to anabolic steroids.

## CASE EXAMPLE

A prevention professional, who coordinates prevention services in the county, receives a call from a local high school coach. The coach suspects that some of his athletes are considering taking steroids. He does not know the effects of steroids but wants information so he can pursue a specific course of action. During the phone call, the prevention professional is immediately able to discuss the effects of steroids and to encourage the coach to offer a prevention program aimed at athletes.

# Inhalants

**Inhalants** and volatile hydrocarbons are usually chemicals that can be purchased legally and are normally used for practical purposes. However, inhalants are volatile substances that produce chemical vapors that can be inhaled to induce a psychoactive, or mind-altering, effect. The category of inhalants encompasses a broad range of chemicals found in hundreds of different products that may have different pharmacological effects. As a result, precise categorization of inhalants is difficult. One classification system lists four general categories of inhalants based on the form in which they are often found in household, industrial, and medical products: volatile solvents, aerosol, gases, and nitrites.

Because inhalants are usually inhaled through the nose and/or mouth or sprayed directly into the nose or mouth, they are quickly absorbed through the lungs and bloodstream. There are no known withdrawal symptoms of inhalants. Tolerance develops in response to nitrous oxide but does not appear to develop with other inhalants.

Prevention professionals and other adults should not place information about household products that can be used to get high in places where kids can see the information. The information about the effects of all drugs—but especially those of inhalants and the products that are easily accessible to most youth—may spark curiosity and lead youth to try inhalants. However, it is important to give them warnings about the dangers of inhaling substances in general.

## Volatile Solvents

Volatile solvents—liquids that vaporize at room temperature—are found in multiple household products, including paint thinners and removers, dry-cleaning fluids, degreasers, gasoline, glues, correction fluids, and felt-tip marker fluids. Inhaling these substances produces temporary stimulation, mood elevation, and reduced inhibitions before the CNS depressant effect is felt. Long-term effects of inhaling volatile solvents include lack of coordination, inability to concentrate, weakness, disorientation, and weight loss.

## Aerosols and Gases

Aerosols—sprays that contain propellants and solvents—include spray paints, deodorants and hair sprays, vegetable oil sprays for cooking, and fabric protector sprays. Gases include medical anesthetics such as chloroform, halothane, and nitrous oxide, commonly called "laughing gas." Household or commercial products that contain gases include butane lighters, propane tanks, whipped cream dispensers, and refrigerators. The chemicals found in aerosol sprays and gases can produce a variety of effects during or shortly after use that are related to inhalant intoxication, including belligerence, apathy, impaired judgment, impaired functioning in work or social situations, dizziness, drowsiness, slurred speech, lethargy, depressed reflexes, general muscle weakness, stupor, nausea, and vomiting. Exposure to high doses can cause confusion and delirium.

## Nitrites

Nitrites-based inhalants include aliphatic nitrites, including cyclohexyl nitrite, which is available to the general public in room odorizers; amyl nitrite, which is available only by prescription; and butyl nitrite, which is now an illegal substance. Nitrites, which dilate blood vessels and relax the muscles, are mainly used as sexual enhancers. Amyl and butyl nitrites have been associated with Kaposi's Sarcoma (KS), the most common cancer reported among AIDS patients. Early studies of KS showed that many people with KS had used volatile nitrites.

### CASE EXAMPLE

After a tutoring session with several elementary-age students, a prevention professional is asked by one of the parents about inhalants. The parent has noticed things missing in the garage and refrigerator and has heard about teens using inhalants. The parent has noticed that when his teenage son arrives home from work at a local ice cream parlor he seems extremely tired and disoriented. The next day the same parent's teenage son shows up to pick up the young child. The teenager appears intoxicated, has slurred speech, and is having trouble walking. The prevention professional immediately recognizes the symptoms of inhalant abuse and takes proper action.

## Drugs of Abuse Chart

Table 4.1 (pages 92–96) summarizes the information described in the text, along with a few added facts. Only general information is provided, since the goal is to give prevention professionals a broad understanding of the effects of ATOD. For every pharmacological category, the major effects are described. The symptoms of overdose, the possible effects of withdrawal, and acute and chronic effects are described. The street names of the drugs are provided in parenthesis.

## Gateway Drugs

**Gateway drugs** are thus called because their use typically precedes the use of illicit drugs such as heroin, cocaine, and LSD. Gateway drugs, or drugs of entry, serve to initiate the beginner into the culture of drug use. Gateway drugs include tobacco, alcohol, and in some communities marijuana and inhalants. In prevention, it makes sense to focus efforts on gateway drugs since these drugs are readily available and their use is considered exciting and adult-like. Further, research has shown that the age of first use of any drug is related to later drug use by adolescents. Also, young people who begin using drugs before the age of 15 are twice as likely to have problems with drugs than those who wait until after the age of 19 (Hawkins, Catalano, & Miller, 1992).

Alcohol and tobacco cause more health and related problems than do other drugs. More people die each month from alcohol- and tobacco-related problems than from all illicit drugs combined (Torabi, Bailey, & Majd-Tabbari, 1993). In 1998, the total cost of alcohol use by youth was $52.8 billion. This figure includes pain, medical care, lost quality of life, work loss, and other costs. Some of the problems included in the above categories are traffic crashes, violent crimes, burns, drowning, suicide attempts, fetal alcohol syndrome, alcohol poisoning, and treatment (Levy, Miller, & Cox, 1999). Annually, tobacco use causes more than 43,000 deaths and costs approximately $50 to $73 billion in medical expenses alone (Centers for Disease Control and Prevention, 1999).

A study at the University of Michigan Institute for Social Research found that among high school seniors, daily smokers were 10 times more likely to use cocaine regularly that those seniors that had never smoked regularly. The study demonstrated that high school seniors were much more likely to use every kind of controlled substance than were non-smoking students. The more cigarettes a student smoked, the more likely he or she was to use marijuana and cocaine (Johnston, O'Malley, & Bachman, 1987).

Children who begin using alcohol in late elementary school or junior high school are more likely to use illicit drugs. Heavy drinkers are more likely to use controlled substances than are nondrinkers or moderate drinkers. A study conducted at the Center for Addiction and Substance Abuse at Colombia found that children who use gateway drugs (tobacco, alcohol, and marijuana) are up to 266 times more likely to use cocaine. The study also demonstrated that almost 90 percent of people who have ever tried cocaine used all three gateway drugs first. Analysis of the study further showed that children who drank alcohol were 50 times more likely to use cocaine that nondrinkers (Center on Addiction and Substance Abuse, 1994).

For these reasons it is logical and reasonable for prevention professionals to focus on reducing the initiation of gateway drugs.

# Trends in Drug Use

The constant introduction of new drugs and the rediscovery of old drugs help keep the drug epidemic going. Some drugs, such as LSD, PCP, cocaine, heroin, and methamphetamines have made a comeback after information about their adverse effects faded from people's memories. This process is termed "generational forgetting" because one generation forgets the lessons learned about a certain drug by the previous generation. The implications for prevention are that young people need education about each drug because the knowledge about negative effects of one drug will not generalize to another drug. Further, as stated in Chapter 2, prevention efforts should focus on the use of *all* drugs (except prevention efforts for tobacco, because prevention efforts have shown effectiveness when focusing on *just* tobacco). Attitudes and beliefs about the perceived benefits of specific drugs help, in part, to explain the popularity of various drugs over time. Likewise, the perceived risks and disapproval of the use of certain drugs help explain the decline in popularity of certain drugs. New drugs often have a period for which adverse effects and negative consequences are not yet known. For example, crack (introduced in the 1980s) and Rohypnol and GHB (introduced in the 1990s) were highly used until the news about the dangers were accumulated and disseminated.

Although overall drug use has declined since 1979, there was a slight increase during the early to mid-1990s, with a decline in use in the late 1990s. According to Monitoring the Future, a long-term study of adolescents in 8th, 10th, and 12th grades, college students, and adults through age 40 in the United States, in the year 2000 illicit drug use remained steady overall, as did the use of certain significant drugs such as marijuana, amphetamines, tranquilizers, barbiturates, and alcohol. The use of inhalants, LSD, Rohypnol, and cigarettes decreased, and the use of MDMA (ecstasy), steroids, and heroin increased (Johnston, O'Malley, & Bachman, 2000b).

## Drugs Holding Steady

Marijuana is the most widely used illicit drug in the survey. A rise in marijuana during the 1960s and 1970s peaked in 1979 and steadily declined until 1992. In 1992 there was a resurgence of use until 1997 when annual prevalence rates peaked and have steadily declined since. However, no one year has shown a significant decline. Disapproval of use declined between 1991 and 1997. Although there was a small increase in disapproval of use among 8th graders there was not very much change among 10th and 12th graders in 2000. Perceived availability of marijuana has been high since the survey began in 1975. In 2000 nearly half of 8th graders reported that marijuana was accessible, as did 89 percent of 12th-grade students (Johnston et al., 2000b).

**TABLE 4.1  Drugs of Abuse**

| Drug | Major Effects | Symptoms of Overdose | Possible Effects of Withdrawal | Acute and Chronic Effects |
|---|---|---|---|---|
| **Central Nervous System Depressants** | | | | |
| ■ Alcohol (in beer, wine, liquor) | ■ Muscle relaxation | Alcohol: | ■ Anxiety | Alcohol: |
| ■ Barbiturates (Seconal ["reds," "red devils"], Nembutal ["yellows," "yellow jackets"], Tuinal ["rainbows"], Amytal ["blues," "blue heaven"], Phenobarbital) | ■ Disinhibition | ■ Staggering | ■ Irritability | ■ Memory loss |
| | ■ Reduction in anxiety | ■ Slurred speech | ■ Loss of appetite | ■ Gastritis |
| | ■ Impairment of judgment | ■ Extreme disinhibition | ■ Tremors | ■ Esophagitis |
| | ■ Impairment of motor coordination | ■ Blackouts | ■ Insomnia | ■ Ulcers |
| | ■ Decrease in reflexes | ■ Vomiting | ■ Seizures | ■ Pancreatitis |
| | ■ Decrease in pulse rate | ■ Possible coma and death | ■ Fever | ■ Cirrhosis of the liver |
| ■ Nonbarbiturate sedative-hypnotics (Doriden ["goofballs"], Quaalude ["ludes"], Miltown, Equinil) | ■ Decrease in blood pressure | Depressants have a synergistic, or potentiation, effect. | ■ Rapid heartbeat | ■ High blood pressure |
| | ■ Slurred speech | | ■ Elevated blood pressure | ■ Weakened heart muscles |
| | ■ Staggering | | ■ Hallucinations | ■ Damage to fetus |
| | ■ Sleep | | ■ Death | Other depressants: |
| ■ Benzodiazepines (Valium, Librium, Dalmane, Halcion, Xanax, Ativan) | ■ Activate gastric juices | | | ■ Family, social, occupational, financial problems |
| ■ Over-the-counter medications (Nytol, Sominex) | | | | ■ Accidents |
| | | | | ■ Violence |
| **Opioids** | | | | |
| ■ Opium | ■ Suppression of pain | ■ Slow breathing rate | ■ Running eyes and nose | ■ Death from overdose from injecting opioids |
| ■ Codeine | ■ Constipation | ■ Decreased blood pressure | ■ Restlessness | ■ Criminal activity |
| ■ Morphine | ■ Euphoria | ■ Decreased pulse rate | ■ Goose bumps | ■ Prostitution |
| ■ Heroin ("smack," "horse") | ■ Sedation | ■ Decreased temperature | ■ Sweating | ■ Malnutrition |
| ■ Vicodin | ■ Constricted pupils | ■ Decreased reflexes | ■ Muscle cramps or aching | |
| ■ Dilaudid | | ■ Drowsiness | ■ Nausea | |
| ■ Percodan | | ■ Loss of consciousness | ■ Vomiting | |
| ■ Methadone | | ■ Flushing and itching | ■ Diarrhea | |
| ■ Darvon | | | ■ Drug craving | |

- Demerol
- Talwin
- LAAM

- Abdominal pain
- Nausea
- Vomiting
- Death

## Central Nervous System Stimulants

- Cocaine ("coke," "blow," "toot," "snow")
- Smokable forms of cocaine ("crack," "rock," "base")
- Amphetamines (Benzedrine ["crosstops," "black beauties"], Methedrine ["crank," "meth," "crystal"], Dexedrine)
- Nonamphetamine stimulants (Ritalin, Cylert, Preludin)
- Caffeine (in coffees, teas, colas, chocolate, No Doz, Alert, Vivarin)
- Phenylpropanolamine (in Dexatrim)
- Nicotine (in tobacco)

- Psychomotor stimulation
- Alertness
- Euphoria
- Elevation of mood
- Increase in heart rate
- Increase in blood pressure
- Suppression of appetite
- Death

- Tremors
- Sweating and flushing
- Rapid heartbeat
- Anxiety
- Insomnia
- Paranoia
- Convulsions
- Heart attack
- Stroke

Caffeine:
- Chronic headache
- Irritability
- Restlessness
- Anxiety
- Fatigue
- Lethargy

Cocaine and amphetamines:
- Intense drug craving
- Irritability
- Depression
- Anxiety
- Lethargy
- Suicidal ideation and attempts

Nicotine:
- Increased anger
- Hostility
- Aggression
- Loss of social cooperation

- Heart attacks
- Strokes
- Seizures
- Respiratory depression
- Strokes
- Cardiovascular problems
- Depression
- Suicide
- Paranoid schizophrenia
- Perforation of the nasal septum
- Malnourishment

*(continued)*

TABLE 4.1 Continued

| Drug | Major Effects | Symptoms of Overdose | Possible Effects of Withdrawal | Acute and Chronic Effects |
|---|---|---|---|---|
| **Hallucinogens**<br>■ LSD ("acid," "fry")<br>■ Psilocybin ("magic mushrooms," "shrooms")<br>■ Morning glory seeds ("heavenly blue")<br>■ Mescaline ("mesc," "big chief," "peyote")<br>■ STP ("serenity," "tranquility," "peace")<br>■ MDMA ("ecstasy")<br>■ PCP ("angel dust," "hog")<br>■ Ketamine | ■ Altered state of consciousness<br>■ Increased suggestibility<br>■ Delusions<br>■ Depersonalization<br>■ Dissociation<br>■ Increase in pulse<br>■ Increase in blood pressure | PCP:<br>■ Acute intoxication and psychosis, including agitation, confusion, excitement, blank state, violent behavior<br>■ Coma<br>■ Analgesia<br>■ Death<br>"Bad" trips of other hallucinogens:<br>■ Paranoid ideation<br>■ Depression<br>■ Undesirable hallucinations<br>■ Confusion | ■ Drug craving | LSD:<br>■ Flashbacks<br>■ Increase in heart rate<br>■ Increase in blood pressure<br>■ Higher body temperature<br>■ Dizziness<br>■ Dilated pupils<br>■ Sensory distortions<br>■ Dreaminess<br>■ Depersonalization<br>■ Altered mood<br>■ Impaired concentration<br>■ Acute anxiety<br>■ Paranoia<br>■ Fear of loss of control<br>■ Delusions |
| **Cannabinols**<br>■ Marijuana ("grass," "pot," "weed," "joint," "reefer")<br>■ Hashish<br>■ Charas | ■ Euphoria<br>■ Enhancement of taste, touch, and smell<br>■ Relaxation<br>■ Increased appetite<br>■ Altered time sense<br>■ Impaired immediate recall<br>■ Increase in pulse rate<br>■ Increase in blood pressure<br>■ Bloodshot eyes<br>■ Dry mouth | Unusual to overdose | ■ Irritability<br>■ Restlessness<br>■ Decreased appetite<br>■ Insomnia<br>■ Tremor<br>■ Chills<br>■ Increased body temperature | ■ Impairment of ability to drive vehicles<br>Chronic use:<br>■ Suppression of immune system<br>■ Decrease of hormones |

- Impairment of motor skills
- Slowness of reaction time

## Inhalants and Volatile Hydrocarbons

- Aerosol sprays, gasoline, kerosene, chloroform, airplane glue, lacquer thinner, acetone, nail-polish remover, model cement, lighter fluid, carbon tetrachloride, fluoride-based sprays, metallic paints, typewriter correction fluids
- Volatile nitrites (amyl nitrite ["poppers"], butyl, isobutyl ["locker room," "rush," "blot," "quick silver," "zoom"])
- Nitrous oxide ("laughing gas")

- Disinhibition
- Euphoria
- Dizziness
- Slurred speech
- Unsteady gait
- Drowsiness
- Constant involuntary movements of the eyes
- Giddiness
- Headaches

- Hallucinations
- Muscle spasms
- Headaches
- Dizziness
- Loss of balance
- Irregular heartbeat
- Coma

- Loss of consciousness
- Coma
- Death from lack of oxygen
- Brain damage
- Lung damage
- Kidney damage
- Liver damage

(continued)

**TABLE 4.1** Continued

| Drug | Major Effects | Symptoms of Overdose | Possible Effects of Withdrawal | Acute and Chronic Effects |
|------|---------------|----------------------|-------------------------------|---------------------------|
| **Anabolic Steroids**<br>■ Depo–Testosterone<br>■ Durabolin<br>■ Danocrine<br>■ Halotestin<br>■ Veterinary anabolic steroids (Finiject 30, Equipoise, Winstrol, Delatestryl, Testex, Maxibolan) | ■ Increase of muscle strength<br>■ Reduction of body mass<br>■ Increased aggressiveness, competitiveness, and combativeness | | ■ Depression<br>■ Fatigue<br>■ Restlessness<br>■ Insomnia<br>■ Loss of appetite<br>■ Decreased interest in sex | ■ Increased risk of coronary artery disease<br>■ Mood swings<br>■ Periods of unreasonable and uncontrolled anger and violence<br>Males:<br>■ Atrophy of testicles<br>■ Impaired production of sperm<br>■ Infertility<br>■ Early baldness<br>■ Acne<br>■ Enlargement of breasts<br>Females:<br>■ Increase in facial and body hair<br>■ Lowered voice<br>■ Irregularity or cessation of menses |

*Source:* Adapted from G. L. Fisher and T. C. Harrison, (2000), *Substance Abuse: Information for School Counselors, Social Workers, Therapists, and Counselors* (2nd ed.). Boston: Allyn and Bacon.

Amphetamine use peaked in 1981; however, it made a comeback in the 1990s. By 1997 amphetamine use leveled off and has steadily declined every year until 2000. During 1991 and 1995 there was a decline in the perceived risk of amphetamines, during which time use rates were rising. There was a small increase in the perceived availability during the mid-1990s followed by a decline in the late 1990s. Although methamphetamines and ice are a type of amphetamine, they were listed separately on the survey. These drugs have followed a similar trend as amphetamines as a whole but had a sharper decrease in 2000 (Johnston et al., 2000b).

The nonmedical use of tranquilizers made a small comeback during the 1990s. Annual prevalence rates peaked in 1996 and steadily declined until 2000. Questions about perceived risks and disapproval are not asked on the survey (Johnston et al., 2000b).

Through the mid-1970s to the early 1990s the use of barbiturates fell in popularity. However, there was a resurgence of use from 1992 through 2000. Use of methaqualone, a type of tranquilizer, also increased from 1993 to 1999, then dropped significantly in 2000. There was an increased perception of risk between 1975 and 1986, during which time use was also declining. In 1991 the perceived risks were higher, as the rates of use were falling. Although there has been some change in the levels, the majority of students have continually disapproved of the illegal use of barbiturates. In general, the perceived availability of barbiturates has declined since 1975 (Johnston et al., 2000b).

The use of alcohol remains high. Eighty percent of students have consumed alcohol by the end of 12th grade and 52 percent have done so by 8th grade. However, just as illicit drug use, binge drinking has steadily declined since its peak in 1979, with the lowest rate in 1992. Binge drinking did not rise as much in proportional terms as the use of illicit drugs during the 1990s, about 4 percentage points among high school seniors from 1992 to 1998. From 1998 to 2000 binge drinking remained level for 8th, 10th, and 12th graders. Between 1982 and 1993 there was an increase in the perceived risks associated with binge drinking; however, there was a small decrease in the perceived risks from 1993 to 1997. The levels of disapproval moved generally in conjunction with the perceived risks, the implication being that peers' favorable attitudes toward binge drinking had declined. The perceived availability of alcohol was high and steady all through the 1990s to 2000. One theory frequently put forth is the "displacement effect," which points to the belief that youth are using marijuana instead of alcohol. According to Johnston et al. (2000b) there is no evidence of this hypothesis.

## Drugs Decreasing in Use

Inhalants are more common among younger adolescents than older teens, and their use tends to decline as adolescents grow older. From 1976 to 1987 the use of inhalants rose slowly, which was unusual considering the trend that the use of other illicit drugs was going down. From 1991 to 1995 inhalant use continued to rise, then started to exhibit a steady decline until 2000. Among 8th-grade students, lifetime use of inhalants declined from 21.0 percent in 1997 to 17.9 percent in 2000. Although this represented a decrease, it is not a statistically significant one. Eighth- and 9th-grade students (12th graders were not asked these questions) perceived only small risks with trying inhalants once or twice, although from 1995 to 1996 there was a sharp increase in the perceived risks. Between 1995 and 1999 there was an increase in students reporting that they disapproved of inhalant use, but this leveled off in 2000. As inhalants are found in most households, questions about availability were not asked (Johnston et al., 2000b).

Although the use of LSD has remained under 10 percent for the past 25 years, during 1991 and 1996 its use increased. From 1996 to 2000, its use has continually gone down. Among high school seniors, lifetime use rates declined from 13.6 percent in 1997 to 11.1 percent in 2000. The rates of use in 2000 were below the peak level of 1996 for all three grade levels. From 1991 to 1997 there was a steady decline in the perceived risks associated with LSD, before this leveled off. Along with the decline in perceived risks of LSD, disapproval of use also began to decline after 1991. After 1996 there was an increase in disapproval of use. From 1986 to 1995 there was a steady increase in the perceived availability of LSD. In 2000 there was a drop in the perceived availability in all three grade levels (Johnston et al., 2000b).

In 1996, questions about Rohypnol were added to the survey. In all three grade levels, reported lifetime use was less than 1.5 percent at that time. There were several fluctuations between 1996 and 1999 but levels returned back to the original 1996 level by 1999. Between 1999 and 2000 all three grade levels showed a decline, although not a statistically significant one. Questions about perceived risks, disapproval, and availability were not asked (Johnston et al., 2000b).

During the 1990s smoking began to rise significantly in all three grade levels. Smoking rates peaked for 8th and 10th graders in 1996 and for 12th graders in 1997. From 1998 to 2000 smoking rates declined among all three grade levels. Among 8th graders, past-month use of cigarettes declined from 17.5 percent in 1999 to 14.6 percent in 2000 and among 12th graders from 34.6 percent to 31.4 percent. Perceived risk of smoking increased among 8th graders from 54.8 percent in 1999 to 58.8 percent in 2000 and from 62.7 percent to 65.9 percent among 10th graders. In 2000, perceived availability was more than 60 percent for 8th graders and more than 85 percent for 10th graders, but this has been declining since 1996. Overall rates of smokeless tobacco remained stable in past-year and past-month use by seniors and decreased from its peak level in 1995 (Johnston et al., 2000b).

## Drugs Increasing in Use

The use of the "club drug" MDMA (ecstasy) began to rise in 1995 with a sharp increase in use in 1999 and 2000 among 8th-, 10th-, and 12th-grade students. Young adults in their early 20s have also experienced a sharp increase in MDMA use. There has been no change in the perceived risks or disapproval of MDMA since 1997 but there has been an increase in perceived availability since 1991. In 1999, the increase in MDMA use occurred mainly in the Northeast and in large cities; however, in 2000 the increase spread to all other regions. According to Johnston, "Young people have not yet come to see 'ecstasy' as a very dangerous drug and until they do, it seems unlikely that we will see the situation turn around" (Johnston et al., 2000a, p. 4).

Between 1998 and 2000 there was a significant drop in the perceived harmfulness of steroids among 12th-grade students (this question was not asked of 8th- and 10th-grade students). The significant drop suggests that a specific event(s) occurred that changed adolescents' beliefs about the adverse effects of steroids, who in 1993 perceived high risks in using steroids. In 1999 and 2000 there was a sharp increase in steroid use among male adolescents. In 2000, the increase in use continued among 10th-grade boys and remained the same for 8th- and 12th-grade boys. Basically, from 1999 to 2000 there was a 50 percent increase in steroid use among boys (Johnston et al., 2000b).

Heroin use among high school seniors rose from 1.1 percent in 1999 to 1.5 percent in 2000. The increase among 12th graders was all via methods other than injection (snorting and smoking). Although the rate of use is still below 2 percent this rate is the highest it has been since the annual survey began in 1975. Although adolescents have generally perceived heroin to be one of the most dangerous drugs, there have been changes in perceptions about risks. In 1992, the percentage of perceived risks lowered, and levels of use started to increase in the following years. The level of disapproval of use has been fairly consistent; nevertheless, the changes in the last years of the 1990s are consistent with the current higher levels of use (Johnston et al., 2000b).

The history of substance use was discussed in Chapter 1. The more recent history described here suggests that the drive to alter states of consciousness and the problems with substances remain widespread. Over half of all students have tried an illicit drug by the time they graduate from high school and nearly 35 percent have done so by eighth grade. The implication for prevention is that education, skills, and instruction to young people are needed earlier and more often. Along with individual prevention efforts, environmental strategies are needed to reduce the easy availability of drugs.

# Summary

The information in this chapter provides a general overview of frequently abused drugs. A thorough understanding of the pharmacology of drugs would require far more than one chapter in a book. Further, just as in prevention, research in this area is constantly being conducted and information about the pharmacology of drugs may soon be outdated. Some drugs that current research has shown to be highly addictive were considered safe in past medical journals. Therefore, remaining informed on the latest pharmacological research and on emerging trends in drug use is critical for prevention professionals, especially when communicating information to students or to the community.

Central nervous system depressants, opiates, central nervous system stimulants, hallucinogens, cannabinols, steroids, and inhalants were covered in this chapter. The effects of use, withdrawal symptoms, overdose effects, tolerance, and short- and long-term effects were described for each category. Further, for each category a case example pertaining to the relevance of this information for prevention professionals was discussed. An overview of the concept of gateway drugs and its importance to prevention was provided, as well as information about recent trends in drug use.

The information provided in this section is intended for prevention professionals. However, prevention programs should not be designed to share this information with students. Although sharing the negative consequences of specific drugs may be an important part of a comprehensive program, information about the general effects may increase use.

## KEY TERMS

| | | |
|---|---|---|
| addiction | designer drugs | raves |
| cannabinols | gateway drugs | sedatives |
| central nervous system (CNS) | hallucinogens | steroids |
|    depressants | hypnotics | substance abuse |
| central nervous system (CNS) | inhalants | substance misuse |
|    stimulants | intoxication | substance use |
| chemical dependence | overdose | tolerance |
| club drugs | psychedelic | withdrawal |
| dependence | psychoactive | |

## DISCUSSION QUESTIONS

1. Since the beginning of time people have altered their state of consciousness. Do you think it is normal for people to want to do this? Why or why not?

2. Why do you think some drugs are seen as more favorable, while others are considered 'bad" in our society?

3. Why do you think some people can experiment with drugs and then easily stop using them while others become addicted?

## APPLICATION EXERCISES

1. Choose a behavior that you are accustomed to doing (eating a certain food, drinking caffeine or alcohol, smoking, nail biting, etc.) and stop doing the behavior during the semester. Keep a journal regarding your feelings and emotions about the abstinence experience. Describe any relapses and coping mechanisms.

2. Search data sources and identify what the most prevalent drugs are in your community. Search for substance-abuse-related issues; for example, the cost of underage drinking in terms of traffic crashes and medical bills in your community.

3. Interview a doctor and ask about the effects of alcohol, tobacco, and other drugs on his or her patients.

## SUGGESTED READINGS

Goldberg, R. (2000). *Taking sides: Clashing views on controversial issues in drugs and society* (4th ed.). Guilford, CT: Dushkin/McGraw-Hill.

Inaba, D. S., & Cohen, W. E. (2000). *Uppers, downers, all-arounders: Physical and mental effects of psychoactive drugs* (4th ed.). Ashland, OR: CNS Publications.

# REFERENCES

Addiction Technology Transfer Center, School of Medicine. (1997, February). *Introduction to addiction studies: A curriculum reference manual.* La Jolla, CA: Author.

Center on Addiction and Substance Abuse. (1994, November 18). *National study shows gateway drugs lead to cocaine use.* Columbia University Record Archives. Retrieved April 30, 2001 from the World Wide Web: www.columbia.edu/cu/record/record2010.24.html.

Centers for Disease Control and Prevention. (1999). *Best Practices for Comprehensive Tobacco Control Programs—August 1999.* Atlanta, GA: U.S. Department of Health and Human Services, Centers for Disease Control and Prevention, National Center for Chronic Disease Prevention and Health Promotion, Office on Smoking and Health. Reprinted, with corrections.

Conners, G. J., & Rychtarik, R. G. (1989). The Supreme Court versus disease model case: Background and implications. *Psychology of Addictive Behavior, 2,* 101–107.

Fisher, G. L., & Harrison, T. C. (2000). *Substance Abuse: Information for school counselors, social workers, therapists, and counselors* (2nd ed.). Boston: Allyn and Bacon.

Hawkins, J. D., Catalano, R. E., & Miller, J. Y. (1992). Risk and protective factors for alcohol and other drug problems in adolescence and early adulthood: Implications for substance abuse prevention. *Psychological Bulletin, 112,* 64–105.

Hester, R. K., & Miller, W. R. (1995). *Handbook of alcoholism treatment approaches: Effective alternatives* (2nd ed.). Boston: Allyn and Bacon.

Inaba, D. S., Cohen, W. E., & Holstein, M. E. (1997). *Uppers, downers, all arounders: Physical and mental effects of drug abuse* (3rd ed.). Ashland, OR: Cinemed.

Inaba, D. S., & Cohen, W. E. (2000). *Uppers, downers, all arounders: Physical and mental effects of psychoactive drugs* (4th ed.). Ashland, OR: CNS Publications.

Jacobs, M. R., & Fehr, K. O. (1987). *Addiction research foundation's drugs and drug abuse: A reference text* (2nd ed.). Toronto, Ontario, Canada: Addiction Research Foundation.

Jellinek, E. M. (1952). Phases of alcohol addiction. *Quarterly Journal of Studies on Alcohol, 13,* 673–684.

Jellinek E. M. (1960). *The disease concept of alcoholism.* New Haven, CT: Hillhouse Press.

Johnston, L. D., O'Malley, P. M., & Bachman, J. G. (1987). *National trends in drug use and related factors among American high school students and young adults, 1975–1986* (NIDA Publication No. 87-1535, pp. 248–255). Washington, DC: U.S. Department of Health and Human Services.

Johnston, L. D., O'Malley, P. M., & Bachman, J. G. (2000). *Drug and alcohol press release and tables: "Ecstasy" use rises sharply among teens in 2000, use of many other drugs steady, but significant declines are reported for some.* Ann Arbor: University of Michigan News and Information Services. Retrieved from the World Wide Web: http://www.monitoringthefuture.org/data/00data.html.

Johnston, L. D., O'Malley, P. M., & Bachman, J. G. (2000b). *Monitoring the future: National Results on adolescent drug use, overview of key findings.* (NIH Publication No. 00-4690). Washington, DC: U.S. Department of Health and Human Services.

Jones, K. L., & Smith, D. W. (1973). Recognition of the fetal alcohol syndrome in early infancy. *Lancet, 2,* 999–1001.

Julien, R. M. (1998). *A primer of drug action: A concise, nontechnical guide to the actions, uses, and side effects of psychoactive drugs* (8th ed.). New York: W.H. Freeman and Company.

Karch, S. B. (1996). *The pathology of drug abuse.* Boca Raton, FL: CRC Press.

Kleinfeld, J., & Wescott, S. (Eds.). (1993). *Fantastic Antone succeeds! Experiences in educating children with fetal alcohol syndrome.* Fairbanks: University of Alaska Press.

Levy, D. T., Miller, T. R., & Cox, K. C. (1999). *Costs of underage drinking.* Rockville, MD: U.S. Department of Justice and Pacific Institute for Research and Evaluation.

Marlatt, G. A. (1985). Relapse prevention: Theoretical rationale and overview of the model. In G. A. Marlatt & J. R. Gordon (Eds.), *Relapse prevention: Maintenance strategies in the treatment of addictive behaviors* (pp. 3–70). New York: Guilford Press.

Miller, W. R., & Kurtz, E. (1994). Models of alcoholism used in treatment: Contrasting AA and other perspectives with which it is often confused. *Journal of Studies on Alcohol, 55,* 159–166.

Palfai, T., & Jankiewicz, H. (1997). *Drugs and human behavior* (2nd ed.). Dubuque, IA: W. C. Brown.

Roizen, J. (1997). Epidemiological issues in alcohol-related violence. In M. Galanter (Ed.), *Recent developments in alcoholism.* New York: Plenum Press.

Schultes, R. E., & Hofmann, A. (1992). *Plants of the gods.* Rochester, VT: Healing Arts Press.

Stafford, P. (1992). *Psychedelics encyclopedia, 1,* 157. Berkeley, CA: Ronin.

Torabi, M. R., Bailey, W. J., & Majd-Jabbari, M. (1993). Cigarette smoking as a predictor of alcohol and other drug use by children and adolescents: Evidence of the gateway drug effect. *Journal of School Health, 63,* 302–306.

U.S. Department of Justice. (1998). *Alcohol and crime.* Washington, DC: Bureau of Justice Statistics.

# CHAPTER

## 5

# The Cultural Context and Ethics of Prevention

When many people think of **culture**, the concept of ethnicity dominates their thinking. No wonder, since our ethnicity can significantly impact our view of the world. When implementing prevention programs, think not only of ethnicity but also of culture in its broader sense, such as cultures of socioeconomic status, sexuality, spirituality, and others. Culture involves every aspect of an individual's external and internal life. Drawing conclusions about a person based on her or his external culture or appearance can be tempting. These conclusions may or may not apply to the individual, but it is important to be aware of the thought process when forming these opinions. People may choose to keep certain aspects of their life a secret while others are shared. Similarly, some aspects of internal life may be hidden in certain environments, but naturally exposed in others. An example might be when a person prays publicly but only within a certain church.

All aspects of culture, whether exposed or hidden, must be considered, understood, and accepted when working with individuals and communities. Therefore, this chapter will discuss various aspects of culture in the broader sense and identify many different types of culture so that prevention professionals will come to understand the relevance of cultural competence in prevention program planning. When planning and implementing prevention programs, thoroughly understanding the community served and involving community members is critical. In order to be effective, prevention professionals must understand the community's perception of the problems that exist. Then, professionals must work with community members to address these identified problems in ways that "make sense" to the community members.

In addition, this chapter will cover the related topic of ethics in prevention, because decisions made by prevention professionals directly affect people's lives. As the field of prevention continues to develop and to become more credible as a profession, the general population must learn to develop trust in prevention professionals. Establishing formal, written codes of ethical conduct provides a much-needed tool in the professionalization of the prevention field. An example of a code of **ethics** will be shared, which can be used to assist in the development of codes that specifically meet the needs of prevention providers working in unique communities.

## Culture Defined

Many definitions of culture exist. One way to define culture is the knowledge, experience, values, ideas, attitudes, skills, tastes, and techniques that are passed on from more experienced members of a community to new members. Carriers of culture include families, religious organizations, peer groups, neighbors, social groups, and professional organizations. Some cultural experiences are related to biological factors, such as physical stature and skin color, while others are related more to sociological factors, such as socioeconomic status and religious affiliation. Many experiences are not related to a specific ethnic group, especially in the United States where many people do not identify strongly with any one ethnic population. For example, many European Americans who are several generations removed from their European ancestors and who equate culture with ethnicity have difficulty identifying characteristics of their culture. Frequently their European "roots" are not addressed at all as they search the broader meaning of culture to express their identity.

Language plays a significant role in the formation of culture by providing a framework in which individuals organize and assimilate experiences, perceptions, and ideas into existing belief systems. The framework is tested as individuals communicate with others and this constitutes part of the process of socialization. The framework then becomes a dynamic system of meaning, reflecting the reality of the individual. If the socialization is relatively complete, the framework reflects the reality of the cultural group as well. This invisible reality is impossible for others to "see," and the resulting behaviors can be difficult to interpret (Gilbert, 1995).

Messages and behaviors cannot always be correctly interpreted when the thoughts that spur them might be unrecognized. For example, during a group session at a university, a clergy member counseled a young woman who was not of the same faith about her desire to have a child. The woman clearly explained to everyone that she contemplated having and raising the child by herself, without finding a life partner. Because this value was unexpected and inconceivable to the clergy member, he could not hear her accurately. He assumed that any further contemplation would naturally be delayed until she had a partner. In this case, the clergy member's personal and professional beliefs within the context of his culture altered his perception of the young woman's intent. This example demonstrates the dynamic connection between language, behavior, and culture that allows us to understand our world, create personal systems of beliefs, and communicate messages based on our unique perspectives. Effective communication is a shared responsibility between the sender and receiver of specific messages. Chapter 9 explores communication strategies that can be helpful to prevention professionals in greater depth.

## Elements of Culture

When looking at culture in a broad sense, there are many considerations to examine, because humans are so complex and dynamic. There are numerous elements of culture to consider as prevention professionals develop knowledge and deepen their understanding of individuals in the communities served. Critically examining these elements can help prevention professionals avoid cultural blunders that can affect efforts adversely and can also directly guide the development of prevention messages. Gonzales (1978) shared elements of culture that are adapted and discussed in some detail as they relate to prevention efforts.

Examining attitudes and behavior related to literature, art, and other forms of expression can help to identify not only cultural ties, but also beliefs about formal and informal education in general. These beliefs may affect the community's receptivity to formalized prevention education. In some communities, receiving formal education may be viewed as "selling out" to the dominant culture. In such instances, youth and other community members may be reluctant to attend a formal meeting to learn about substance abuse issues.

In addition, examining formal codes related to wellness and sickness can be relevant when dealing with prevention-related issues. For example, messages fostering respect for body and mind can be received ineffectively by individuals who are unable to take care of basic needs, such as food and shelter, in an environment of extreme poverty. Preoccupation with basic needs and/or the desire to self-medicate undiagnosed psychological disorders can overrule any desire to achieve greater (perceived as lofty, in this instance) ideals of wellness. Sometimes tied to issues of wellness are beliefs about recreation and methods of spending leisure time. For example, some people enjoy forms of risk-taking activities, whether they are perceived as somewhat safe or not. Because alcohol, tobacco, and drug use and abuse are forms of risk-taking, they can become desirable to some individuals.

Understanding another's use of verbal and nonverbal communication is instrumental in determining the way in which messages are sent and received. Effective communication will be reflected by an increasing openness in the exchange of ideas. In the absence of this positive sign, another method of communicating must be sought. Likewise, interpreting nonjudgmentally the attitudes and behaviors related to physical appearance and grooming is imperative; for example, when dealing with cross-generation self-expression. Chapter 6, on human development theory, will discuss the harm that can occur as a result of stifling an adolescent's urge to develop and express individuality through personal appearance.

Understanding the expectations of ceremony, both for special and ordinary occasions, can assist the prevention professional in understanding the unique codes of behavior expected when working in the community. In addition, understanding the principles of ethics, especially with regard to honesty and fairness, can help one avoid violating cultural taboos.

Another consideration in avoiding cultural taboos is honoring the space requirements of individuals, meaning the accepted distance between individuals depending on the status of their relationship. Understanding attitudes toward being on time or being early can also be critical in avoiding conflicts in newly formed relationships. For example, in some cultures where telephones are uncommon, courtesy may dictate that an uninvited guest remain in the car in front of the house for a specific amount of time to allow the residents to prepare for the unexpected visit by tidying up and making coffee. Various cultural groups also have complex beliefs regarding those of differing status, with regard to age or wealth, which can also lend valuable cultural clues. For example, some groups may regard elders as the wisest members of the community, while other cultural groups may devalue the elderly. When identifying influential members of the community to assist in developing the prevention program, it is important to understand how community members regard these people.

Attitudes and behaviors related to heroes, traditions, legendary characteristics, and superstitions can also be very beneficial when learning about a group of people. For example, incorporating a popular, traditional story can be a powerful way of reaching youth with a prevention message. Determining values about crime, aggressiveness, and violence, versus those about security and freedom can also be instrumental in framing prevention messages. Attitudes toward merit and motivation can contribute to prevention-related issues. For example, some people may regard a peaceful walk in the park for the entire family as a reward for a hard week at work or school, while others regard "happy hour" at the local bar or smoking cigarettes on the corner with friends as a reward.

Beliefs about gender roles can also play a role in substance use and abuse. In some cultures, substance use can be considered taboo for females while males may be able to use in moderation with little or no scrutiny from family and peers. Examining roles within relationships, including attitudes toward family and friends, can be instrumental in understanding the unique perspectives of individuals. Certainly, attitudes about romance and sex are related to relationship roles, which can be strongly influenced by the individual's preference, whether gay, lesbian, bisexual, transgender, questioning, or heterosexual.

The significance of spirituality, whether internalized or connected formally to a specific religious organization, must also be considered. Framing prevention messages within the context of the unique spiritual beliefs of an individual or group can be a powerful tool in gaining acceptance for the message. For example, church newsletters can provide a media resource for advertising prevention-related activities while symbols that are commonly accepted by church members can be incorporated into the design of the prevention message.

Some elements of culture described above are evident by simply meeting someone for the first time. By and large, however, elements of culture cannot be determined without interpersonal communication. Frequently, extensive contact is necessary to understand an individual's various aspects of culture. Even then, some elements of culture may never be revealed or understood.

When thinking of culture, it is important to recognize both the elements of **surface culture** and the elements of **deep culture**. Surface culture includes characteristics that we can determine about someone by looking at them. Deep culture includes those characteristics that are invisible by simply seeing someone. While becoming acquainted with people, do not assume that specific deep cultural elements exist based on the presence of some surface cultural elements. For example, encountering a teenager wearing a shabby tee shirt with a representation of a marijuana leaf might provoke certain assumptions. For example, one might think, "this teenager is making a counterculture statement" or "this teenager uses drugs." It is possible, however, that the teenager has no money for clothing and is wearing a borrowed or hand-me-down shirt. As an alternative, perhaps the teenager is a journalist covering a story for the school newspaper. She might even be doing an assignment for sociology class where she looks for different reactions to her shirt from members of society.

Prevention professionals may be unaware of strong cultural factors influencing the people served. For example, some religious cultures incorporate the use of drugs—specifically tobacco, alcohol, marijuana, or peyote—into ritualistic use. Consequently, motivating people to change (e.g., developing the goal to create a healthy lifestyle and/or to give up using drugs) may be dependent on understanding these cultural values. Requesting that a person give up ceremonial use is not the same as suggesting that someone give up unhealthy, nonceremonial use. Making the distinction between the spiritual aspects of the situation and the health aspects is critical.

In general, culture can serve as either a powerful tool in preventing substance abuse or factors related to culture can place an individual at increased risk for substance abuse. Many prevention programs effectively reinforce healthy cultural norms within the community. Other prevention programs reunite community members with their lost cultural traditions in order to prevent substance abuse. "If people participate in their native traditions and are proud of their heritage, culture builds resiliency and helps to heal the wounds caused by prejudice, racism, and discrimination" (U.S. Department of Human Services, 1996, module 4, p. 17). Still other programs attempt to do this, but are largely unsuccessful in preventing substance abuse using this approach. In some cultural contexts, such as those that openly encourage alcohol consumption as the community norm, individuals may be at increased risk for substance abuse.

In general, understanding the elements of culture among individuals and within communities is the key to successfully working with communities to create healthy norms and behavior changes. It is equally important to understand all the different types of culture, which will be described below.

# Types of Culture

Just as it is important to note that culture is not limited to ethnicity, it is important to acknowledge that any one person belongs to more than one culture. In fact, we are surrounded by numerous cultures, including but not limited to cultures of sexuality (e.g., gay, lesbian, bisexual, transgender, questioning, heterosexual); residence (e.g., urban, suburban, rural, frontier); socioeconomic status (e.g., upper class, middle class, working class); ethnicity (e.g., Mexican, Polish, Syrian); race (e.g., Black, White, Asian); sex (e.g., female, male, transgender); drugs (e.g., smokers, drinkers); age and school grade; religion (e.g., Jewish, Christian, Islamic, Buddhist); and groups (e.g., gangs, civic groups, professional groups).

The concept of "biculturalism" demonstrates that we are capable of belonging to more than one culture. "Biculturalism is the ability to function effectively in the mainstream culture, also called dominant culture, and yet maintain positive and significant cultural connections to the ethnic community" (Moran, 1995, p. 49). Many people find it both necessary and possible to straddle cultures, coming and going between their culture(s) of origin and mainstream or other cultures. Consequently, when working with different individuals and communities, prevention professionals must ensure that all aspects of culture are considered instead of concluding that any one aspect defines the identities and needs of those served.

# Cultural Competence

**Cultural competence** is the ability to serve individuals and communities in ways that demonstrate understanding, caring, and valuing of the unique characteristics of those served, including the cultural differences and similarities within, among, and between groups. This process of developing cultural competence involves both a willingness and an ability to draw on community-based values, traditions, and customs and to work with knowledgeable persons from the community in developing prevention strategies.

When considering one's cultural competency, one question for the prevention professional to ask is whether it is easy or difficult to remain neutral about all cultures. It is also important to note the biases people might generally have about different cultures, including their own. The point in examining these critical issues is to determine how these biases might affect one's service as a prevention professional. Although it is completely normal for the brain to react to images and to form assumptions, these assumptions must not govern behavior. Expressing some assumptions can be damaging to others.

The importance of developing cultural competence cannot be overstated. "Danger emerges when the researcher [prevention professional] is ignorant of [his or her] limitations. Without self-criticism there is no corrective process. Without humility there is no true respect for the need to be self-critical" (Robinson, 1995, p. 59). However, prevention professionals can understand that developing cultural competence is an evolving process with infinite boundaries. In other words, it is acceptable to acknowledge that individuals are a work in progress. Cultural competence does not develop simply because one wishes it to do so. The following section will introduce strategies prevention professionals can use to develop cultural competence.

## Strategies to Become Culturally Competent

Moran (1995) notes that the first step in becoming culturally competent prevention professionals is to become more aware of the various cultures that exist. The second step is to assess personal cultural values while acknowledging the existence of a "cultural lens" that shapes interpretation of the world (Moran, 1995, p. 47). The third step is to understand the dynamics that may occur when members of different cultures interact.

Learning about other cultures is a lifelong evolutionary process that is influenced greatly by an existing framework of beliefs. A competent prevention professional understands that this framework can affect one's cultural perspective, perhaps causing limitations in the ability to provide services professionally in some situations. These limitations must not be ignored. Instead, assistance must be sought to overcome these limitations in order to ensure that the services provided are done so competently, even if by another professional. The process of developing cultural competence is ongoing, often involving an ebb and flow, as individuals evolve in the dynamic process of living.

The U.S. Department of Human Services (1996) offers several strategies that one can enlist in the effort to become culturally competent when working in communities. A powerful first step, and a strong testament to the dynamic process involved, is developing one's own self-concept and self-respect. These can be perceived differently from day to day depending on the successes or struggles of the day. By working through personal issues related to self-esteem, prevention professionals can enhance the ability to regard community members without bias and judgmental values.

Another step is to learn as much as possible about and understand all aspects of one's own cultural history. Developing self-awareness about intercultural relating, communicating, and problem solving is best achieved by developing friendships with members of different cultural groups. This is also a positive step in obtaining a rich and rewarding life in general.

Critically thinking about the way in which different group members are portrayed in the media, instructional materials, and movies is another valuable step. Through both subtle and devious advertising practices, tobacco and alcohol manufacturers have become even more successful by targeting many specific ethnic and age groups. Once one becomes aware of these strategies, one can educate others about them in hopes of protecting them from substance abuse.

It is also important to respect individual boundaries. Relationship building needs to occur before some cultural information can be shared. Asking someone, rather than assuming what he or she wants to be called, constitutes a respectful courtesy. Since language has played a powerful role in oppression, one must understand and accept that names used today for a cultural group will change as our society evolves. Then, respectfully listening, observing, and asking for information, while demonstrating a willingness to learn and accept cultural behavior different from one's own, can help to provide a bridge to sharing. At the same time, the prevention professional must only share personal information about cultures if it is offered unconditionally. The prevention professional must not have the expectation that others will accept and adapt to the cultures shared.

The prevention professional must also understand and acknowledge the historical relationship of one's own cultures with that of other cultural groups. This can be an uncomfortable challenge for those representing the "dominant culture" when working with specific ethnic groups that have experienced discrimination. Forces still exist that foster institutionalized oppression and the culturally competent prevention professional will systematically work to discover and change these forces. Also, the prevention professional can be an ally for others and can also develop ally relationships with members from various cultural groups, strengthening the message of equal rights through cross-cultural collaboration. As an ally, the prevention professional must demonstrate commitment to human rights and justice for others.

Prevention professionals can diligently strive to improve specific skills that are necessary for working in communities, including communication and group facilitation skills. Communication skills are critical in both learning about communities and in teaching community members about prevention. Quality communication must be designed to bridge cultural differences while conveying a sense of value regarding such differences. When delivering prevention messages, recognize that different communication techniques work with different people. For example, teaching adults and teaching children involve different strategies, just as discussing evaluation practices with grassroots youth workers will differ from discussing the same topic with prevention researchers. Understanding the needs and beliefs of clients helps prevention professionals frame prevention messages while providing meaningful services.

When facilitating community meetings and prevention training sessions, prevention professionals can allow members of a group to share experiences related to cultures. This is a powerful strategy for promoting understanding and cohesiveness among group members. Further, drawing upon the cultural experience of community members in order to include authentic cultural perspectives in the prevention curriculum or activity is both imperative and richly rewarding. In general, when facilitating sessions each participant must be recognized as integral to the strength of the program with unique qualities to offer. Communication and group facilitation strategies are discussed in greater detail in Chapter 9.

Conversely, cultural competence is not stereotyping and overgeneralizing or even romanticizing a cultural experience. It does not involve paternalism, tokenism, or trivializing the experience or history of a people. Culturally competent prevention professionals never make offensive comments or jokes, never use terminology such as "those people" or "you people." Nor do they speak for other cultural groups. Culturally competent prevention professionals do not presume to know what others want or need, do not deny or reject their own culture, and never ask an individual to speak for the interests or needs of an entire culture.

## Cultures and Prevention Programs

In addition to prevention professionals becoming more aware of cultural factors, prevention programs must also demonstrate awareness of cultural factors. Programs are culturally competent when they demonstrate sensitivity to cultural differences and similarities while also demonstrating effectiveness in using cultural symbols to communicate a message.

One important aspect of cultural competency is that prevention professionals and agencies must work with communities in developing and implementing prevention programs, instead of providing services to community members without seeking their input. This strategy, to be discussed in greater detail below, will assist in empowering the community to meet the needs identified by community members in ways that match the values and beliefs of those served. The prevention agency must be committed to building relationships throughout the community, at all levels and all phases of planning and decision making, while seeking to facilitate community empowerment.

The following paragraph offers some additional characteristics of a culturally competent prevention program (Banks, 1995; U.S. Department of Human Services, 1996). Knowing these characteristics can assist prevention professionals in forming a plan of action to ensure that their organizations reflect cultural competency.

One sign of cultural competency in an organization is that the program staff, administrators, and board members have high expectations and positive attitudes toward all program participants, regardless of their cultures, while recognizing, valuing, respecting, and building on the diversity within the community. Additionally, prevention agencies must develop written codes that help to guide the cultural competence of program staff. The written codes must mandate that the agency's staff (board, facilitators, evaluators, etc.) demonstrate respect for the participants' first language and dialects, while developing formalized policies, practices, and procedures that respect the cultures of the community. The written codes must also mandate that the composition of the organization must reflect the cultural diversity of the community itself. The agency must provide guidance to ensure that the program's formalized curriculum and activities reflect the cultural beliefs and values of the participants. Instructional materials must reflect various perspectives of ethnicity and other aspects of culture. Just as critical, evaluation materials, procedures, and reports must be culturally sensitive. Finally, the organizational leaders must continually assess cultural competence by periodically reviewing all programs, policies, practices, and procedures. Just as prevention professionals must engage in the lifelong pursuit of becoming increasingly culturally competent, so too must organizations.

Developing formal codes for an agency's cultural competence greatly enhances the probability that each member understands the specific guidelines that will ensure his own cultural competency. The codes must acknowledge culture in its broader sense, as incorporating many more factors than just ethnicity. Issues related to spirituality, sexuality, socioeconomic status, and other factors are just as critical when developing organizational guidelines. The following section will offer further guidelines for individual and organizational cultural competency to be considered for inclusion in prevention agencies' standards and practices.

# Working in the Community

The key to having a culturally competent prevention program is working with, instead of for, the community. There are four critical steps in working with the community to foster positive changes in behavior: gather academic information about the community from external resources, gather information from within the community, involve the community in prevention program planning and implementation, and evaluate programs with cultural competency. Although these steps are always critical, they have particular relevance when working with communities other than one's own. Note too that these steps are typically not conducted in isolation from each other. For example, gathering information from resources outside the community will often co-occur with information gathering from within the community. Learning from community members is also an ongoing process because members will be involved with prevention program planning and implementation throughout the life of the project. In addition, designing evaluation strategies and instruments occurs simultaneously with program planning.

## Gathering Academic Information about the Community

Working in the community must be preceded by gathering information about the community by reading about it, visiting it to observe and listen, talking to members, asking questions, and becoming involved in community events. All this occurs while maintaining objectivity about the community's characteristics. First, gather information from sources outside the community—for example, from the library and from experts. Then gather information from within the community. Although it is not always possible to gather information in such a methodical and linear way, collecting information in this order can help prevention professionals avoid some cultural blunders when working with communities other than their own.

When gathering information from resources outside the community, search for relevant historical issues; current social, economic, and political concerns; traditional or culture-specific issues; languages spoken; ideas about health and health practices, including medical orientation and diet; educational levels of community members; existence of formal and informal community leaders; and religion and/or spirituality (Gonzalez, Gonzalez, Freeman, & Howard-Pitney, 1991). It is imperative to understand the historical relationship between the target community and the dominant culture, especially if that relationship has been particularly problematic. Many ethnic groups in particular have a justifiable distrust of dominant society, especially as it relates to the forced acculturation of Native Americans and the enslavement of African Americans (Moran, 1995).

One word of caution when obtaining information from academic resources on the target community, especially with regard to ethnicity: note that much of the epidemiological data on specific ethnic groups are only of marginal use since they do not take into consideration the distinct dynamics of the target community. For example, Hispanic/Latino populations from different countries do not share one culture. Communities are dynamic based on the diversity within the community. Additionally, varying levels of **acculturation**, or the transfer of culture from one ethnic group (typically to the dominant culture) to others (such as newly arrived immigrants), will create unique dynamics within each community (Gonzalez et al., 1991). Information gathered must be specific to the community served and must not perpetuate stereotypes.

## Gathering Information from within the Community

The second part of gathering information from the community comes from direct contact with the community, specifically by visiting it to observe and listen, talking to members, asking questions, and becoming involved in community events. The success of the prevention project relies greatly on the ability of program planners to establish good relationships within the community. Without this critical relationship building, the community will not "buy in" or support the prevention program (Gonzalez et al., 1991).

Through observation, determine appropriate codes of dress and conduct. For example, it might not be appropriate to mimic common linguistic expressions when conversing with community members. This may imply a familiarity that could be interpreted as offensive by the target population. When in doubt, it is preferable to "be one's self," behaving in respectful ways that are particular to one's own cultures. However, attempting at least a few words or phrases in the native language(s) spoken within the community, instead of speaking only the language(s) of the dominant culture, can demonstrate respectfulness.

Also note that having good intentions is not enough to ensure cultural competence. By developing a thorough understanding of all the values and beliefs existing among community members, a person working within that community can greatly enhance the probability of not making cultural mistakes that can jeopardize the success of the prevention program. In particular, through dialogue, discover all the community values that influence behavior with regard to substance use and abuse. Additionally, identify all external factors that influence community values, such as media and public policies (Gonzalez et al., 1991).

Another important consideration during preliminary contact within the community is that members likely do not want an "outsider" providing information about what is wrong within the community along with the proposed solution. Instead, work with community members to assist them in determining their self-identified needs and then in encouraging them to participate in the solution as noted in the following section.

Once all relevant information about the community has been obtained and the organization's staff has been briefed and trained on how to work in the community in culturally competent ways, then a more formalized effort can be made to involve the community in the prevention effort.

## Involving the Community in Prevention Program Planning and Implementation

The third step in working with communities is involving the community in prevention program planning and implementation. Although this step will be influenced largely by the relationships forged within the community when gathering information from members, obtaining community "buy-in" of a prevention program will depend on whether the program matches the social structures and beliefs of the community. In short, the program must "make sense" to community members (Gilbert, 1995). The best way to ensure success is to involve community members in not only identifying the problems to be addressed, but also in developing the solution—in this case, the prevention program. When the community has a sense of ownership of the program, the probability of success becomes vastly greater. In short, community members must be involved in all stages of the prevention program planning discussed in Chapter 3 of this book.

"Become involved with the target community in a way that allows for the acquisition of meaningful cultural knowledge" (Moran, 1995, p. 51). By establishing meaningful relationships with members of the community, prevention professionals can often gain access to important meetings and events that will further enhance the collection of cultural knowledge; for example, events where binge drinking is likely to take place. Participating in such community events can assist in opening the dialogue about the needs, strengths, and characteristics of the community. In addition, community members can offer insider interpretations to relevant behaviors among community members.

A critical step in working with communities is identifying formal and informal leaders by getting to know them and then selecting those who would be suitable partners to have an active role in program development. A critical component of selecting community leaders is that they "practice what they preach." In other words, they must serve as positive role models in representing the program. Some of these leaders can become members of the advisory board for the program. The advisory board members can be active in prevention program planning. Specifically, they can help assess and improve the level of readiness of the community, conduct a needs assessment, prioritize data, conduct a resource assessment, select the target population, implement guiding principles or select a best practice, and evaluate the program. The advisory board members will be instrumental in ensuring that the program and strategies implemented will be consistent with the community's beliefs, values, and traditions, and that they will meet the needs of the target population.

Youth play an important role in the program, not just as participants, but as resources. Youth can serve on the advisory board to help guide the development of the prevention program. Youth can be provided with opportunities for meaningful participation, along with the resources and skills to maximize their participation. One must ask whether youth will be able to participate in a way that provides them with gratification and feelings of well-being. Also, youth must not be placed in the overwhelming role of being asked to serve as spokespeople for all members of their generation.

Once members of the advisory board and other key community leaders are chosen, assess the needs of the group before expecting them to work with the group. Based on the identified needs of the group, create strategies that will help meet these needs, particularly to help individuals relate to one other. This extra effort will go far in meeting individual needs and in sustaining the group. Specifically, the group may require team building or training on research-based prevention strategies to become effective members of the program planning effort. Specific strategies to enhance team building include "getting to know you" activities, social gatherings, and retreats that help to start relationships. In order to strengthen the team, members must work together to clarify the vision for the community. In order to sustain the team, a formalized process must be developed to spread recognition and share power (U.S. Department of Human Services, 1996). This can be accomplished by allowing each member to share leadership roles and decision-making activities. Offering training to team members in conducting research-based prevention practices can be another critical component of building or sustaining the team. Providing training empowers community members by offering them a meaningful sense of participation in the prevention efforts.

Focus groups are another valuable tool, because they offer advice and assistance in developing and/or adapting program materials for cultural appropriateness. This step involves more than simple linguistic interpretation. All materials must be culturally modified as necessary, reflecting the beliefs and practices of the target population. At the same time, however, materials must not reflect ethnic stereotypes. Instead, they must portray a variety of social groups and lifestyles. Additionally, the use, or lack, of terminology and/or jargon must be consistent with the normal usage and knowledge base of the target population. Remember, however, that information obtained from focus groups can be imperfect. Obtaining a random selection of community members will help guard against gathering incorrect information.

## Evaluating the Program with Cultural Competence

Evaluating prevention programs is part of prevention program planning, as discussed above and in Chapter 3 of this book. Program evaluation will also be discussed in more detail in Chapter 8. There are, however, a few important considerations in evaluating prevention programs that are particularly relevant when working in communities other than one's own. First, program goals must be jointly agreed upon between the program planners and the community members involved in the program. This is particularly relevant as community criteria for the success of the program may differ greatly from those of the project evaluators and these criteria must be considered in the evaluation design (Gilbert, 1995). For example, community members may consider a program successful if a certain number of youth choose to learn traditional songs or dances, as this indicates a return to traditional values. Youth who choose this path may be required through community norms to abstain from all drugs, including alcohol. Evaluators may not consider these factors without direct knowledge obtained from community members.

Community members must also be involved with the creation of evaluation tools. For example, an evaluator might create a survey or questionnaire with questions that will be interpreted differently by the target population than intended. In this case, the evaluation tool could be detrimental to the data-collecting effort. Sensitivity to these issues can only evolve through direct involvement of community members during the creation of evaluation instruments.

Additionally, program evaluators must assure the community that information gathered will be disseminated to the community in a form that is understandable. Information must be presented in a way that is culturally sensitive and not derogatory. For example, issues related to the norms and beliefs within the community must be portrayed in a nonjudgmental, unbiased way. Issues of confidentiality must also be addressed.

As always, program evaluation must be used to determine the successes and shortcomings of the program. For example, if some events are well attended while others are not, this information can help determine which events to modify or abandon. Community members can offer valuable insight into why some efforts succeed while others fail.

In short, by involving the community members in every phase of the prevention effort, successful prevention programming becomes a reality. The key lies in effective collaboration and in the sense of involvement and empowerment of all people involved in the effort, both as planners and as participants.

## Ethics in Prevention

As stated in the previous section, imposing one's culture on someone else is unethical. Ensuring cultural competency is one issue related to ethical conduct for prevention professionals, but there are many other ethical issues in prevention as well. Many of them are complex, often defying consensus among prevention professionals. The goal in studying ethics is to recognize that decisions made by prevention professionals directly affect people's lives, and that people need to be able to trust prevention professionals both as individuals and as professionals. Therefore, prevention agencies must have formalized policies and standards that can be used to educate staff and volunteers on appropriate ethical guidelines and conduct. Further, these formalized ethical policies and standards must be custom fit to the unique characteristics of the community.

Having a written code of ethics for each prevention agency is imperative. Prevention professionals can be faced with difficult issues; some are overwhelming and require consultation with legal counsel. With other issues, prevention professionals can use reason to establish an official procedure. Each person is responsible for his or her own behavior. Newcomers to prevention and existing prevention professionals must continue to evaluate their words and actions. The process of self-discovery and self-improvement is eternal.

Thinking through and discussing difficult ethical issues and then establishing a written code of ethics assists prevention professionals in identifying and addressing difficult situations. For example, suppose that after an evening event for youth, all but one child are picked up by a parent or responsible adult. Is it appropriate for you to offer the child a ride home? Does it matter if the child is of the same sex? Would it be better to insist that another available adult come along, if possible, as a third party? If a program staff member provided transportation for the child, but on arriving at her home, discovered that her parent is extremely intoxicated, would it be appropriate to leave the child with this parent? What other options are there? The answers to these questions may depend a great deal on the unique characteristics of the community and whether the adult in charge is a paid staff member or a volunteer.

Another important issue to address in agency policy is the necessity of conducting criminal background checks for staff and/or for volunteers. The decision must be based on the specific dynamics of the community, including all statutes that might apply. Establishing a written protocol for such situations can be very effective in avoiding possible legal problems as well as avoiding embarrassing situations that could damage the credibility of staff members or the agency itself. Whenever these difficult issues arise, prevention program planners must thoroughly discuss all implications and revisit established policies and standards.

The issues mentioned above are far from exhaustive. Specific issues to consider will vary among agencies and communities. Valuable resources in creating a formal code of ethics include all local, county, and state statutes, along with all agency regulations (such as

**BOX 5.1**

## National Association of Prevention Professionals and Advocates (NAPPA)

### Code of Ethics

**Preamble**

The Principles of Ethics are a model of standards of exemplary professional conduct. These Principles of the Code of Ethical Conduct for Prevention Professionals express the professional's recognition of his or her responsibilities to the public, to service recipients, and to colleagues. They guide members in the performance of their professional responsibilities and express the basic tenets of ethical and professional conduct. The principles call for commitment to honorable behavior, even at the sacrifice of personal advantage. These principles should not be regarded as limitations or restrictions, but as goals for which prevention professionals should constantly strive. They are guided by core values and competencies that have emerged in the development of the field.

**Principles**

*I. Nondiscrimination*  A prevention professional shall not discriminate against recipients or colleagues based on race, religion, national origin, sex, age, sexual orientation, economic condition, or physical or mental disability, including persons testing positive for HIV. A prevention professional shall broaden his or her understanding and acceptance of cultural and individual differences, and in so doing render services and provide information sensitive to those differences.

*II. Competence*  A prevention professional shall observe the profession's technical and ethical standards, strive continually to improve personal competence and quality of service delivery, and discharge professional responsibility to the best of his or her ability. Competence is derived from a synthesis of education and experience. It begins with the mastery of a body of knowledge and skill competencies. The maintenance of competence requires a commitment to learning and professional improvement that must continue throughout the professional's life.

   **A.** Professionals should be diligent in discharging responsibilities. Diligence imposes the responsibility to render services carefully and promptly, to be thorough, and to observe applicable technical and ethical standards.
   **B.** Due care requires a professional to plan and supervise adequately any professional activity for which she or he is responsible.
   **C.** A prevention professional should recognize limitations and boundaries of competencies and not use techniques or offer services outside his or her competencies. Each professional is responsible for assessing the adequacy of his or her own competence for the responsibility to be assumed.
   **D.** When a prevention professional is aware of unethical conduct or practice on the part of an agency or prevention professional, he or she has an ethical responsibility to report the conduct or practices to appropriate authorities or to the public.

*III. Integrity*  To maintain and broaden public confidence, prevention professionals should perform all professional responsibilities with the highest sense of integrity. Integrity can accommodate the inadvertent error and the honest difference of opinion. It cannot accommodate deceit or subordination of principle.

    **A.**  Personal gain and advantage should not subordinate service and the public trust. All information should be presented fairly and accurately. Each professional should document and assign credit to all contributing sources used in published material or in public statements.

    **B.**  Prevention professionals should not misrepresent either directly or by implication professional qualifications or affiliations.

    **C.**  A prevention professional should not be associated directly or indirectly with any services or products in a way that is misleading or incorrect.

***IV. Nature of Services***  Above all, prevention professionals should do no harm to service recipients. Practices shall be respectful and nonexploitative. Services should protect the recipient from harm and the professional and the profession from censure.

    **A.**  Where there is evidence of child or other abuse, the prevention professional shall report the evidence to the appropriate agency and follow up to ensure that appropriate action has been taken.

    **B.**  Where there is evidence of impairment in a colleague or a service recipient, a prevention professional should be supportive of assistance or treatment.

    **C.**  A prevention professional should recognize the effect of impairment on professional performance and should be willing to seek appropriate treatment for himself or herself.

***V. Confidentiality***  Confidential information acquired during service delivery shall be safeguarded from disclosure, including—but not limited to—verbal disclosure, unsecured maintenance of records, or recording of an activity or presentation without appropriate releases.

***VI. Ethical Obligations to Community and Society***  According to their consciences, prevention professionals should be proactive on public policy and legislative issues. The public welfare and the individual's right to services and personal wellness should guide the efforts of prevention professionals who must adopt a personal and professional stance that promotes the well-being of all humankind.

*Source:* S. H. Mowrer, & T. N. Strader, National association addresses tough prevention issues, *The Journal of Primary Prevention,* 13:1, 73–77. Kluwer Academic/Plenum Publishers (1992). Reprinted with permission.

those in the school district), especially with regard to confidentiality issues and mandatory disclosure reporting. Prevention professionals who create a formal code of ethics should do so by using these resources and continually updating references to them as statutes and regulations change.

    For example, if a young participant discloses personal drug use or drug use by another family member, reporting requirements to the school, to other agencies involved in the prevention training, and/or to Child Protective Services may vary based on the specific circumstances. Reporting requirements may also vary based on the employment status and the role of the prevention professional providing the services. For example, a teacher may be required to report the incident, whereas a visiting prevention professional may not be required to complete a report. Knowing current and specific guidelines for individual circumstances could help prevention professionals and programs avoid legal complications.

The National Association of Prevention Professionals and Advocates (NAPPA) code of ethics is presented in Box 5.1. Although NAPPA no longer exists, its code of ethics can offer a stimulus for discussion within agencies and a guideline for creating a customized code of ethics. Ultimately, however, prevention professionals and their agencies must determine a code of ethics that is appropriate for them and their clients. As an emerging discipline, ethical codes of conduct need to be developed and advanced to act as a positive benchmark for positive professional behavior.

The NAPPA code of ethics helps prevention professionals identify issues related to creating agency standards. The American Association for Health Education, a division of the American Alliance for Health, Physical Education, Recreation, and Dance (http://www.aahperd.org) has also developed a code of ethics that can serve as a helpful resource.

Standards can also be regarded as an ongoing work in progress, updated continuously as difficult issues are addressed by program staff and volunteers. The goal is not to create a laborious and bureaucratic document, but instead to offer guidelines for all of the agency's members and volunteers that will help prevent difficult situations from becoming disastrous ones.

## Summary

As mentioned in the NAPPA code of ethics, when studying prevention, above all else it is important to do no harm. Setting clear guidelines for cultural competency and for ethics are crucial steps to ensure that prevention professionals are prepared to practice prevention and to affect the lives of others in positive ways that promote well-being. Cultural competence and ethical conduct are not practiced over and above regular prevention program planning. Instead, they are an integral part of everything that a prevention professional does when conducting prevention program planning.

The community is the heart of all prevention efforts. The prevention professional must not inflict prevention on the community. Instead, he or she works in harmony with the community and its members. To do so, one must demonstrate cultural competence and ethical conduct during every interaction with the community. To circumvent these goals is to invite alienation from the community. Only by achieving harmonious relations in the community can the prevention professional produce the desired effect of fostering an environment in which individuals are empowered with the choice to make healthy decisions.

## KEY TERMS

| | | |
|---|---|---|
| acculturation | culture | ethics |
| cultural competence | deep culture | surface culture |

# DISCUSSION QUESTIONS

1. Review the seven steps to prevention program planning, discussed in Chapter 3. In which ways can prevention professionals incorporate culture into prevention planning?

2. Imagine the cultures to which you belong, perhaps already mentioned or perhaps not. Think of an object that illustrates one or more of your cultures. This can include food, a photograph, clothing, jewelry, or some other object. How would you describe this object to others to offer a better understanding of you?

3. How would you develop an action plan to make yourself or your organization more culturally competent?

4. Appendix C contains three case studies involving ethical issues in prevention. How would you respond to the questions following each study?

5. What issues must be considered when designing a code of ethics for use in your community?

# APPLICATION EXERCISE

Prepare an essay that addresses the following questions (U.S. Department of Human Services, 1996):

1. Who lives in your community? List all the cultural groups.

2. Identify some of the significant events, issues, struggles, contributions, leaders, and history of each of the cultural groups.

3. What is the history of your community as you know it? Who were the first inhabitants? Who moved into the area and when? What were the economic, social, and political forces at work in forming your diverse community?

4. Which cultural groups are currently active in the community and collaborating together? Which groups are not yet actively involved or working together?

5. What changes or events have occurred that have affected your community? This could include the influx of a new culture or cultures, economic development or decline, or governmental regulations.

6. Describe any current conflicts that exist in your community. Identify the cultures represented in the conflict and whether the conflict has been long-term or has developed recently.

7. Describe any successful examples of collaboration between cultures that have occurred or are occurring in your community and identify the cultures represented.

8. Share the substance abuse prevention history of your community.

# SUGGESTED READINGS

Gonzalez, V. M., Gonzalez, J. T., Freeman, V., & Howard-Pitney, B. (1991). *Health promotion in diverse cultural communities: Practical guidelines for working in and with diverse cultural communities.*

Stanford, CA: Health Promotion Resource Center, Stanford Center for Research in Disease Prevention in cooperation with the Henry J. Kaiser Family Foundation.

U.S. Department of Human Services, Public Health Services, Substance Abuse and Mental Health Services Administration. (n.d.). *The Challenge of Participatory Research: Preventing Alcohol-Related Problems in Ethnic Communities.* (DHHS Publication No. SMA 95–3042). Washington, DC: U.S. Government Printing Office.

# REFERENCES

The Addiction Counselor Certification Board of Oregon Website. *Certified prevention specialist application.* Retrieved September 19, 2001, from the World Wide Web: http://www.accbo.com/prevent.pdf.

Banks, J. A. (1995). Multicultural education and the modification of students' racial attitudes. In W. Hawley & A. Jackson (Eds.), *Toward a common destiny: Improving race and ethnic relations in America.* San Francisco, CA: Jossey-Bass.

Gilbert, M. J. (1995). Conducting culturally competent alcohol prevention research in ethnic communities. In U.S. Department of Human Services, Public Health Services, Substance Abuse and Mental Health Services Administration, *The challenge of participatory research: Preventing alcohol-related problems in ethnic communities.* (DHHS Publication No. SMA 95–3042). Washington, DC: U.S. Government Printing Office.

Gonzales, P. F. (1978, May). *Mexican American culture in bilingual education classrooms grades 1 through 3: A description of three Spanish/English programs in Texas.* Unpublished doctoral dissertation, University of Texas at Austin.

Gonzalez, V. M., Gonzalez, J. T., Freeman, V., & Howard-Pitney, B. (1991). *Health promotion in diverse cultural communities: Practical guidelines for working in and with diverse cultural communities.* Stanford, CA: Health Promotion Resource Center, Stanford Center for Research in Disease Prevention in cooperation with the Henry J. Kaiser Family Foundation.

Moran, J. R. (1995). Culturally sensitive alcohol prevention research in ethnic communities. In U.S. Department of Human Services, Public Health Services, Substance Abuse and Mental Health Services Administration, *The challenge of participatory research: Preventing alcohol-related problems in ethnic communities.* (DHHS Publication No. SMA 95–3042). Washington, DC: U.S. Government Printing Office.

Mowrer, S. H., & Strader, T. N. (1992). National association addresses tough prevention issues. *The Journal of Primary Prevention,* 13:1, 73–7.

Robinson, R. G. (1995). The relevancy of cultural sensitivity in alcohol prevention research in ethnic/racial communities. In U.S. Department of Human Services, Public Health Services, Substance Abuse and Mental Health Services Administration, *The challenge of participatory research: Preventing alcohol-related problems in ethnic communities.* (DHHS Publication No. SMA 95–3042). Washington, DC: U.S. Government Printing Office.

U.S. Department of Human Services, Public Health Services, Substance Abuse and Mental Health Services Administration. (1996). *Crossroads: Building cross-cultural collaboration: Facilitator manual.* Washington, DC: U.S. Government Printing Office.

# 6 Incorporating Human Development Theory into Prevention

$E$ffective prevention strategies are grounded in theory. Chapter 2 discusses three theories that are specific to prevention: risk and protective factors theory, the developmental assets model, and the resiliency approach. Human development theory also offers prevention professionals valuable insight into designing and implementing prevention programs that meet the developmental needs of clients.

Learning about human development theory can help prevention professionals enhance the services for clients by providing the tools to custom-fit programs to the developmental stages of participants. This section will discuss four developmental theories that address physical, emotional, mental, and spiritual development among individuals. The theories include Abraham Maslow's hierarchy of needs, Erik Erikson's psychosocial developmental stages, Jean Piaget's cognitive developmental stages, and the medicine wheel view of human development. The first three theories that are discussed are well-known academic theories that provide a framework from which prevention professionals can design and select prevention programs that are developmentally appropriate. In other words, programs will be more able to address the specific needs of clients based on their developmental stages. The fourth theory, that of the medicine wheel, is discussed as a nonlinear model and one that addresses spirituality as a developmental quality in humans.

In comparing and selecting theories to apply to prevention program participants, it is important to know what questions to answer about the clients served. For example, what are the cognitive needs of the youth served? What might be the causes of potential academic failure, placing youth at increased risk of substance abuse? Developmental theories can help provide clues to answer these questions. Youth might be failing academically because they are malnourished. Perhaps they and their parents devalue education. Perhaps they need assistance in developing specific cognitive skills. Developmental theories can also help to uncover the other considerations that might apply.

Theories naturally focus on specific issues and have underlying philosophical and methodological convictions. Not all theories seek to answer the same questions or give the same importance to a given question. There are many theories to choose from, and readers are encouraged to maintain a healthy curiosity about other developmental theories that may apply to the services that they provide to clients.

# Abraham Maslow's Hierarchy of Needs

Contemporary psychology typically focuses on the negative aspects of the human personality, including deficits, struggles, frustration, and other unhealthy aspects of the human condition. Abraham Maslow introduced his hierarchy of needs in the 1960s, a time in which people, in general, were interested in searching for and finding higher, more positive, and even mystical, purposes in life. Maslow's theory matched the emerging paradigm by providing a mechanism through which individuals could guide their own progression. Individuals could do this by ensuring that certain needs were met in order to transcend to the next level of being.

Maslow (1968) notes, "destructiveness, sadism, cruelty, malice, etc., seem so far to be not intrinsic but rather they seem to be violent reactions *against* frustration of our intrinsic needs, emotion and capacities. . . . Human nature is not nearly as bad as it has been thought to be" (p. 5). At the same time, Maslow's theory does not deny the existence of negativity in the world or in human personality. "Most people experience *both* tragedy and joy in varying proportions. Any philosophy which leaves out either cannot be considered comprehensive" (p. 21).

This section will include a discussion on Maslow's hierarchy of needs (Figure 6.1), including the concepts of "basic needs" and "growth needs." Following that will be a discussion of Maslow's concept of "peak experience." Although this concept is meant to capture the best of experiences for healthy adults, some of whom are prevention professionals, the pursuit of peak experiences can have implications for some people who choose to abuse substances as well. Maslow's concepts will then be applied to the work that prevention professionals perform within the community.

## Hierarchy of Needs

Maslow's theory illustrates a developmental progression, or hierarchy, based on human needs. Some of the needs are called **basic needs**, such as those for safety, a sense of belonging with others, love, respect, and esteem. Higher needs are called **growth needs**, which involve the motivation to obtain one's unique potential. During the course of healthy development, individuals will progress from focusing on meeting basic needs to focusing on meeting growth needs. The ultimate goal of this theory is to obtain **self-actualization**, or to reach one's maximum potential.

## Basic Needs and Growth Needs

Basic needs, sometimes called "deficiency needs," are "deficits in the organism, empty holes, so to speak, which must be filled up for health's sake, and furthermore must be filled from without by human beings *other* than the subject" (Maslow, 1968, p. 28). Maslow believed in the innate potential of humans and noted that the environment must provide the nourishment to help individuals realize their unique potential. Depending on others to provide the elements of basic needs, of course, produces a lack of control for determining one's own fate. If needs are unmet, the individual may fear the environment, and become anxious and even hostile.

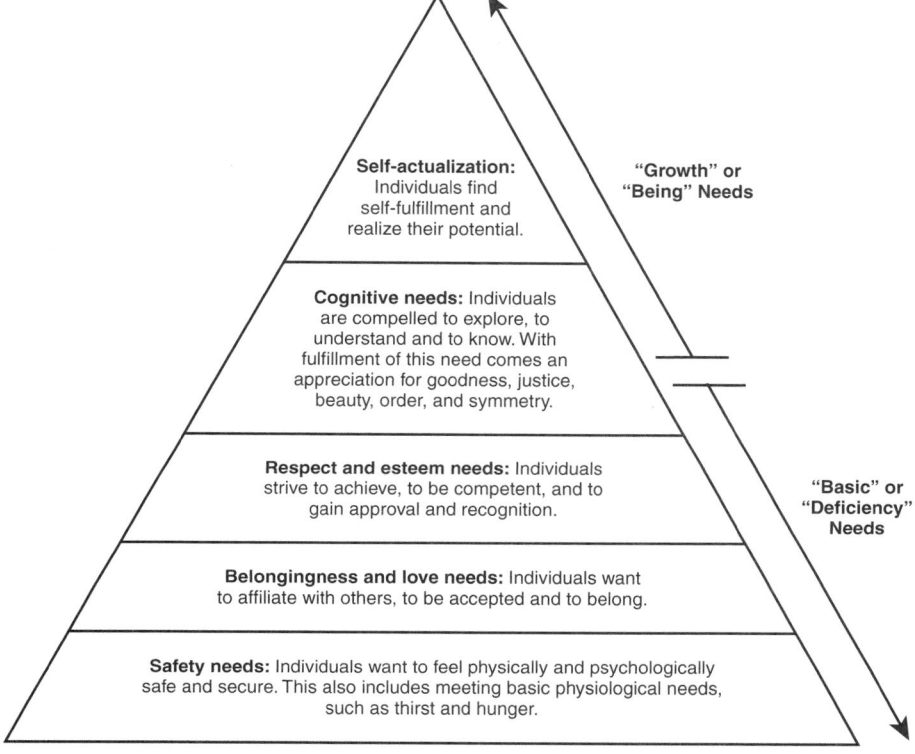

**FIGURE 6.1    Maslow's Hierarchy of Needs**

Safety, the first of the basic needs, is a survival-related need, involving a sense of security in both the physiological and psychological sense. Physiological needs, including shelter, food, and water, are the most basic of all safety needs. When one is preoccupied by these survival needs, one cannot think beyond meeting these needs. Meeting the need for physical safety can provide an everyday struggle. For example, for those who live in an unsafe, crime-ridden neighborhood, or for a child hassled by a bully each day at school, physical safety is a constant issue. Concern over meeting physical safety needs can also be situational, even for those who typically do not have daily worries about their physical safety. For example, a person may suddenly encounter a frightening and dangerous situation, perhaps a threatening animal, and therefore cannot think beyond the immediate moment. Ensuring psychological safety can present a challenge when one is in an emotionally abusive relationship, for example, or when one has psychological disabilities.

Once a person is established in an environment where safety needs are met, that person can begin to focus on filling the needs of belonging and love. In this pursuit, one will seek affiliation with and acceptance from others. Once accomplished, one can begin to focus on meeting respect and esteem needs. One's focus will be on experiencing achievement and building competence, all while seeking approval and recognition from significant sources.

Once a person meets all the above basic needs, then that person is free to work toward meeting growth needs, sometimes also called "being needs." Meeting growth needs involves the motivation to obtain one's potential by developing talents that are unique to one's destiny and by pursuing greater knowledge of the world and of one's unique nature. The focus for an individual who is growth-need motivated is on meeting cognitive needs, including the quest for knowing, understanding, and exploring various aspects of the world. Within the world of knowledge, one will develop an appreciation for goodness, justice, beauty, order, and symmetry.

Each time a need is met, a new awareness evolves of the next "higher" need. Consequently, the individual becomes motivated to move to the next highest level. During the developmental cycle, children grow and become healthy from having their basic needs consistently met. As they come to trust that safety needs will be met, they develop an awareness of their need for love, then esteem, then cognitive stimulation. Therefore, they will demand that others provide the appropriate stimulus, whether love, esteem, or cognitive stimulation, to encourage further growth.

Further, unhealthy adults are motivated by basic needs, while healthy adults are motivated by growth needs. People can accept and welcome the emergence of a newly presented need if in the past they have had rewarding experiences in meeting their needs. For example, if one likes to eat and food is available, as it has been in the past, then hunger will be welcomed.

After 12 years of psychotherapeutic work and research, and 20 years of conducting personality studies, Maslow concluded that neurosis is caused when someone is deprived of having needs met, including those for safety, belongingness, love, and respect. However, if these needs are eventually met, the neurosis tends to disappear.

During the course of healthy development, each individual will experience the need to meet both basic and growth needs. Further, people generally experience immature love before developing the ability to love maturely. One must also learn to cast aside safety in order to explore the world and grow cognitively. The concepts of deficiency-love and being-love will be discussed below, along with deficiency-cognition and being-cognition.

## Deficiency-Love vs. Being-Love

Maslow discusses love needs in some detail (1968). There are two types of love. Deficiency-love, also called **D-love**, is an unhealthy, selfish love. Conversely, being-love, or **B-love**, is an unselfish love for the total being of another. All of those who report the experience of B-love also report having known D-love in the past. So it appears that D-love relationships occur naturally.

Those who are experiencing D-love do not view others as whole, unique individuals. Instead, others are simply a means to fulfill basic needs. Whatever qualities or characteristics another possesses that are not directly related to the needs of the D-lover are viewed as boring, irritating, or threatening, if they are noticed at all. Further, one person can fill the needs of a D-lover just as easily as another. Therefore, the objects of D-love are interchangeable and relationships are highly transient. For example, when a D-lover requires admiration, the admirer is of little consequence so long as she or he admires.

Conversely, a B-lover can perceive realities and potentialities in the beloved that others cannot see. B-lovers accept each other and encourage growth in the other. However, the experience of B-love is not limited only to romantic love. Parents see the potential of their own children from birth and B-love their children for more than they can be at that moment. B-love produces great happiness and fulfillment.

## Deficiency-Cognition vs. Being-Cognition

Maslow (1968) discussed the role of developing cognition in some depth. He defines deficiency-cognition, or **D-cognition**, as that which is organized by the basic needs. Being-cognition, or **B-cognition**, conversely, revolves around the growth-needs of an individual.

Every person has two impulses. One is to cling to safety, hanging on to the knowable past, afraid to grow, learn, and know. This is D-cognition. The other impulse urges one to grow and learn, to risk failure and ridicule in order to become more oneself. This is B-cognition. As an example, a child experiencing D-cognition will hide behind the knees of the caregiver, looking at the environment from this safe stance. After determining that the environment provides some measure of safety, the child will venture forth independently to discover the environment more closely, at which point the child is in an active state of B-cognition. If the caregiver disappears, then curiosity is replaced with panic and the child will abandon the quest for knowledge until once again feeling safe. Adults too can experience this fear of knowing, exploring, and growing. The unknown can be frightening, but gaining knowledge about the unknown factor can help relieve the resulting anxiety.

## Self-actualization

Meeting basic and growth needs provides the method of obtaining self-actualization, which is the ultimate goal in this developmental theory. The term "self-actualization" was created by Kurt Goldstein (1934), a neuropsychiatrist who worked with brain-injured soldiers. Goldstein postured that these patients would reorganize their capacities and strive to reach potential through whatever means remained. Maslow uses the term to capture one's drive to discover self-fulfillment and to realize one's own unique potential. However, self-actualization is not necessarily a permanent state. It can also be experienced in brief moments of insight. Maslow (1968) offers the following definition of self-actualization:

> An episode, or a spurt in which the powers of a person come together in a particularly efficient and intensely enjoyable way, and in which he is more integrated and less split, more open for experience, more idiosyncratic, more perfectly expressive or spontaneous, or fully functioning, more creative, more humorous, more ego-transcending, more independent of his lower needs. . . . He becomes in these episodes more truly himself, more perfectly actualizing his potentialities, closer to the core of his Being, more fully human. (p. 106)

Because this is described as an "episode" or a "spurt," it is clear that self-actualization is *not* static or a "perfect" state in which all human problems are transcended as one enters a state of perpetual serenity. However, there is a continuum for those who are moving toward self-actualization where they enjoy life more fully while others only experience random moments of joy.

Maslow uses the term "healthy people" to describe those who are on a path to self-actualization, also called "self-actualizers." Some of these qualities include an increased acceptance of self, increased spontaneity, greater appreciation, and emotional reaction to favorable occurrences, improved interpersonal relations, and increased creativity. Self-actualizers are governed by inner laws, not by the environment, to develop potential, creativity, talents, and self-knowledge. As a result, they are less affected by adverse external circumstances, such as unfortunate occurrences, deprivation, and even stress.

Additionally, they also have an increased desire for privacy and increased independence, self-sufficiency, autonomy, and resistance to acculturation. In fact, they might be hampered by the presence of others when they need solitude for meditative reflection. Self-actualizers also have an increased sense of identification with the human species. These latter qualities indicate an interesting paradox, where the person feels less connected to and dependent on those in the immediate environment, but more connected to humanity in a global sense.

For the healthy person, creative impulses and expanding talents promote pleasurable tensions. Self-actualizing people are "relatively unfrightened by the unknown, the mysterious, the puzzling, and often are positively attracted to it, i.e., selectively pick it out to puzzle over, to meditate on and to be absorbed with" (Maslow, 1968, p. 154). Maslow describes this as a second childhood or "second naïvéte," in that it is similar to the way that children can be completely absorbed in the moment and the task at hand.

## Peak Experiences

Related to self-actualization, Maslow also identified the term **peak experience**. This is a mystical or transcendental experience in which the individual feels valuable, sincere, expressive, good, intelligent, stronger, spontaneous, worthwhile, unselfconscious, creative, unique, and free of doubt and fears. Peak experiences often involve a sense of wonder, awe, and unity with the universe. These appear serendipitously and are happy, thrilling experiences. At these times, the individual reaches levels of great maturity, individuation, fulfillment, and psychological health (Maslow, 1968). After such an experience, individuals have a profound love for everyone and everything and they are driven to repay the experience through services to others.

Anyone can have a peak experience, although "highly evolved [healthy, self-actualizing] personalities have more peak-experiences, and these seem to be more profound" (Maslow, 1968, p. 130). This does not mean that healthy, highly evolved, self-actualizing people who have peak experiences do not have problems. They do, but they are typically of a higher nature, and not based on meeting basic needs. However, healthy people do enjoy pleasures in a greater and richer fashion. Not only do self-actualizing people have more frequent peak experiences, anyone who has a peak experience, no matter his or her state of personal evolution, takes on temporarily the characteristics of self-actualizing people.

During a peak experience, one can become absorbed in an object or person in a completely nonjudgmental way. Maslow refers to this as **concrete thinking**, which involves perceiving all aspects of an object as unique and completely disconnected from any other system of ideas. In other words, a person takes in all information about the object simultaneously or in rapid succession. Self-actualizers and others during a peak experience think concretely; the perceived object is regarded as whole, unique, as more than "the sum of its parts." This perspective is nonjudgmental and can help prevention professionals to value all clients as uniquely valuable. Children, too, have the ability to regard objects concretely.

Conversely, **abstract thought** involves categorizing, classifying, and schematizing an object of thought in order to fit information about it into one's existing system of thought. While doing so, individuals screen out all information that is incompatible with existing beliefs, not useful or frightening, or which does not fit within the confines of language. Perceiving abstractly results in distortion, as some information is retained and some is discarded.

## Applying Maslow's Theory to Prevention

Whether working with youth or adults, understanding the principles of Maslow's theory can help prevention professionals determine the specific needs of clients in order to help them to grow from basic needs toward growth needs, thus moving them closer to self-actualization. Understanding individuals' needs helps prevention professionals to select prevention strategies that compliment youth development through the hierarchy. Peak experiences also have implications for prevention. Thinking concretely can help prevention professionals to assess clients without judgmental assumptions. In addition, some people may attempt to create something similar to a peak experience through the abuse of substances. This knowledge can help prevention professionals understand the motivation of some clients to experiment with substances.

## Helping Clients Meet Basic Needs

There are many ways to apply Maslow's theory when working with clients that will help them to meet their basic needs. As an example, many school programs have adopted a policy of providing breakfast for youth from low-income families who might not otherwise have access to a healthy, well-balanced meal in the morning. The premise is that until children have their basic physiological needs met, they will be unable to concentrate on their studies, or in other words, strive to meet their cognitive needs. As discussed in Chapter 2, academic failure is a risk factor for substance abuse. Therefore, leveraging resources from the community to help improve nutrition may promote improved cognitive functioning. This in turn may help to reduce the risk for substance abuse.

As another example, many disorganized communities have dangerous gang activities. As noted in Chapter 2, disorganized communities place their members at greater risk for substance abuse. Because gang affiliation can offer some protection in an unsafe environment, a child may become involved with a gang and its negative behaviors in order to have the basic needs of safety and belonging met. Once the safety need within the neighborhood is met, the child is free to progress to other needs. However, if the newly acquired negative behaviors include substance abuse, then the child is at risk of physiological danger and cognitive disorientation, thus moving the child backward through the hierarchy of needs. Working in the community to organize leaders and law enforcement to make the neighborhood safe from drug dealing and other crime would be a way to incorporate Maslow's theory into prevention program planning. Once youth are safe in their environment, then bonding to positive peers and caring adults can become one focus for prevention efforts.

Prevention professionals are not limited to working with youth. Frequently, adults are targeted in order to reduce risk factors in the family domain. In some communities, especially those with extreme economic deprivation, families are unable to provide for their children's basic needs. If, for example, a parent is involved with a prevention activity but is unsure of finding food and shelter for the evening, then that parent will not be able to participate fully in the prevention activity. If the activity involves training where the parent will be expected to learn about effective parenting strategies for reducing the risk of substance abuse, then the parent will not likely be able to maintain the cognitive functioning necessary to retain and apply these improved parenting techniques. In this case, the prevention professional must remain open and aware of the difficulties faced by clients and then utilize professional contacts within the community to help provide necessary resources for the family. Only by first ensuring that the family's basic needs are met can further prevention efforts be attempted with any hope of success.

Many prevention professionals facilitate coalition meetings and administer training to clients or other professionals. In order to create an environment where sharing ideas and learning can take place, more than physiological needs must be met. Participants must have a sense of belonging and acceptance in order to participate fully. To create this environment, prevention professionals can create ground rules at the beginning of the meeting or training that address respectful communication among participants. In addition, prevention professionals can demonstrate appreciation for all ideas that participants share.

Maslow's theory can help prevention professionals understand the complex relationships that youth experience. It is important for prevention professionals and other caring adults to understand that many adolescents will meet their needs for belonging and esteem through D-love. However, as they develop to meet these needs through a variety of relationships with caring people, including prevention professionals, they can progress to experiencing a more gratifying B-love. Additionally, Maslow (1968) notes that healthy infants and children live in the moment spontaneously and joyfully, without thinking about distant goals. This knowledge helps prevention professionals understand why antitobacco posters depicting bad breath, an immediate outcome from using tobacco, is more effective than depicting ill health in adulthood.

## Helping Clients Meet Growth Needs

In his discussion of cognitive development, Maslow (1968) notes that healthy, happy, secure children enjoy growing, learning, and becoming competent. However, once the child masters a particular task, repeating this mastery becomes boring. Then, more complex tasks are sought and mastered. Under ideal circumstances, each step forward offers a more satisfying experience. The very intelligent child poses special challenges for adults because it takes more effort to provide stimulus to keep the child from becoming bored, to validate curiosity, and to encourage further growth. The child's curiosity must not be ignored or used to ridicule the child.

Prevention professionals can help others grow to B-cognition by minimizing the attractiveness of safety while making growth more attractive. To do so, make learning activities fun for youth and point out advantages to learning that are specific to the occasion. Additionally, individuals learn about themselves by gravitating toward what motivates them. Therefore, one must select opportunities that motivate and interest youth. Then one can point out the personalized advantages of taking the opportunity and of learning the new skills needed to participate in the opportunity. This is important, as some youth may become fearful of exploring the new opportunity.

Another way to encourage B-cognition is to minimize the danger of exploring by encouraging small steps toward growth. Obtaining knowledge successfully will then provoke a positive reaction. For example, understanding an intricate poem or political theory or discovering something new under the microscope causes illumination and exhilaration, along with the impulse to explore further. Success with small steps will produce enjoyment and the increased likelihood of continued growth.

Resources needed for youth to participate successfully must also be provided as appropriate to ensure that the opportunity is not overly daunting. The enjoyment gained from the opportunity, the new skills gained that enable youth to participate fully and succeed, and the esteem that youth receive when they succeed will lead to bonding with those who provide the opportunities, skills, and recognition. As noted in the social development strategy, prevention professionals must infuse healthy beliefs and clear standards into the equation to assist in the mission to protect our youth from substance abuse.

Caring adults, including prevention professionals, cannot force or be solely responsible for someone else's cognitive growth. Individuals must determine their own level of readiness to experience risk. If young persons do not enjoy the risk, they will likely retreat to review the situation at some safe distance in order to recover strength to attempt growth again. They may even regress to remastering a task from the past in order to build up courage.

Children with a dysfunctional parent may experience cognitive conflict. Because a child relies on the opinions of others and needs "love, respect, approval, admiration, and reward from others," the child with an uninvolved or unloving parent must consciously deny knowledge about the parent (Maslow, 1968, p. 59). Acknowledging that the parent cannot meet these critical needs would provoke the child to fix the situation or abandon the parent. This course of action is impossible if safety needs are to be met. As a result of denying obvious truths and in order to reduce anxiety, cognitive needs suffer in the young person. Providing a completely nonthreatening environment for such children where basic needs are met will help the children learn to express themselves. If this intervention does not occur, the children may never grow to healthy maturity, learning to live free of the fear of disapproval from others in the childish, dependent sense. They may feel helpless and fear abandonment, just as they felt as children, instead of developing a healthy distance from others' disapproval as adults.

## Peak Experiences and Prevention

Peak experiences can have implications in the field of prevention because many healthy adults, some of whom are prevention professionals, demonstrate positive aspects of the peak experiences. Conversely, some people may strive to achieve something similar to a peak experience through the abuse of substances.

One positive aspect of the peak experience is concrete thinking. Ideally, prevention professionals and others in the helping professions must regard each client concretely, in that each individual is perceived as whole, unique, and as having personal needs and desires. Abstract thinking about clients, conversely, involves categorizing them—regarding them as less than whole persons with unique qualities. Being perceived this way can be insulting and damaging to the client.

As an example, youth are frequently categorized in ways that are useful to the field of prevention, but damaging to individuals. Many prevention professionals refuse to use the term "high-risk youth," preferring instead "youth at risk." Others refuse to use any risk-related language when referring to youth. It is imperative that youth remain unfamiliar with such terminology as it applies to them, just as they must not be aware of labels such as "troubled," "unhealthy," or other such derogatory terms. Such categorizing is an insult to the person's individuality. This is also true when we minimize someone's experience. For example, one may diminish the significance of adolescent angst by mentioning that all teenagers feel that way. Mentioning that it is only a stage that all young people go through negates the young person's individuality. Individuals each believe that their situation is uniquely personal.

Additionally, a self-actualizing person or one experiencing a peak experience becomes more playful, in both a childish and mature sense simultaneously. This can be a helpful attribute when attracting youth to prevention programs. The ability to perceive and respond to people and objects in a genuinely childlike way can help to establish relations with youth participants in a way that feels familiar and intimate to the youth involved.

There are a few other attributes worth noting of those involved in peak experiences, as these attributes may relate to the impulse for some to use drugs. One involves a perception of an object, a person, or the world that is richer and more beautiful than ordinary reality. Another is the tendency to have bursts of insight and creativity. Yet another involves disorientation in time and space, where one becomes completely unaware of personal surroundings. These, along with a sense of unity in the world, can be similar to some experiences with drugs. Just as some note that the peak experience is a welcome and awesome experience, others say the same about the drug-induced similar experience.

Understanding a person's motivation to use drugs can be an important key in preventing substance abuse. During the 1960s, many people began to experiment with marijuana use and with a psychoactive substance, then legal, known as LSD. The experience that they recorded when using LSD in particular is similar in some ways to that of a peak experience. Golas (1971) describes the phenomena as "expansion . . . comprehension, understanding . . . a feeling of total awareness, of being one with all life . . . timeless, bliss, with unlimited choice of consciousness, perception, and feeling" (p. 14). He further notes that "total expansion is always there, beyond time, within and around you. You need only open your awareness at the pace you find safe and comfortable. If LSD is too fast, go slower" (p. 22). Golas refers to his experience as available to everyone at anytime, similar to Maslow's teachings. LSD can be a contributing factor to creating the environment for a pseudopeak experience that may include sensory distortions, dreaminess, and an altered mood. As noted in Chapter 4, however, use of LSD is not without negative consequences, including acute anxiety, paranoia, fear of loss of control, and delusions. These experiences are completely different from a peak experience. Additionally, flashbacks may occur that are similar or opposite to the peak experience and these may come at completely inopportune times. Since the 1960s, a host of other drugs have emerged that create similar experiences.

Knowing that some people choose to use drugs to produce a pseudopeak experience must provoke a different strategy than one created for those who seek to self-medicate because of chemical imbalances, physiological or psychological disabilities, or personal problems. In the case of the former, information on the dangers of drugs might be more effective than in the latter case, where the person is seeking to meet basic needs through self-medication. In the case of the latter, one must devise other strategies to meet the basic needs of the client, specifically through affiliation with medical personnel.

## Hierarchy for Prevention Professionals

Many prevention professionals spend each day accomplishing or overseeing numerous activities. These may include collecting data and other information from within the community, implementing and evaluating prevention programs, developing agency standards, administering budgets, creating reports, managing and training personnel and volunteers, planning logistics for events, writing grants, coordinating with various media, conducting literature reviews and Internet searches, and a host of other activities that ensure the success of prevention programs and agencies. This assortment of intellectual and creative activities, along with involvement in an altruistic and optimistic profession, can provide extreme job satisfaction. However, during evenings and weekends, frequently there are youth activities, parent trainings, and other community events to attend.

Unfortunately, many enthusiastic and dedicated prevention professionals soon get burned out because they are overcommitted to their projects. This results in a high turnover rate of highly qualified staff members within many prevention agencies. At the risk of stating the obvious, but largely overlooked rule, prevention professionals must schedule time to nurture themselves. Maslow's hierarchy provides a guide for accomplishing this. First, prevention professionals must ensure that their basic physiological needs are met by eating healthy foods, exercising, and getting sufficient sleep and rest. After a long day, prevention professionals may consider taking time off the following morning. Even when workloads are heaviest, prevention professionals are advised to spend quality time with family and friends and to allow themselves the freedom to further explore the intellectual and creative world both within and outside of the field of prevention. Only by maintaining balance in life between work and leisure can prevention professionals ensure that they will have the stamina to continue their work in this helping profession while guiding their own evolution toward self-actualization. Volunteers and staff can provide a valuable resource in maintaining balance. Others involved with the program will feel rewarded and gain a sense of belonging when trusted with meaningful program activities. Offering meaningful opportunities to staff and volunteers can provide needed relief. However, they must also be encouraged to maintain balance and to voice difficulties encountered in this regard.

## Conclusion

Maslow's theory offers prevention professionals tools for determining what clients need in order to thrive. By evaluating a client's interpersonal status with regard to the hierarchy, prevention professionals can gain valuable knowledge about what the client needs to move further into the realm of the higher needs.

Because basic needs must be filled by someone other than the individual, prevention professionals can play a critical role in helping clients evolve through the hierarchy. First, determine whether a client's basic needs are met. Clients will only be receptive to prevention information if they have their basic needs met. If any are not, ensure that they become met through established community resource networks. If a client has all basic needs met, then one can encourage cognitive development by offering and fostering opportunities to explore and learn about the world. As clients move closer to self-actualization, prevention professionals will gain the satisfaction of knowing that they have encouraged the growth of a healthier community—client by client.

Additionally, by assessing one's own needs in relation to the hierarchy, prevention professionals can aspire to move themselves closer to self-actualization. By developing concrete thinking, prevention professionals can provide services to clients without generating judgmental assumptions. In addition, by critically analyzing one's relationship to the hierarchy to ensure that all needs are met, one can avoid professional burnout.

## Erik Erikson's Psychosocial Developmental Stages

In the middle of the 1900s, the Danish clinical psychologist Erik Erikson (1950) posited a theory of development that organized people's lives into discrete stages. Erikson's contention was that if people could not solve the task at the appropriate stage, they would remain "stuck" on that conceptual problem, with psychological implications throughout their lives. For example, some people may not learn to trust their environments during infancy. Such people may not learn to trust themselves or others as adults. Conversely, successfully transcending the task results in the development of a new competence, along with increased good judgement and personal wholeness (Erikson, 1959). Erikson's theory provides a tool that prevention professionals can use to implement developmentally appropriate prevention programs. By understanding the task that clients must solve at a particular developmental stage, prevention professionals can determine how to offer developmentally appropriate prevention programs. In addition, when working with clients who are stuck at a particular stage, Erikson's theory also offers insight into how to help clients transcend the task of that stage.

Even though Erikson's stages have ages attributed to them, these are fairly arbitrary ones, based on individual and cultural variances. Similarly, each stage seems isolated and distinct from the others, when in fact each conflict and task exists in some form before its critical time (Erikson, 1959). The following are Erik Erikson's developmental stages, each discussed in further detail below:

- Birth to 18 months—Basic Trust versus Mistrust
- 18 months to 3 years—Autonomy versus Shame and Doubt
- 3–5 years—Initiative versus Guilt
- 5–12 years—Industry versus Inferiority
- 12–18 years—Identity versus Identity Diffusion
- 18–35 years—Intimacy versus Isolation

- 35–65 years—Generativity versus Stagnation
- 65 years and up—Integrity versus Despair

## Basic Trust versus Mistrust—
## Birth to Approximately 18 Months

During this stage, infants learn to either form trust that their needs will be met, including those for food, shelter, and sleep, or that their needs will not be met and that the environment is not supportive of survival. Information about the environment is gained through the senses. The mouth is the focus of life, as evidenced by the all-important tasks of sucking and feeding. The eyes, too, play a critical role in learning about the world, as the infant learns to distinguish familiar faces from others that are not familiar. Tactile senses allow the infant to determine what feels good.

Erikson (1959) describes trust as the "cornerstone of a healthy personality" (p. 56). Forming trust will produce a sense of well-being and a sense of confidence that one is capable of becoming what others expect him or her to become. The concept of trust is twofold. Not only must children learn that caregivers will meet their needs; they must also learn to trust their own bodies and cope with their own urges, such as learning not to bite others during teething episodes, especially during nursing. Also, letting infants cry briefly before meeting needs, such as providing food, rather than anticipating every need, helps them to trust their own feelings and responses.

The crisis of this stage derives from three developments: (1) the urge to appropriately observe and grasp items close by, (2) increasing awareness of oneself as a distinct person, and (3) the caregiver's turning attention to other pursuits that were given up during later pregnancy and postnatal care (Erikson, 1959).

The first development—grasping items close by—becomes complicated when the infant begins teething. Suddenly, the infant has the urge to bite the mother while nursing and to grasp and to bite other caregivers as well. Caregivers can offer little relief from teething, and once bitten can instinctively pull away from the infant, even expressing hostility that the infant perceives. From the natural and instinctive reaction of adults to withdraw from pain, the infant can develop a sense of innate badness. Caregivers can guard against reflexive, extreme reactions and demonstrate a calm and loving reaction instead.

The second development—becoming aware of the self as a distinct person—can arouse separation anxiety when caregivers leave sight of the infant. Infants may fear that they will be abandoned. The first social achievement is letting the caregiver out of sight without excessive anxiety, which is achieved through the formulation of trust based on consistent, quality caregiving. Separation anxiety from the parent is also complicated by the third development, in which the caregivers return to day-to-day duties, such as caring for other children, returning to the workplace, and resuming other roles aside from parenting. These duties naturally result in less one-on-one contact between the caregivers and the infant.

In order to facilitate the development of trust in the infant, caregivers must provide care with consistency and continuity, doing the same things in the same way, throughout this developmental stage and especially during the above crises. Caregivers must deliver stimuli, including smiles and nurturing touches, with the proper intensity and at the proper time. The amount of trust derived from early experience is not based on quantities of food or quantities of "demonstrations of love" (Erikson, 1950, p. 221). Instead, the amount of trust is based on the quality of the nurturing relationship.

Building trust within the infant will result in the development of "ego identity," which is the matching up of the inner world of the infant, including remembered and anticipated images, with what is happening in the environment (Erikson, 1950, p. 219). This consistency concerning what is real in the external world and what is perceived within the mind of the infant is critical to the development of a healthy personality. In the absence of trust, individuals can demonstrate either "introjection," or "projection." Introjection occurs when people internalize the attitudes, beliefs, or desires of an admirable person as if they were their own. In this way, the goodness in the world can be perceived as coming from within. Projection occurs when people perceive that the ill intent within is actually coming from others in the environment. For example, bullies who desire to pick on smaller children may perceive that the children are in fact after them, justifying their aggression toward the children. In short, there is an unhealthy, unrealistic split between the individual's internal and external worlds that affects behavior in potentially negative ways.

## Autonomy versus Shame and Doubt— Approximately 18 Months to Approximately 3 Years

In this stage, children need to learn that they are individuals separate from their caregivers, establishing autonomy without a sense of shame or self-doubt. During the previous stage, at about eight months of age, the infant began to be aware of separateness from the caregivers. Involved with this process is learning to distinguish the faces of the caregivers from others' faces, along with adapting to occasional separation from the caregiver. These developments set the stage for children to discover the world while growing in autonomy.

While working to develop autonomy, children discover their own will. The sense of basic trust gained during the previous stage will permit children to express, sometimes demandingly, their wish to have a choice. On occasion, children will seem pliable and agreeable, doing exactly what is expected. This is because the children choose to behave this way at this time. Other episodes may prove much more frustrating. When caregivers impose their will onto the children, even when the goal is to protect them, the imposition may produce anger and defiance. However, by learning to exercise choice and free will during safe and appropriate situations, children will learn to make appropriate choices in adulthood and to set healthy limits for themselves.

This stage is also marked by the all-important task of toilet training as it coincides with muscular maturation, helping the child become physically prepared for the task. Because of the anal-muscular maturation, two sets of social modalities evolve during this stage: one of holding on and another of letting go. These concepts are not restricted to the sphincter muscles, however. A general ability and need develop to alternately withhold objects and then to drop them or to throw them away. Thus, for example, beloved stuffed animals are flung from the car window onto the highway. Similarly, the child will alternate between affection and pushing away from others.

During this stage, caregivers can offer children simple choices, supporting their wish to "stand on their own feet." This will help them experience and develop autonomy. Simple choices might include which cup to drink from or which toy to take in the car. "Would you like this or that?" rather than "what do you want?" helps to limit the choice and to make the discussion manageable. At the same time that caregivers offer choices and as the child is encouraged to experience independence, the child must also be protected from "meaningless and arbitrary experiences of shame and of early doubt" (Erikson, 1950, p. 223). This is especially true with regard to teaching critical lessons and to toilet training.

To do so, caregivers must guard against initiating toilet training too early or too rigidly. Children should experience gradually controlling toilet functions willingly. If these needs are not met, the children will experience doubt in their ability to master their bodies along with a sense of self-consciousness. The children may respond by sucking their thumb, becoming hostile, or pretending to be autonomous even though they really feel dependent, confused, and incompetent. In short, overcontrolling caregivers will produce children with a lasting sense of shame and doubt, even paranoia.

Caregivers must be both firm and tolerant with children during this stage so they will learn to be firm and tolerant with themselves throughout life. Not only will they feel pride in their autonomy, but they will freely grant autonomy to others as adults. Similarly, shaming children will lead to internalized shame. For both adults and children, "there is a limit to endurance in the face of demands which force him to consider himself, his body, his needs, and his wishes as evil and dirty, and to believe in the infallibility of those who pass such judgment" (Erikson, 1959, p. 69). In other words, the children will develop an innate belief in their own "badness" because they believe that others who shame them are right in their judgment.

Erikson (1950) describes shame as a self-consciousness, of being visible when one does not feel comfortable being visible. Those who harbor such shame may have dreams of being exposed undressed or have the impulse to bury their faces or to sink into the ground. This experience is actually rage turned against the self, a wish for invisibility, instead of "destroying the eyes of the world" (Erikson, 1950, p. 223). This rage can produce a defiant child or even a young criminal.

Another lasting consequence related to turning rage against the self is the tendency to overmanipulate oneself by becoming obsessed with creating repetitiveness, or with having everything "just so." This phenomena of the compulsive personality, often referred to as "anal," has normal aspects in "abnormal exaggerations" (Erikson, 1959, p. 73). "The question is always whether we remain the masters of the rules by which we want to make things more manageable, instead of more complicated, or whether the rules master the ruler" (Erikson, 1959, p. 73). People can go through life apologetic, afraid to be seen, and sorry to be themselves.

## Initiative versus Guilt—
## Approximately 3 Years to Approximately 5 Years

In this stage children learn about their identities. This is an extension of the previous task in that they discover more about how they as individuals can do things to influence their world and their lives. "Being firmly convinced that he is a person, the child must now find out what kind of person he is going to be" (Erikson, 1959, p. 74). This is accomplished as children compare themselves to grown-ups, attempt to comprehend future roles, and attempt to understand which roles are worth imitating. In the process of learning about roles, children will desire to be like the caregivers who appear to be powerful and beautiful. In order to become more like caregivers, children will try on meaningful roles of participation within the family, using tools and toys, and caring for younger siblings.

During this time, children will also begin to associate with peers. The process of learning is vigorous. Erikson (1959) notes that "at no time is the individual more ready to learn quickly and avidly, to become big in the sense of sharing obligation, discipline, and performance rather than power, in the sense of making things, instead of 'making' [manipulating] people, than during this period of development" (p. 81). During this time, children will work with other children without directing their actions in a bossy way. Additionally, children profit fully from their association with teachers during this stage.

Three developments bring children to crisis at this time. One is related to their ability to move about freely and establish what seems to them to be unlimited goals. Another is related to the development of their language skills as they become perfected just enough to enable them to ask many things but to misunderstand the answers. The third is related to the expansion of their imaginations so that they can frighten themselves with their own dreams and thoughts.

As the children move about exploring the world physically and mentally, they may experience a sense of guilt resulting from their thoughts and actions, which in the case of the latter will often provoke interference on behalf of the caregivers. This is especially so because children will be particularly intrusive during this time. They may intrude on others physically by moving about aggressively and even by directly attacking others on occasion. The child may also intrude on others' minds and ears through aggressive talking resulting from his or her consuming curiosity. Compliance and defiance, as seen in the last stage, will continue to appear alternately.

Children must emerge from these conflicts with unbroken initiative. Caregivers can help support this by reassuring children that they are loved and have strengths, even when they demonstrate needs and are challenged when working through a learning process. Also, reassuring children that they will still be taken care of when sick or hurting and that they can express their needs in a straightforward manner is important. When children gain a sense of initiative, they will be more relaxed and brighter in judgment, they will seem to have a surplus of energy, they will forget failures quickly, and they will approach what they desire with enthusiasm (Erikson, 1959).

## Industry versus Inferiority—
## Approximately 5 Years to Approximately 12 Years

In this stage, children's sense of industry and self-esteem become more fully developed. Learning to do things their own way, developing industry, is part of the process. Industry is a sense of being useful, with an ability to make things and make them well in order to gain recognition. Before this stage, children learn by watching how things are done and then by trying them. Now children want to develop a sense of industry, gained when people show them how to do things. Additionally, more is learned about making choices and experiencing consequences appropriate to the choices made.

Toys become useful to the child in acquiring a sense of industry (Erikson, 1959). Successfully mastering imagined conflicts about the adult world through the use of toys helps children prepare to master real-world conflicts with anticipated success. For example, children may manipulate dolls, demonstrating a successful compromise after an imaginary disagreement. The same children during a different game may simulate a sturdy, upright architectural structure using building blocks.

At this time, children go to school. Not all cultures have schools based on literacy, as in reading, writing, and arithmetic. In some cultures, skills of technology are transmitted instead. Similarly, sometimes there are formal teachers and sometimes not. However, all cultures have some form of education. Because of this, the primary caregivers become less important during this stage. At the same time, society in its broader sense becomes significant in showing children the way to contribute meaningfully. Children win recognition by producing things and gain gratification in using tools and personal skills to complete tasks.

The challenge of developing industry arises when children are not prepared for school life by the caregivers or when school life does not measure up to the children's expectations. Also, the teachers must master a balance between play and work, between games and study, or in other words, between teaching to the children within the framework of childhood and that of adulthood. Teachers must also recognize special efforts by children and encourage their special gifts. They must nudge the child along who is not yet ready for school, offering extra time and attention. The child who is not ready may not enjoy working or might not feel pride at doing something well. The child may also experience inferiority if identifying too strongly with the teacher, always seeking praise from the teacher. This child may become the "teacher's pet," thereby limiting identity to that of "good little worker."

Children who develop a sense of inferiority might feel inadequate in the mastery of using tools or else despair that their personal skills are inferior to those of others, especially to other children. These children may fear that others will not accept them, leading to a feeling of mediocrity. If teachers are too strict, emphasizing self-restraint and a sense of duty, children may grow up unable to unlearn this and will then make their own and others' lives miserable, including those of their own children. This strict approach will spoil the natural desire of children to work and to learn. The lenient teacher who lets children learn by playing and doing only what they like to do is not meeting their needs either. A child must be guided to the "adventure" of learning to "accomplish things which one would never have thought by oneself" (Erikson, 1959, p. 84). Children are attracted to learning that is not "the product of play and fantasy but the product of reality, practicality, and logic" (Erikson, 1959, p. 84). This offers children the thrilling sense that they are participating in the real world of adults.

Another danger during this stage lies in the fact that many children will face their first encounter with "division of labor" and of "equality of opportunity" based on the color of their skin, the background of their parents, or the cost of their clothes (Erikson, 1959). Children may decide that their social worth is more important than their own will to learn. This can harm not only the children's sense of industry, but also their sense of identity as discussed in the next stage. Discrimination can also create the foundation for the risk factor in the individual domain, "alienation and rebelliousness," placing youth at increased risk for abusing substances.

Adults can help children experience that their ideas and beliefs are valued as uniquely their own by helping them to share thoughts, feelings, and beliefs in a straightforward manner and without demonstrating judgment. This is also a stage of separation from the caregivers as children venture into the realm of school. Creating opportunities for children to experience their independence from their families in appropriate ways may prepare them for healthier independence later.

## Identity versus Identity Diffusion— Approximately 12 Years to Approximately 18 Years

The task in this stage is to learn about personal identity in order to become a separate, independent person. During this stage, children develop their own interests, values, and beliefs. They also develop a clearer sense of responsibility for meeting their own needs. They are primarily concerned with their social roles and preoccupied with how they are perceived instead of how they perceive of themselves. This factor places youth at increased risk of succumbing to peer pressure, whether positive or negative. They want to match the roles and skills they have mastered with the social contexts that they choose for themselves and the opportunities with which they are provided.

In this stage, childhood ends and adolescence begins as individuals develop physical, sexual maturity. As a result, youth are inundated by unfamiliar drives, leading them toward physical intimacy, even though they may fear it. Conflicting possibilities and choices appear, such as "Should I do what my parents tell me or would I rather smoke cigarettes like someone else who is popular?" Youth get through these by forming cliques and stereotyping themselves, their ideals, and their enemies. Hero worship for youth is like falling in love, which may or may not be sexual. Adolescent love is an attempt to define one's identity by projecting oneself onto another, determining what is similar and different, and then interpreting the reflection that they perceive. From the information gathered, youth can adjust their self-perception or their behavior as desired to become more like the ideal that they hold.

In this stage, youth struggle to maintain sameness and continuity in themselves to avoid inner turmoil, while searching for sameness and continuity within the environment. This also helps them to stabilize emotions and to feel safer. This aspect of the search for identity has a correlation with the issue of sameness and continuity experienced in the basic trust versus mistrust stage. Conflict arises in this quest from the constantly changing body that causes change internally. However, it also provokes changed reactions from others as the individual develops and matures. As a result, youth tend to fight many of the battles of earlier years all over again. To do so, they appoint well-meaning people to "play the role of enemies" (Erikson, 1950, p. 228). Youth shift away from the worldview held by caregivers while broadening social contacts, learning to adapt to new social situations, and learning to become more independent.

Developing positive self-esteem and identity is related to three factors. One involves the conviction of approaching a tangible future. The second involves developing a personality matching one's social reality and values. The third involves developing an awareness that one's mastery of challenges matches that of other people; that is, one "measures up" to the performance of peers. The development of a healthy personality depends on specific psychological necessities, specifically that one perceives that the world offers both freedom and viable choices for a successful and meaningful life.

**Identity diffusion** is based on a doubt of one's identity, specifically regarding ethnicity and sexuality. Youths' primary concern involves an inability to settle on an occupational identity, including but not limited to the choice to obtain higher education. Youth may compensate for identity diffusion by overidentifying with heroes of cliques and by demonstrating intolerance of others who are regarded as "different" in various cultural ways. Additionally, if youth perceive that the environment will not permit the methods of self-expression that help them to form their identity, then the youth will lash out with a force rivaling the instinct for survival. In fact, without a fully formed identity, there will be no sense of being alive. This can be particularly problematic as members of each generation select methods of self-expression that may seem peculiar to members of the generations before. In an attempt to create their identities and to express them, youth will select appearances that are different from the norm. Whether the expression involves new hairstyles, "body art," or other methods of altering appearance, intolerance of this creative expression will result in an intense reaction resembling an animal's fight for survival. Delinquent and psychotic incidents are not uncommon during this stage. If treated appropriately, these incidents do not have the same significance and permanence as when they occur in other developmental stages.

## Intimacy versus Isolation— Approximately 18 Years to Approximately 35 Years

In this stage, the first of adulthood, people must acquire a sense of intimacy and sociability while avoiding a sense of isolation. A critical component of forming intimacy is forming a sense of identity in the previous stage. This is needed to face fear of identity loss and to experience self-abandon through sexual union, close friendships, and physical combat. The capacity for intimacy is needed to experience inspiration by teachers and to trust one's own intuition. During this time, people prepare for their life's work through job selection or studies and find mentors, all while attempting to form a capacity for intimacy without losing the self.

The conflict of this stage lies in the paradox of needing commitment while simultaneously being unwilling to commit. Erikson (1980) notes that the unwillingness can be based on the desire to remain independent and to retain identity, neither of which is compromised by true intimacy, and on fear of commitment. Because of an unwillingness to form commitments, some may surrender to sexual relations without emotional commitment. This leads to isolation and consequent self-absorption. Without intimacy one's relationships are "highly stereotyped" and "formal interpersonal relations [lack] spontaneity, warmth, and real fellowship" (Erikson, 1959, p. 95). In these cases, the quest for intimacy may be attempted repeatedly with subsequent failures. One must become oneself before becoming an intimate partner.

## Generativity versus Stagnation—
## Approximately 35 Years to Approximately 65 Years

During this stage people attempt to obtain what Erikson referred to as **generativity** while avoiding stagnation. Erikson (1950) coined the term "generativity" because existing words such as "creativity" and "productivity" were insufficient. He defines generativity as the "primary interest in establishing and guiding the next generation or whatever in a given case may become the absorbing object of a parental kind of responsibility" (p. 231). Some channel this drive, not in procreation and child rearing, but instead in altruistic concern and in creativity. In short, generativity requires a concern for others, whether care for children, contributions to community, or production of meaningful work or art.

In the absence of generativity, there is stagnation, which manifests as a preoccupation with self-health and with enjoyment of life. One might also strive for pseudointimacy with others while experiencing a troubling sense of interpersonal impoverishment. In short, those who stagnate indulge themselves "as if they were their one and only child" (Erikson, 1959, p. 97). Ultimately, those who aspire to generativity must achieve a healthy balance between self-interest and the interest of others.

## Integrity versus Despair—
## Approximately 65 Years and Over

In this stage, people try to achieve a sense that life has had meaning and that their lifelong process has been worth the effort. They also try to face not being in the future. Integrity is a "post-narcissistic love of the human ego—not of the self—as an experience which conveys some world order and spiritual sense, no matter how dearly paid for" (Erikson, 1950, p. 232). Erikson clarifies that at this stage one gains an acceptance of one's own life cycle and of the significant people in one's life without feeling the desire to change any of the details of the past. In short, one loves one's own life history and all of the players contained there unconditionally, even if the events or people caused significant hurt or other unfavorable emotions. In a sense, integrity reflects Maslow's attributes of self-actualizers who obtain a sense of higher meaning in the world and a sense of connectedness with others in the world.

One who achieves integrity will have a new unconditional love of one's own parents, along with all their imperfections. One will also accept responsibility for the life encountered, without finding fault with others for imperfect situations or events. One will have a sense of comradeship with people of different historical times, who have created artifacts that portray the best qualities of humanity (Erikson, 1959). However, in order to become a mature adult with integrity, each person must develop all of the qualities throughout the stages already discussed.

Ultimately, one who lacks integrity fears death and revels in despair. One who despairs will not regard this life as ultimate and will fear that time is too short to start another path to integrity. This person will show disgust, misanthropy, and chronic displeasure, which is really directed at the self even though it appears outwardly directed.

## Applying Erikson's Theory to Prevention

Erikson's theory can be applied to prevention in two ways. First, prevention professionals can understand the developmental task that their clients naturally experience by virtue of their age and stage of development. In addition, prevention professionals can look for signs among clients that they might be stuck in a particular developmental stage. Ideally, clients will transcend each stage successfully, thereby enhancing their happiness and overall quality of life. Those who do not transcend a particular stage may have doubts, insecurities, or other negative feelings that adversely affect their quality of life. The following offers a few examples of how to incorporate Erikson's theory into prevention program planning at various stages of development.

Children who do not develop basic trust during the first developmental stage (birth to 18 months) can become depressed adolescents or adults. Some who display mistrust will withdraw into themselves when at odds with themselves or others, refusing food and comfort and becoming oblivious to companionship. In this event, one can work with them to help instill a sense of trust in the world by being a trustworthy, dependable, and caring person and by encouraging other relations with healthy, dependable persons. One can also help them develop a sense of trust that becomes innate within themselves by helping them notice and acknowledge the presence of basic needs, such as hunger and that for love and belonging, while acknowledging their emotional responses to specific situations. This is the first step in learning to care for oneself, by providing essential self-nurturing and by protecting one's emotional self from situations that feel unhealthy or unsafe.

Erikson (1959) also notes that the kind and degree of the caregivers' sense of autonomy will determine the level to which they can grant it to their small children during the second stage (18 months to three years). The caregivers themselves must have a sense of personal independence and dignity. Sometimes the best way to protect and develop a child is to help the caregivers develop the essential awareness and skills needed to raise healthy children. Many substance abuse prevention programs for parents focus on this very topic. They work to ensure that the parents' developmental needs have been met, while offering them the skills necessary to become competent, effective, and caring parents. The parents then gain a sense of satisfaction instead of insecurity about their own parenting skills, resulting in more enjoyable relationships with their children.

Children who experience guilt instead of initiative during the third stage of development (three to five years) will repress their wishes because of a feeling of inadequacy, or else will "show off" when feeling scared. The consequences of ingrained guilt show up later in life as self-restriction. This keeps the individual from living to full potential. It can be seen in those who fear challenges and who consistently back away from positive, growth-oriented opportunities. One might also overcompensate feelings of inadequacy by showing tireless initiative at all cost or by developing a sense of self-worth based entirely on what one is doing instead of what one is. This can be seen when a person strives to achieve goals at the great personal cost of health and relationships, never slowing down enough to enjoy life.

In order to help youth develop initiative and avoid the negative consequences of its absence in their adulthood, prevention professionals can incorporate the social development model (discussed in Chapter 2) into prevention efforts. For example, showing and allowing a small child to assist with grown-up activities such as picking up the toys or folding up the chairs in the recreation center may require more time and patience on the part of the adult than when performing the task alone. However, this will allow the child to have an age-appropriate experience in initiative. During these next few years, while youth express an eagerness to try new things, one can provide them with the opportunities, give them the skills to participate safely, and provide recognition for having taken the opportunities and used the new skills, in order to help them through this phase.

Also during the initiative versus guilt stage, the child's conscience becomes firmly established. The child will feel guilty for thoughts and deeds that are undiscovered. The child will fear being found out and will feel ashamed when finally discovered for a wrong-doing. Related to this is the danger that the child will develop lasting resentments if the caregivers or other adults do not live up to the "new conscience" that they instill in the child. Some caregivers live by the motto, "Do as I say, not as I do," which could damage their credibility as ethical people. For this reason, it is important for caregivers, prevention professionals, and other adults to model behavior that they in turn expect from young people.

Beginning in the industry versus inferiority stage (five to 12 years), children enjoy assuming roles of adults and participating in real-world activities. During this stage and continuing into the next, peer-led prevention programs can become particularly beneficial. Offering training to youth leaders to help them to serve as role models and activity leaders during prevention programs benefits the peer leaders by allowing them the opportunity to act as responsible, caring adults. Similarly, research demonstrates that the other youth involved in the program will be persuaded more and ultimately benefit more from partici-pating in a peer-led program, as opposed to one led by adults. Of course, providing the training to peer leaders can result in a much more complex prevention program with added inconstant variables, such as peer leaders moving away from the area. However, the benefit of working with peer leaders can far outweigh the disadvantages. Additionally, youth can provide expert counsel in improving prevention programming efforts.

Many prevention professionals work with youth who are experiencing the identity versus identity diffusion stage (ages 12 to 18). Prevention professionals must ensure that they understand the need for youth to express their individual identities as they create them. For this reason, prevention professionals must maintain a nonjudgmental posture when youth express themselves in ways that are unappealing aesthetically to the professional.

Puberty rites can help youth to integrate and to affirm their new identity. In order to facilitate this process, adults can show appreciation for their changing intellectual, social, emotional, physical, and sexual identities and affirm independence by initiating separation where appropriate. Youth can also see through empty praise and condescending encourage-ment. Conversely, youth gain strength from "whole-hearted and consistent recognition of real accomplishment" (Erikson, 1959, pp. 89–90).

Erikson (1959) and Maslow (1968) agree that the important thing is not to judge or label youth for their delinquent and psychotic incidents during their development of iden-tity. Doing so can result in further rebellion, which places them at increased risk for sub-stance abuse. Additionally, when grouping youth with varying levels of problems together, youth who are experimenting with drug use may become exposed to those who are frequent users actively involved in a drug culture. The experimental users may be compelled to join the new drug culture, as society has formally determined that they belong there.

When clients are experiencing the conflict of intimacy versus isolation (ages 18 to 35), one can help to provide opportunities that enable others to discover and develop meaningful relationships. Forming affiliations with organizations and finding meaningful life work may assist in the development of a sense of usefulness.

Maslow's discussion of deficiency or D-love from the previous section can prove useful when working with clients in this stage. D-lovers do not regard others as whole, unique individuals and because of this, they will obviously experience difficulties in forming intimacy. However, Erikson notes that developing a strong sense of identity is the critical developmental precursor to experiencing intimacy. Therefore, some individuals who cannot establish intimate, meaningful relationships with peers, teachers, mentors, and romantic partners may first need to return to the previous stage's conflict in order to develop the capacity for intimacy.

For those in the generativity versus stagnation stage (ages 35 to 65), common manifestations of stagnation include fixation on personal health, happiness, and materialistic gain. Helping such persons to develop meaningful interests and providing them with opportunities to participate meaningfully in a variety of activities can help them to transcend this conflict. People in this stage may enjoy greatly and benefit from participation in prevention programs and other altruistic and creative activities.

More and more frequently, prevention professionals express concern for preventing substance abuse with aging populations, especially those in the integrity versus despair stage (ages 65 and over). Such individuals often deal with loss of economic and social power within cultures that can devalue them. Additionally, they can experience the loss of loved ones as their own life cycle approaches closure. Some individuals increasingly turn toward the use of substances to alleviate a sense of despair. Additionally, increased presence of health issues, changing physiology, and multiple prescribed medications can all create unexpected chemical reactions within the aging person's body, sometimes with devastating effects. Because existing prevention research provides very few clues for administering effective prevention strategies for the elderly and other adult populations, this is an extremely valuable direction for researchers and prevention program developers to venture. Creating much-needed support systems, offering prevention education, and providing opportunities for aging people to share their many wonderful gifts and insights with others may be some of the ways to assist this population in sustaining a happy, healthy lifestyle.

Sometimes prevention professionals work with families where many developmental issues are involved. For example, a single, 18-year-old woman raising a child may experience intimacy issues based on her limited availability to peers and potential romantic partners. She may need help in establishing meaningful relationships with others or may need to work on establishing a sense of identity before this can occur. If she has not selected or obtained meaningful life work, then this may further inhibit the development of a healthy personality.

If the teen parent is emotionally detached from the child based on romantic preoccupation, then the child may suffer from mistrust or shame issues. In such a case, the prevention professional may be able to provide parenting education information that will help the parent to recognize the importance of remaining emotionally and physically available to the child. This can be done while the parent creates a balance in life that allows for her development of intimate relationships as long as support systems are in place that allow for this.

If the mother and child are living with the grandparents, then the grandparents will also have the challenge of assisting with the care of their grandchild while supporting their child into the adult years. This situation can produce a heightened sense of generativity, but might also produce a redundant sense of purposelessness. In such cases, the needs of each individual client must be considered when providing services.

Prevention professionals may not be able to address all developmental issues for every client. However, having a working knowledge of Erikson's developmental theory can offer insight into the healthy developmental issues of clients. This theory also helps prevention professionals detect when clients may be struggling with a developmental issue that may limit their ability to function as healthy individuals. Many times, prevention professionals can work with members from other community resources to meet the needs of clients.

## Conclusion

According to Erikson, the process of accomplishing each developmental task allows people to face challenges in life and provides them with the means of coping with a complex world. Erikson's stages demonstrate the significance of caregivers setting children on the path to a healthy personality, as all subsequent development is contingent on the mastery of the initial stages. Erikson notes, however, that the ever changing world makes it difficult for parents to be genuine and sure of themselves. Caregivers with developmental challenges will have particular difficulty in raising healthy children. Providing prevention programs for children and caregivers simultaneously is an excellent method of meeting the needs of the entire family.

Unfortunately, Erikson's discussion of the stages incurred during adulthood, specifically dealing with the formation of intimacy, generativity, and integrity, are brief. Although prevention efforts typically focus on youth, many members of the community become involved in comprehensive prevention efforts and often parents are targeted in specific strategies in order to help their children. Regardless of the developmental stages of clients, it is important for prevention professionals to thoroughly understand the types of prevention strategies that are appropriate for different age groups and for individuals in unique developmental patterns.

# Jean Piaget's Cognitive-Developmental Stages

Jean Piaget, a native of Switzerland, developed a theory of cognitive development largely influenced by his earlier background as a biologist. His cognitive-developmental theory for humans was developed through observation over the course of 60 years. His work in later years involved rigorous research methods. Although his work was widely accepted in Europe much earlier, it did not reach the educational systems within the United States until the 1960s, largely because his work was written in French. Piaget created a complex system of terminology reflecting thought processes. Understanding the terminology helps to build comprehension of the theory, which can be helpful to prevention professionals in meeting the cognitive needs of clients.

Piaget's theory can be applied to teaching strategies for those providing prevention education. It can also be helpful to prevention professionals providing services, particularly within the school domain when addressing academic failure. Additionally, Piaget's theory can be applied to helping youth accept prevention messages as meaningful and valuable. Finally, the following theory can be very useful in creating prevention messages that can reach target audiences in ways that specifically match their cognitive developmental stage.

## Piaget's Terminology and Concepts

Piaget coined several terms that helped to explain why cognitive development occurs, including **schema**, **assimilation**, **accommodation**, **equilibrium**, **disequilibrium**, and **equilibration**. Piaget also identified three types of knowledge and discussed the methods that children use to develop these types of knowledge. Understanding how children learn can help guide prevention professionals' attempts at sharing information about alcohol, tobacco, and other drugs. Piaget also discussed the concept of **affective development** that addresses children's motivation to learn. Understanding Piaget's use of these terms and concepts can help prevention professionals to incorporate his theory into prevention work. Therefore, they will be described in some detail below.

### Schema

Schemata (the plural of schema) are "the cognitive or mental structures by which individuals intellectually adapt to and organize the environment" (Wadsworth, 1971, p. 14). Schemata provide a sort of invisible, intellectual filing system within the brain that can adapt and change as an individual develops cognitively. When an individual is faced with incoming information, or stimuli, from the environment, the schemata offer a frame of reference for processing, identifying, classifying, and generalizing the new information. Suppose a child sees a young pig for the first time and her father asks her what it is. After looking at the pig, she determines that it is most similar to what she knows about dogs because it has a tail, four legs, and a longish nose. She tells her father that the pig is a dog. In this way the child is adapting new information into existing beliefs.

Young children have only a few schemata, but the system continues to grow throughout life. Each time new information presents itself, the schemata adapt to the new information so that the child does not think that pigs are dogs forever. Further, the child's placement of stimuli into schemata is "always appropriate for his or her level of conceptual development. There is no wrong placement. There are just better and better placements as intellectual development proceeds" (Wadsworth, 1971, p. 20). The processes that allow for the development of schemata are assimilation and accommodation.

### Assimilation

Assimilation is the cognitive process of classifying and placing new information into existing schemata. This occurs constantly as individuals make sense of the environment around them. The child above has determined that the pig is a type of dog and therefore she has assimilated the information about pigs into her existing dog schema. She now thinks that dogs may have curly tails, a wrinkled nose, and make grunting noises.

As another example, suppose a child is learning about barnyard animals and learns that females are usually smaller than males. The child spots a seemingly large, wooly lamb and a smaller goat; instead of recognizing that they are two different animals, the child assumes that the larger lamb is the male. Because they are perceived as the same species, the goat is logically the female. The conclusion fits with the existing schemata that the child has developed and does not result in a change to the system except that it grows somewhat to include the new concept. Because the individual creates schemata that can only reflect the individual's current understanding and knowledge of the world, the schemata are not accurate reflections of reality. This, in part, results in differing perceptions of the same event by various individuals. Even among prevention professionals, this can result in various interpretations of individuals, their cultures, and other significant events as discussed in Chapter 5.

## Accommodation

In contrast, accommodation involves changing some thinking in order to cope effectively with a new problem. Accommodation occurs when new information cannot be assimilated because there are no existing schemata that match the new information. In this case, the individual can either create a new schema or modify an existing schema. Once accommodation has taken place, an individual can try again to assimilate the new information and it will fit because the schema has changed. Assimilation is always the eventual goal in accommodation.

For example, suppose a child is learning about the American Revolution and the significance of national flags. The child assumes that all flags are red, white, and blue, like the flags of England and the United States. Suddenly the child is confronted with the image of Mexico's flag bearing green, white, and red. The child's impulse is to believe that Mexico's flag is not a flag at all, but must be something else. After social interaction with others, however, the child learns to acknowledge that flags can come in many different colors. The child has changed a fundamental conviction to accommodate new information that would not otherwise fit into the existing belief system.

As another example, suppose a teenager has witnessed his parents' drug use on numerous occasions. In order to justify their open drug use, the parents tell him that occasional use of certain drugs is not harmful, so he has adopted this belief. Suddenly, one of his friends uses the same drug, suffering fatal consequences due to an overdose or a traffic fatality. He must then reconcile the realization that use of this particular drug can be harmful with the formerly held misconception that it is not. This can be done through accommodation.

The processes of assimilating and accommodating information help to advance cognitive development. However, one more ingredient must also be present: action. A child's cognitive development is dependent on his *active involvement* in seeking out new stimuli through the senses, through play, and through the manipulation of objects. Searching for information to assimilate and accommodate is necessary for the development of cognitive structures.

## Equilibrium, Disequilibrium, and Equilibration

A balance between assimilation and accommodation is necessary for normal intellectual development. In other words, we function maximally when assimilation and accommodation are balanced or in equilibrium. This means that we are able both to draw on past experience and to respond to changed circumstances with new ways of thinking. Equilibrium is always accomplished through assimilation. An imbalance between assimilation and accommodation is called disequilibrium. Equilibration is the process of moving from disequilibrium to a balanced state of equilibrium.

The teenager mentioned above who loses a friend through the use of a drug formerly perceived as harmless experiences disequilibrium. This occurs because the two facts cannot coexist. The first fact is that the drug is not harmful. The second fact is that his friend died from using it. His disequilibrium is caused by his inability to hold both beliefs simultaneously. In order to achieve equilibrium, the teenager must go through the process of equilibration. To do this, he must acknowledge that his previous belief is false and that the drug can be harmful. When he changes his previously held belief, he is in the process of accommodating his schema by changing his thinking to cope with this problem. Once he accommodates his schema, he can then assimilate the view that all drugs are potentially harmful into his drug schema. Once the information is assimilated, the teenager has achieved equilibrium. Of course, establishing equilibrium is temporary as individuals are constantly exposed to new information that challenge existing schemata. This example illustrates the concepts of schema, assimilation, accommodation, equilibrium, disequilibrium, and equilibration. Piaget also defined specific types of knowledge that individuals acquire, as noted below.

## Types of Knowledge: Physical, Logical-Mathematical, and Social

Piaget identifies three types of knowledge: **physical knowledge**, **logical-mathematical knowledge**, and **social knowledge**. Children develop these types of knowledge through active involvement, not by simply listening to information. Understanding these types of knowledge and how children learn can help prevention professionals understand better how to deliver information about alcohol, tobacco, and other drugs.

Physical knowledge is that of the physical properties of objects and events, including size, shape, texture, and weight. The child learns about these properties by physically manipulating the object and taking in information through various senses. For example, in order to learn about sand, the child must play with sand. Reading about sand, looking at pictures, or listening to a discussion about sand will not help the child to gain accurate knowledge about sand (Wadsworth, 1971).

Logical-mathematical knowledge, also called logico-mathematical knowledge, derives from thinking about objects and events. This form of knowledge is invented by the child and is not inherent in the objects themselves. Social knowledge involves that which is agreed upon by social groups in the environment regarding rules, laws, morals, values, ethics, and language systems. This knowledge evolves through children's social interactions with people.

Because these three forms of knowledge cannot occur by simply listening to teachers or by reading books, the transfer of knowledge must be done in a more comprehensive way. Specifically, teachers and prevention professionals must actively engage those who are learning by providing hands-on activities and by encouraging youth to actively think about topics, such as substance use issues. This is consistent with the statement in Chapter 2, which supports that didactic communication techniques are largely ineffective in reaching people with prevention messages to create behavior change or changes in attitudes toward substance use.

## Affective Development

Piaget also describes affective development, including the development of "feelings, interests, desires, tendencies, values, and emotions" (Wadsworth, 1971, p. 31). Motivation to learn about a specific topic is obviously influenced by one's interest in the subject. Fatigue and boredom impair motivation. Feelings of accomplishment, or conversely, feelings of failure, related to the experience of learning can also affect motivation to learn. When prevention professionals provide training to youth or adults, these factors must be considered. Is parenting education held late at night after a full day of work when the parents are exhausted? When children receive prevention messages, are they encouraged to see how the information is related to them? Does the trainer spend time establishing relations with the students and creating a safe environment for learning? Other issues for effectively communicating prevention messages will be discussed later in this section.

## Stages of Cognitive Development

Piaget (1963) distinguished three stages of cognitive development. First is the **sensory-motor stage**, the second is the **concrete operations stage**, and the third is the **formal operations stage**. Because understanding the latter two stages will help prevention professionals communicate effectively with clients when framing prevention messages, these will be discussed in more detail than as the first stage. Table 6.1 compares Piaget's and Erikson's stages of development.

The sensory-motor intelligence stage lasts from birth to approximately two years of age. During this period, infants "think" with their bodies, through action in which they attempt to affect their surroundings. By sucking on a blanket and then sucking on a bottle, infants will learn how they are different in meeting their needs. There is a transition phase between this stage and the next, typically occurring from about ages two to seven, called the preoperational period. The learning of language characterizes this stage.

The second stage is the concrete operations stage, which lasts from about age 7 to about age 11. During this stage children can apply logical thought to concrete problems occurring in the present. The third stage, formal operations, begins at about age 11 to 15 for many but not all people. Those with formal operations can apply logical reasoning to all classes of problems existing in the past, present, and future. Information about the concrete and formal operations stages can provide valuable clues about how to communicate with individuals during the different cognitive-developmental stages.

**TABLE 6.1    Comparing Erikson's and Piaget's Developmental Stages**

| Age | Erikson's Stage | Piaget's Stage |
| --- | --- | --- |
| Birth to 18 months | Basic Trust vs. Mistrust | Sensory Motor Stage |
| 18 months to 3 years | Autonomy vs. Shame and Doubt | Preoperational Stage |
| 3–5 years | Initiative vs. Guilt | Preoperational Stage |
| 5–12 years | Industry vs. Inferiority | Preoperational Stage/ Concrete Operations |
| 12–18 years | Identity vs. Identity Diffusion | Concrete Operations/Formal Operatons |
| 18–35 years | Intimacy vs. Isolation | Concrete Operations/Formal Operatons |
| 35–65 years | Generativity vs. Stagnation | Concrete Operations/Formal Operatons |
| 65 years and up | Integrity vs. Despair | Concrete Operations/Formal Operatons |

## Concrete Operations

During the concrete operations stage, individuals can process problems that are concrete in nature. In other words, the problems are based on physical reality in the present environment. Even when problems are concrete, there are certain limitations for individuals during this stage in solving them. For example, people often cannot solve multiple, concrete problems at the same time or solve concrete problems that are presented verbally only. However, individuals become competent at mentally grouping objects according to similarity. For example, they can sort objects first by color and then by shape. As they do so, they recognize multiple factors related to similarities and differences.

There are many characteristics of concrete thinkers that can help prevention professionals to understand their abilities and limitations. These are related to the development of cooperation, reasoning, morality, autonomy, and the recognition of others' intentions behind their deeds.

At about the age of seven or eight, children begin to develop the skills needed for cooperation and mutual respect. They do this in the process of working problems out with peers. Children also begin to understand and value the existence of rules for games. Additionally, they come to realize that rules are not unchangeable, but instead can be changed if everyone playing agrees. Game playing becomes organized and competitive, whereas formerly, game pieces were manipulated randomly. As children develop relations with peers that are based on equality, they begin to respond with adults in ways that reflect their differing, inferior status in the world of adults. Through relationships with adults, children learn about moral reasoning and unilateral respect. They begin to internalize the values that they accept from the adults they hold in esteem.

Additionally, children begin to recognize the viewpoints of others through their social interactions and they begin to realize that others may develop different solutions to the same problem. Because of this, children will often question their own reasoning and ask for validation from others to ensure they are following a good course of reasoning. The resulting disequilibrium can result in the cognitive restructuring that will stimulate further cognitive development.

During the concrete operations stage, children develop an internal sense of morality through the development of their will. Often in life, individuals experience simultaneous impulses to do that which they should and that which would give them pleasure; for example, "Should I do my homework or go to the ball game?" As the individual debates about the virtues of fulfilling the obligation versus the quest to fill a desire, the individual will create a personal "scale of values" that the individual will feel an obligation to follow. This value system is a permanent construct, though it can change over time as the individual develops further.

Individuals also form a sense of autonomy during the concrete operations stage. They do this by developing an internalized set of norms rather than automatically accepting these norms of others. However, their self-selected values and norms are most frequently based on those of the adults that the child holds in esteem.

Children also begin to recognize the intentions behind others' actions during the concrete operations stage. For example, if someone bumps them accidentally, they will not automatically assume a negative intent. As with other learning, children cannot learn this concept simply by having an adult explain it to them. They must learn this through their social interactions with peers. Additionally, children begin to consider intentions when determining whether a statement is a lie rather than assuming that every incorrect statement is a lie.

During this stage, children will also understand and regard punishment that matches the crime rather than simply accepting arbitrary punishment. For example, if a child does not put a toy away properly or treats the toy badly, an effective punishment would be to deny the right to play with the toy for the remainder of the day, rather than to deny the child dessert that evening.

## Formal Operations

The final stage is called formal operations; this *usually* becomes possible in adolescence as the individual's cognitive structures reach maturity. After this stage, there are no further cognitive structural improvements, although the system in place can become more sophisticated as the adolescent or adult develops additional schemata.

Formal operations are abstract and deal with the logic of the possible or the hypothetical. Science, philosophy, advanced mathematics, and logic represent formal operations at their most abstract and sophisticated level. Individuals begin to think in a way that reflects the scientific method of establishing a hypothesis, performing experiments, and drawing conclusions in a systematic way. Formal operations involve an awareness of cause and effect in solving problems. Further, the individual will be able to reason about a hypothesis that is believed to be untrue, or a false premise, and still arrive at a logical conclusion. For example, an instructor might begin a train of thought with a question such as, "Suppose that the sky is green . . ." with the students successfully solving the problem.

During the formal operations stage, individuals can deal effectively with all classes of problems dealing with the past, present, and future, including those about hypothetical situations and those presented in verbal form. Individuals also become capable of introspection and of thinking about their own thoughts and feelings as if they were objects. Lies during this stage are only perceived as such when the false information is delivered intentionally. The individual will avoid lying not to avoid punishment, but in order to get along with others.

During adolescence, an individual in the formal operations stage develops two affective characteristics. The first involves the development of idealistic feelings and the second involves the continued formation of personality. Adolescents are capable of reasoning at the same level as adults; however, they see what is most logical as ideal rather than including "real world" factors in their reasoning. Therefore, they become very idealistic rather than seeing the practical applications and solutions to problems. Adolescent idealism is related to adolescent egocentrism, both of which are developmentally normal and a direct result of the individual's adaptation to formal operations (Wadsworth, 1971). This egocentrism involves:

> The inability to differentiate between the adolescent's world and the "real" world. The adolescent is emboldened with an egocentric belief in the omnipotence of logical thought. Because the adolescent can think logically about the future and about hypothetical people and events, he feels that the world should submit itself to logical schemes rather than to systems of reality. (Wadsworth, 1971, p. 131)

As a direct result, the adolescent will often criticize various aspects of society, causing adults to view him as defiant, rebellious, and ungrateful. However, Piaget notes that this is developmentally normal (Wadsworth, 1971). Regarding adolescent idealism and egocentrism, there is a word of caution for parents, teachers, prevention professionals, and others who serve as role models to youth. Many caregivers smoke, drink, and use drugs, yet instruct youth not to do so. To the adolescent, this seems illogical and hypocritical. The adolescent will be compelled to argue logically that if caregivers, other adults, or peers engage in these behaviors, then there is no reason to avoid them personally. Prevention professionals and other role models for youth must be very careful to model desired youth behavior in order to avoid a moral and an idealistic conflict. This also helps us to see why youth who have peers who use substances are more likely to use substances themselves, as was noted in Chapter 2. Similarly, research also shows that youth who have a family history of substance abuse are more likely to abuse substances themselves.

As adolescents enter the real world—that is, establish careers and become contributing members of society—they will try to implement their lofty, idealistic dreams. They will then experience disequilibrium as they trip over real-world factors. This provokes adjustments in their assumptions about the world so that they become less idealistic and more realistic.

Additionally, the complete formation of the personality occurs after the individual achieves the capacity for formal operations. The development of the personality is less related to the individual's self and more related to the individual's role within society and the ability to fit in. When the individual enters the workforce, only then can the personality become fully developed. As mentioned above, the "rose-colored," logical, idealistic perspective of the world can then advance to a more reality-based perspective. At this point, the individual will learn to appreciate the logical and illogical complexities of the world.

Piaget described cognitive development as a process through which an individual's thinking becomes freed from dependence on immediate, concrete situations. In other words, the individual progresses from concrete operations to formal operations. However, several studies have concluded that within the American population, no more than half of all people experience formal operations (Ekind, 1962; Kohlberg & Mayer, 1972; Kuhn, Langer, Kohlberg, & Hann, 1977, as cited in Wadsworth, 1971). Most children attain concrete operations with or without attending school. However, the development of formal operations is related to attending school and to direct experience with learning. Social interaction also helps to provoke the development of formal operations, along with the development of intelligence, respectful relations, cooperation, will, personality, and healthy social adjustment. Social interaction plays a significant role in the development of formal operations because when children's thinking conflicts with the thinking of others, they begin to question their own egocentric thoughts. This causes disequilibrium and subsequently the quest for equilibrium. This helps to explain why peer-led prevention programs can have such a profound effect on participants. Children learn actively through socially interacting with their peers, evaluating their own thinking, and advancing their thoughts through accommodation, the development of new and improved schemata, and assimilation.

Motivation is also affected by the development of formal operations. No longer will a reward system alone, such as an offer of candy, motivate young people. Motivation becomes stimulated as the individual experiences disequilibrium while experiencing different points of view during social interactions. Individuals are also motivated by having an interest in the topic and by understanding its relevance to them. Individuals also enjoy facing the unknown and performing some detective work to reestablish equilibrium. Unknown and unpredictable factors add an element of surprise that fosters motivation.

Developing an understanding of the qualities associated with concrete and formal operations can be beneficial. These qualities offer insight into the cognitive abilities and limitations that individuals experience. The discussion below will offer practical tips for incorporating Piaget's theory into prevention work.

## Piaget's Theory Applied to Prevention Learning

There are numerous ways that caregivers, teachers, and prevention professionals can apply Piaget's theory when working with young people. One way is to help them to develop a capacity for formal operations. Another is to foster their moral development.

## From Concrete to Formal Operations

One of the goals of educating youth is to help them to develop the capacity for formal operations. This in turn will inspire academic success and prepare them for adulthood. In summary, Wadsworth (1971) offers the following guidelines for helping healthy children advance from concrete to formal operations within the parameters of Piaget's theory. The key to success is promoting disequilibrium among children. *This can never be accomplished through the use of didactic teaching.*

Children construct knowledge through exploration of their environment. Their actions may be physical, as when they manipulate objects; or mental, as when they ponder specific information. Learning must be based on active exploration. Children become motivated when they encounter disequilibrium. Prevention professionals should develop methods that encourage this cognitive conflict. To do so, allow children to explore their own interests in legitimate ways. Asking questions based on children's personal interests motivates their interest and helps them to reason.

Prevention professionals can structure unexpected experiences that motivate children to learn in order to provoke disequilibrium. Wadsworth (1978) described an experience where he learned through the use of surprise. When he was in elementary school, he and his classmates visited a whale grounded on the beach. The children looked at it, listened to it, touched it, and ran away when it opened its mouth. "From that day on we all knew exactly what a whale was" (p. 55, as cited in Wadsworth, 1971). Learning through surprising events can happen mentally, not just physically. Prevention professionals can accomplish this by posing a problem verbally which has a surprising resolution. As an example, a teacher could begin a story about a teenager who uses drugs three times and remains unharmed. The teacher can stop the story and engage in dialogue. The youth may conclude that the drug is not harmful. The teacher could then continue the story where the teenager becomes harmed as a result of further use of the drug. This outcome would be surprising based on the former logical conclusion that the youth held.

Social interaction is both a source for learning cooperation and for creating cognitive conflict, causing disequilibrium. Prevention professionals should provide legitimate opportunities for social interaction. Peer interactions are particularly important from the time a child enters school. Supporting research states that peer-led prevention programs can be more effective in persuading youth to avoid substance use.

Allowing children to function autonomously as they struggle with learning gives them the opportunity to learn how to self-regulate, control, and direct the self efficiently, effectively, and responsibly. Prevention professionals should let children learn in their own way, either through active manipulation of objects or through an active reasoning process. Engaging youth in interesting dialogues, instead of providing didactic lessons, can encourage the latter.

Helping youth to develop the capacity for formal operations will help them become free from the limitations of thinking only in terms of the concrete, present situation. By achieving formal operations, youth will be better prepared for academic success. Because academic failure is a research-based risk factor for substance abuse, reducing the risk for academic failure can be an effective prevention strategy.

Youth who struggle excessively to develop formal operations, half of whom may not, may experience academic failure or else find coping strategies that will help them succeed as much as possible. For example, some youth may resort to memorizing or cheating on tests instead of understanding the new information. Those who fail academically may learn to hate the information, hate learning in general, or hate themselves (Wadsworth, 1971). These students must have referrals to education specialists who can help them to develop the capacity for formal operations. Those who have learning disabilities, such as attention deficit disorder, must have early diagnosis and interventions from education specialists and other professionals as needed. Tutoring from prevention professionals without additional interventions may not be sufficient to assist those with learning challenges.

## Moral Development

In additional to offering tips to help youth develop cognitively, Wadsworth (1971) also offers tips for helping youth to develop moral reasoning and moral behavior based on an internalized value system. First, prevention professionals should assume mutual respect with youth in nonauthoritarian relationships while encouraging youth to resolve issues themselves. In addition, when disciplining youth is necessary, prevention professionals must base it on reciprocity. In other words, the punishment must "fit the crime." For example, the child who throws candy wrappers onto the playground can be asked to fill a bag with litter from the playground area.

In addition, encourage the development of affective autonomy, "the basis for what many call self-discipline because it is a guide for behavior selection that is grounded in one's constructed values and a sense of obligation to adhere to those values" (Wadsworth, 1971, p. 154). To do this, prevention professionals or peer leaders can pose questions about substance abuse that stimulate meaningful dialogue among peers. When peers share anti–substance use information, other youth will more readily question their own values, especially if they are favorable toward substance use. This creates disequilibrium, causing youth to struggle to achieve equilibrium in their own way. This will assist them in internalizing prevention messages into their value systems. Mentors can also provide a valuable resource for reaching youth with prevention messages and provoking this process.

Application of Piaget's theory helps youth to progress to formal operations and encourages moral development. However, Piaget's theory also offers important information that can help prevention professionals to communicate effectively with all clients based on their cognitive-developmental stage.

## Concrete and Formal Operations Applied to Communication

The concepts of concrete and formal operations are especially significant when developing communication strategies that will effectively reach listeners. Frequently, in a classroom where many students are transitioning into formal thought processes, teachers will assign a project where formal operations come into play. Some students will become stimulated by the intellectual challenge and rise to the occasion. However, many others will not be ready to move to the formal realm of thinking and will struggle, then fail at the assignment. In addition, many prevention professionals must develop prevention materials, press releases, and other messages to communicate with the community. This section will explore some of the lessons learned for creating prevention messages. These lessons specifically address the cognitive development of those receiving the messages.

## Communicating with Youth

Prevention messages are communicated in a variety of ways when working with youth. It is important to understand the cognitive-developmental stage of the children involved in order to communicate with them effectively. For example, during a prevention event at a local park, young people were offered a handout with a sketch of a face. The instructors asked the children to write 10 nice things about their personalities on the sketch. This prevention activity was intended to enhance self-esteem, *which is not a science-based approach to prevention,* but is still commonly practiced. However, this activity proved painful for those struggling with self-esteem issues, those who could not think of a single favorable adjective to describe themselves, let alone 10 of them.

Additionally, the children who were unable to create abstract concepts of themselves based on their cognitive development in the concrete stage struggled needlessly. The problem was compounded by the fact that there were large groups of children with only a few instructors and the instructors present did not personally know the youth. For this reason, the instructors were unqualified to suggest anything more than superficial compliments to the children to help them describe themselves. The adults did not actually know, for example, if each child was loyal, generous, or compassionate. If an assignment such as this is done with youth, teachers or prevention professionals must be very knowledgeable about the youth so that they encourage each child's development of abstract concepts. These concepts should be deduced collaboratively, between the children and others, to help them learn more efficiently. This will also help children to internalize their belief in the positive adjectives that describe them.

The use of media campaigns for sharing prevention-related messages has been popular and can be effective when used with other strategies. Through the years, media campaigns have helped to demonstrate effective communication strategies and also those that have been ineffective at reaching their intended audience.

## Lessons Learned through Media Messages

Through the use of media, prevention messages have been received by masses of people. Through trial and error in creating and analyzing the effects of these messages, the prevention field has learned some lessons regarding how to communicate effectively with the public about addiction issues. Some of these messages were largely ineffective in providing meaningful information. Other messages effectively reached the intended audience. Examples of ineffective and effective methods of creating messages follow. Learning from these examples can help prevention professionals develop prevention materials, press releases, and other messages for community members that will reach all members of the intended audience.

Some years ago, a popular public service announcement was aired frequently as a prevention tool for young people to warn against the danger of drug use. The announcement depicted an egg in a frying pan with the catchy slogan, "This is your brain on drugs." Although the announcement provoked a strong emotional appeal among adults, young children typically missed the point. Concrete responses to the message include, "That looks good. I think I am hungry" or "Fried eggs are greasy and gross."

More recently, a public service announcement depicted a young girl, perhaps eight or nine years old, who was noted to be inhaling chemicals, or "huffing." The announcement showed her experiencing the sensation of drowning as her bedroom suddenly became filled with water. The point of the announcement was that inhaling chemicals robbed her brain of oxygen. Although this creative and provocative message had strong appeal to older youth and adults, the young children targeted for this announcement did not have the capacity for formal operations needed to equate drug use with the real effect of the drug—oxygen deprivation, not drowning in water.

The frying pan was revisited in the world of public service announcements more recently, but this time the character and the target audience were in their early 20s. The warning in the announcement was about the harmful consequences in all aspects of life resulting from heroin use. The announcement depicted an attractive, young woman destroying everything in her kitchen with the frying pan. Because the target audience for this lesson is older, the opportunity is greater for viewers to interpret the message that heroin use is dangerous. When viewing this ad, young children will not necessarily make the assumption that heroin is destructive. They may think instead that women with frying pans are dangerous. However, older youth and adults who are more likely to become exposed to heroin were warned about the dangers in a way that provoked a memorable, emotional response of distaste for the drug.

Messages intended for concrete thinkers must be direct, logical, and situated in the present. Antismoking posters that warn against the dangers of bad breath and yellow teeth provide concrete, visible, short-term consequences of using tobacco. In contrast, those that warn against the future manifestations of lung disease and other health-related risks provide a challenge for the concrete thinker. Similarly, research demonstrates that depicting short-term consequences of tobacco use has greater efficacy than does showing long-term dangers in deterring youth from using tobacco.

Another public service announcement depicted a young adult who appears beautiful, but then removes her teeth, hair, and makeup, exposing someone physiologically devastated by the effects of using heroin. These are concrete, visible examples of how use can affect a person's appearance. In this way, concrete thinkers can understand the message that heroin use can cause damage to one's body and appearance. However, if a viewer knows someone who has used heroin and that person has not been physically ravished by the drug in observable ways, then the message loses its potency and becomes just another scare tactic.

Not all prevention professionals develop public service announcements. However, all must choose methods of communication that effectively reach clients. Analyzing information about these public service announcements demonstrates guidelines that can help prevention professionals select methods of communicating. This knowledge can be applied when communicating verbally to individuals or to groups of adults and/or youth. They can also be applied when developing prevention messages to be used with posters, flyers, and other prevention resources. Knowing that some prevention messages must reach individuals who think in varying ways can help prevention professionals to guide the development of prevention messages.

Before the section of applying Piaget's theory to prevention ends, there is still one more important aspect to explore. Specifically, the following offers a discussion about working with families with a history of substance abuse as it relates to concrete and formal operations.

## Working with Families with a History of Substance Abuse

Many prevention professionals work with high-risk youth and their families based on family history of the problem behavior; that is, substance abuse. Some family members may have fetal alcohol syndrome (FAS) or fetal drug effect (FDE). FAS, now the leading cause of mental retardation, is completely preventable. Prevention professionals working to reduce risk factors in the school domain and in the family domain will likely experience some individuals who are diagnosed with FAS or who may be affected but are not yet diagnosed.

The term "FAS" is not used to describe all individuals exposed to or affected by alcohol in utero. Instead, FAS describes those at the severe end of the continuum who have disabilities caused by maternal use of alcohol. FAS is diagnosed according to three criteria, all of which must be connected to knowing or strongly suspecting a history of maternal alcohol use. The first is prenatal and/or postnatal growth retardation, in which the infant is born at five pounds five ounces or less. The second is a pattern of facial anomalies and other physical abnormalities. These might include shortened eye slits that cause the appearance of a wide space between the eyes, a flattened mid-face, a thin upper lip, and a flat nasal bridge, among others. The third is central nervous system dysfunction, which may include diminished intelligence, learning disabilities, attention deficit disorder with or without hyperactivity, and many others. Those who are affected by FAS are incapable of formal operations, so they are not able to differentiate cause and effect. Therefore they will strive unsuccessfully to learn about the consequences of their actions. For this reason, prevention messages that warn of the dangerous consequences of substance use must be shared in concrete ways that depict immediate negative consequences.

Individuals with FDE may have similar characteristics to people with FAS. However, FDE has been difficult to diagnose and to describe. This is true because the effects of many drugs on the fetus must be studied. This is also complicated by the fact that many pregnant women who use drugs other than alcohol are polydrug abusers, making the distinct effects of any one drug difficult to determine. Children diagnosed with FAS or FDE will need special assistance from educators in order to succeed academically. A prevention program that attempts to reduce academic failure through tutoring will not be sufficient in meeting their needs.

Prevention professionals may also work with members of families who abuse or have abused alcohol. Chronic alcohol abuse can cause persistent cognitive impairment for abstinent alcoholics (National Institute on Alcohol Abuse and Alcoholism, 1989). For this reason, either family members who are abusing or have abused alcohol may experience cognitive impairment, even long after establishing sobriety. When communicating with the abuser's family members, it is important to remember that information must be relayed in a very concrete fashion. Examples used must be meaningful and immediately applicable to participants' real lives. In addition, many individuals are quick to accuse birth mothers of children with FAS. Understanding the complexities of the cycle of addiction can help prevention professionals empathize with the cause of FAS without judging others harshly and unproductively.

## Conclusion

Prevention professionals can encourage the development of formal operations in healthy youth by asking critical and relevant open-ended questions. Youth can be encouraged to challenge their current ways of regarding the world as they learn new and exciting information. The primary goal is to communicate important messages effectively. This sometimes requires extra effort in carefully constructing messages, asking for feedback from focus groups to ensure that messages are received effectively, and paraphrasing messages when necessary, to ensure effective communication.

# Medicine Wheel

*If a child hasn't been given spiritual values within the family setting, they have no familiarity with the values that are necessary for the just and peaceful functioning in society.*
—Eunice Baumann-Nelson, Ph.D., Penobscot (Native American Elder)

*When we are born, we start with a beautiful empty mind ready to be given our beliefs, attitudes, habits, and expectations. Most of our true learning comes from watching the actions of others. As we watch our family or relatives, whatever their actions and values are, so will be the children's values and acts. If we see our families living a just and peaceful way of life, so then will the children. If we see our family shouting, arguing and hateful, so will it be for the children. The cycle of life—baby, youth, adult, and Elder—is all connected. If the older ones have good values, it will be connected to the children*
—White Bison Website, page 1

White Bison's quote demonstrates the value that society's teachings play in raising healthy children. Additionally, healthy children with healthy values grow into healthy care-givers who again perpetuate a healthy developmental cycle. White Bison's quote also helps to demonstrate the storytelling quality of teaching through a **medicine wheel** approach. The medicine wheel concept is a valuable teaching tool because the stories can help us to see and understand things that are difficult to understand because they are ideas or abstract concepts instead of physical objects (Bopp, Bopp, Brown, & Lane, 1989). Often, stories of concrete, observable events in nature are used to represent symbolically the inner development of human beings and communities. The medicine wheel teachings can be applied to prevention work in a similar way to the developmental models discussed previously in this chapter.

Although most academic developmental models are linear, including those of Maslow, Erikson, and Piaget, the Native American concept of the medicine wheel symbolically demonstrates a nonlinear model of human development. This section will explore the ideas shared through a medicine wheel approach to generate an understanding of the concept of the medicine wheel. Next, the concepts will be explored as they relate to systems, including organizations, coalitions, and communities. Finally, bridges between the medicine wheel approach and the field of prevention will be suggested. The medicine wheel is shared with respect to those who have practiced this tradition through various Native American cultures.

## The Medicine Wheel Approach

Not all Native American people have a medicine wheel in their tradition. In addition, those who do have one do not all share the same medicine wheel. For that reason, the information provided is generalized in order to show that the medicine wheel offers symbols and stories as a way to instruct others about the values of life. This method of storytelling, sharing con-

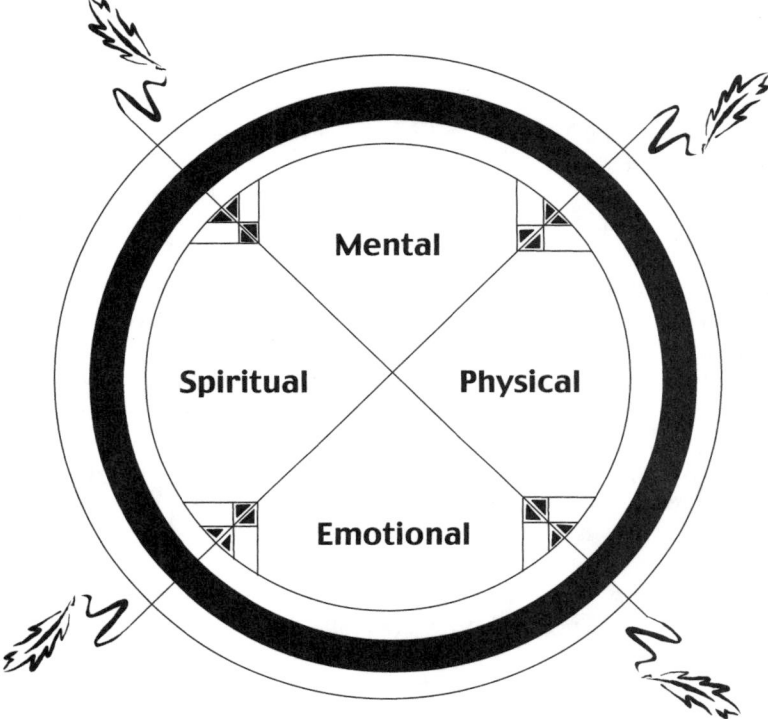

**FIGURE 6.2    Medicine Wheel.**    Reproduced with permission from *The Sacred Tree* by Four Worlds International Institute for Human and Community Development, published in the USA by Lotus Press, P.O. Box 325, Twin Lakes, WI 53181. Copyright © 1984. All rights reserved.

crete examples of abstract ideas, can be an effective way to communicate difficult concepts to clients. Prevention professionals who seek to advance their personal development can use the teachings of the medicine wheel to stimulate their own growth. In addition, prevention professionals can apply the teachings to their organizations and coalitions, in order to understand the developmental cycles that they also encounter.

The number four is sacred in many Native American traditions; thus the medicine wheel is divided into four sections, often called directions. Lessons that come from the medicine wheel generally have four dimensions or approaches. For example, the human being has four aspects: the physical, the emotional, the spiritual, and the mental. Many developmental models address physical, emotional, and mental development. Maslow's theory has implications for spiritual development. However, the medicine wheel directly incorporates spiritual development as equally important to the other aspects.

There are other examples of how the number four is used in the medicine wheel. The directions of the medicine wheel can also symbolically represent the time of day. Each day's journey begins in the east as the sun enters the sky. Then the sun moves to the south, to the west, and finally exits the sky to leave us without sunlight. The medicine wheel directions can also represent the time of the year. The east is the place of spring, the south of summer, the west of autumn, and the north of winter. The directions can also represent the development of individuals. The east is the direction of birth, the south of childhood, the west of adulthood. The north is the direction for the respected Elders. The four directions can also represent the four areas of emphasis in substance abuse fields, including prevention in the east, intervention in the south, treatment in the west, and recovery in the north.

Coyhis (n.d.) noted that the medicine wheel helps to teach and to share concepts about the Great Spirit's (or Creator's) system. Many teachings of the medicine wheel come from the wise Elders, who say that the Creator's system still exists today. The system includes both the seen (physical) world and the unseen (spiritual) world. The medicine wheel can help each individual to "see" them both.

The Creator's system and the teachings of the medicine wheel also contain principles, laws, and values that help individuals live in harmony. Organizations and communities living by these principles, laws, and values will also obtain harmony and positive results. Those who do not will experience chaos, fighting, injustice, and fault-finding (Coyhis, n.d.).

Each direction on the wheel (east, south, west, and north) offers lessons and gifts that help an individual to develop. Typically, animals, plants, herbs, and minerals are used to demonstrate developmental lessons in a storytelling fashion. The idea is to remain balanced at the center of the wheel while equally developing the physical, emotional, spiritual, and mental aspects of one's personality continuously throughout the life cycle. When individuals or communities become unbalanced, not living within the center of the teachings of the wheel, they suffer and even die. Addiction, violence, and other harmful consequences damage the individuals or communities (Coyhis, n.d.).

The medicine wheel also teaches us that all people are part of the same human family, regardless of race or ethnicity. The colors that symbolically represent all races are yellow, red, black, and white. The underlying principle of the medicine wheel is that everything on earth is interconnected and we can only understand something or someone if we understand how it is connected to everything else (Bopp, 1984; Coyhis, n.d.). Coyhis (n.d.) noted that because of this interconnectedness, "The honor of one is the honor of all; the pain of one is the pain of all." This is true of all systems, including families, schools, organizations, and communities. What is done to one creature on the earth has a profound affect on all other creatures. Learning this lesson can help individuals to treat others with respect.

Because all humans are interconnected, individuals are able to perceive the intent behind words and deeds. As an example, sometimes a person will smile and ask about someone's health while behaving as though she is late for an appointment, distractedly looking at her wristwatch. The other person will perceive that her health is not a priority in this conversation. As another example, a politician will make a grandiose gesture on behalf of the people, but everyone will perceive correctly that there is an ulterior motive and will suspect wrongdoing (Coyhis, n.d.). The medicine wheel teaches us that individuals have the capacity to intuit the spirit and intent behind words and deeds because all creatures are interconnected through the unseen world (Coyhis, n.d.). When people are out of harmony with the principles, laws, and values of the medicine wheel, they may demonstrate insincerity behind their words and deeds. Returning to the teachings of the medicine wheel can help them to return to harmony and joy.

---

BOX **6.1**

## The Gifts of the Medicine Wheel

Lessons and gifts from the east, the place of first light, spring, and birth, include:

- Warmth of spirit.
- Seeing complex situations clearly.
- Purity, trust, and hope.
- Unconditional love.
- Courage.
- Truthfulness.
- Guidance and leadership.
- Remaining in the present moment.

Lessons and gifts from the south, the place of summer and youth, include:

- Generosity, sensitivity, loyalty, compassion, and kindness.
- Healthy romantic love.
- Testing the physical body/self-control.
- Gifts of music and arts.
- Idealism and passionate involvement.
- Capacity to express feelings openly in ways respectful to others.

Lessons and gifts from the west, the place of autumn and adulthood, include:

- Dreams, prayer, and meditation.
- Perseverance when challenged.
- Balance between passionate loyalty and spiritual insight.
- Prayer and meditation.
- Use of personal, sacred objects.
- Life's meaning.
- Fasting, ceremony, self-knowledge, vision and sacrifice.

Lessons and gifts from the North, the place of winter and elders, include:

- Intellectual wisdom.
- Completing tasks that began as a vision.
- Detachment from hate, jealousy, desire, anger and fear.
- Ability to see the past, present and future as interrelated.

---

The specific concepts of the medicine wheel vary among Native peoples, including the gifts attributed to each position on the wheel. Bopp et al. (1984) offered an overview of some lessons and gifts connected to the developmental process. These are summarized in Box 6.1.

Bopp et al. (1984) noted that the lessons of each of the directions can be used to develop the unique potential within each human being. Each individual will perceive the teachings of the medicine wheel uniquely, because each human being is unique. Not only that, but the developmental process never ends because human potential is infinite.

The narrative given in Box 6.2 comes from *The Sacred Tree* (Bopp et al., 984) and helps to demonstrate the effectiveness of storytelling in the medicine wheel approach. The story helps to communicate multiple, complex ideas. By using animals and elements of the earth, abstract ideas concerning interpersonal growth of individuals can be viewed in concrete ways.

---

BOX **6.2**
## From *The Sacred Tree*

It is in the East of the medicine wheel that all journeys begin. When a path is new, it totally occupies our attention. Our sights are focused on the next few steps. One of the most important gifts to be acquired in the East is the capacity to focus our attention on the events of the present moment. As young children (the East is also the direction of childhood), we knew instinctively how to do this. When as children we watched a beautiful butterfly or examined any interesting new aspect of the world, we were completely absorbed by what we were doing. We were able to submerge our total awareness into that butterfly, that patch of ground, or that toy. The animal that many have used to symbolize this capacity is the mouse. Our little mouse sister does what she does with all of her tiny being.

Many people cannot do this. They are always looking to the future, or to the past, or inside, or far away, but seldom to the activity of the present moment. It is this capacity of being fully in the present moment that enables a person to accomplish physical tasks that require the alertness of all the senses and the complete giving of ourselves to what we are doing. Examples might include acquiring excellence in hunting, in craftsmanship such as fine beadwork, sewing, or woodwork, in the healing arts, in competitive sports or in the playing of a musical instrument. All of these require a merging of the person's total being with the activity at hand. This is the special gift of our little mouse sister. Learning to do this is the first stage in the development of volition (the power of the human will).

But like the mouse who is caught unaware by the owl because she is so absorbed in gathering seeds that she becomes oblivious to her own danger, a person who has learned this quality in the East must also learn to listen to inner warning signs that rumble like thunder or flash like lightning within us (a lesson of the West), and must have the foresightedness (a lesson of the North) to look at the overall picture (another lesson of the East) in order to ensure his own happiness and well-being.

A person who is too proud or insensitive to listen to others (a gift of the South) or who has never stood in the West of the medicine wheel and looked over to the East to see how vulnerable our little mouse sister really is—such a person may well be too filled with a false sense of his own greatness to be of assistance to the people.

It is no accident that (from one symbolic view) one of the humblest creatures (the mouse) and one of nobility (the eagle) are the twin teachers of the East. For greatness of spirit and humility are opposite sides of the same reality. The essence of true leadership is service to the people.

Indeed the essence of what it is to be a human being is to be found in service to others. This is the greatest of all the lessons of the medicine wheel. In a lifetime, most people must journey many times to the East to relearn this one lesson. (pp. 45–47)

*Source:* Reproduced with permission from *The Sacred Tree* by Four Worlds International Institute for Human and Community Development, published in the USA by Lotus Press, P.O. Box 325, Twin Lakes, WI 53181. Copyright © 1984. All rights reserved.

In the narrative in Box 6.2, Bopp et al. (1984) discussed the concept of volition, or will. Volition, "the force that helps us make decisions and then act to carry out those decisions," is a critical component in developing humans physically, emotionally, spiritually, and mentally (Bopp et al. 1984, p. 14). Bopp et al. (1984) outlined five steps that can help individuals develop their volition. First, focus attention on the matter at hand. Second, set goals. Third, initiate the action. Fourth, persevere as obstacles arise. Fifth, complete the action. Bopp et al. (1984) placed volition at the center of the medicine wheel, as this helps individuals to learn the teachings of the medicine wheel.

The medicine wheel concepts included above are not inclusive of all the teachings of the medicine wheel. However, they may help to develop an interest in exploring the teachings further in order to help prevention professionals develop interpersonally. The teachings can also be applied to systems, including organizations, coalitions, and communities. Some of these key teachings will be explored below.

***The Medicine Wheel for Systems.***    Coyhis (n.d.) noted, as told to him by the Elders, that the medicine wheel also has teachings that apply to systems. Systems, including organizations, coalitions, and communities, are constantly evolving. "That which is built is constantly being destroyed; that which is loose is being used to build new things" (Coyhis, n.d.). When a log cabin is left unattended, it will eventually crumble back into the earth and provide nourishment for the plants that will eventually grow there. The principle of constant evolution applies to systems as well as to objects. The following section explains the four laws of change for systems.

The first law that Coyhis (n.d.) mentioned notes that all *permanent and lasting* change comes from within the individual and then works its way into the system. Everything that one needs to know in order to make the change is already within each individual waiting to be discovered. Discovery can be accomplished only by living in accordance with the principles, laws, and values of the medicine wheel. When working in communities, the community members will already know the best course of action for their community. The prevention professional must ask them for their ideas instead of dictating the course of action, as noted in Chapter 5.

The second law notes that in order for a development to occur, it must be preceded by a vision. Individuals move toward that which they think about, whether the thought is healthy or not. In other words, thought manifests reality. For this reason, one must pay attention to the thoughts that emerge. In order to effect positive change, one must first create a vision of the benefits of the change. When a community is unhealthy, the first step to becoming healthy is to build a positive vision with all the community members, aligning each person with the vision.

The third law notes that a great learning must occur that includes all people within the system. Many times adults will gather in the community to talk about how youth are and what they need. They conclude, "someone needs to do something" about the problem they have identified. For example, they may say, "The youth drink too much and someone needs to stop them" (Coyhis, n.d.). This law tells us that all people must participate in the solution. If the youth should not drink, then the adults and Elders should not drink either. If the children should be respectful, then adults and Elders must treat the children with respect. Everyone in the community or system must be actively involved in the change if it is to take place.

The fourth law of change that Coyhis (n.d.) shared notes that communities or other systems must create a healing forest. The story of the healing forest involves a sick forest containing many sick trees. One tree is removed from the forest and planted temporarily in a healthy place. The tree is nurtured back to health and then replaced within the sick forest once again. However, the healthy tree cannot remain well in a sick forest and becomes sick again. So is it for humans. It is very difficult for healthy individuals to remain that way in an unhealthy environment. Nor can children develop in a healthy way within unhealthy families and communities. Communities must create support groups, solution groups, and healing circles in order to create and sustain healthy individuals within healthy systems.

The four laws of change are not applicable only to Native American communities. They can be applied to schools, prevention agencies, and other communities to promote changes at the individual and the systems level that will foster healthy development.

***Organizational Seasons of Development.***    In addition to the four laws of change, Coyhis (n.d.) discussed the four seasons of growth for organizations. Organizations will experience seasons, each lasting about a year, that will resemble spring, summer, autumn, and winter. These organizational seasons will be described to provide an understanding of how complex organizations are with regard to their development. Understanding the cyclical nature of organizations can help prevention professionals to accept potentially unsettling cycles of change.

Just as an oak tree will sprout new leaves in the spring, this is a season when the individuals within an organization will be full of energy, generating new ideas and separating from old ways that no longer work. During the summer, just as the leaves of the oak reach maturity and splendor, the members of the organization will solidify the plans initiated in the spring. The system will mature and the members will experience harmonious balance. Members of the organization will have fun at work and have a sense of goodness and perfection about the organization. During the autumn, the members of the organization will perceive that the organization is even more perfect than in the summer, just as the beautiful oak tree of the summer suddenly becomes full of brilliant, autumn color. Members of the organization will have a strong sense of belonging with the organization and with other members, perceiving that all is perfect.

As the cold wind blows the leaves off the oak tree, winter is a painful time for organizations as they shed old beliefs that no longer prove useful. This season involves uncomfortable work and the members will have a strong sense that something is wrong with the organization. Management will frequently serve as the scapegoat responsible for whatever is perceived to be wrong. Relationships within the organization suffer disharmony and many individuals have a sense of being burned out and will be unable to stay within the organization.

Winter is an intense time of reflection and introspection. Each individual within the organization must answer three questions: Why am I? Who am I? Where am I going? In other words, people will question why they are doing what they are doing and consider doing something else. They will wonder if it is time to create a new identity. They will wonder why they are restless. Individuals will have a sense of craziness as they explore the answers to these questions. Many people have a need to withdraw and isolate themselves from others and their peers will ask, "What is wrong?" However, the person in winter will not be able to identify exactly what it is that is wrong.

Each of the four seasons is valuable. Similarly, no one season is better than the others are. Organizations and individuals all experience the seasons, which do not necessarily match those of the physical environment. Although individuals in winter may feel nostalgic for the optimistic days of the other seasons, this shedding time is necessary for the growth of the organization. The winter can be spent letting go of systems and ways that no longer work effectively. Winter's contemplation also serves the purpose of helping to renew the energy of the group in preparation for spring's growth.

## The Medicine Wheel and Prevention

Only a few of the principles, laws, and values of the medicine wheel are covered in this chapter, since the teachings last a lifetime. However, prevention professionals who are interested in using the medicine wheel approach for personal reasons or when working with community members can view the suggested readings and references that conclude this chapter. Some suggestions for incorporating the medicine wheel teachings in prevention work follow.

Using the medicine wheel to teach children principles, laws, and values can help them to make healthy choices. Initiating dialogue with children about the teachings can help to stimulate the development of their internalized value system, as noted in the discussion of Piaget's theory. The principles can also be applied to adults, prevention agencies, and communities to help them develop in healthy ways.

Because the focus of the medicine wheel approach is to obtain balance between the physical, emotional, spiritual, and mental aspects of one's personality, this model can be useful when working with clients. For example, a person who intellectualizes all aspects of life without "feeling" what life has to offer may have emotional barriers to living life fully. Establishing meaningful friendships with mentors or other youth might help that person to "open up" emotionally. This in turn might encourage the formation of a well-rounded personality. Also, because of the spiritual component within this model, the medicine wheel might offer a valuable tool for prevention efforts in some faith-based communities, even outside of Native American communities.

Because all humans are interconnected, prevention professionals must ensure that services are provided with genuine enthusiasm and passion. If prevention professionals go through the motions of providing services dispassionately, then the clients will perceive the disinterest and will not bond to the prevention professional, to the prevention program, nor to the healthy beliefs and clear standards conveyed. When feeling overwhelmed, beyond harmony, and dispassionate about the prevention work to be done, prevention professionals can review and return to the principles, laws, and values of the medicine wheel to regain harmony, joy, appreciation, and a love of one's work.

Prevention program planners can apply the principles of change in programs by including all members of the community in forming the vision and in working within the community to create a healing forest. Prevention professionals can also demonstrate understanding and respect for the four seasons of their agencies and their colleagues as they evolve. Understanding that the wintertime of strife and disharmony is a naturally occurring phenomenon making way for innovative system changes can help to build a tolerance for the painful process.

## Conclusion

The medicine wheel's principles, laws, and values can be beneficial to prevention professionals who strive for interpersonal growth, balance, and harmony. The medicine wheel can also be a valuable resource when working with youth to explore difficult ideas or concepts. In addition, the teachings of the medicine wheel provide valuable insight into the organizational evolution that prevention agencies experience. In short, the holistic approach of the medicine wheel can serve individuals and communities in a variety of ways.

# Summary

To utilize human development theory in prevention program planning, first identify the target group that will be involved in the prevention program. Next, determine the developmental stages that participants are likely to be experiencing and learn about them. Then, select programs and strategies that are appropriate to that developmental stage. Specifically, always ensure that the teaching and learning methods, physical activities, tasks, and discussion topics are developmentally appropriate for the intended audience. Next, determine whether members of the group might be "stuck" at a particular stage. For example, some individuals may be dealing with safety needs within their environment, they may have difficulty trusting others, they may be on the threshold of developing formal operations, or they may respond to the world in an intellectual and completely unemotional way. Take action, through the use of other community resources if necessary, to help these individuals transcend their developmental barriers.

There may be many developmental theories that prove helpful when working with clients. Others may be of no benefit. Prevention professionals can select the theories to work with that are most beneficial in forming an understanding of clients' needs. Of course, using research-based prevention strategies and demonstrating cultural competence when working with clients are just as critical, as discussed in previous chapters.

Further, the use of human development theory can assist in identifying problems among individuals that cannot be handled through the efforts of prevention professionals alone. Remember that for ethical reasons, prevention professionals must identify and examine potential weaknesses when providing services to clients and then make the necessary accommodations for the benefit of the client. Referral to a professional counselor may be needed for some individuals. Maintaining ties to community resources can assist prevention professionals in linking youth with cost-effective services from other agencies. Just as prevention professionals cannot treat drug addiction without specialized training in the field of addiction, prevention professionals cannot serve as professional counselors without specialized training.

# KEY TERMS

abstract thought
accommodation
affective development
assimilation
B-cognition
B-love
basic needs
concrete operations stage
concrete thought

D-cognition
D-love
disequilibrium
equilibration
equilibrium
formal operations stage
generativity
growth needs
identity diffusion

logical-mathematical
  knowledge
medicine wheel
peak experience
physical knowledge
schema (schemata)
self-actualization
sensory-motor stage
social knowledge

# DISCUSSION QUESTIONS

1. Consider your own developmental process. List one change you have gone through in each of the following categories and write down how old you were when the change happened.

   - Physical change
   - Family change
   - Intellectual change
   - Social change

   - Emotional change
   - Spiritual change
   - Financial change

   - Career change
   - Philosophical change
   - Political change

   After reviewing your responses, consider the following questions:

   - Did your changes seem to occur around certain ages or were they spaced out across your lifetime?
   - Do you think major changes occur more at certain ages than at others?
   - What implications does this have for prevention strategies?

2. Compare Piaget's concept of concrete and formal operations with Maslow's concept of concrete and abstract thought. How are they similar? How are they different? Are there value judgments inherent in either view? How do these perceptions of concrete and abstract thinking match the mouse's experience in the excerpt from *The Sacred Tree*?

3. Look for similarities that exist among the theories. Do these similarities help to reinforce the importance of concepts that can be applied to prevention?

4. Which of these theories addresses the issue of caregivers, teachers, prevention professionals, or other adults modeling behavior that they expect from youth? Specifically, which ones suggest that adults should not use substances in the presence of youth? What is your opinion about this?

## A P P L I C A T I O N   E X E R C I S E

1. Think of a prevention program that you have worked with, are currently working with, or are otherwise familiar with. Identify the developmental stage of the target population and think of ways to make the program more developmentally appropriate using ideas from all the developmental theories presented in this chapter. If you do not have direct experience with a program, consider the following: The Parenting Plus Program offers parents workshops to help them develop effective parenting skills. Their children, ages 7 to 12 years, who are identified by their teachers as at risk for low academic achievement, attend information sessions on alcohol, tobacco, and other drugs. What developmental issues would you identify as relevant for the adult participants? For the children? What recommendations would you make to ensure that the program is appropriate developmentally?

## S U G G E S T E D   R E A D I N G S

Bear, S., Wind, W., & Milligan, C. (1992). *Dancing with the wheel: The medicine wheel workbook.* New York: Simon and Schuster.

Bopp, J., Bopp, M., Brown, L., & Lane, P. Jr. (1984). *The sacred tree: Reflections on Native American spirituality.* Twin Lakes, WI: Lotus Light Publications.

Kleinfeld, J., & Wescott, S. (Eds.). (1993). *Fantastic Antone succeeds! Experiences in educating children with fetal alcohol syndrome.* Fairbanks: University of Alaska Press.

Lefrançois, G. R. (1999). *The lifespan* (6th ed.). Belmont, CA: Wadsworth Publishing.

Maslow, A. H. (1968). *Toward a psychology of being* (3rd ed.). New York: John Wiley and Sons.

Wallen, J. (1993). *Addiction in human development: Developmental perspectives on addiction and recovery.* Binghamton, NY: The Haworth Press.

## R E F E R E N C E S

Bopp, J., Bopp, M., Brown, L., & Lane, P. Jr. (1984). *The sacred tree: Reflections on Native American spirituality.* Twin Lakes, WI: Lotus Light Publications.

Coyhis, D. (n.d.). *Teachings of the medicine wheel for personal growth.* (Audio Cassette Recording). Colorado Springs, CO: Coyhis Publishing.

Elkind, D. (1962). Quantity conceptions in college students. *Journal of Social Psychology, 57,* 459–465.

Erikson, E. H. (1950). *Childhood and society.* New York: W. W. Norton.

Erikson, E. H. (1959). Identity and the life cycle: Selected papers. *Psychological Issue Monograph* Series I (No. 1). New York: International Universities Press.

Erikson, E. H. (1980). *Themes of work and love in adulthood.* Cambridge, MA: Harvard University Press.

Golas, T. (1971). *The lazy man's guide to enlightenment.* Redway, CA: Bantam Books.

Goldstein, K. (1934). *The organism.* New York: American Book Company.

Kohlberg, L., & Mayer, R. (1972, November). Development as the aim of education. *Harvard Educational Review, 42*(4), 449–496.

Kuhn, D., Langer, J., Kohlberg, L., & Hahn, N. S. (1997). The development of formal operations in logical and moral judgment. *Genetic Psychology Monographs, 95,* 97–188.

Maslow, A. H. (1968). *Toward a psychology of being.* (3rd ed.). New York: John Wiley and Sons.

National Institute on Alcohol Abuse and Alcoholism (NIAAA). (1989). Alcohol and cognition. *Alcohol Alert, 4,* 14.

Piaget, J. (1963). *Problems of the social psychology of childhood.* (T. Brown and M. Gribetz, Trans.). Originally published in *Traité de sociologie* [Treaty of Sociology] (G. Gurvitch, ed.), pp. 229–254. Paris: Presses Universitaires de France [Universities of France Press].

Wadsworth, B. J. (1971). *Piaget's theory of cognitive and affective development: Foundations of constructivism* (5th ed.). White Plains, NY: Longman.

Wadsworth, B. J. (1978). *Piaget for the classroom teacher.* White Plains, NY: Longman.

White Bison Website. *Elder's Meditation.* Retreived August 17, 2001 from the World Wide Web: http://www.whitebison.org/usercgi/whtbison/med.cgi.

# 7 The Media and Prevention

The media plays an important role in substance abuse prevention, either by competing against or complementing prevention messages. The effects of advertising and other media messages can have a tremendous impact on youth's attitudes and behaviors toward alcohol, tobacco, and other drugs. Each year brewers and distributors spend millions of dollars on advertising, which includes sponsoring college events, concerts, sports, cultural events, and other special events. Between 1995 and 1999, in the United States the beer industry alone spent $3.74 billion on advertising (Center for Science in the Public Interest, 2000). And in 1999, cigarette manufacturers spent $8.24 billion on advertising and promotions (Federal Trade Commission, 2001) in the United States. The advertising and sponsoring of events help persuade youth and adults alike that alcohol and tobacco are normal and commonly used within our culture. However, the media can also be a powerful ally to prevention professionals. In this chapter, three tools that prevention professionals can use to advance prevention efforts in their communities will be discussed. These tools include media advocacy, media literacy, and social marketing. Although all three are related to the media, they are distinct prevention strategies.

## Media Advocacy

**Media advocacy** is the strategic use of media to advance a social or public policy initiative (Center for Substance Abuse Prevention [CSAP], 1993). In the past, the media has been used by prevention and health professionals to build awareness about the dangers of individual behavior related to the use of alcohol, tobacco, and other drugs (ATOD). Media advocacy shifts the focus from the individual to society's laws, norms, and policies. It is based on the public health perspective, described in Chapter 4. The public health model calls for communities to implement strategies that target the individual, the drug itself, and the environment. Media advocacy targets changes in the environment.

Media advocacy can help shape the debate around public policy. The goal of media advocacy is not only to obtain media coverage but to effect changes in policy. Media advocacy moves the focus away from individual behaviors to policies that impact the environment where individuals make decisions. Community groups can use media advocacy to communicate their stories in their own words for the purpose of implementing changes in tax laws, school rules, industry promotional practices, community norms, and other issues associated with substance abuse. For example, Mothers Against Drunk Driving (MADD) utilizes the media to tell their story and gain support for Drinking While Intoxicated (DWI) laws. Some characteristics of policy advocacy include:

> Advocacy assumes that people have rights, and those rights are enforceable; advocacy works when focused on something specific; advocacy is chiefly concerned with rights and benefits to which someone or some community is already entitled; and policy advocacy is concerned with ensuring that institutions work the way they should. (Amidei, 1991, p. 6)

In terms of alcohol, tobacco, and other drugs, youth have a right to have the community protect them from unhealthy products and unfair marketing tactics that target them. In turn, the community has an obligation to protect youth. Additionally, youth have a right to live in a safe environment free from the crime and violence that is often derived from drug dealing and high alcohol outlet density. For example, across the nation advocates have been instrumental in passing clean indoor air ordinances to protect the rights of citizens to eat, work, and play in smoke-free environments. Legislators and policymakers enacted most of these policies partly because of media advocacy.

In a case study that will be discussed later in the chapter, advocates working to restrict alcohol and tobacco advertising argued that their community was unfairly targeted by those industries. They compared the number of store-front advertisements and billboards in their neighborhood to the number of ads in a nearby affluent community and fought for the same right—to live in an environment free from the eyesore of billboards that exploited their culture and targeted young people.

Another example of media advocacy is when, in 1961, advocates urged President John F. Kennedy to establish a commission for the study of the health consequences of smoking, which led to the 1964 Surgeon General's report on smoking and health. The report led to a multitude of policies and activities, such as a ban on cigarette broadcast advertising in 1971.

Media advocacy can also be used to change unethical practices related to social norms. The following excerpt illustrates this point:

> A few years ago community members were concerned about an announcement at an Oakland Athletics baseball game about a promotion for Bud Lite at a future game. Small flashlights with Bud Lite inscribed on them would be given away to anyone who came to the ballpark who was 16 years of age or older, although the legal drinking age is 21. Community members decided to challenge Anheuser-Busch for promoting this particular product to underage youth through the use of a novelty item—Bud Lite flashlights. Using contacts with the media, they raised public concern about the beer promotion and Anheuser-Busch canceled its planned giveaway.
>
> This is one way of focusing on alcohol policy through the media in a way that contrasts with the traditional focus on behavior change. It focused public attention on the policy issues. The question was, shouldn't the alcohol industry know when to say "when" in their efforts to promote alcohol to underage youth? (Center for Substance Abuse Prevention [CSAP], 1993, p. 79)

## Skills to Advocate in the Media

Media advocacy relies on building coalitions and organizing communities and is based on the premise that people can use their knowledge, skills, and resources to create positive changes in society. By using specific skills to advocate using the media, community prevention providers can offer reporters interesting stories and information to advance prevention issues further. According to Wallack, Woodruff, Dorfman, and Diaz (1999) those skills include having a strategy, framing the issue, knowing the research, and gaining access to media outlets.

## Having a Strategy

When groups come together to address prevention policy issues, it is important that they have a common goal and focus activities on specific tasks they want to accomplish and policies they want to change. When community members decide to make a change in a policy, it is important that they have a strategy. Media advocacy includes the "strategic use of media" (CSAP, 1993, p. 79). Having a media advocacy strategy can assist organizers is allocating resources. The answer to the following questions can help advocates form a media advocacy strategy (Dorfman, 1996; Wallack, Woodruff, Dorfman, & Diaz, 1999):

- What is the problem?
- What is the solution or policy approach?
- Who has the power to make it happen?
- Who must me mobilized?
- What message will be most effective in persuading those with power to act?

Knowing exactly what the problem is will help advocates develop a solution. The way in which a problem is worded can have an effect on what the solution will be. Advocates are usually knowledgeable about the problem but it is important to break it down into manageable pieces. For instance, the problem might be binge drinking (five or more drinks in one sitting) by college students. In this example, if the problem is that college students do not know about the harmful effects of binge drinking, then the solution would be to provide them with information about the effects of binge drinking. The problem may also be that there are not enough alcohol-free activities. In this case, the solution would be to offer alcohol-free activities. These are the types of strategies that are usually recommended.

However, in terms of advocacy, the problem may be addressed by changing characteristics in the environment that contribute to the binge drinking. For example, the solution might be a policy banning happy hours and/or enforcing underage drinking laws. When forming a media advocacy strategy, an advocate should spend his time and energy describing the exact nature of the solution in clear and concise terms. Calling for specific steps to eradicate the problem is more interesting, effective, and further promotes the goal of solving the problem rather than simply talking about it or its complexity.

The people who have the power to make the solution in this example—merchants, representatives, city council members, county commissioners, and law enforcement or nonconventional community leaders—may have the power to make the policy change that is needed. Although society usually blames the person with the problem and places responsibility on her or him to solve it, advocates must address the dilemmas in terms of what society can do about the problem. This calls for addressing key people that have the power to make changes in the environment which will benefit the entire community.

Media advocacy can be very time- and cost-effective compared to prevention approaches that focus on the individual. For instance, college administrators could create a curriculum to teach students about the harmful effects of binge drinking, have speakers address the topic in classes, teach refusal and decision-making skills, and provide alcohol-free activities—which would take a lot of time, energy, and money. In terms of advocacy, prevention professionals can target the regulatory body to limit the hours of alcohol sales, restrict reduced product pricing of alcohol, or limit the number of alcohol outlets close to the campus. These approaches would impact large numbers of people and would ultimately cost less than the other strategies described.

Media advocates need to formulate the answers to the questions listed earlier (the questions that can help advocates form a media advocacy strategy), and be able to discuss them with reporters in a clear and succinct manner. The answers to these questions should be strategic and applicable immediately. It is important that media advocates be specific about the outcomes they want to see, such as a policy banning cigarette sales through vending machines, a policy banning alcohol billboard advertising, a policy limiting the hours of alcohol sales or locations of alcohol sales, or a policy mandating server training.

Effective media advocacy focuses on establishing a long-term social movement, not just short-term policy goals, in order to tackle influential commercial interests (Wallack, Dorfman, Jernigan, & Themba, 1993). Building a broad-based, representative, and united collaborative will establish a sense of community and empowerment, which are necessary in order to battle large corporate interests that will not go away after a coalition victory focused on a short-term accomplishment. To do so, the policy initiative must come from within the community. In order to achieve this, it is important to involve parents, youth, community-based and faith-based organizations, individuals, and groups from all sectors of the community. Allies can include health organizations, researchers, members of the media, businesses, authorities in the field, all cultural and ethnic groups, and other key leaders or institutions.

After advocates identify the specific problem and determine the solution, they find out who has the power to resolve the problem. Media messages do not need to target everyone in the community—only those that have the ability to make the policy change. Next, the message must be developed. Advocates should consider what arguments will be most likely to appeal to those with power to make the changes. For example, they may be receptive to arguments about the health and safety of community members, or they may need to become aware that there is a demand from the community to take action, or they may want to hear about other communities that have had success with a similar strategy. Also, advocates must determine whether the message may be more effective coming from a parent, a student, or an expert in the field. Credibility of the messenger is very important. Finally, advocates must determine the best media channel through which the message can reach the target audience. Advocates can write an editorial, write a letter to the editor, or generate an investigative report (Wallack, Woodruff, Dorfman, & Diaz, 1999; Wilbur & Stewart, n.d.).

## Framing the Issue

An additional skill necessary to implement media advocacy successfully is being able to frame an issue. Framing has to do with the information that is included in the story and the elements that are left out. Since media advocacy is about changing the environment, it is important always to frame the issue in a way that demonstrates the policies that need to be adopted in order to provide a healthy environment for all individuals. Advocates should keep the focus on the policies rather than on individual behavior. Something as simple as the language used can help frame an issue. For example, drinking is an individual behavior but alcohol is a product, and its harmful effects are a societal problem. In this example, the language lays the groundwork for a policy issue. In terms of a solution to a possible problem, framing becomes important, because the word "drinking" will elicit an individual change, while use of the word "alcohol" lays the groundwork for policies to restrict its sale or other preventative strategies. Understandably, this can be difficult since most news media reinforces individualism. Both sides—policy advocates and industry proponents-will attempt to frame the issue in a way that seems rational. For example, when prevention professionals oppose the alcohol and tobacco advertising practices for unethically marketing to youth and vulnerable populations, they frames the issue by discussing individual responsibility or First Amendment rights to free speech. Further, the alcohol industry not only shifts the focus from its marketing techniques, but it moves the attention to their positive contributions of supporting sporting events, minority organizations, charities, scholarships, and other favorable endeavors (Wallack et al., 1999).

The way in which an issue is framed helps the public to determine who is responsible for a problem as well as what can be done to solve it. Most news events frame stories in such a way that individual responsibility is identified as the solution to a problem. Advocates must work harder to present information that makes the audience consider broader factors, making a solution society's responsibility. Advocates can help frame a story by providing statements, metaphors, and information that focus on institutional responsibility and social accountability (Wallack et al., 1993).

## Knowing the Research

A third skill that media advocates need is knowledge of the current facts and figures about the problem that is being addressed, the populations most affected, and the variables in the environment that could impact the problem. Also, advocates should be familiar with the research documenting how the proposed solution has proven effective in other communities and be able to discuss the research implications for alcohol, tobacco, and other drug policies. For example, a community may seek to increase alcohol or tobacco taxes. Advocates should know the research, which documents the impact of this strategy. Or a community may seek to restrict advertising or promotional practices. In this case advocates should be able to articulate clearly the effects of advertising on youth. It is also important to document what the community need truly is. For example, a community may want to reduce the hours of alcohol sales, but after completing a thorough planning process, described in Chapter 3, they may find that their resources might be better spent in limiting the number of alcohol licenses or the outlet density rate.

Statistical data can be dry and boring; however, using the information creatively can be an effective strategy for advocacy. By using statistics creatively, advocates can capture the attention of their audience. The following example illustrates the point: "12 million U.S. college students annually consume over 430 million gallons of alcoholic beverages" (CSAP, 1993, p. 80). Although this is true, it doesn't mean much to the general public. It is hard to figure out whether this is too much or whether this is normal. Another way to present the information is: "The total alcohol consumption of college students exceeds the volume of an Olympic-size swimming pool for every one of the 3,500 colleges and universities in the United States" (CSAP, 1993, p. 80). This statement is more likely to impress the audience. It is easy for people to imagine all those pools filled with alcohol. This also provokes people to wonder what is being done about it or what could be done about it. Consequently, it is valuable for media advocates to distribute data and statistics in creative ways.

Another reason why it is important for media advocates to have knowledge of research, statistics, and facts is that the media is more likely to contact sources they know to have credible and factual information. If advocates are knowledgeable, credible, and have access to useful information, over time media advocates can build relationships with journalists.

However, in addition to knowing the facts and understanding the research, prevention media advocates also need to research how the media operates. By researching the practices of the local media, making phone calls, and developing relationships, advocates can learn which reporters are concerned with the issues surrounding alcohol, tobacco, and other drugs. Advocates should learn the names of relevant news editors and submit news releases to specific people. Advocates should know how the media prefers to receive information.

## Gaining Access to Media Outlets

Gaining access to the media is a crucial skill for media advocates. Media advocates need to monitor the media in order to determine whether and how an issue is being covered and when is the best time to contact the media. The media should be observed to find out what are the main themes and arguments regarding the issue (e.g., enforcement of underage drinking laws, increasing taxes, limiting alcohol advertising, etc.), who appears as the spokesperson, what solutions are presented, who is named as being able to solve the problem, and what perspectives or facts could improve the case for the advocate's side. Also monitoring the media will provide information about which reporters cover health and substance abuse issues, who the target audience is for the media outlet, which feature columns or television talk shows could provide more in-depth coverage (i.e., local talk shows or specific sections of the newspaper), and which newspapers are likely to be sympathetic to substance abuse prevention issues. Further, monitoring the media can assist in compiling an inventory of media outlets to be used by the media advocate, depending on the strategy and goals (Wallack et al., 1999).

Media advocates must learn the best methods for contacting members of each media outlet. Contact may be made through news release, press conference, letter to the editor, guest editorials, holding a newsworthy event, writing an op-ed piece, or calling an individual reporter to build interest in a story since they are often looking for ideas. News releases can be used to announce a milestone, an anniversary, or a seasonal event but should not be overused. News releases should be short, to the point, and include all relevant details such as contact information, speakers, date, time, and location. Media advocates should always follow up after sending a news release to ensure receipt and answer additional questions.

Advocates can organize letter-writing campaigns and send them to the newspaper editors. One point per letter is better than presenting many arguments. Press conferences should be used cautiously. If the information is not newsworthy, the media may not attend future press conferences held. Press conferences should be held only if there is significant, dramatic, or controversial news to announce. The media always wants a good photo opportunity; imagination and creativity can help advocates get the media to their event. For example, in an effort to restrict alcohol and tobacco billboards, a group of youth organized a march on a Mexican holiday to honor the dead. The youth carried frogs, representing the Budweiser frogs, in coffins and skeletons with cigarettes and beer bottles in their mouths. They criticized the alcohol and tobacco companies for the death their products cause.

Op-ed pieces usually appear opposite the editorial page and feature articles or columns that present personal and often contrasting viewpoints and are generally more in depth. Although they are longer than a letter, the piece should still be kept simple with no more than three to four main points.

Another way to make contact with the media is to develop relationships with journalists by creating a media list and sending an introductory letter to let them know the issues for which you can serve as a resource. Also, advocates can send complimentary letters to reporters about a well-presented story. It takes patience and perseverance, but gaining access to the media can be done.

Advocates should prepare for an interview with the media by developing two to three main points and several key phrases that clearly communicate the argument. During the interview the points should be made regardless of the questions that are asked by the reporters. It is also important to avoid jargon, acronyms, and other technical data that will obscure the message. Advocates should anticipate questions and practice answering them with other colleagues who can provide feedback. Most importantly, if advocates do not know the answer to a question, they should be honest and offer to find out the correct answer (Wilbur & Stewart, n.d.).

Rural residents may also follow these tips for gaining access to the media. In some instances advocates in rural areas may need to get creative in terms of reaching people through the media. Some rural towns have colleges that have public access television, which can be used by the community. Also, advocates can use school newspapers or community weekly or monthly newspapers, and radio. Oftentimes, small communities read newspapers and watch television stations from nearby bigger cities. Advocates can use these media outlets. Interpersonal and informal communication can also be an effective way for advocates in rural areas to communicate their message.

Although it takes time, media advocates can build credibility and eventually the media will contact them when stories about alcohol, tobacco, and other drugs arise. By using contacts with media editors and reporters, advocates can create public interest in changing the alcohol and tobacco industry's marketing practices, tax laws, law enforcement practices, labeling laws, school rules, workplace policies, healthcare policies, community norms, and other factors that may contribute to youth alcohol, tobacco, and other drug use.

**TABLE 7.1     Gaining Access to the Media**

| Method | Tip |
| --- | --- |
| Monitor the media | a. Determine how an issue is being covered. |
| | b. Observe main themes and arguments. |
| | c. Determine who appears as the spokesperson, what solutions are being presented, who is named as the problem solver, what facts could improve the case for the advocate's side. |
| | d. Determine which reporters cover what issue. |
| | e. Determine who the target audience is for what media outlet. |
| | f. Determine which media could provide more in-depth coverage on an issue. |
| | g. Determine which media is more likely to be sympathetic to the advocate's issue. |
| Contact the media members | a. News releases (short, to the point, include all relevant information, and follow up with a phone call). |
| | b. Press conference (use cautiously, event should be newsworthy, dramatic, significant, or controversial news to announce). |
| | c. Letter to the editor (make 1 point per letter). |
| | d. Holding a newsworthy event (provide a good photo opportunity for the news). |
| | e. Writing an op-ed piece or guest editorial (simple with no more than 3 to 4 main points). |
| | f. Calling an individual reporter (send an introductory letter about the issue(s) for which you can be a resource). |
| | g. Develop relationships with journalist (send complimentary letters to reporters about a well-presented story). |
| Conduct interviews | a. Develop 2 to 3 main points. |
| | b. Develop several key phrases. |
| | c. State points and phrases regardless of questions. |
| | d. Avoid jargon and acronyms. |
| | e. Anticipate questions and practice answering them. |
| | f. Be honest. |

## Applying the Skills of Media Advocacy

In theory, the skills to advocate in the media may seem complex or unclear. The following is a summary of a case study entitled *Chasing the Camels and Frogs out of Los Angeles* (Gallegos, 1999), which documents how the skills of media advocacy were applied to effect a policy change.

***Having a Strategy.***    Residents of Los Angeles were tired of their community being the alcohol and tobacco industry's paradise. Billboards covered the landscape of almost all parts of Los Angeles County. Holiday celebrations and sporting events seemed always to be sponsored by alcohol and tobacco companies. Popular entertainers and sports figures openly endorsed and glamorized alcohol and tobacco consumption. Community members noticed that cultural symbols, kid-friendly images, ethnic minority entertainers, and advertisements in Spanish, Korean, and hip-hop slang, were all being used to target many cultural and ethnic groups, including children in their community. The community decided to do something about it. In 1997, the Los Angeles County campaign to restrict alcohol and tobacco billboards and storefront advertising was initiated by the Los Angeles County Alcohol, Tobacco, and Drug Policy Coalition, a multiracial coalition of more than 60 organizations. The 15 Los Angeles City Council members became the target of the coalition's effort—they had the power to enact the ordinance.

The coalition not only wanted to pass the ordinance restricting billboard and storefront advertising. Most importantly, it also wanted to establish a countywide, multiracial, multisector movement that would continue to work toward creating a healthy environment and build a social movement that could oppose the powerful alcohol and tobacco companies. Although passing the ordinance was their goal, they knew that would only be the first step in protecting youth from the impact of alcohol and tobacco advertising. Initially the coalition focused on developing a strategy. The strategy included the following goals: "getting the right players at the table; developing a vision and setting clear goals and objectives; creating a winning message; identifying the core constituency and key allies; focusing the target and assessing the opposition; and utilizing creative tactics" (Gallegos, 1999, p. 4). The coalition members knew the key was to develop a consistent message through consensus (B. Gallegos, personal communication, July 5, 2001).

***Framing the Issue.***    Although there were many arguments that could be made to support the ordinance, such as the degrading images of women on the advertisement or that the restrictions could help people in recovery from addiction, the campaign focused on the issue of overconcentration of alcohol and tobacco billboards in low-income, minority communities, compared with the few billboards in the nearby affluent communities, and on protecting youth from their images. They also knew the opposition would focus on the First Amendment issue of free speech, blaming parents for underage drinking, and arguing that advertising had no impact on youth behavior. The coalition mobilized youth to tell policy makers about the advertisements they saw on their way to school every day, the appealing messages encouraging them to smoke and drink, and the large numbers of advertisements they saw in their neighborhoods. Parents also spoke to council members and told policy makers that they do talk with their children about not smoking and drinking but that it was so difficult to compete with the glamorous advertisement messages their kids were receiving outside of the home. Coalition experts educated the council members about the legality of restricting alcohol and tobacco advertising.

***Knowing the Research.***     The coalition gathered research about the community. They provided fact sheets to the council members and the media outlining facts such as the average age that a child starts smoking and that internal tobacco company papers demonstrated they research and target youth; they also provided research demonstrating that youth who are exposed to more alcohol advertising are more likely to hold favorable attitudes toward alcohol than those who are exposed to less alcohol advertising, and statistics that documented the percentage of underage violent offenders that were under the influence of alcohol at the time they committed their crimes; and research documenting that alcohol was the leading cause of death or injury among youth ages 15 to 24. The coalition also used studies, research, and community surveys documenting the problems associated with alcohol and tobacco billboard advertising to assist the city planning team that drafted the ordinance.

Parents and youth surveyed the number of alcohol and tobacco billboards in their neighborhoods and near their schools and found a disproportionate number of billboards and store-front advertisements in communities of color. A petition was circulated in support for the ordinance and the coalition eventually generated several thousand signatures. These creative ways to gather data proved to the city council that there was indeed a problem, that there was support for the ordinance, and that community members were mobilized to resolve the problem.

***Gaining Access to Media Outlets.***     The alcohol and tobacco industries had been sponsoring cultural events for decades in Los Angeles in order to promote their product and the coalition used their own strategy against them. Several of the coalition's member organizations planned a march on "El Dia de los Muertos," a Mexican holiday to honor the dead. Press releases were sent and follow-up calls were made to the media. The media interviewed the youth who spoke about the importance of honoring the dead and criticized the alcohol and tobacco industries for the deaths their products cause. The youth called for city council members to pass the ordinance restricting alcohol and tobacco billboards.

On days of important council hearing meetings or subcommittee meetings, the coalition organized press conferences on the steps of City Hall (B. Gallegos, personal communication, July 5, 2001). Youth and parents always addressed the media about the importance of passing the ordinance and the problems of alcohol and tobacco billboard advertisements in their communities. The powerful images of youth, parents, and community members of many ethnic groups speaking with one voice to make a political change were a great way to gain further support from community members and to show the city council the importance of passing the ordinance.

***Conclusion.***     In September 1998, the Los Angeles City Council passed the ordinance to restrict alcohol and tobacco billboard and storefront advertising. The measure took effect in October 1999. The coalition continues to work with the Los Angeles City Department of Building and Safety and the Los Angeles Unified School District to ensure that it is properly enforced. They continue to work to improve substance abuse issues and "to address the race and class inequalities that underlie many of the alcohol, drug, and tobacco problems in Los Angeles, and to create an empowered citizenry that can develop its own safe and healthy neighborhoods" (Gallegos, 1999, p. 15).

In 2001, the United States Supreme Court agreed to hear a case brought by tobacco companies regarding limits on tobacco advertising in the State of Massachusetts. The Massachusetts law banned outdoor cigarette advertising within 1,000 feet of any elementary or secondary school or public playgrounds (this ordinance is similar to the L.A. County ordinance, but specific to tobacco). The Court ruled that federal laws pertaining to cigarette advertising block any parallel state regulations. Therefore, states do not have authority to implement advertising restrictions on tobacco that exceed federal law. The Supreme Court did allow states to pass zoning restrictions on tobacco advertising as long as tobacco was on the same provisions as other products (Supreme Court of the United States, 2001). For instance, if billboard advertising were banned for all products then it would be legal to ban tobacco billboards. Considering this ruling, it is important for communities to enact ordinances that comply with the federal law. This decision may reverse the ordinance that was passed in Los Angeles County. However, as stated in the beginning of the case study, the coalition was not just focused on the short-term goal of passing the ordinance, but rather on establishing a long-term social movement. The victory of the grassroots coalition members will no doubt serve as a reminder of the positive social changes that can occur when community members work together in advocacy.

## Media Advocacy Tips

There are many details involved in working with the media. Ideally, prevention professionals will be working with community members who have some expertise with the media. If not, training may be available from other prevention coalitions working on similar issues. Government offices many times have a press office that might be able to provide guidance and **media access**. In addition, business organizations may be able to provide pro bono help to community nonprofit groups. The following list provided by Wilbur and Stewart (n.d., p. 35) offers tips on media advocacy:

- Take the initiative. Do not wait for the media to contact you; make news happen.
- Know your goal. What are you trying to accomplish? How will working with the media help you get there?
- Be strategic in everything you do and say. Do not go after media for media's sake; have a purpose. What do you want people to do? What change do you want to take place? What solutions do you have for the problems you raise? What messages will advance your cause? Who do you need to influence and how can you reach them?
- Be newsworthy. Keep in mind what constitutes newsworthiness; highlight what is significant, timely, and groundbreaking when you contact the media. If your story doesn't receive good coverage, find out why. Is there a different aspect you can highlight next time?
- Be timely. Do not wait to take advantage of media advocacy opportunities; be prepared to respond to events as soon as they come up.

- Practice. Role-play phone calls to reporters; rehearse your media bites out loud before your interview; hold practice question-and-answer sessions with your colleagues. Practice will help make you more comfortable and effective in your contacts with the media.

- Frame your story. Always consider how the story is framed. Are you emphasizing an **environmental** approach? Are you emphasizing the social aspects of the problem and avoiding putting all of the responsibility on the individual? Are you highlighting policies that will solve the problem?

- Think locally. If there is a national story, offer local spokespeople to talk about what impact that story has on your state or community.

- Be strategic in selecting your spokespeople. Be creative; the head of your coalition may not be the best spokesperson available. Are there parents, police officers, teenagers, or others who will have inherent credibility with the media? Once you've selected them, give them plenty of practice through training or role-playing. Even people with a lot of media experience can benefit from becoming more familiar with your issues.

- Tend your relationships. Relationships with journalists, like any relationships, require two-way efforts. Get to know the reporters, editors, and producers in your area. What kind of information do they like to have? What kind of stories do they want to cover? On any given day, ask yourself how you can help them.

Additionally, prevention professionals should not be embarrassed or afraid to ask for help from more experienced media advocates. Media advocates may be able to share stories about how they have used the tips described above and which ones have worked best. Ultimately, advocates will learn by working with other advocates and by "doing" media advocacy.

## Media Advocacy in Action

**Media advocacy** can be a difficult concept to comprehend, especially for prevention professionals that have been working to implement strategies targeted to individuals. However, it is a tool that can be used to help journalists and the general public view the issues from a public health perspective. Box 7.1 provides an example of how state and community leaders used media advocacy to convince legislators not to pass a bill that would reduce the penalty to vendors caught selling alcohol to minors.

This local media coverage and activism by San Diego residents made it clear that the senator's local constituency opposed the bill. These statements also demonstrated that citizens had done the research to learn about the alcohol industry in their community. They also framed the issue in a manner that stated the policy that needed to be kept and not the youth or parents' individual behavior.

Despite all the attention and criticism in San Diego, the bill moved along with only minor revisions. Policy advocates opposing the bill believed the bill was going to pass and decided to strengthen their efforts in the media to defeat the bill. The advocates knew the media statewide would be interested in the story. They had data on the amount of money

BOX **7.1**

## Case Study: Senate Bill 1696

In 1994, the California State Legislature passed the "three strikes and you're out" law (Ryan & Mosher, 270). The law permits revocation of an alcohol license if a vendor is caught selling alcohol to minors three times in a three-year period. The law gave community members concerned with underage sales to minors the mechanism to shut down retailers that would not comply with the law. The law also gave business owners warning about taking measures to prevent sales to underage youth if they wanted to stay in business. In addition, during that same year, the California Supreme Court ruled that minors could be used as decoys to conduct compliance checks on licensees. Further, the following year the California State Department of Alcoholic Beverage Control (ABC Department) provided grants to communities for partnerships with law enforcement to reduce problems associated with alcohol. Communities used the majority of the grant money to establish minor decoy programs. The minor decoy programs began to yield noncompliant retailers and the three-strikes provision began to pose a real threat to businesses selling to minors.

In 1998, a California state senator from San Diego introduced Senate Bill 1696 in the legislature. In essence, the bill allowed a fourth violation in a three-year period and restricted the ABC Department's grant funding for decoy programs. Multiple food and beverage retail associations, big breweries such as Anheuser-Busch and Miller, as well as the Wine Institute supported the bill. However, when prevention advocates learned about Senate Bill 1696, they mobilized and made defeating it a top priority.

The California Council on Alcohol Policy sent out legislative alerts to people around the state. Members of the North City Prevention Coalition in San Diego wrote letters to their senator (the author of the bill) opposing it. Members of the coalition also signed a petition opposing the bill. Members of the San Diego Council on Alcohol Problems (SANDCAP) also called, wrote, and complained to the senator and demanded the bill be dropped or dramatically changed. Other prevention and recovery organizations also opposed the bill and wrote letters and spoke to the senator. The director of the San Diego Policy Panel on Youth Access to Alcohol urged its influential members from a cross section of the community to take appropriate measures to ensure the defeat of the bill. One prevention services director estimated that the senator received over 57 calls opposing the bill. California alcohol policy activists met with the senator and wrote letters to the members of the policy committee.

Policy advocates used their relationship with a San Diego newspaper to gain public support in San Diego for defeating the bill. The newspaper editor wrote an editorial describing the bill as beneficial to a special interest group and not the public interest, which prompted many letters to the editor. The newspaper ran eight more pieces on the topic within the next few months. The newspaper articles allowed both sides to voice their arguments. However, alcohol policy advocates made strong arguments. Some of the points made by the prevention advocates were as follows:

- What's our priority, industry profit or safety for our children?
- The beer industry sells an estimated 1.1 billion cans of beer each year to junior and high school students.
- Kids already have ready access to booze. We should be making it more difficult to sell to them, not easier.
- The industry is trying to "buy" a bill in the legislature to get itself off the hook. It made $2.4 million dollars in donations in the 1996–97 legislative year.

- Why let these "three-strike" violators off the hook? Prevention strategies should be implemented without giving violators a break.
- Ninety-five percent of Californians want stricter, not weaker, enforcement." (Ryan & Mosher, 270, p. 15)

---

the alcohol industry donated to political campaigns, and they "had a frame that would attract attention: the industry was trying to protect their right to sell to kids" (Ryan & Mosher, 2000, p. 22). Although the advocates had been reluctant to criticize the senator and the bill statewide because they did not want to anger her and risk their ability to work with her in the future, they decided to be more explicit. James F. Mosher, JD, Senior Policy Advisor at the Marin Institute for Prevention of Alcohol and Other Drug Problems, sent an op-ed piece on Senate Bill 1696 to newspapers in Sacramento and San Jose, outlining the principle reasons why it was a bad bill. The piece ran a few days later. Soon other major newspapers in the state were running stories and editorials about the bill. The stories generated letters to the editor, mainly in support of defeating the bill. The media took the frame and called it the "fourth strike bill." One headline in San Jose read, "Responsible retailers do not need SB 1696. And the Community doesn't need irresponsible retailers" (Ryan & Mosher, 2000, p. 24).

Apparently the media coverage worked. The senator agreed to meet with policy advocates and seriously discuss their concerns. She amended the bill by removing the fourth strike provision and keeping the grant funding for the minor decoy programs. In this case, grassroots organizing helped generate media coverage at the local level but did not seem to be enough to defeat the bill. Nearly everyone involved in defeating the bill felt these changes would not have happened without the media attention the bill received. The surprise victory for the alcohol policy activists proved they could do it and helped to strengthen their confidence and commitment. Further, and most important because of the relationships that were developed, alcohol policy advocates now sit at the table with legislators to assist in drafting bills related to prevention issues and they continue to work with the media (Ryan & Mosher, 2000).

## Summary

Media advocacy can be used to advance many public policy issues. Prevention professionals can use the skills described to advocate for policies that are consistent with prevention practices. Advocating in the media may be a new experience for some prevention professionals, but with a well-thought-out strategy, a little practice, and perseverance anyone can become a media advocate.

# Media Literacy

Oftentimes the media glamorizes and normalizes unhealthy lifestyles and behaviors. For example, tobacco and alcohol are frequently portrayed as a normal and routine part of life. Additionally, advertising campaigns, movies, videos, and television programs portray alcohol and tobacco users as fun, successful, and sexy. **Media literacy** is about giving young people the skills and knowledge to analyze media messages critically and to become smart consumers. The most widely used definition of media literacy is "the ability to access, analyze, and produce information for specific outcomes" (Aufderheide, 1997, p. v). Another definition used by the Centers for Disease Control (CDC) (1998) is "the ability to 'read' and produce media messages" (p. 9). According to Aufderheide, a person that is media literate "can decode, evaluate, analyze, and produce both print and electronic media" (p. 1). Media literacy can focus on several skills, such as analyzing or production. For the purposes of this chapter, the focus will be on analyzing media messages. While media literacy involves educating people about how all media influences virtually every aspect of their lives, this chapter will focus on alcohol, tobacco, and other drugs in the media.

Media literacy is considered a promising practice (McCannon, 2000) for helping reshape youth's interpretation of unhealthy behavior portrayed in the media. A study on the general and alcohol-specific effects of media literacy training on third-grade students and their decisions about alcohol found positive effects on the training (Austin & Johnson, 1997). Immediate effects included an increase in children's understanding of persuasive intent, decreased desire to be like the characters, decreased expectation of positive consequences of alcohol, and decreased chance to select alcohol-related products (Austin & Johnson, 1997). By teaching young people to "read" media messages, in other words, making them "media literate," youth can resist messages that encourage and reinforce the use of alcohol and tobacco. Media literacy can be easily incorporated into existing academic and prevention curricula and into youth programs. In addition, the skills emphasized in media literacy—critical thinking, analysis, effective communication, and problem solving— apply across many disciplines, making media literacy applicable within many courses and with many age groups.

Teaching media literacy can be a tool prevention professionals can use to help youth minimize the consequences of their exposure to so many images glamorizing substance use. Media literacy can help youth understand the powerful messages that shape their attitudes toward alcohol, tobacco, and other drugs.

## Bandura's Social Learning Theory

Although there are many theories that can be used to explain the effects of media on behavior, the theory of social learning (Bandura, 1977) most adequately informs the research in substance abuse and media. Social learning is based on the proposition that most of a child's learning comes from modeling what others do. The behavior is then shaped by the consequences that follow it. Therefore, if the behavior is reinforced, it is more likely to be acquired even if the reinforcement is vicarious. According to Bandura, the main reason children learn from seeing or hearing a model is that they are able to interpret and understand if initiating the behavior will help or hinder them in fulfilling their needs in the future.

In terms of learning to use alcohol and tobacco, social learning can be used to explain how youth view media messages, process the information, and adopt the behavior.

The process of learning consists of five main functions. First, children must pay attention to the behavior and monitor for clues. Second, they must accurately record the image in their memory. A third factor influencing the success of learning is retaining the information or image in memory. The more children see the behavior, the more likely it will stay in their memory. Fourth, children carry out the behavior, receive feedback, and then correct the technique. Fifth, learners must be motivated to carry out all of the steps of the process. The consequence of the behavior is a crucial function of motivation. According to Bandura (1977), consequences tell a learner under what circumstances it is appropriate to try a certain behavior. They tell a child if the behavior will lead to a pleasant or unpleasant outcome. Children will be more likely to learn modeled behavior if they value the consequences (Bandura, 1977).

Social learning theory applied to the learning of alcohol consumption, cigarette smoking, and illicit drug use means that children observe others or hear about others engaging in this behavior on television, in movies, in music, on advertisements, in person, and in other places. The child is motivated to pay attention because the people engaging in the behavior may seem mature, glamorous, prestigious, famous, or rich, or they may be in positions of authority. The images of people drinking alcohol, smoking cigarettes, or using other drugs are recorded in their memories. And since the images are repeatedly shown through various communication channels, the stored information is readily retrieved. Once children engage in the behavior, they learn from others how to do it, under what circumstances to engage in the behavior, what brands are more popular, which methods they can use to get a high quicker, and other techniques used to perfect drug-taking behavior. In most cases, the consequences are usually positive (or at least, they are not negative). The behavior is accepted and encouraged by peers. Also, the children perceive that others who engage in the behavior receive positive reinforcement. Therefore, their behavior is both vicariously and actually reinforced.

The media has the ability to transmit information, shape attitudes, and provide "models" for behaviors. When young people encounter media depictions in advertisements, movies, or songs, the potential exists for that behavior to be imitated. The media influences young people in terms of social learning by portraying a "reality," contributing to the cultural norms, and conveying messages about the behaviors and the substances that are portrayed (Bandura, 1977). For example, according to Chassin, Presson, and Sherman (1984), youth do in fact overestimate the number of peers and adults that smoke, and this overestimation is a predictor of smoking initiation. They also underestimate the disapproval of peers and the risks associated with smoking. Another literature review found that "cigarette advertising appears to influence young people's perceptions of the pervasiveness, image, and function of smoking. Since misperceptions in these areas constitute psychosocial risk factors for the initiation of smoking, cigarette advertising appears to increase young people's risk of smoking" (U.S. Department of Health and Human Services [DHHS], 1994, p. 195).

## Marketing to Special Populations

Alcohol and tobacco advertisers use multiple techniques to reach special subgroups of the general population. Symbols that appeal to children, young adults, and various ethnic groups are used to associate alcohol and tobacco as normal products that everyone uses.

Alcohol and tobacco advertisers sell their product by linking alcohol and tobacco with success, social acceptance, sexuality, youthfulness, attractiveness, and physical vigor.

Alcohol companies often seem to target youth. Animated or cartoon characters have been used to sell alcohol and tobacco by making risky and unhealthy behavior look normal. Alcohol advertising creates brand recognition among children, which is associated with children holding favorable attitudes toward drinking alcohol, an intention to drink alcohol in the future, and the belief that peers hold favorable attitudes toward drinking alcohol. Although children may be aware of and recognize slogans, they are not more aware of the negative consequences of alcohol (Leiber, 1996; Grube & Wallack, 1994). For example, one study found that children ages 9 to 11 were more aware of the slogan associated with Budweiser frogs ("Bud-weis-er") than Tony the Tiger ("They're Grrreat!") or Smokey the Bear ("Only you can prevent forest fires") (Leiber, 1996). Another study found sufficient evidence to conclude that beer and wine commercials were indicators of adolescent alcohol use and drunk driving (Atkin, 1990). A study of high school students found a relationship between television viewing and drinking alcohol (Tucker, 1985).

Alcohol companies also appear to heavily target college students. A study published by the Harvard School of Public Health found that binge drinking is prevalent on campuses in the United States. The study found that 84 percent of college students nationwide drink alcohol and half of them are binge drinkers (44% of the total student population; the range for binge drinking is from 1 to 70 percent). The effects of binge drinking include injury to self and others, lost educational achievement, antisocial and illegal involvement, high-risk sexual practices, harassing others, and disturbing the peace (Lyall, 1995).

Despite all the problems associated with alcohol among college students, advertisements in college newspapers and nearby bars continue to promote heavy drinking through pictures, phrases, or promotions. Marketing techniques include extremely discounted drinks, using women as "bait" (i.e., "ladies night") to attract male drinkers, price increases as the evening progresses ("ladder pricing" or "beat the clock" specials), or offering students all they can drink for a single low price ("cover charge"). Oftentimes, promotions that encourage heavy drinking are disguised as responsible safety programs. For example, some bars offer "a ride home" program and offer free nonalcoholic drinks to the designated driver. These programs appear responsible; however, the message to the nondriving student is to drink excessively (Erenberg & Hacker, 1997).

The alcohol and tobacco industries also appear to heavily target communities of color. For example, various studies have shown that ethnic minority communities have higher numbers of alcohol and tobacco billboard advertising (Allen-Taylor, 1997; Hackbarth, Silvestri, & Cosper, 1994) and higher concentrations of alcohol outlets (Alaniz & Wilkes, 1998; Scribner, MacKinnon, & Dwyer, 1995). Alcohol and tobacco companies often sponsor cultural holidays and events, such as Cinco de Mayo, St. Patrick's Day, Pow Wows, and Black History Month. They also contribute to community agencies and organizations, support education by providing scholarships, and contribute to political campaigns.

One brewery, in its efforts to target Native Americans, used the image of Crazy Horse, a Lakota Sioux warrior on a malt liquor bottle. Names that mean certain things to groups have been used to market products. For example, cigarettes named "Uptown" and "X" were targeted toward African Americans, "Dorado" and "Rio" toward Hispanic

Americans, and "American Spirit" toward Native Americans (U.S. DHHS, 1998). Alcohol and tobacco industries use cultural symbols, historical figures, ethnic holidays, and heroes in their advertising to minorities to promote ethnic pride and nationalism while creating an association between culture, drinking, and smoking. The advertising's impact is increased due to the invisibility of minorities in the media, in school textbooks, in other communication channels, and in other historical, economical, and political issues (Alaniz & Wilkes, 1995). For ethnic minorities that feel excluded from society, the alcohol and tobacco's recognition of their culture fosters a sense of belonging.

In spite of many alcohol-related problems among Hispanics, the alcohol industry aggressively targets the Hispanic community, and Mexican Americans specifically (the largest Hispanic group), using culture symbols and other symbols of nationalism. Although Hispanics in general consume less alcohol than Caucasians, Mexican American men have higher rates of heavy drinking and alcohol-related problems (Aguirre Molina & Caetano, 1994). Further, although the national trend is a decrease in heavy drinking, among Hispanics there has been an increase (Caetano & Clark, 1997). An example of how Hispanics have been targeted by the alcohol industry is an advertisement for tequila that featured an ancient Mayan pyramid as the base for a blender to be used in making margaritas. Other print advertisements for beer often include the Mexican flag or the Mexican map with a beer bottle superimposed on the image. One brewer printed a map with the pre-Columbian borders, representing Mayan nationalism. A few years ago community members challenged one billboard that exploited the Hispanic community's religious beliefs. The wine company-sponsored billboard featured a priest and a monk holding a glass of brandy gazing toward a light from the sky. The ad read in Spanish, "To drink is not a sin." To summarize, alcohol marketers exploit Hispanic values and symbols to sell their product.

African Americans have also been heavily targeted by the alcohol industry. Many alienated African American young people living in pervasive poverty consider rap music to be a form of social protest and regard rap artists as heroes. Although not all rap music advocates violence and some rap artists have criticized alcohol and drug use as destructive to the Black community, "gansta" rap supports it. "Gangsta" rappers have embraced the use of alcohol and other drugs to perpetuate their image of violence and sexuality. African American "gangsta" rap artists have been used to sell malt liquor to young black men by portraying images and practices that would be considered unacceptable and inappropriate among Caucasians. One malt liquor company signed a rapper that almost had his eye taken out in a suicide attempt. The horrific image of his eye was actually glorified in the advertisement. Another rapper's ad stated, "Get your girl in the mood quicker, get your jimmy thicker, with St. Ides malt liquor." Traditionally, African Americans have had lower alcohol consumption rates; this tactic is seen as a way to widen the base of consumers among African Americans (Herd, 1993).

There are multiple examples of exploitation and unethical marketing strategies by tobacco companies as well. During the years of the Joe Camel campaign, one study concluded that by age six, the character was as well known as Mickey Mouse (Fischer, Schwartz, Richards, Goldstein, & Rojas, 1991). After a law suit filed by the Federal Trade Commission against RJ Reynolds Tobacco for using the Joe Camel character to appeal to children, the company ended the campaign in 1997.

An example of tobacco's advertising to minorities includes a campaign targeting ethnic minority women that portrayed women of various ethnic backgrounds, often in traditional dress, and directed messages of empowerment toward them. One tobacco company has attempted to link smoking with success and equality for women by using the slogan, "You've come a long way, baby."

Generally, alcohol advertising encourages drinking in all situations, downplays potential risks of drinking, and actively discourages abstinence. Further, alcohol advertisements encourage heavy drinking and, as stated earlier, focus their message about responsibility on the individual while denying the effects of their unethical marketing practices. Tobacco advertising encourages children to experiment with smoking, deters current smokers from quitting, encourages former smokers to start again, and increases the number of cigarettes that current users smoke. There is a great amount of evidence that tobacco advertising is a contributor to the onset of smoking and that restricting tobacco industry sponsorship of social and cultural events, sporting events, and musical festivals will reduce adolescent exposure to tobacco messages (U.S. DHHS, 1994; CSAP, 1997). Media literacy can help minimize the impact of the alcohol and tobacco industry's advertising by teaching young people about the methods used to persuade them to hold favorable attitudes toward their product.

## Substance Use in Movies, Music, and Television

Youth also receive messages about alcohol, tobacco, and other drugs through media channels other than advertising. Media literacy can assist youth in analyzing those messages as well. Music lyrics, movie scripts, and television programs often glorify and promote the use of alcohol, tobacco, and other drugs. Ultimately, the impact of the media on youth depends on multiple factors. Based on the theory of social learning (Bandura, 1977), it is reasonable to hypothesize that positive portrayals of substance-taking behavior in movies, music, and television may be influencing young people to use substances.

In 1999, the Office of National Drug Control Policy (ONDCP) explored the frequency and context of alcohol, tobacco, and other drugs in the most popular home movie rentals and music recordings of 1996 and 1997. The study examined the 200 most popular movie rentals and the 1,000 most popular songs. The music sample included songs from five genres: country and western, alternative rock, hot 100/top 40, rap, and heavy metal (ONDCP & U.S. DHHS, 1999).

Ninety-eight percent of the movies depicted substances of some kind. Alcohol was depicted in 22 percent, tobacco in 89 percent, and illicit drugs in 22 percent of the movies. One or more lead characters used alcohol in 85 percent of the movies depicting substance use. Fifteen percent of movies depicted substance use by characters who appeared to be younger than 18 years old. Only 7 percent of movies depicted long-term consequences of substance use. Positive expressions about substance use occurred in 29 percent of all movies, with most pro-use statements referring to alcohol. When alcohol was depicted, it was associated with wealth or luxury in 34 percent, sexual activity in 19 percent, and crime or violence in 37 percent of the movies. When illicit drugs were depicted they were associated with humor 26 percent of the time, portrayed at parties 16 percent of the time, 9 percent of the time with sexual activity, and 12 percent of the time in wealthy or luxurious settings. Few movies portrayed the illegal nature or the legal consequences of illicit drug use (ONDCP & U.S. DHHS, 1999).

Twenty-seven percent of music lyrics referenced substances in some form. Alcohol was mentioned in 17 percent, tobacco in 3 percent, and illicit drugs in 18 percent of the songs. When alcohol was described, it was associated with wealth or luxury in 24 percent of the songs, with sexual activity in 34 percent of the songs, with bravery in 21 percent, and with crime or violence in 13 percent. Consequences of alcohol use were mentioned in 9 percent of the songs containing a reference to alcohol. When illicit drugs were mentioned, their consequences were described in 19 percent of the songs. Of the songs that referenced illicit drug use and alcohol use, 42 percent cited mental consequences (i.e., diminished thinking skills) and 52 percent cited physical consequences (i.e., disease or weight loss) of use. Tobacco did not appear in enough songs to make a meaningful analysis of the association or consequences (ONDCP & U.S. DHHS, 1999).

An analysis of program episodes on prime time television found that alcohol appeared in 64 percent of the episodes and was consumed in 50 percent of them (Grube, Wallack, Madden, & Breed, 1990). Alcohol consumption occurred more than eight times per hour. The drinkers tended to be higher status, White, upper-class professionals. Regularly appearing characters tended to drink more than non–regularly appearing characters. Another analysis of broadcast television programs from ABC, CBS, FOX, and NBC from fall 1994 to spring 1995 found that alcoholic beverages were the most frequently portrayed food or drink (Mathios, Avery, Bisogni, & Shanahan, 1998). When adolescents were portrayed in episodes involving alcohol, they were portrayed with significantly more negative personality characteristics than older characters. Although cigarette smoking is not as prevalent on television as is alcohol consumption, higher rates of smoking appear on television than in real life. One analysis of prime-time television programming found that 24 percent of programs contained at least one event including tobacco (Hazan & Glantz, 1995). Ninety-two percent were pro-smoking events and 8 percent were anti-smoking. Fifty-five percent of the smoking characters were "good guys" or high-status characters.

In general, there are many opportunities in the media for children to learn how to use substances, under what circumstances it is acceptable to use substances, and how to improve their substance-taking techniques. Most portrayals of substances in the media are associated with positive outcomes and rarely are the negative consequences of substance use portrayed.

## Media Analysis

The media provides youth with encouragement, acceptance, fun, and entertainment. Oftentimes the media helps adolescents define who they are by providing role models to study, then accept or reject them. The media shows a wide variety of behaviors and can indicate which are valued and which are not. Therefore, it is essential to help youth understand what the media does and does not tell them. Decoding media messages, or **media analysis,** can be complex but it can also be fun. Media literacy can easily be incorporated into an existing prevention curriculum. The following questions from *Media Sharp: Analyzing Tobacco &*

*Alcohol Messages* (Centers for Disease Control, 1998, p. 37) can provide a guideline for youth and adults on understanding media messages:

- Who is communicating and why? Every message is communicated for a reason: to entertain, inform, and/or persuade. However, the basic motive behind most media is to profit through the sale of advertising space and sponsorships.
- Who owns, profits from, and pays for media messages? Media messages are owned. They are designed to yield results, provide profits, and pay for themselves. Both news and entertainment programming try to increase listenership or viewership to attract advertising dollars. Movies also seek to increase box-office receipts. Understanding the profit motive is key to analyzing media messages.
- How are media messages communicated? Every message is communicated through sound, video, text, and/or photography. Messages are enhanced through camera angles, special effects, editing, and/or music. Analyzing how these features are used in any given message is critical to understanding how it attempts to persuade, entertain, or inform.
- Who receives media messages and what sense is made of them? Messages are filtered through the "interpretive screens" of our beliefs, values, attitudes, and behaviors. Identifying the target audience for a given message and knowing its "filters" and the way in which it interprets media messages helps make you media sharp!
- What are the intended or underlying purposes and whose point of view is behind the message? Behind every message is a purpose and point of view. The advertiser's purpose is more direct than the program producer's, though both may seek to entertain us. Understanding their purposes and knowing *whose* point of view is being expressed and *why* is crucial to being media sharp.
- What is *not* being said and why? Because messages are limited in both time and purpose, rarely are all the details provided. Identifying the issues, topics, and perspectives that are *not* included can often reveal a great deal about the purposes of media messages. In fact, this may be the most significant question that can uncover answers to the other questions.
- Is there consistency both within and across media? Do the political slant, tone, local/national/international perspective, and depth of coverage change across media or messages? Because media messages tell only part of the story and different media have unique production features, it helps to evaluate multiple messages on the same issue. This allows you to identify multiple points of view, some of which may be missing in any single message or medium. This is typically referred to as the "multisource rule."

Answering these questions can provide youth with an understanding of how media messages are designed to influence them. By thinking about the answers to these questions that relate to media messages, youth can become smart consumers instead of passive consumers.

## Persuasion Techniques

As stated in the discussion on social learning, behavior is motivated by the urge to meet certain needs. Motivation is the drive that directs people toward a certain target. Showing people their need then letting them know how to fulfill it is a tremendous persuasive technique used by advertisers. According to Abraham Maslow (1970), all humans have five fundamental needs, arranged in order of priority or hierarchy, that motivate their behavior. Although Maslow was discussed in Chapter 6, this section will provide a brief overview of Maslow's theory as it applies to persuasion techniques.

At the basic level are physiological needs, such as food, air, and water. When these needs are aroused they dominate behavior. For instance, advertisers can gain the viewer's attention by showing a picture of an ice-cold beer on a hot day. The beer is intended to meet the basic need for water. Advertisers also use sex to arouse the basic needs of humans. For instance, models with little clothing are often used to sell many different types of products. The second level in the hierarchy is safety and security needs. These include the need to feel protected from threats and the need to be able to depend on specific things to happen or to be a certain way. Advertisers may use this to sell alarms, locks, and other antitheft devices. Certainly, in most advertisements people are in a secure and comfortable setting. The third level is belongingness needs. These include the need for family, friends, affection, intimacy, loyalty, and acceptance. People want to be with others and want the companionship of others, therefore advertisers will often communicate the message that everyone is doing "it" or that engaging in this behavior or buying this product will bring love and friends. The fourth level is esteem needs. These include prestige, self-respect, attention, and pride and can be satisfied through accomplishments and recognition by others. Advertisers usually appeal to the esteem needs. Their product is associated with expensive cars, luxurious homes, extravagant clothing, and being the "best." The message that advertisers want to send is that this product is a status symbol. The fifth level is self-actualization needs. These include the need to realize potential, to seek knowledge, and to develop an identity. This appeal may be particularly effective for people who are idealistic or do not have their identities firmly established. Terms such as "achievement" or "accomplishment" may be used to appeal to the self-actualization needs. In summary, advertisers attempt to link their product with something the target audience needs, wants, or finds desirable.

The New Mexico Media Literacy Project (NMMLP) is an American media education project providing media literacy curricula, videos, and CD-ROMS that are used in schools all over the world. According to the NMMLP, several media techniques can be used to persuade consumers (McCannon, 2001). They are symbols, hyperbole (glittering generalities), fear and scapegoating, humor, lies (big), maybe, testimonials, repetition, plain folks, strength, name-calling or ad hominem, flattery, bribery, diversion (straw man), denial, card stacking, bandwagon, simple solutions, scientific evidence, group dynamics, rhetorical questions, nostalgia, and timing (McCannon, 2001, pp. 1–2).

One technique that is used by the media to persuade consumers is the use of symbols. These are used to relate to the consumer by appealing to emotions such as patriotism, power, religion, sexuality, traditions, and more. Symbols can include ethnic artifacts, music, places, heroes, or sexually implicit female bodies. Alcohol and tobacco advertisements often include symbols that connote product use, such as young attractive models engaged in fun activities. By combining language and symbols, advertisers strengthen the message. Music can be used to enhance the mood and conjure up feelings, such as excitement, romance, suspense, fear, anger, or power and distract people from their immediate concerns.

Hyperbole, fear, and scapegoating are other persuasion techniques. Hyperbole, or exaggerations, also appeal to the emotions in order to make the audience less likely to think about the advertising pitch. Statements are vague, unclear, and meaningless. For example, "The greatest beer in the world." Hyperbole can cause confusion, which wears people down. "Fear," another emotional appeal, is used as a threat. "Scapegoating" blames problems on a person or subsets of the general population based on race, gender, ethnicity, or religion.

The humor technique usually involves something out of place or unexpected. It is used to make people laugh and forget about the logic behind the sales pitch. Humor is a commonly used persuasion technique, which breaks up the monotony of other boring ads. Humor is also used as a diversion technique to move the attention away from important issues.

Lies are used by omitting details or changing the meaning of words to imply something different. For example, a print advertisement for cigarettes may read, "No additives." Although it is probably true that the cigarette contains no additives, this implies a safer and healthier tobacco product. Omissions can be used to deliberately mislead or conceal. As in the case of the tobacco product, does "no additives" mean a lower risk of cancer? The words "maybe," "almost," "could," or "might" are often used with lies but the listener has to pay attention to notice them.

Another persuasion technique is testimonials. This technique uses famous and respected people and institutions to sell a product. There is usually no logic behind why a certain person or institution makes the claim. The spokesperson or model is usually someone who appears to be caring or knowledgeable, like a television mom or a doctor. Celebrities are often used by advertisers if they are well-liked and trusted by the target audience.

Repetition is a technique that creates intensity, which is a simple and effective way to persuade. Messages can be repeated in various mediums, such as television, radio, magazines, newspapers, music, movies, billboards, music, the Internet, and in-store promotions. The purpose is to imprint the message in the memory of the receiver so that receivers can recognize and respond to the advertised product. Often people are able to recognize brand names, logos, trademarks, and even packaging. For example, one convenience store in a small community was upset that tobacco companies were not able to advertise on billboards since the store generated large profits from the sale of tobacco. They created a billboard advertisement for the convenience store, which did not mention tobacco. The advertisement looked like a Marlboro billboard and everyone immediately recognized the colors, the font graphics, and other characteristics of the billboard as an advertisement for Marlboro. The fact that neither tobacco nor the brand name were mentioned, and yet people understood that it was an advertisement for Marlboro, implies the power of repetition in marketing strategies.

The "plain folks" technique is used to promote the image of common origins and humility. For example, in an advertising strategy targeting Hispanics by assisting with citizenship information, Coors Brewing Company describes its founder, Adolph Coors, as an immigrant with a dream that he was able to realize by becoming a United States citizen. By portraying the founder of the brewing company as an ordinary person, the ads are hoping to establish a bond between the Hispanic community and Coors.

The media uses the "strength" technique by portraying athletic and energetic people in advertising and through sponsorship of sport events. The use of this persuasion technique is ironic considering the effects of alcohol and tobacco on the body and on athletic performance. Consider the advertisements for Marlboro that portray a strong cowboy in a rugged environment who looks completely in control. These images conjure up feelings of individualism, freedom, health, and strength.

Name Calling, or ad hominem, is a technique that attempts to discredit the message by attacking the person rather than the issue. For instance, when alcohol companies are asked to remove or reduce advertising, they blame parents for underage drinking. On the other hand, flattery is used by advertisers—namely, they give people compliments to make them feel good. Advertisers attempt to make the audience feel like society's elite, the social and political leaders, movie stars and millionaires, artists and athletes, scholars or celebrities. This technique is based on the premise that people like and trust people who like them.

Media uses the technique of bribery by offering a reward for using the product. The bribe may be tangible or abstract. For example, a person may symbolically be "given" sex, success, or beauty by purchasing a specific product. The reward may also be tangible, as in the case of the "Bud Gear" campaign. In this marketing strategy, points could be accumulated by Budweiser and redeemed for merchandise. An analysis by Cal Partners Coalition revealed that large quantities of beer purchases were required to get most of the merchandise (Hernandez, 1998).

Diversion is a technique used to detract or downplay from other important issues or the harm that a product may cause. For example, many alcohol ads include the statements, "drink responsibly" or "do not drink and drive." These statements attempt to present the alcohol industry as responsible. However, the messages divert attention from the alcohol industry's marketing techniques, the outlet density rates, health issues, sexually transmitted diseases, and other social problems commonly caused by the availability and use of alcohol.

Denial is used by the media to cover up responsibility for doing or saying something unpopular. For example, when the tobacco companies were asked about their marketing strategies, they denied that they studied and targeted youth, which would have been condemned by the public.

Card stacking refers to providing only part of the information, usually only the favorable part. For example, one alcohol advertisement depicted a young male at a bar looking at a woman and perhaps preparing to approach her. The slogan read "the WD-40 of conversation." While it is true that alcohol reduces inhibition and may get people to talk more, alcohol also causes people to do things they would not ordinarily do. The ad did not show all the possible negative consequences of alcohol, such as sexually transmitted diseases, which can occur as a result of going home with someone from a bar.

Bandwagon implies that "everyone is doing it." In the case of alcohol and tobacco, the products are normalized. In other words, their use is made to appear as a routine or normal part of life. In alcohol advertisements, usually everyone portrayed in the advertisement is drinking and drinking is occurring in all situations (weddings, graduations, after work, at the beach). This is an effective technique because most people want to be like others, especially young people.

The simple solution technique means that a simple solution is provided for confusing and obscure problems. The problems are illustrated using ambiguous language that is so complex and chaotic that the average person cannot understand. However, a simple solution is offered, in a way that appears to make sense, as a way to tackle and resolve many issues. For example, an advertisement for Johnnie Walker depicted a man and a woman apparently getting ready for an evening out, with the message, "Men are from Earth. Women are from Earth. End of story." The advertisement ignores the complexities of dating relationships and downplays the importance of the difficulty men and women often have in understanding each other. The implication is that the simple solution to relationships is Johnnie Walker.

Group dynamics are used to demonstrate that many people agree on the message. The message is imbued with power because a group of people is delivering it and is enjoying the benefits of the product. One person may not be as believable, but a group of people cannot all be wrong.

Scientific evidence is used by advertisers to imply that there is "proof" for the message. Advertisers show lists, graphs, and charts to convey the message that their product or result is scientific. Scientist-like people (wearing lab coats or stethoscopes) may be portrayed to convey accuracy and authority.

Rhetorical questions are used to prompt an internal response from the target. Advertisers want the audience to say yes or another specific response, then give the sales pitch. For example, an advertisement for alcohol may say, "Do you want to have fun?"

Nostalgia is used to make people forget about the bad things in the past and remember only the good things. Advertisers will often bring back old or former slogans, spokespeople, or advertisements that were once popular to jog people's memory about why they liked that product.

Timing is a technique about planning the message delivery when the audience is most susceptible or vulnerable to the sales pitch. When people are hungry, angry, lonely, or tired, advertisers can let them know how to meet their needs more easily.

### Summary

Sophisticated marketing strategies employ a combination of these and other appeals to make people do what they customarily would not do (McCannon, 2000). Understanding how these media persuasion techniques work can help youth become media literate. Furthermore, prevention professionals can assist youth in rethinking the media messages they receive by making them aware of the psychological motivations used to manipulate their thinking and behaviors.

# Social Marketing

Social marketing is based on the premise that one can "sell" certain healthy behaviors, such as avoiding alcohol, tobacco, and other drugs, just as one would sell toothpaste. The term **social marketing** was coined in 1971 by Phillip Kotler, a professor at Northwestern University. Kotler and Gerald Zaltman (1971) further defined social marketing as the "design, implementation, and control of programs calculated to influence the acceptability of social ideas, and involving considerations of product, planning, pricing, communication, distribution and marketing research." According to CSAP (1993) the definition of social marketing is "the design, implementation, and control of programs developed to influence the social acceptability of a social idea or cause by a group" (p. 116). Social marketing techniques are applied to social issues and are centered on the target audience. They include recognizing the need of a specific group, providing information to allow people to make decisions, and offering programs or services that meet the needs. Social marketing is more complex than product marketing because the product being promoted is a behavior or a belief.

The following describes the differences between social marketing in the public health arena and product marketing campaigns:

- *Type of change expected:* Health campaigns aim to change fundamental behaviors, whereas much product advertising aims to mobilize an existing predisposition, as in switching brands. However, some product advertising does aim to create new markets.
- *Amount of change expected:* Health campaigns aim to change a large portion of the population. Product advertising is usually satisfied with small shifts in market share.
- *Time frame of expected benefits:* Health campaigns usually ask their target audience to wait for delayed statistical probabilities. Product advertisers promise immediate certainty.
- *Presentation of the product:* Product advertisers can dress up their product as much as they want or need to. Health campaigns do not, and probably cannot be seen to oversell benefits or the ease of their acquisition.
- *Available budgets:* Product advertisers have massive budgets. Health campaigners usually operate on relatively minuscule budgets.
- *Trustworthiness:* People often distrust advertising. Health campaigners cannot allow distrust to develop.
- *Level of evaluation:* Product advertisers stress formative research: market research conducted before campaigns. Health campaigners tend to stress summative evaluation, conducted after the campaign, if they stress any evaluation at all. (CSAP, 1993, pp. 116–117)

## The 4 Ps of Social Marketing

When developing a social marketing campaign, prevention professionals need to keep the "4 Ps" in mind: production, **price**, **place**, and **promotion**. Traditional **product** marketing techniques include marketing analysis, planning, and control; which in turn includes market research, product positioning and conception, pricing, physical distribution, advertising, and promotion (Walsh, Rudd, Moeykens, & Moloney, 1993). For a commercial marketer the "product" may be soap or cereal but for social marketing it is a healthy behavioral change or a changed attitude. In substance abuse prevention the product is the knowledge, attitudes, or behavior that the target audience should adopt. The price for a bar of soap may be $2.00, but for a healthy behavior the "price" is what the person must give up in order to receive the benefits. For instance, the price may be the cost of separating oneself from peers that use alcohol, tobacco, and other drugs. The "promotion" is the overall strategy or message used to persuade the target audience to pay the price for the product. It is the means for persuading the target audience that the product is worth the price. The "place" is the communication channel, such as the mass media, schools, churches, or work-places. Some social marketers also define "place" as the location where the audience can partake in the healthy behavior. It is important to note that social marketing does not have to include mass media. The following example illustrates how the 4 Ps of social marketing can be applied to a media campaign:

> *Product:* Refusing to have a drink when offered one by peers
> *Price:* Not fitting in with one's peers (the price perceived by preteens)
> *Promotion:* Not drinking or using other drugs is smart and fashionable
> *Place:* Mass media and community programs

## Steps for Social Marketing Program Development

The Center for Substance Abuse Prevention recommends that social marketing planners follow specific steps in developing their campaign (Substance Abuse and Mental Health Services Administration [SAMHSA] & Center for Substance Abuse Prevention, n.d.). First, campaign developers should plan their approach, which includes knowing the community and the audience and establishing the goals and objectives. The plan should include the primary, secondary, and tertiary target audience. Although generally the target audience will probably be defined (i.e., teenagers, college students, teenage mothers), it is important to know which segment of that general audience is the primary target (i.e., Hispanic teenagers residing in a certain area of town or college students under the age of 21). Categories such as age, sex, ethnicity, socioeconomic status, education levels, or occupation should be considered when defining the primary target audience. The secondary target audience may be the family members, peers, teachers, or employers of the primary target audience (Breitrose, 1992). And the tertiary target audience may be the policy makers and community leaders that have influence to impact prevention efforts (Breitrose, 1992).

Defining the goals and objectives is the second part of step one in the social marketing planning process (SAMHSA & Center for Substance Abuse Prevention, n.d). The goals and objectives should be clearly defined in the plan. This will permit the developers to judge clearly their progress and success. The goals may be simply to raise awareness about an issue, increase knowledge, provide information about resources, generate support for an issue, recruit volunteers, influence attitudes, demonstrate skills, influence norms, or refute myths. The ultimate goal, however, should be behavior change or maintenance of a healthy behavior. A social marketing campaign can assist with a comprehensive approach to achieving this goal, which should include multiple strategies, such as environmental policies that support a healthy environment and implementing prevention programs that reduce various risk factors and increase protective factors. It is also important to teach skills that instruct the target audience in how to adopt or maintain the healthy behavior.

The second step in the social marketing planning process is to define the messages and communication channels. The message must be meaningful and appeal to the target audience. It should also be based on fact and linked to the present rather than to the future, especially if the target audience is youth. For example, a message about not smoking can provide information about bad breath, yellow teeth, or reduced energy instead of the threat of cancer many years from now. Scare tactics, which include fear arousal and proving information about the most extreme consequences of substance use, should be avoided, as they have failed to influence long-term behavior change. The behavior that people should adopt or change should be clear as well as the benefits of adopting the new behavior. If the target audience is involved in the issue, the message will be different than if they are not involved (Breitrose, 1992). For example, a message to smokers wanting to quit will be different than one to smokers who think smoking is cool and are not interested in stopping.

When determining the communication channels, the number of people exposed to the messages during a specific time period should be considered. Repetition helps make the point but unnecessary repetition may turn the audience off to the message. Campaign developers need to be aware of where the target audience usually gets information, what media or communication channels they prefer and find credible, and how much time they spend watching, listening, or reading various media channels. For example, if the target audience for a message is youth, then it would not make sense to play a message on all radio stations in the area; instead, social marketers should find out which stations are the most popular among youth in the area. It is also important to be aware of the target audience's preference of magazines, newspapers, television programs, and other media channels. Television advertisements are costly, so messages should be simple and short. If more details need to be given, then print media might be a better option.

The third step in a social marketing campaign is to develop and pretest or pilot materials. The target audience should be involved in both. The arguments used to persuade the audience should be carefully considered. The messages can appeal to the emotions, including fear (also fear of social disapproval), self-esteem, patriotism, and humor, but they are usually more effective if they appeal to positive emotions (Breitrose, 1992). Social marketers can also learn from traditional marketers in this area. The persuasion techniques described in the media literacy may be helpful in developing messages to persuade youth to live healthy, drug-free lifestyles. For example, fear may be used to get attention about a harmful substance; humor can be used to describe the irony of using substances and participating in sports, or group dynamics may be used to persuade youth that not everyone is using drugs. The appeals will depend on the target audience.

If the target audience does not care about an issue, then an emotional appeal may be a way to get their attention. Fear may be a way to get the audience involved. However, if fear is used, make sure to provide information about how people can protect themselves or avoid the fearful situation. Further, the level of fear aroused should not be so high as to elicit inappropriate reactions, such as denial or perceived invulnerability. If people feel there is no hope or that nothing can be done, they are unlikely to listen to the message. Emotional appeals often focus on describing the effects or consequences of a substance. The appeals are more likely to be effective if they are short-term. For example, with smoking cessation campaigns, messages about increased lung capacity may be more effective than the promise of a longer life. In general, the use of fear is unlikely to work in terms of affecting behavior change and may reduce the effectiveness of subsequent health promotions, as these messages may lose credibility with the audience. Therefore, this appeal should be used cautiously (Soames, 1988).

Messages can also appeal to logic or reason. A logical or reasonable approach may be effective if the target audience already cares or is involved in the issue. A logical or reasonable approach may include proving a simple argument about why alcohol, tobacco, and other drugs should not be used and providing ways to say no. Humor can also be a way to engage the audience if used effectively. It is important not to be offensive, and the message should be funny to the target audience. Further, as stated earlier in this chapter in the discussion on Bandura's social learning theory, modeling behavior is a great way to show the desired behavior. A message that shows the positive behavior as opposed to one that shows a negative behavior which the audience is told not to do, is more likely to have success (Breitrose, 1992). For example, if you want the target audience to avoid smoking cigarettes and drinking alcohol, do not portray kids in the advertisement engaging in that behavior, but instead show the other activities they could be doing. Positive modeling shows the target audience that people do practice the healthy behaviors. The choice for the model should have similar attributes as the target audience. If the model is too different from the audience, the audience will have a reason to discount the message. This can occur because the possible benefit will not seem germane to their situation. For example, if the audience is teenage boys living in rural areas, then 30-year-old males in an urban setting should not be delivering the message.

The last part of creating a message is to pretest the messages on the target audience. Pretesting assesses the target audience's responses to the messages. Examples of pretesting methods include focus groups, interviews, theater testing, self-administered questionnaires, and readability testing. Focus groups can be comprised of 8 to 12 people from the target audience to provide feedback on the themes, images, and general issues. Focus group members can explain the pitfalls to avoid, rate the messages in terms of like or dislike, provide information about their media habits, give feedback on the appropriateness of the message or appeals used, and provide information about the extent to which they are involved in the issue. Interviews can be used to assess an individual's reactions to sensitive issues or emotions. Informal interviews can be held in places where the target audience gathers, such as restaurants, churches, parks, schools, malls, or other places. Theater testing is used when a group of people in one location are shown the messages rooted in another agenda. For example, a group of people may be invited to watch a free movie. Before the movie, a social marketing message will be demonstrated and participants can then be asked about the message. Self-administered questionnaires may be mailed or delivered to people who may not be able to participate in focus groups, or to other target audience members. Readability testing is used to measure the reading level of the materials.

The fourth step in the social marketing planning process is to implement the campaign. If the campaign includes negotiating for free airtime, then it should be planned for a time when local stations have the least number of paid advertisements (this will increase the chance of the messages being broadcast). Negotiations will include talking to station managers in the area. Also, create spots that vary in length (i.e., 10-second, 15-second, 30-second, and 60-second) to allow stations flexibility in terms of when they can air the spots. The messages need to be distributed through the chosen channels. To ensure more coverage, use multiple channels and methods. Communication channels include radio spots, posters, newspapers, billboards, small groups, television spots, take-home projects, music and visual arts programs, among others. At this step an evaluation method for the effectiveness of the materials should be in place (more information on evaluation will be discussed in the following step). The messages that are aired or published should be monitored in order to ensure delivery and appropriate distribution. If the messages include free public service announcements, determine which ones were broadcast and which ones were not broadcast.

The fifth step in a social marketing campaign is evaluation. Social marketing campaign staff members need to conduct process evaluation, answering such questions such as, "What did we do?" "How often?" "Who received the messages?" "What needs to be improved?" This would include monitoring the media in order to determine how often messages were broadcasted or published and to determine the number of people who were exposed to the messages. Social marketing campaigns also need to conduct outcome evaluations, which describe what the campaign's immediate effects on the behavior, attitudes, or beliefs of the target audience were. Outcome evaluations answer such questions as, "Did the target audience show an increase in knowledge, attitude, or perception?" and "Did their awareness of alcohol, tobacco, or other drugs increase?" An impact evaluation must also be conducted. An impact evaluation answers questions such as, "What was the long-term impact of the campaign on the target audience or on the community?" "What changes have occurred in the target audience's behavior relating to alcohol, tobacco, and other drugs?" For more information about evaluation, refer to Chapter 8.

The last step, step six, requires that feedback and evaluation results be used to refine the program. Feedback can be acquired by asking community members about the campaign's strengths and weaknesses, then using the information to continuously improve the campaign. The same pretesting techniques can be used to refine the campaign. It is also important to provide positive feedback to all of the people involved in developing the campaign, such as the media, committee members, funders, focus group participants, and campaign spokespersons.

There are also other guidelines to consider when planning a social marketing campaign (SAMHSA & Center for Substance Abuse Prevention, n.d). Social marketing campaigns can be one part of a community's comprehensive plan by helping to build awareness, increase knowledge, and positively influence attitudes and norms. As was discussed in Chapter 3, community prevention program planning should be comprehensive and include all of the six CSAP strategies described in Chapter 2. Another consideration when planning a social marketing campaign is that it should not focus only on individual behavior, but should also focus on the environment. For example, focusing only on individual risk factors and ignoring risk factors in the community, such as community laws and norms favorable toward drug use, ignores the influence of the environment on individuals. Cultural issues should also be considered when implementing a social marketing campaign. Cultural issues may include assimilation, immigration, and discrimination issues. Knowing the answers to questions such as, "Has the group adopted the mainstream's beliefs or do they still hold traditional values?" will help shape an effective message. Furthermore, it is important to know how long the group has been in the United States and what the political issues have been. Messages targeting specific ethnic groups should promote cultural understanding and pride in the heritage. For additional sources on how to gather information on diverse communities and on working with various cultural groups, refer to Chapter 5 of this book.

Another consideration when planning a social marketing campaign is the use of innovative communication channels such as music videos, on-line computer databases, computer-generated animation, and the use of computer-generated art to create flyers, posters, and other print materials. Remember not to reinvent the wheel. Research other communities with similar dynamics in order to find out how they started their campaign, what challenges they had, what worked, and how they evaluated their efforts. Finally, long-term campaigns are essential. Lessons in social marketing in the areas of cardiovascular risk reduction, antismoking, and family planning suggest that it may take up to 10 years to see social changes (Walsh et al., 1993).

## Applying the Skills of Social Marketing

In 1998, the Office of National Drug Control Policy (ONDCP) launched the National Youth Anti-Drug Media Campaign. The primary target audience of the campaign was at-risk adolescents ages 11–13 who were nonusers or occasional users. The secondary target audiences were at-risk nonusers or occasional users in late elementary and high school students. The term *at-risk nonusers* was defined as youth who do not use illicit drugs but have behavioral, psychological, or environmental characteristics that place them at greater risk, and those youth who have tried alcohol or tobacco during the previous year. An occasional user was defined as a youth who has used illicit drugs between 1 and 10 times during the previous year. Although alcohol and tobacco use are illegal for youth, the campaign did not address these substances. The campaign also focused on a parent/caregiver audience (ONDCP, 1998). Several of the many groups the campaign was designed to reach include African Americans, Hispanics, Native Americans, Asian Americans, and Alaskan Natives.

The overall goal of the National Youth Anti-Drug Media Campaign was to "educate and enable America's youth to reject illicit drugs" (ONDCP, 1998, p. 3). The campaign included several communication objectives. The objectives for the youth audiences included correcting misperceptions about youth drug use rates, informing about the negative consequences of drug use, informing about the positive consequences of a drug-free lifestyle, and reinforcing positive use of time. The communication objectives for the parents/caregiver audiences included informing parents about the harmful effects of marijuana and inhalants, about their children's at-risk status, about what they could do to make a difference, and providing simple skills that parents could use to protect their children from drug use. The communication objectives were tailored to each specific audience group. For example, information about the psychological benefits of a drug-free lifestyle, such as achieving personal growth, was targeted to middle school and high school youth. Information regarding the norm of marijuana and inhalants was targeted toward late elementary school and middle school students (ONDCP, 1998). All of the campaign's activities were focused on one message at a time. For example, if the message was on "norm education," then this message appeared on all media channels (ONDCP, 2000c). The messages were delivered in multiple languages in addition to English to ensure that the target audiences received the messages. Languages included Spanish, Mandarin Chinese, Cantonese Chinese, Korean, Cambodian, and Native American languages. The campaign also included outreach to the U.S. territories of Guam, the U.S. Virgin Islands, American Samoa, and Puerto Rico (ONDCP, 2000b).

All of the campaign messages underwent a rigorous pretesting process. Input from the target audience was sought early in the development of the messages. The messages were tested for audience reaction and interpretation. Advertising professionals judged the ads' creativity and persuasiveness. Experts on behavioral change judged the ads' observance of the theories of substance abuse, communication, and behavior change. Focus groups comprised of target audience members provided feedback on the relevance, credibility, and appeal of the messages. Several federal agencies and a private organization double-checked the content for accuracy (ONDCP, 2000a).

The campaign used paid advertising in 102 local markets in the United States, through more than 2,250 media outlets nationwide, including television, cable, radio, and magazine ads. According to the mandate from Congress, 100 percent of the media outlets receiving paid advertisements were required to contribute an equal amount (in-kind match). This "pro bono" match can take many forms, such as free advertising space or time, newspaper inserts, broadcast programming, and sponsorship of community events (ONDCP, 2000a, p. 2). In addition, the campaign coordinators worked with the entertainment industry to ensure that when a drug was portrayed in the media, the consequences and risks were clearly demonstrated. Other communication channels included school-based educational materials, playground basketball backboards, home videos, ads in movie theaters, Internet Websites, and parenting brochures (ONDCP, 2000a).

The campaign was designed to be implemented in three phases over five years. Phase one was piloted in 12 U.S. cities during a 26-week time period. Phase two was launched nationwide shortly after the pilot, using 80 different ads in a variety of media outlets. Phases one and two contributed to over 50 television program scripts with antidrug storylines. The ads exceeded their pro bono match requirements and reached more than 90 percent of the target audiences. Phase three incorporated more messages to parents and multicultural audiences, produced fewer yet more specific ads, and focused on "sensation seekers" and "at-risk" middle school students. Feedback from the target audience and monitoring the media during each phase provided essential information to the campaign's subsequent phases (ONDCP, 2001; n.d.).

The campaign included an extensive process-and-outcome evaluation. Televised spots were tested quantitatively for effectiveness prior to airing. A study tracking the marketplace among parents and youth was implemented in order to provide ongoing feedback for fine-tuning the campaign. The outcome of the campaign on changing attitudes and reducing drug use was evaluated through scientific surveys of parents and youth over the five-year duration of the campaign. The National Survey of Parents and Youth (NSPY) was administered to 40 million youth and 43 million parents over a three-year period. The *Evaluation of the National Youth Anti-Drug Media Campaign: Third Semi-Annual Report of Findings* processes data reports on the media campaign's activities, such as statistics on level of exposure and media purchases (Westat, 2001). In terms of outcomes, the report states that parents and youth have substantial levels of recalled exposure to the campaign's antidrug messages. Further, the evaluation reports overall positive changes in four of the five outcomes for parents, including talking about drugs with their children and monitoring their children. Parents who report more exposure to the campaign's messages also report better scores on the campaign's intended outcomes. The media campaign's effect on youth is not statistically significant. However, the report indicates that there is preliminary evidence for association between the amount of exposure to the campaign and changes in beliefs, attitudes, and intentions to use. In terms of long-term impact, the authors state that future reports will examine the impact that occurs through other routes, including through parents, social networks, or institutions.

In order to sustain the campaign's efforts over the long term, ONDCP expanded the Web-based components, expanded outreach to multicultural audiences, involved participation from corporations, and maintained relationships with news media as well as other partners formed during the campaign (ONDCP, n.d.).

## Challenges of Social Marketing

There are many challenges associated with social marketing (Linkenbach, n.d.). First is the rigor of the process. As demonstrated in the above example, each step of the campaign requires input from the target audience. Second, there is great competition from the highly financed alcohol and tobacco campaigns. Lack of funding makes it practically impossible for government agencies and prevention organizations to compete with the alcohol and tobacco industry's marketing efforts. For example, in 1993 the alcohol industry spent $1 billion on advertising, while the National Institute on Alcohol Abuse and Alcoholism's budget was $176 million (CDC, 1998). A third challenge of social marketing is that the "product" must be presented in a way that reinforces core needs. An adolescent wants to be autonomous, and often the use of alcohol, tobacco, and other drugs may superficially provide that, whereas the benefits of health and safety may not reinforce the core need to belong. Fourth is the challenge of evaluating the campaign. Campaign staff often stop at process evaluation, only counting the number of times a person saw a message or assessing whether the audience liked a message. Unfortunately, it can be challenging to evaluate the impact of social marketing campaigns on behavior. As a result, the case for social marketing essentially lies in the established science of marketing. A fifth limitation is that social marketing campaigns traditionally have focused on negative approaches. Messages have described the horrific effects of alcohol, tobacco, and other drugs but they are largely ineffective at affecting behavior. These approaches have been popular because they appeal to emotions. However, as discussed in Chapter 3, the use of scare tactics, fear arousal, and moral appeals have been ineffective in causing behavior change. Furthermore, as was discussed in Chapter 2, effective use of the media for prevention education is primarily demonstrated when it is combined with other prevention strategies. When used alone the media's prevention messages are largely ineffective in influencing long-term behavior changes, but are a good way to promote a healthy norm in communities. Finally, social marketing usually focuses on individual behavior, not on environmental facts. Consequently, social marketing campaigns need to be implemented along with other prevention strategies that affect policies, laws, and norms.

One additional challenge is that some researchers view social marketing as ineffective. For example, according to Wallack (1990), a proponent of media advocacy, social marketing is a tool that is contradictory to public health because it applies the principles of marketing, which fosters passivity, dependence on experts, and consumption. He further explains that social marketing diverts attention from public policies and issues that promote and advance the unhealthy behaviors. For example, in underdeveloped countries, social marketing strategies have focused on changing individual habits instead of working to ensure clean and healthy water supplies (Wallack et al., 1993). However, social marketing supporters counter this by stating that social marketing promotes activism and partnerships, media literacy, and the development of skills.

## Social Norms Marketing

**Social norms marketing** is a strategy used to promote the healthy behaviors practiced by the majority of the public. The focus of social norms marketing is to change youths' perceptions of how much alcohol, tobacco, and other drugs their peers use. The assumption is that correcting misperceptions about the rates of use will decrease use by youth because they want to be part of the crowd. For example, surveys conducted across college campuses indicate that young adults on college campuses have a much higher perception of alcohol, tobacco, and other drug use by their peers than is actually occurring (Perkins, Meilman, Leichliter, Cashin, & Presley, 1999). Research also indicates that young adults typically underestimate the support for abstinence or moderate drinking. As a result, the perception of heavier ATOD use becomes in part a self-fulfilling prophecy.

One possible explanation for the inflated misperceptions about actual peer use of alcohol, tobacco, and other drugs may be found in the attribution theory (Perkins, 1997). According to this theory, people are constantly gathering information about the environment by observing themselves and others in a variety of situations in an effort to understand why things happen. The information is then used to bring order to the social environment. According to Perkins (1997), this theory is applied to misperceptions about alcohol, tobacco, and other drug use in the following manner: When students drink, even when they drink more than they intended, they are able to attribute their behavior to situational factors. For example, a student who had too much to drink rationalizes that he was celebrating a special occasion, was upset about a breakup, or simply misjudged how much he drank and had too much. Regardless of how wise the decision was, the person contextualizes or rationalizes the situation. However, the same person may see another person who had too much to drink and, because he is unaware of the person's situation, will attribute the behavior to the character of the person. Consequently, the person makes a general conclusion about the overall social environment based on pieces of isolated incidences, which helps to create an overall misperception about what is really happening. Attribution theory helps explain how misperceptions progress.

Another reason why students may have misperceptions about the rates of peer ATOD use provided by Perkins (1997) is "public peer behavior and conversation" (p. 189). According to Perkins, inebriated people make a vivid impression. Oftentimes they may act violent, funny, or out of character and therefore others are likely to remember the experience. Conversely, the noninebriated persons do not make such lasting impressions. A person is unlikely to remember all the people who were drinking in moderation and were not acting out of the ordinary. Thus, the person is probably going to distort the level of alcohol use in the entire student body based on those observed incidences.

Conversations may also alter perceptions about alcohol, tobacco, and other drug use (Perkins, 1997). Students are likely to talk about the one party where many students got drunk or the behavior of intoxicated party-goers. They are also more likely to talk about their experiences while being intoxicated and exaggerate or overstress how drunk they got. Students may receive reinforcement by their peers by gaining their attention and thus their behavior and topic of conversation is encouraged. Their friends are unlikely to be impressed with stories about remaining sober at a party. Therefore, conversations can contribute to misperceptions and, in turn, to higher rates of drinking.

## Social Norms Marketing in Action

An example of a social norms marketing campaign includes one that was undertaken by Northern Illinois University (NIU). The NIU Health Enhancement Services conducted a student survey and discovered that less than half of the students had engaged in binge drinking during the previous two weeks. However, the students believed that more than two out of three were binge drinkers. After receiving information from the students about the best communications channels and testing the materials and messages, the campaign organizers placed news stories and advertisements in the college newspapers and posters around the campus. The message that more than half of NIU students did not binge drink when they partied saturated the university. The same messages appeared in classified newspaper ads, a newspaper column, press releases, and flyers. Other parts of the campaign included giving money to students that knew the correct rate of binge drinking and informational flyers to those who did not. In an effort to provide incentives, students were also given $5.00 if they put up campaign posters in their dorms (student office workers were used to find the posters). Health Enhancement Services staff spoke in classrooms, the residence hall, and sorority houses, conveying the message about the correct binge-drinking rate (Haines, 1996).

After the campaign, another survey was conducted. Students' perception of the binge-drinking rate was closer to reality, and the rate of binge drinking had also declined. There was an 18 percent reduction in perceived binge drinking and a 16 percent reduction in actual binge drinking. Further, surveys revealed there was a 5 percent reduction in alcohol-related injuries to self and a 33 percent reduction in alcohol-related injuries to others. Five years after the campaign started (it was implemented each year), the binge-drinking rate fell by 35 percent (Haines, 1996).

The four Ps still apply to social norms marketing campaigns. In this example, the "product" is to stop binge drinking, the "price" is fitting in with one's peers, the "promotion" is that most students at NIU do not binge drink, and the "place" is the college newspaper and other locations on campus.

## Seven Steps toward Success

There are a number of considerations when planning a social norms marketing campaign (Linkenbach, n.d.). First, as in social marketing, the campaign should be focused on outcomes and not on activities. The campaign should be designed, implemented, and evaluated with the end result in mind. Second, in a social norms marketing campaign the goal is to ultimately prevent or reduce substance use. Therefore, if the goal is to reduce the age of onset of drinking alcohol, then the target population should be those who have not yet tried alcohol. Third, the target audience's misperceptions should be corrected because perceptions affect behavior more than reality does. For example, instead of saying, "almost half of all college students surveyed admit to binge drinking" a message should say, "Most of the college students surveyed drink moderately or not at all." Fourth, for many youth it is more important to be considered normal than to be healthy. If the norm is that the population is engaging in healthy behaviors, for example not smoking, then the normative behavior should be promoted so that being healthy is the best way to be normal. Fifth, the focus should be on the healthy behavior in which you want the target audience to engage. Focusing on the problem and/or consequences is not effective in changing behaviors. Sixth, policies that impact the environment should be addressed. Targeting individuals and ignoring the social environment communicates the message that alcohol, tobacco, and other drug problems are solely the responsibility of individuals. And seventh, the messages should be targeted toward a specific population. For example, should a county allocate 90 percent of its resources to the 15 percent of seventh-graders who have started smoking, or to the 85 percent who have not?

Successful implementation of a social norms marketing campaign includes collecting baseline data to determine the rate of ATOD among the target population. Then simple, truthful, and consistent messages should be developed that highlight the nonuse norm. For example, a message can state, "Did you know that 85 percent of the students at the University of Nevada, Reno have never smoked marijuana?" The source on the messages should be credible by the target audience. Deliver the nonuse norms messages to the target audience. Communication channels may include posters, flyers, billboards, bulletin boards, screen savers, and presentations. The target audience should be frequently exposed through a variety of communication channels. Also, incentives and rewards may be given to those who remember the message. If the baseline data indicates that a high rate of ATOD use is the norm, then the campaign may focus on reducing the higher misperception. For example, if 60 percent of the students do in fact binge drink, but most students believe 95 percent of the students binge drink then the campaign can focus on correcting the misperception. If the baseline data indicates a high rate of abstinence or there is little misperception about the norms (the target audience's perception about the rates of use is accurate), then other strategies should be used to delay onset and reduce ATOD (Haines & Spear 1996; Haines, 1996).

## Summary

The information in this chapter provided an overview of how prevention professionals can use the media to advance prevention efforts. Media advocacy can be used to generate interest and support for environmental strategies. Media literacy can be used to educate young people about the alcohol and tobacco industry's marketing strategies. Teaching youth to analyze advertisements and other media critically can help them resist the persuasiveness of the messages. Social marketing uses traditional marketing strategies to sell healthy behaviors. Social marketing campaigns and media literacy should be used in combination with other prevention strategies.

## KEY TERMS

environmental strategies
framing the issue
media access
media advocacy

media analysis
media literacy
place
price

product
promotion
social marketing
social norms marketing

# DISCUSSION QUESTIONS

1. Discuss how the media has been used to change a public policy issue in your community. Discuss national movements or issues that have used the media to implement policy changes.

2. Discuss the alcohol and tobacco promotional practices in your community and how you believe they affect the community. What can be done?

3. Discuss advertising appeals or persuasion techniques that are not described in this chapter. Discuss how advertising persuasion techniques influence your behavior as a consumer.

4. Discuss your opinion about the messages in local, state, or national social marketing campaigns. Discuss your opinion regarding their effectiveness for changing behavior.

# APPLICATION EXERCISE

1. Read Box 7.1, the case study of Senate Bill 1696. Discuss how the skills to advocate in the media were used in the case study.

2. Select an environmental policy issue that puts kids in your community at risk. Develop a strategy to change the policy using the skills for media advocacy.

3. Select alcohol or tobacco advertisements from popular magazines, billboards, or television. Use the seven critical media questions and the media persuasion techniques (from the Media Analysis section of this chapter) to analyze the advertisements.

4. Develop a marketing message for a product you want to sell. Determine who the target audience is and describe which persuasion techniques could be used to appeal to that target audience.

5. Using the 4 Ps of social marketing, develop a social marketing message. Describe the target audience, how misperceptions will be corrected, and how the effectiveness will be evaluated.

# SUGGESTED READINGS

Center for Science in the Public Interest. (1989). *Marketing disease to Hispanics.* Washington, DC: Center for Science in the Public Interest.

Kotler, P., & Eduardo, R. (1989). *Social marketing.* New York: Free Press.

Strasburger, V. C. (1995). *Adolescents and the media: Medical and psychological impact.* Thousand Oaks, CA: Sage.

Streicker, J. (Ed.). (2000, October). *Case histories in alcohol policy: A project of the Trauma Foundation.* San Francisco: Trauma Foundation.

# REFERENCES

Aguirre Molina, M., & Caetano, R. (1994). Alcohol use and alcohol-related issues. In C. W. Molina & M. Aguirre-Molina (Eds.), *Latino health in the United States: A growing challenge.* Washington, DC: American Public Health Association.

Alaniz, M. L., & Wilkes, C. (1995). Reinterpreting Latino culture in the commodity form: The case of alcohol advertising in the Mexican American community. *Hispanic Journal of the Behavioral Sciences, 17,* 430–451.

Alaniz, M. L., & Wilkes, C. (1998). Pro-drinking messages and message environment for young adults: The case of alcohol industry advertising in African American, Mexican American, and Native American communities. *Journal of Public Health Policy, 19*(4), 447–472.

Allen-Taylor, J. D. (1997, July 24). Liquid lunge: Beer industry takes aim at young Latinos with high-octane malt beverage. *San Jose Metro, 13*(21), 20–28.

Amidei, N. (1991). *So you want to make a difference: Advocacy is the key.* Washington, DC: OMB Watch.

Atkin, C. K. (1990). Effects of televised alcohol messages on teenage drinking patterns. *Journal of Adolescent Health Care, 11,* 10–24.

Austin, E. W., & Johnson, K. K. (1997). Effects of general and alcohol-specific media literacy training on children's decision making about alcohol. *Journal of Health Communication, 2,* 7–42.

Aufderheide, P. (1997). Media literacy: From a report of the national leadership conference on media literacy. In Robert Kubey (Ed.), *Media literacy in the information age.* New York: Transaction Press.

Bandura, A. (1977). *Social learning theory.* Englewood Cliffs, NJ: Prentice Hall.

Breitrose, P. (1992). *PSAs that work: Guidelines to help you select or produce effective health promotion public service announcements.* Palo Alto, CA: Health Promotion Resource Center & Office for Substance Abuse Prevention.

Caetano, R., & Clark, C. (1997). *Trends in alcohol consumption patterns among Whites, Blacks, and Hispanics: 1984 and 1995.* Berkeley, CA: Public Health Institute.

Center for Science in the Public Interest (CSPI). (2000, December 14). *Fact sheet: Putting Anheuser-Busch's consumer responsibility campaign into perspective.* Washington, DC: CSPI. Retrieved July 23, 2001, from the World Wide Web: http://www.cspinet.org/booze/A-B_Campaign.html.

Center for Substance Abuse Prevention (CSAP) (1993). *Prevention primer: An encyclopedia of alcohol, tobacco, and other drug prevention terms.* (DHHS Publication No. SMA 94–2060). Rockville, MD: National Clearinghouse for Alcohol and Drug Information.

Center for Substance Abuse Prevention (CSAP) (1997). *Reducing tobacco use among youth: Community-based approaches. Prevention Enhancement Protocols System.* (DHHS Publication No. SMA 97–3146). Rockville, MD: National Clearinghouse for Alcohol and Drug Information.

Centers for Disease Control. (CDC). (1998). *Media sharp kit: Analyzing tobacco and alcohol messages,* CDC. Video and 98-page leader's guide.

Chassin, L., Presson, C. C., & Sherman, S. J. (1984). Cognitive and social influence factors in adolescent smoking cessation. *Addictive Behaviours, 9,* 383–390.

Dorfman, L. (1996, May 4–8). *The news on alcohol—Media advocacy strategies to promote prevention policy.* Paper presented at Alcohol Policy X, the Tenth International Alcohol Policy Conference, Toronto, Canada. Retrieved May 14, 2001 from the World Wide Web: http://www.apolnet.org/sano/apn9609g.html.

Erenberg, D. F., & Hacker, A. (1997). *Last call for high-risk bar promotions that target college students.* Washington, DC: Center for Science in the Public Interest.

Federal Trade Commission. (2001). *Federal Trade Commission cigarette report for 1999.* Washington, DC: Federal Trade Commission. Retrieved June 22, 2001 from the World Wide Web: http://www.ftc.gov/opa/2001/03/cigarette.htm.

Fischer, P., Schwartz, M., Richards, J., Goldstein, A., & Rojas, T. (1991). Brand logo recognition by children aged 3 to 6 years. *Journal of the American Medical Association, 266,* 3145–3148.

Gallegos, B. (1999). *Chasing the frogs and camels out of Los Angeles: The movement to limit alcohol and tobacco billboards.* San Rafael, CA: Marin Institute for the Prevention of Alcohol and Other Drug Problems.

Grube, J. W., & Wallack, L. (1994). Television beer advertising and drinking knowledge, beliefs and intentions among schoolchildren. *American Journal of Public Health, 84,* 254–259.

Hackbarth, D. P., Silvestri, B., & Cosper, W. (1994). Tobacco and alcohol billboards in 50 Chicago neighborhoods: Market segmentation to sell dangerous products to the poor. *Journal of Public Health Policy, 16*(2), 213–230.

Haines, M. P. (1996). *A social norms approach to preventing binge drinking at colleges and universities.* Newton, MA: The Higher Education Center.

Haines, M. P., & Spear, S. F. (1996, November). Changing the perception of the norm: A strategy to decrease binge drinking among college students. *Journal of Applied College Health, 45,* 134–140.

Hazan, A. R., & Glantz, S. A. (1995). Current trends in tobacco use on prime-time fictional television. *American Journal of Public Health, 85,* 116–117.

Herd, D. A. (1993). Contesting culture: Alcohol-related identity movements in contemporary African-American communities. *Contemporary Drug Problems, 24,* 739–758.

Hernandez, E. (1998). *The effects of alcohol on Latinos in California.* Sacramento, CA: CalPartners Coalition.

Kotler, P., & Zaltman, G. (1971). Social marketing: An approach to planned social change. *Journal of Marketing, 35,* 3–12.

Leiber, L. (1996, April). *Commercial and character slogan recall by children aged 9 to 11 years: Budweiser frogs versus Bugs Bunny.* Berkeley, CA: Center on Alcohol Advertising.

Linkenbach, J. (n.d.). *Beyond health terrorism: Social marketing for healthy norms.* [Brochure]. Montana State University: Health and Human Development.

Lyall, K. (1995). *Binge drinking on American college campuses: A new look at an old problem.* Winston-Salem, NC: Robert Wood Johnson Foundation.

Maslow, A. (1970). *Motivation and personality* (2nd ed). New York: Harper & Row.

Mathios, A., Avery, R., Bisogni, C., & Shanahan, J. (1998). Alcohol portrayal on prime-time television: Manifest and latent messages. *Journal of Studies on Alcohol, 59,* 305–310.

McCannon, B. (2000, Fall/Winter/Spring). *SIG Grant: Cutting-edge program fires up kids, parents, & faculty for prevention.* New Mexico Media Literacy Research Project. Retrieved May 14, 2001 from the World Wide Web: http://www.nmmlp.org/research/.

McCannon, B. *(2001).* Specific media tools for analysis. New Mexico Media Literacy Research Project. Retrieved July 23, 2001 from the World Wide Web: http://www.nmmlp.org/resources/specifictools.pdf.

Office of National Drug Control Policy (ONDCP). (n.d.). *Media campaign update fact sheets: Campaign performance in year one.* Washington, DC: ONDCP. Retrieved June 29, 2001 from the World Wide Web: http://www.mediacampaign.org/newsroom/080299/update3.html.

Office of National Drug Control Policy (ONDCP). (1998). *The national youth anti-drug media campaign: Communication strategy statement.* Washington, DC: ONDCP.

Office of National Drug Control Policy (ONDCP). (2000a). *Media campaign update fact sheets: Campaign overview.* Washington, DC: ONDCP. Retrieved June 29, 2001 from the World Wide Web: http://www.mediacampaign.org/newsroom/080299/update1.html.

Office of National Drug Control Policy (ONDCP). (2000b). *Media campaign update fact sheets: Multicultural outreach.* Washington, DC: ONDCP. Retrieved June 29, 2001 from the World Wide Web: http://www.mediacampaign.org/newsroom/080299/update8.html.

Office of National Drug Control Policy (ONDCP). (2000c). *Media campaign update fact sheets: Strategic focus message platforms.* Washington, DC: ONDCP. Retrieved June 29, 2001 from the World Wide Web: http://www.mediacampaign.org/newsroom/080299/update12.html.

Office of National Drug Control Policy (ONDCP). (2001). *Media campaign update fact sheets: Summary of campaign accomplishments.* Washington, DC: ONDCP. Retrieved from the World Wide Web: http://www.mediacampaign.org/newsroom/080299/update4.html.

Office of National Drug Control Policy & U.S. Department of Health and Human Services. (1999, April). *Substance use in popular movies and music* (Publication No. BKD305). Washington, DC: U.S. Government Printing Office.

Perkins, H. W. (1997). College student misperceptions of alcohol and other drug norms among peers: Exploring causes, consequences, and implications for prevention programs. In *Designing alcohol and other drug prevention programs in higher education: Bringing theory into practice* (pp. 177–206). Newton, MA: The Higher Education Center for Alcohol and Other Drug Prevention.

Perkins, H. W., Meilman, P. W., Leichliter, J. S., Cashin, J. R., & Presley, C. A. (1999). Misperceptions of the norms for the frequency of alcohol and other drug use on college campuses. *College Health, 47,* 253–258.

Ryan, B. E., & Mosher, J. F. (2000). *The campaign against SB 1696: No 4th strike for California retailers who sell alcohol to minors.* San Rafael, CA: The Marin Institue for the Prevention of Alcohol and Other Drug Problems.

Scribner, R. A., MacKinnon, D. P., & Dwyer, J. H. (1995). The risk of assaultive violence and alcohol availability in Los Angeles county. *American Journal of Public Health, 85,* 335–340.

Soames Job, R. F. (1988). Effective and ineffective use of fear in health promotion campaigns. *American Journal of Public Health, 78,* 163–167.

Substance Abuse and Mental Health Services Administration. (1997). *Reducing tobacco use among youth: Community-based approaches.* Rockville, MD: U.S. Department of Health & Human Services.

Substance Abuse and Mental Health Services Administration & Center for Substance Abuse Prevention. (n.d.) *Social marketing and health communications.* Retrieved May 29, 2001 from the World Wide Web: http://www.preventiondss.org/MacroHQ/54curricula/THEORY/communications.htm.

Supreme Court of the United States. (2001). *Lorillard Tobacco Company et al., Petitioners v. Thomas F. Reilly, Attorney General of Massachusetts et al.* Washington, DC: Supreme Court of the United States. Retrieved on July 21, 2001 from the World Wide Web: http://a257.g.akamaitech.net/7/257/2422/28jun20011130/www.supremecourtus.gov/opinions/00pdf/00-596.pdf.

Tucker, L. (1985). Television's role regarding alcohol use among teenagers. *Adolescence, 20,* 593–598.

U.S. Department of Health and Human Services. (1994). *Preventing tobacco use among young people: A report of the Surgeon General.* Atlanta: U.S. Department of Health and Human Services, Public Health Service, Centers for Disease Control and Prevention, National Center for Chronic Disease Prevention and Health Promotion, Office of Smoking and Health.

U.S. Department of Health and Human Services. (1998). *Tobacco use among racial/ethnic minority groups—African Americans, American Indians and Alaska Natives, Asian Americans, and Pacific Islanders, and Hispanics: A report of the Surgeon General.* Atlanta: U.S. Department of Health and Human Services, Centers for Disease Control and Prevention, National Center for Chronic Disease Prevention and Health Promotion, Office of Smoking and Health.

Wallack, L. (1990). Improving health promotion: Media advocacy and social marketing approaches. In C. Atkin and L. Wallack (Eds.) *Mass communication and public health: Complexities and conflicts* (pp. 147–163). Newbury Park, CA: Sage.

Wallack, L., Dorfman, L., Jernigan, D., & Themba, M. (1993). *Media advocacy and public health: Power for prevention.* London: Sage.

Wallack, L., Woodruff, K., Dorfman, L., & Diaz, I. (1999). *News for a change: An advocate's guide to working with the media.* Thousand Oaks, CA: Sage.

Walsh, D. C., Rudd, R. E., Moeykens, B. A., & Moloney, T. W. (1993, Summer). Social marketing for public health. *Health Affairs,* 104–119.

Westat. (2001). *Evaluation of the National Youth Anti-Drug Media Campaign: Third Semi-Annual Report of Findings.* Rockville, MD: Westat. Retrieved February 8, 2002 from the World Wide Web: http://www.mediacampaign.org/publications/westat_report_2001/westat_report_2001.pdf.

Wilbur, P. M., & Stewart, K. (n.d.). *Strategic media advocacy for enforcement of underage drinking laws.* Rockville, MD: Pacific Institute for Research and Evaluation.

# 8 The Logic Model and Evaluation

Evaluation is the one of the critical components of prevention program planning and implementation. Yet it is often allotted less time and/or priority by many prevention professionals. Some have a fear of evaluation; others believe that they do not have enough time to "bother" with evaluation. However, **evaluation** is the key to saving much time, energy, and funding on programs and strategies that are not having the desired effect. An evaluation can assist in deciding whether to continue a program, identifying areas in the program that need improvement, pinpointing what is working well in a program, and assisting in replicating effective programs. A strong evaluation also provides prevention professionals with the leverage to access additional funding.

Although professional program evaluators have developed many designs to help them better identify specific causes of outcomes (e.g., was it this program or something else that prevented substance abuse?), it may not be critical that a program evaluation provides this information. For many prevention programs, if demonstrated changes in knowledge, skills, and/or behaviors occur within a group of program participants, this is sufficient evidence that the program is working. Further, in terms of preventing substance abuse, it is widely recognized that no one program is going to have a strong overall effect in isolation. However, this does not excuse the prevention professional of the responsibility of evaluating a prevention program. Instead, it is important that prevention professionals proceed with these thoughts in mind when designing and implementing an evaluation.

This chapter will assist professionals in designing and implementing an evaluation. The chapter begins with an introduction into a version of the **logic model** developed by the Western Center for the Application of Prevention Technologies. The logic model is one tool that can assist prevention professionals in designing their evaluations. It captures information about what the prevention strategy/program is and what it is expected to accomplish. This information in turn creates the evaluation questions that lead to the desired designs and methods of evaluation. In short, the logic model creates a map for prevention professionals to follow in evaluating their programs/strategies.

Although the logic model is presented in a chapter separate from the rest of the program planning steps discussed in Chapter 3, it cannot be done in isolation. The results of the other steps of program planning are incorporated directly into the logic model. Therefore, a logic model cannot be completed until the prevention professional or coalition has information from the other program planning steps. Even though it is presented as the last step in the planning process, it is essential that the logic model be developed *before* a program or strategy is implemented.

After the logic model is presented, a discussion regarding internal and external evaluations is covered. This section provides prevention professionals with tools to decide whether or not they will be able to answer the evaluation questions from their logic models themselves or if they need to hire a consultant to assist them. The subsequent sections, "Developing a Design to Answer Evaluation Questions" and "Developing Methods to Carry Out the Evaluation Design," provide information on evaluation design and methods. Finally, the chapter concludes with a discussion of how to create an evaluation plan. This is an essential step in evaluation planning, whether an internal or external evaluation will be done, because it can ensure that the evaluation is implemented with fidelity.

# Logic Model

Before implementing an evaluation, it is useful to develop a program logic model. The logic model lays out what the program is expected to achieve and how it is expected to work—essentially forming a "map" linking together a project's goals, activities, services, and assumptions. In turn, evaluation questions, designs, and methods are developed out of the program's logic model.

Prevention programs and community prevention coalitions often do not want to spend time at the outset of their work to develop a logic model. For some, creating a map of the program may seem overly rational or unrealistic. However, this process is a crucial part of evaluation and program planning. Experience shows that taking time to develop a logic model—thinking through the model of action—not only makes explicit the intended outcomes and assumptions of the project, but also makes evaluation more feasible and effective. It also assists in focusing the evaluation on appropriate questions that have meaning and are useful to the program and to key stakeholders.

The benefits of using a logic model are numerous. First, a logic model develops understanding among program developers, program implementers, funders, and other stakeholders. It helps build understanding, if not consensus, about what the program is, what it is expected to do, and what measures of success will be used. Next, a logic model helps to monitor progress. It provides a plan against which changes can be tracked so that successes can be replicated and mistakes avoided. Furthermore, a logic model serves as an

**TABLE 8.1   Blank Logic Model**

|  | 1. Logic Model | 2. Evaluation Questions | 3. Designs and Methods |
|---|---|---|---|
| A. Goals |  |  |  |
| B. Strategies |  |  |  |
| C. Target group |  |  |  |
| D. If-then statement |  |  |  |
| E. Short-term outcomes |  |  |  |
| F. Long-term impacts |  |  |  |

evaluation framework. It makes it possible to identify appropriate evaluation questions and relevant data that are needed.

Yet another benefit of a logic model is that it helps to expose assumptions. It helps program planners be more deliberate about what they are doing and identifies assumptions that may need validating. For example, a common assumption voiced during community substance abuse prevention meetings is: "If kids only had something to do, they would stay off drugs." However, experience has shown that services and activities to "keep kids busy," such as youth drop-in centers and drug-free dances, have not alone led to nonuse attitudes and behaviors. In fact, some evaluations have shown that "some extracurricular activities and alternative programs seem to increase the use of alcohol and some drugs" (Center for Substance Abuse Prevention [CSAP], 1996, p. 19).

A logic model also helps to restrain overpromising. It helps program planners and others realize the limits and potential of any single program. Finally, a logic model promotes communication. It creates a simple communication piece useful in portraying and marketing the program to others.

In order to build a useful logic model, six questions need to be answered about a prevention program. These include:

- What are the risk and protective factors to be addressed? (The goals.)
- What services and activities will be provided? (The strategies.)
- Who will participate in or be influenced by the program? (The target group.)
- How will these activities lead to expected outcomes? ("If–then" statement.)
- What immediate changes are expected for individuals, organizations or communities? (The short-term outcomes.)
- What changes would the program ultimately like to create? (The long-term impacts.)

These six questions will now be explored in more detail.

## Which Risk and Protective Factors Will Be Addressed?

First, the risk and protective factors to be addressed must be identified. If a community risk assessment has been completed, and priority risk and protective factors identified, then the goal(s) of the prevention program are the reduction of those priority risk factors and enhancement of the priority protective factors. These are Steps 2 and 3 from the program planning model presented in Chapter 3.

## Which Services and Activities Will Be Provided?

Next, the services and activities to be provided must be identified. This is the information generated by the completion of Step 6 of the planning process from Chapter 3. These are the strategies to be implemented by the program. Or in other words, this is what will actually be done. It is very important to specify which activities are planned, because a program that is not implemented in the way that it is designed (without fidelity) is not likely to lead to the expected program outcomes. However, it will be unclear whether the program was implemented as planned, unless it is documented from the start what the services and activities will be. While documenting the services and activities, include answers to the questions, "What is going to happen?" and "When and how much will it be done?" "When and how much" refers to when the program or activities will be delivered (after school every day for three hours, a single day for three hours, etc.).

## Who Will Participate in or Be Influenced by the Program?

The third question, when answered, delineates who will participate in or be influenced by the program. Or, in other words, it identifies the target group to whom the program is being delivered. This includes identifying whether the target group is a universal, selective, or indicated population, as described in Step 5 in Chapter 3. It is important at this point to ensure that the target population selected will be appropriate for the strategy selected. Also, it is crucial to verify that working with this population will reach the goals of reducing your priority risk factors and enhancing priority protective factors. For example, a prevention professional needs to reduce the risk factor of early antisocial behavior. She chooses to work with the fourth-grade class at the local elementary school as her target population (a universal population). The risk factor of early antisocial behavior is specific to kindergarten through third-grade boys (a selective population), so what is the chance that she is going to be effective in reducing the risk factor of early antisocial behavior? Not likely. Consequently, in order to increase the likelihood of success in prevention programs, it is essential that the most appropriate target population be selected.

## How Will These Activities Lead to Expected Outcomes?

The next step involves identifying the assumptions underlying the program. That is, it forces planners to think about why and how program activities are expected to lead to the desired outcomes. This is the pivotal section in the logic model. A very common problem in prevention programs is selecting program activities and strategies that do not lead logically to the goals or outcomes that the program would like to achieve. As a result, it is essential that the assumptions of why and how a program is expected to lead to the desired changes be delineated. It is easiest to view this as a series of "if-then" relationships.

The following is an example of a series of "if-then" statements that is often seen in prevention programs:

If the program invests time and money to develop an inventory of drug-free summer activities, then youth will be more informed about what is available in the community.

If youth know what is available, then they will be more likely to participate in these programs.

If youth participate in alternative activities, then they will be more likely to develop friendships with nonusing peers and then be less likely to use ATOD themselves.

Note that even in this very simple series of "if–then" statements there are a number of assumptions about the problem to be addressed, how the program will work, and what it can achieve. For example, the following assumptions were made in the "if-then" statement above:

- Currently, youth do not know about many available activities.
- Knowing about the activities will lead youth to actually participate in the activities.
- The activities will support development of new, positive peer relationships.
- Once the resource inventory is developed, people will use it, particularly the identified target group.

If a community prevention program implemented the strategies as identified in the "if-then" statement above, what probability of success could be anticipated? With so many assumptions, it is likely that they will not achieve the results they have anticipated.

A stronger "if-then" statement, with a greater chance of success, could be:

> If a parenting education program aimed at reducing family management problems is offered, then parents with family management problems attend.
>
> If parents with family management problems attend, then they gain skills on reducing family management problems.
>
> If they learn skills to reduce family management problems, then they apply those skills to their daily family lives.
>
> If they apply those skills to their daily family lives, then the family management problems decrease in their family lives.
>
> If the family management problems decrease in the family lives, then the likelihood that the children will abuse alcohol, tobacco, and other drugs will decrease.

In this "if-then" statement, many assumptions are identified. However, there is a logical flow to the statements without huge leaps in assumption.

In summary, when developing a logic model, the underlying assumptions must be exposed. These assumptions must be tested to see if they are realistic and sound. And finally, evidence should exist to support the validity of the assumptions made.

## What Immediate Changes Are Expected for Individuals, Organizations, or Communities?

The final two questions in the logic model deal with the outcomes to expect from programs. Before working with these questions, some issues in defining program outcomes must be discussed. First, the way in which the terms **process**, **outcome**, and **impact** are used in this book must be clear. Different organizations and materials define these terms in different manners. In this book, **process evaluation** is documenting program implementation. "Short-term outcomes" are the immediate program effects that are to be achieved soon after the program is completed. "Long-term impacts," on the other hand, are the long-term or ultimate effects from the program.

For example, documenting that a life-skills training program was held for one hour per week for one school year for 200 middle school students would be a process evaluation. Assessing whether an increase in students' problem-solving skills when the life skills program is implemented would be a short-term outcome evaluation. Prevention programs attempt to increase students' problem-solving skills, the immediate outcome, because it is believed that these increased skills will ultimately help to prevent or reduce student drug use, the long-term impact.

Some additional issues about outcomes and impacts exist. First, there is no right number of outcomes and impacts. The number selected by a program will depend on the nature and purpose of the program, resources, and size and number of constituencies represented. Next, the more immediate the outcome or impact, the more influence the program has over its achievement. In parent training programs, for example, changes in participants' family management skills can be largely attributed to the education and training provided by the program. Conversely, the longer term the outcome or impact, the less direct influence a program has over its achievement and the more likely other extraneous forces are to intervene. For example, if a preschool prevention program is implemented, assessing whether the program created an impact on decreased adolescent substance abuse is difficult. A variety of factors, including sociocultural, political, and economic factors, often have an effect on long-range outcomes and impacts.

Another issue is that just because other forces affect a given outcome or impact, does not mean that that particular outcome should not be included in an evaluation. Despite the influence of other factors on substance abuse, a prevention professional may wish to measure and track these outcomes or impacts in order to understand the rates of use in the community and how a confluence of factors, including the specific program being implemented, may affect overall rates of use. Long-term impacts, however, should not go beyond the program's purpose or target audience. For example, evaluating a long-term impact of "delay of onset of use before age 15" for a prevention program for kindergarten students would be, in most cases, beyond the scope of the program. Think about what the program is designed to do—where its influence is likely to be felt—and focus the outcome/impact measurement at that level. Likewise, keep the outcome/impact measures focused on the targeted audience. For example, it would be a mistake to conduct an evaluation of a substance abuse prevention program using all 600 students in an elementary school if only 20 of the students participated in the program. In this case, the program may have been effective with those 20 students, but the effects of the program would not be evident if the other 580 students were included in the evaluation.

Finally, it is important to avoid confusing outcomes with **outputs**. This is an important distinction. It is important to have goals about how many outputs a program will achieve (i.e., how many clients served, how many teachers trained, and how many community events implemented). Outputs are documented in the process evaluation. If a program does not successfully provide services, train teachers, or host events, it is impossible for a program ever to affect people and therefore reach its goals. However, outputs do not provide evidence that the program is creating change. Outcomes and impacts refer to changes produced (in individuals, communities, or systems) by the program. Outputs, however, refer to the number of opportunities the program has to create these changes, such as the number of clients served and for how many hours the program is held.

Now that several issues surrounding outcomes and impacts are clear, the next question in the logic model can be explored. Namely, the immediate changes expected for individuals, organizations, or communities must be identified. Or, in other words, the short-term outcomes must be defined. The short-term outcomes are likely to include some, if not all, of the risk and protective factors that were specified as program goals in the first question in the logic model. It is important that a connection exists between the risk and protective factors being addressed and the short-term outcomes.

## What Changes Would the Program Ultimately Like to Create?

Finally, the last question to be answered in the logic model is the identification of what changes the program ultimately would like to create. These are the long-term impacts desired by the program. Again, the long-term impacts identified here should relate to the program's goals, target population, and short-term outcomes. The long-term impacts for substance abuse prevention programs are typically related to substance abuse. For example, long-term impacts are often "prevent substance abuse in target population," or "delayed onset of use."

## Sample Logic Model

The following is a sample logic model related to the questions outlined above. In the example below, a community coalition conducted a needs assessment and identified the risk factor of "academic failure" as a priority. Furthermore, they identified a selective population of children in grades one through three who were having academic problems as

**TABLE 8.2    Logic Model**

| 1. Logic Model | |
| --- | --- |
| A. Goals | Reduce academic failure. |
| B. Strategies | Tutoring: 3 hours per week for one school year; 50 students. |
| C. Target group | Children in grades 1–3 at the local elementary school who are struggling academically as identified by teachers (selective population). |
| D. If-then statement | If tutoring is offered to students having academic problems, then students will have the opportunity to improve their academic skills. If the students take the opportunity, then they will improve their academic skills. If they improve their academic skills, then they will not fail in school. If they don't fail in school, then they are less likely to abuse alcohol, tobacco, and other drugs. |
| E. Short-term outcomes | Participants' grades improve; participants move to next grade level on time. |
| F. Long-term impacts | Participants do not begin using alcohol, tobacco, and other drugs within 3 years after participating in the program. |

their target population. Finally, they selected the research-based practice of "tutoring" to address the identified needs.

Once a logic model is complete, it is essential to continue to use it for planning an evaluation. It is also important to review and update the logic model regularly in order to see what has changed, keep track of progress, make modifications in how the program is being implemented, and communicate to others about what the program is doing. Programs are usually not implemented exactly as planned, but are changed, adapted, and improved. If this occurs, the logic model should be revised to provide a "picture" of these changes.

## Developing Evaluation Questions

After a logic model is completed, evaluation questions need to be developed for each part of a logic model. To do this, simply take the logic model's information and turn it into clear and concise questions. For example, if the goal of the program were to reduce the risk factor of academic failure, then the evaluation question would be, "Was academic failure reduced?" or "Was academic success increased?" Although this is not a difficult step in creating an evaluation plan, it is an important step because the cornerstone of any good evaluation is evaluation questions.

Continuing on from the sample logic model in Table 8.2, review how the evaluation questions in Table 8.3 reflect the logic model.

Next, taking all the factors discussed, program planners need to identify the *key* questions that they believe their evaluation should focus on. This is important because most prevention programs do not have the ability to answer all the evaluation questions. Consequently, the issue of whether the questions seem appropriate given the purpose of the evaluation, stakeholder concerns, and the developmental stage of the program must be considered. Also, the ability to answer the evaluation questions must be feasible, given the timelines and resources available. Specifically, the questions described in the following paragraphs need to be answered first in order to ensure that the key evaluation questions are selected.

First, what is the purpose of the evaluation? Is an evaluation needed to ensure that program activities are being implemented as planned (e.g., the number of participants, number of hours, type of activities)? Or does an evaluation need to be designed to collect information that can be used for continuous program improvement? Or is the purpose of the evaluation to collect information about whether a program is effective in creating intended outcomes and impacts? Before selecting which evaluation questions to pursue, it is important that it be clear what type(s) of evaluation needs to be completed for the program.

A second question to be asked when reviewing evaluation questions is, who wants to know what? What is wanted from the evaluation may differ according to what information funders, supervisors, and/or participants want to learn. Consequently, learning what the different stakeholders need or want is crucial when selecting evaluation questions.

Third, when is the information needed? Different kinds of evaluations require different timelines. Process evaluation data is generally needed quickly. In general, outcome evaluation results need to be reported back in a timely manner, in order to achieve continuous program improvement. Impact evaluation results typically are not available until after the program is completed.

**TABLE 8.3    Logic Model with Evaluation Questions**

| | 1. Logic Model | 2. Evaluation Questions |
|---|---|---|
| A. Goals | Reduce academic failure. | Was academic failure reduced in the target population? |
| B. Strategies | Tutoring: 3 hours per week for one school year; 50 students. | How many students participated in a tutoring program for 3 hours per week for one school year? |
| C. Target group | Children in grades 1–3 at the local elementary school who are struggling academically as identified by teachers (selective population). | How many participants were in grades 1–3 and struggling academically? |
| D. If-then statement | If tutoring is offered to students having academic problems, then students will have the opportunity to improve their academic skills. If the students take the opportunity, then they will improve their academic skills. If they improve their academic skills, then they will not fail in school. If they don't fail in school, then they are less likely to abuse alcohol, tobacco, and other drugs. | How many students who were selected for the program participated? How many participants' reading skills improved? How many participants failed in school after participating in the program? How many participants abused alcohol, tobacco, and other drugs after participating in the program? |
| E. Short-term outcomes | Participants' grades improve; participants move to next grade level on time. | How many participants' grades improved? How many participants moved on to the next grade? |
| F. Long-term impacts | Participants do not begin using alcohol, tobacco, and other drugs within 3 years after participating in the program. | How many participants used tobacco, alcohol, and other drugs within 3 years of the end of the program? |

Finally, what resources (time, money, people) are available for the evaluation? The resources that programs have often influence evaluation plans more than any other single factor. It is crucial to determine what resources are available before agreeing to conduct an evaluation. For example, if the funder requests a long-term impact evaluation, but the funding does not allow for money to be spent on evaluation, then the prevention program must negotiate with the funder before agreeing to conduct the evaluation.

One word of caution: When selecting the key questions, do not select only short-term outcome and/or impact evaluations questions. This is sometimes called a "black box" evaluation. Process evaluations "open" the black box of outcome and impact evaluation by defining what the program is, why it is expected to work, for which types of people the program is or is not effective, and in what circumstances the overall program is or is not effective. Evaluations focusing only on outcomes/impacts without information about how the program was implemented, how clients experienced the program, and so on, will be of limited value, especially if the outcomes/impacts are not as positive as hoped. Outcome and impact evaluation only, without a process evaluation component, will not provide information about why the program worked or did not work. For example, a parenting education program was implemented in order to decrease family management problems. A short-term outcome evaluation was done with the parents at the end of the program in order to assess whether family management problems decreased. The evaluation showed no change in the family management problems in participant families. The director of the agency conducting the program reviewed these results and deemed the parent education curriculum ineffective. Was she correct? If a process evaluation had also been conducted, the agency director would have also gained the knowledge that participants attended only roughly half the sessions, and that three of the eight sections of the curriculum were not taught. With this information, the agency director could make a more accurate judgment: that the curriculum may not be ineffective, but that the program implementation may be to blame. Consequently, process evaluations contribute essential information to short-term outcome and long-term impact evaluations.

After completing columns one and two of the logic model, the methods of evaluation and analysis plans must be determined. Before this is done, however, it must be determined whether an internal or external evaluator will assist in completing the analysis and methods portion of the logic model and evaluation plan.

# Internal or External Evaluations?

Evaluations that are done by staff or volunteers, who are also working for the program being evaluated, are called **internal evaluations**. Evaluations done by hired consultants or researchers not working for the same organization as the program are called **external evaluations**. Another popular model for doing evaluations involves a combination of these two approaches, and is called **participatory evaluation**. This usually, although not always, involves an external evaluator who works closely with program management, staff, volunteers, and participants to design the evaluation. Benefits exist for both internal and external evaluations.

Internal evaluators are often more skilled and knowledgeable about program functioning. They also may produce more useful information because of familiarity with the program. Furthermore, internal evaluators may be more successful in getting support from other program staff. Finally, internal evaluators often are less expensive.

On the other hand, external evaluations are usually perceived as being more objective about the program because of less direct connection with the program. External evaluators are usually perceived as more credible, provided that sufficient time is taken to understand program functioning. Finally, they are often more skilled and knowledgeable about evaluation.

## How to Know Whether an Evaluation Consultant or Contractor Is Needed

Although most programs can and should be engaged in their own internal program evaluation activities, there may be occasions in which the assistance of an external evaluator is necessary. Some situations in which one might consider hiring an evaluation consultant or contractor include:

- The evaluation requires more time than program staff and volunteers can provide.
- The program is "under fire" from outside critics and the results of an internal evaluation might be subject to criticism.
- Statistical assistance in analyzing data is needed.
- Help in designing a questionnaire, survey, or other data collection instruments is needed.
- The program is highly complex and major disagreements exist regarding the focus of the evaluation.

### Finding and Selecting a Good Consultant

Depending on a program's situation and needs, different kinds of skills in an evaluator will be necessary, as described by the W. K. Kellogg Foundation (2001). For example, if a controversy exists over the program and how to evaluate it, conflict-resolution skills, team-building skills, and neutrality and objectivity can be useful. Yet if a program is highly visible, then public presentation skills, experience with media and politicians, and a credible reputation and experience are essential. If a program is highly dynamic, then an evaluator must have a tolerance for ambiguity, be flexible, and have skills in qualitative methods. Finally, if the program is a collaborative, then an evaluator needs to have team-building skills, the ability to focus and direct progress, and experience in participatory evaluation. Therefore, according to the program's situation, the evaluator must possess a different set of skills.

## Developing a Design to Answer Evaluation Questions

If at this point in the evaluation planning, it is decided that an external evaluator will be used to complete the evaluation, the logic model with columns one and two completed (shown in Table 8.3) can be shared with the evaluator. Columns one and two of the logic model should provide the evaluator with the information needed to begin designing the evaluation. However, if at this time it is decided that the evaluation will be done internally, then the evaluation design must be selected by the prevention professional.

A review of each key evaluation question from the logic model is needed in order to determine the appropriate evaluation design to answer each evaluation question. For many evaluation questions, it is possible to choose any of the different types of designs. Consequently, one must consider which design will provide the most useful and credible information. The selection of a design can vary according to what type of evaluation questions need to be answered. For example, the designs used for evaluating program activities and outputs are different from those designs that are useful for evaluating outcomes and impacts. These differences are explored in the next sections.

## Evaluating Program Activities and Outputs

Collecting information about program activities and outputs (rows B and C in the logic model, Table 8.1) provides a description of what happened while the program was actually implemented. This includes data such as the number of participants in the program and for how many hours the program was held. Often, program funders require this type of information. Consequently, before collecting information about program implementation, a program's reporting requirements should be reviewed. Any tools developed to collect program implementation data should capture all the information needed in one place, to help make reporting easier.

There are many possible sources of information that might be used to evaluate program activities and outputs, such as observations and program records review (e.g., attendance sheets, staff logs, event logs). The data for program activities and output are usually collected as the prevention program is implemented.

## Evaluating Short-term Outcomes and Long-term Impacts

Designs for evaluating short-term outcomes and long-term impacts are quite similar. There are many different ways to collect data for outcome and impact evaluations. However, the three most commonly used designs will be explored here, including: post-test only data collection; pre-post data collection; and pre-post data collection with a comparison group.

***Post-test Only Data Collection.***   Often, program outcomes and impacts are measured only after the program is completed. This is understandable, as programs must first be developed and operated as planned before they can be assessed. Although collecting data only after the program is implemented cannot tell how much participants have changed (because their status before the program was not documented), this information can contribute additional information to the description of the program and to the overall picture of substance abuse prevention programs at the state and national level.

The measurement of outcomes and impacts only after a program is completed provides information about where participants stand at a given point in time. It may be found, for instance, that students in a substance abuse information program have mastered 85 percent of the knowledge about the effects of alcohol, tobacco, and other drugs as measured by a drug information test. In some cases this information can be compared with already existing information about the standard rate of substance abuse information among students.

The problem with using existing data about student substance abuse information knowledge or other substance abuse-related behaviors is that the data often are not an appropriate standard for students in a particular program. The data may be based on a different grade level, region of the country, social class, or some other factor that can make comparisons with a program's participants misleading. In fact, the lack of good descriptive data about substance abuse information and use with different groups of students in a community and across the country is one of the most important reasons for local program evaluators to collect and share their findings.

What is done with outcomes and impacts measured only after the program if there is no data with which to compare it? There are times when the outcome being measured, such as substance abuse knowledge, seems relatively unlikely to be influenced by the participants' prior knowledge, so the outcome/impact is logically related to the program. In such a case, one might have some confidence that the program had the desired effect on the outcome. Indeed, most classroom teaching and testing operates on a very similar basis: Children are taught a lesson and then given a test to see how well they learned the lesson. Often, however, there is a need to have some basis of comparison before it can be concluded that the program brought about a change from the way things were before the program.

***Pre- and Post-test Data Collection.***   The most direct way to know whether the prevention program changed program participants' knowledge, attitudes, behavior, or some other outcome/impact is to test program participants before the program and then after the program. Comparing the difference between before-program scores with after-program scores (i.e., after-program scores minus before-program scores) will indicate clearly whether a change in the outcome scores has occurred. Students will, for example, have increased their knowledge of substance abuse or will have decreased their acceptance of attitudes toward substance abuse. Change no longer has to be assumed. This moves beyond describing where program participants stand at one point in time to demonstrating that they have changed in important ways. Because of this benefit, a pre-post data collection method is recommended rather than post-test only whenever possible.

However, using a pre-post test strategy for data collection does not ensure that the changes seen were actually caused by a program. Consider the following. The consequences of substance abuse are so serious and often so dramatic that substance abuse–related incidents are a constant topic of interest in the media. As a consequence of this level of media coverage and of personal experience, substance abuse has become a very serious concern to citizens and to all levels of government. Many different uncoordinated efforts are being made to solve the substance abuse problem.

It cannot be assumed that a particular prevention program is the only force affecting program participants' knowledge, attitudes, behaviors, or other outcomes. Most participants are exposed to news programs, TV dramas, magazine articles, or sermons that could change how they stand on some measure. For example, an intoxicated high school student driver and his girlfriend die tragically in a car accident. As a result, a schoolteacher introduces into the curriculum new materials intended to prevent substance abuse, or the student government independently begins an antidrug program. These events and others can all act to change program participants' outcome scores in unanticipated ways. While these events contribute to a common effort to prevent substance abuse, the combination of these events does make it difficult to say decisively that one particular program was the most important event that brought about the desired change.

***Pre- and Post-test Data Collection with a Comparison Group.***   The best way to increase confidence that one particular program led to specific changes is to collect data from a comparison group. Testing both program and comparison groups before and after the program would indicate both how much change had occurred over the course of the program and how comparable both groups were before the program. For example, a local high school conducts an experimental program to change ninth-graders' attitudes toward substance abuse. Another local high school is selected as the comparison group. Both groups have similar student bodies, are located in similar neighborhoods, and have similar before-program scores. With reasonably comparable program and comparison groups, there is a good chance that both groups are exposed to similar outside experiences during the program.

Sometimes these experiences may cause changes in the after-program scores of both groups. For instance, both groups' attitudes toward substance abuse become more negative, but the program group scores change much more dramatically than the comparison group scores. Later, questioning of the ninth-graders reveals that, during the program, a large percentage of both groups viewed a special television series of three programs that dealt with the dangers of teenage substance abuse. The program evaluators were able to detect this unanticipated event and explain why both groups' outcome scores changed. The evaluators demonstrated good program effects and were able to answer questions about other possible influences. Careful monitoring of school, community, and media events can also help detect other possible influences or give some assurance that the most reasonable explanation for changes in outcome scores is the prevention program.

## Cause Attribution

Although professional program evaluators have developed many designs to help them better identify specific causes of outcomes (e.g., was it this program or something else?), it may not be critical to an evaluation to know this information with confidence. For many programs, if demonstrated changes in knowledge, skills, and/or behaviors occur within a group of program participants, this is sufficient evidence that the program is working. Further, in terms of preventing substance abuse, it is widely recognized that no one program is going to have a strong overall effect in isolation. Thus, it is expected that multiple programs are having multiple influences at any given time. This suggests that if a program keeps good information about how well it is implemented, and about the short-term changes that the participants experience, this is sufficient evidence for program effectiveness. Isolating one program's effects may be unrealistic.

## Expectations Regarding Changes in Short-term Outcomes and Long-term Impacts

Evaluating long-term impacts is usually done in the same manner as are short-term outcomes. One important difference between evaluating long-term impacts and short-term outcomes is the amount of change that can reasonably be expected of any individual program.

As stated earlier in this chapter, change in many outcomes (e.g., substance abuse knowledge; attitudes about alcohol, tobacco, and other drug use; accessibility to alcohol, tobacco, and other drugs; and peer group values) can have some effects on the ultimate substance abuse. It is unreasonable to expect any one program by itself to independently and dramatically change existing patterns of substance abuse. It is the combination of many programs and other local, state, and federal responses to the substance abuse problem that will, over time, culminate in significant reductions in substance abuse. Changes in many short-term outcomes must come before changes in long-term impacts are revealed. Good evaluation must first document and evaluate programs' short-term outcome effects. This is not to say that long-term impacts are not important, but they must be evaluated in the context of a longer time perspective and a bigger picture in mind. Prevention professionals should not be discouraged by findings that show little or no program effects on long-term impacts. Serious social problems require the combined efforts of many people and time. Local substance abuse prevention programs and their evaluations are part of the solution.

# Developing Methods to Carry Out the Evaluation Design

## Types of Evaluation Methods

The key evaluation questions and evaluation design have been identified at this stage of the process and decisions can be made about what information is needed to answer the questions and how this information will be collected. The way that the evaluation design is carried out is called the **evaluation method**. Many methods of evaluation exist. A few of these methods will be discussed here.

***Written Surveys or Questionnaires.***   Written surveys or questionnaires are documents containing questions answered by individuals. Survey questions can be self-administered or administered by the evaluator. Survey questions can be open-ended (e.g., "What did you like about this program?") or close-ended (e.g., "How much did you like this program? Not at all, a little, somewhat, a lot"). Surveys and questionnaires can be used to evaluate many different aspects of a program. In particular, they can assess changes in risk and protective factors. Many sources exist, such as the Decision Support System (CSAP, n.d.), which can provide prevention professionals with risk and protective factor survey instruments and/or questionnaires.

The benefits to using written surveys and questionnaires, as identified by the National Center for the Advancement of Prevention (NCAP) (2000), include anonymity provided to the participants, the low cost of analysis, and the standardization that allows comparisons to other data. Drawbacks include results that are easily biased, missed information, and often a low response rate. The cost of implementing written surveys and questionnaires is moderate.

***Interviews.***   Interviews involve one person asking questions of another person. Interviews can be done face-to-face or by telephone. Interviews, like surveys, can involve both open-ended and close-ended questions. Interviews can be used in many different ways in an evaluation.

One of the benefits to conducting interviews (National Center for the Advancement of Prevention [NCAP], 2000) includes the ability to gather in-depth and detailed information. Also, the information gathered during interviews can be used to generate survey questions. However, interviews do take much time and expertise to conduct and analyze, and there exists the potential for interview bias, which often becomes an issue if a program staff person conducts the interview. In this case, respondents are likely to give answers that will please the program staff. Consequently, it is essential to have an interviewer who will not cause bias to occur. Furthermore, interviewing can be an inexpensive method to use if done internally, but can be expensive if interviewers and transcribers are hired.

***Tests and Assessments.***    Tests and assessments are usually tools that have already been developed for particular purposes. They can provide information about different aspects of the evaluation, but are most frequently used for assessing short-term outcomes and long-term impacts. Tests can include physical assessments, knowledge or achievement tests, psychological tests, and attitudinal assessments. Tests and assessments might be included as part of written surveys, questionnaires, or interviews. Standardized assessments have been used on large segments of the population so that test "norms" have been developed.

***Observations.***    Observations of program activities are often used to understand the program context. Observational techniques can also be used to collect some forms of outcome data. For example, conducting observations of parent and child interactions at a parenting class could glean information about the change in parenting skills, family conflict, and family bonding. The benefit to using observations is that they can provide detailed information and an "insider" view (NCAP, 2000). However, the drawbacks of observations are that the observer can be biased and the process can be very lengthy (NCAP, 2000). If done internally, the cost is usually inexpensive.

***Focus Groups.***    Focus groups involve asking a series of predetermined questions to a group. People are encouraged to provide their opinions, but not necessarily to reach consensus. Focus groups can be used in a variety of ways in evaluation. The advantages to using focus groups are as follows: information about needs, community attitudes, and community norms can be gathered quickly; information gathered in focus groups can be used to generate survey questions (NCAP, 2000). The disadvantages to focus groups are that they can be difficult to run (a good facilitator is needed) and analyze, and it may be difficult to gather the appropriate individuals to participate (NCAP, 2000). Focus groups can be inexpensive if done internally, but expensive if a facilitator and/or a transcriber are hired. It is essential to have a trained facilitator conduct the focus group.

***Case Studies.***    Case studies involve collecting in-depth information about a few selected participants. Usually case studies are used to provide examples of particular aspects of the program. Some evaluators also do case studies of programs. Case studies can provide in-depth information and provide insight to the inner workings of a program and its impact on individuals. However, case studies can be time-consuming to complete.

***Document and Program Record Reviews.***    Existing program records and documents (such as meeting minutes, reports, and brochures) can provide excellent information, particularly about program context and history, and about program implementation. Case files often contain a wealth of information about program participants that can be useful in the evaluation. Attendance records and staff logs often contain information about how many people have received services and how many services have been delivered.

Document and program record reviews are quick and objective; furthermore, they already exist and do not require the participation of program staff or participants (NCAP,

2000). However, the data in the documents being reviewed may be difficult to interpret and are often incomplete (NCAP, 2000). Yet document and program record reviews are typically inexpensive evaluation methods.

***Existing Databases and Archives.***    Many kinds of data are collected by public agencies, such as the Census Bureau; school districts; police departments; and other county, state, and federal agencies. This data can be an important source of information for evaluation. Existing databases and archives can provide detailed information about a program (NCAP, 2000). This is typically an inexpensive evaluation method. However, usefulness of data available from databases can be limited because someone else determined what data were collected in what manner. Also, the data is often aggregated for a large geographic region.

## Selecting the Appropriate Evaluation Method

A number of factors need to be considered before deciding which methods to use, as identified by the W. K. Kellogg Foundation (2001). One factor is to stay focused on the questions that **stakeholders** want answered and to select methods that are most appropriate to answering those questions. Do not select the method before selecting the question! Another factor to consider is available resources. Usually, there is more than one way to collect information about any particular question. Some methods involve more time, money, and effort than do others. Realistic decisions need to be made about which method can be used.

Next, it is important to be sensitive to the types of participants in the project and the kinds of information being collected. Some information may place participants at risk if it becomes public (for example, any report of illegal activity). Other information may be sensitive to some people or groups; be sure to consider how respondents will feel if they are asked to provide particular information. Also, consideration of the particular skills of the respondents is also important: if most do not read English, alternative ways of obtaining the information must be available.

Another factor to consider when selecting methods of evaluation is credibility. How credible will the evaluation be as a result of the methods that have been chosen? First, credibility is affected by the validity of the instrument. That is, does the instrument measure what it claims to measure? Do the questions make sense for the program? Next, the reliability of the instrument affects the credibility of the evaluation. That is, will it provide the same answers if administered at different times and places? Furthermore, the methods must be suitable for the target group, and must not be biased toward finding only positive results. Finally, credibility is affected by the importance of the information. In other words, how important is a particular piece of information in the context of the overall evaluation plan?

Finally, before selecting the method of evaluation, it must be determined who will use the information collected through the evaluation. What type of information are they most likely to understand and consider credible? Will they be more receptive to statistics, human stories, or case descriptions? In most cases, users find a mix of data and/or numbers and narratives (individual anecdotes and more generalizable results) most useful.

In summary, prevention professionals must keep in mind several factors before selecting the method(s) of evaluation. In some cases it may be necessary to use several methods of evaluation to have an effective evaluation plan. In other cases, one method may provide all the necessary information for key stakeholders and program staff.

### Qualitative and Quantitative Data

Evaluation often requires measuring or assessing things that are hard to measure. Sometimes what needs to be evaluated may seem vague or subjective. This does not mean that it is not important to evaluate, but that sometimes it can be quite difficult to evaluate. Because of this difficulty, using a combination of qualitative and quantitative methods is recommended whenever possible. Most professional evaluators now acknowledge that both quantitative and qualitative methods contribute important, and complementary, types of information to an evaluation. Both quantitative and qualitative data can be collected through the various evaluation methods discussed above.

**Quantitative data** is information that is reported in numerical form, such as test scores, numbers of people attending, the dropout rate, and percentages. Quantitative data are things that can be counted and measured. Quantitative data is useful for describing concrete phenomenon, and for completing statistical analyses of evaluation results (for example, calculating the percentage decrease in cigarette use among eighth-graders). Surveys and questionnaires often include rating scales that can be used in quantitative analyses.

**Qualitative data** is information that is reported in narrative form, such as written description of program activities, testimonials of program effects, and comments about how a program was or was not helpful. Qualitative information can be used to describe how a project functions and what it may mean to the people involved. Qualitative data provides a context for the project, and can be used to convey information about people's perceptions and reactions to a program using rich description. However, it can be harder to make generalizations with qualitative data, due to the difficulty of aggregating qualitative information.

## Sample Logic Model with Design and Methods

Now it is time to review the logic model again (Table 8.4). Designs and methods must now be identified for each of the key evaluation questions selected. Consider whether pre-tests and post-tests might be feasible. Consider whether comparison group information could be collected. Consider how the data will be used, including what information is needed to answer the concerns of stakeholders.

## Analyzing Evaluation Data

Much data analysis can be done in simple and straightforward ways, using sums, averages, and percentages. Unless a person working on the evaluation enjoys statistical analysis, it is recommended that a professional evaluator or local college class assist in analyzing the data. For more complex analyses, however, professional evaluators or statisticians are recommended.

**TABLE 8.4 Logic Model with Designs and Methods**

| | 1. Logic Model | 2. Evaluation Questions | 3. Designs and Methods |
|---|---|---|---|
| A. Goals | Reduce academic failure. | Was academic failure reduced in the target population? | Pre-post survey conducted with the student participants. |
| B. Strategies | Tutoring: 3 hours per week for one school year; 50 students. | How many students participated in a tutoring program for 3 hours per week for one school year? | Program records from the tutoring program coordinator. |
| C. Target group | Children in grades 1–3 at the local elementary school who are struggling academically as identified by teachers (selective population). | How many participants were in grades 1–3 and struggling academically? | Program records from the tutoring program coordinator. |
| D. If-then statement | If tutoring is offered to students having academic problems, then students will have the opportunity to improve their academic skills. If the students take the opportunity, then they will improve their academic skills. If they improve their academic skills, then they will not fail in school. If they don't fail in school, then they are less likely to abuse alcohol, tobacco, and other drugs. | How many students who were selected for the program participated? How many participants' reading skills improved? How many participants failed in school after participating in the program? How many participants abused alcohol, tobacco, and other drugs after participating in the program? | Program records from the tutoring program coordinator and pre-post test surveys of the student participants. |
| E. Short-term outcomes | Participants' grades improve; participants move to next grade level on time. | How many participants' grades improved? How many participants moved on to the next grade? | Pre-post design using the existing database at the school to examine grades of participants. |
| F. Long-term impacts | Participants do not begin using alcohol, tobacco, and other drugs within 3 years after participating in the program. | How many participants used alcohol, tobacco, and other drugs within 3 years of the end of the program? | Pre-post survey conducted with the student participants 1 year, 2 years, and 3 years after the end of the program. |

# Conducting the Evaluation

Before conducting an evaluation, it is important to create an evaluation implementation plan. Writing an implementation plan will help ensure that the information collected is done so in a timely and efficient way. The implementation plan describes the logistics of the data collection and should address the following issues.

- Will an internal or external evaluator be used? If an external evaluator will be used, what skills will the evaluator need? Who will find the evaluator?
- Who will be responsible for developing the data collection instruments (e.g., surveys, interview protocols)?
- When do the data collection instruments need to be finalized?
- Who will collect the data? Will program staff collect the data? Will volunteers be needed? Will people be hired to collect the data? (Data collectors may need training or other support to collect the information effectively. If the staff is collecting additional information, they must be supported by seeing the time spent on evaluation as a part of their workload.)
- What will be the schedule for data collection?
- When will the information be available?
- When can the information be conveniently collected? When will it be least disruptive?
- Where will the information collection take place?
- When will data collection start and end?
- Who will tabulate, organize, and analyze the information?
- When will reports be generated?
- Who will write the reports?
- Who is responsible for monitoring the implementation plan?

Answering the above questions and creating an evaluation implementation plan can avoid errors and costly mistakes. However, as mentioned above, the implementation plan will only be effective if it is created before implementing the evaluation.

# Using the Answers to the Evaluation Questions

The final step in evaluation, and one that is extremely important, is reporting the information. Information that is not shared effectively with others will not be used effectively. The following questions need to be answered when deciding how to report evaluation results.

## To Whom Is the Information to Be Communicated?

Look back at who was identified early on as a key user. Target key decision-makers with appropriate and hard-hitting information. Share information with colleagues who may need to conduct a similar evaluation. Is there anyone else who might, or should, be interested in the evaluation results?

Remember to communicate findings to the respondents who participated in the evaluation. Not only is this courteous, but it helps to ensure their cooperation in future work. It may be necessary to develop separate brief reports and summaries depending on the audience. Remember, different stakeholders have different information needs.

## When Will the Information Be Reported?

The first step in reporting is determining when information will be made available. A schedule will be needed of when different kinds of information will be available along with a plan describing simple ways of communicating information to the stakeholders on a regular basis. In general, short-term outcome evaluations are less likely to be needed too quickly; for long-term evaluations, a final report may be sufficient.

## How Will the Information Be Communicated?

Time and resources have been expended in conducting an evaluation. Now is the time to maximize the investment in the project. Other ways need to be identified to get some mileage from the effort. Remember that citing a finding or two in informal conversations may have more influence than preparing a formal report.

Communication methods used will depend on the audience. A variety of possibilities exist, including a written report; short summary statements; film or videotape; pictures, photo essays, wall charts, bulletin boards, and displays; slide presentations; graphs and visuals; media releases; and Internet and e-mail postings. Invite audiences to suggest ways they would like to receive the information. For example, ask for dates when evaluation results would be most valuable, what formats would be useful, and what displays or graphs would be desired. Refer to Chapter 7 for information about using the media effectively.

## What Are the Conclusions and Recommendations?

It is recommended that the three to five main points that are most important from the evaluation be summarized—the points that program staff and others should remember. As appropriate, provide recommendations that follow from these findings.

## What Was Learned? What Should Be Done Differently?

If it is agreed that the underlying purpose of any evaluation is to promote understanding and learning about programs, including how to improve them, then the ultimate result is to articulate what was learned about the program, about professional competencies, and about the process of the evaluation. What will be done as a result of these insights? Often, it is useful to design an action plan. When conducting the evaluation in collaboration with others, developing an action plan helps to ensure that the results are used.

# Summary

Evaluation may be the most crucial step in prevention program planning, but is often the one allotted the least amount of time and given the smallest amount of attention. However, using the logic model can assist in creating a solid evaluation plan and can remove the mystery of evaluation. Prevention professionals need first to create a logic model of the prevention program/strategy they plan to implement. Once this logic model is created, then the evaluation can be designed. Evaluation questions are created from the logic model, then the key questions are identified. Next, the best design to answer these questions is selected, followed by the identification of appropriate methods to collect the data. Finally, an implementation plan must be created in order to ensure that the evaluation is conducted appropriately and in a timely manner.

## KEY TERMS

| | | |
|---|---|---|
| evaluation | logic model | process evaluation |
| evaluation method | outcome | qualitative data |
| external evaluation | outputs | quantitative data |
| impact | participatory evaluation | stakeholders |
| internal evaluation | | |

## DISCUSSION QUESTIONS

1. Why is evaluation an important step in prevention program planning? Why do you think that it is a step that is often given the least amount of attention in program planning?

2. What is the difference between process, short-term outcome, and long-term impact evaluations? What is the danger of conducting only a short-term outcome or long-term impact evaluation, without a process evaluation component?

3. Discuss the benefits and drawbacks of using an internal evaluator or an external evaluator.

## APPLICATION EXERCISES

1. Select a research-based substance abuse prevention program and create a logic model for it.

2. Create evaluation questions for the logic model made in application exercise number 1.

3. Select five of the key evaluation questions created in application exercise number 2. Be sure to select at least one evaluation question in the following categories: process, short-term outcome, and long-term impact. Select an appropriate design and method of evaluation for each evaluation question. Provide documentation about why you chose the designs and methods that you selected.

## SUGGESTED READINGS

Campbell, D. T., & Stanley, J. C. (1963). *Experimental and quasi-experimental designs for research.* Boston: Houghton Mifflin.

United Way. (1996). *Measuring program outcomes: A practical approach.* Alexandria, VA: Author.

W. K. Kellogg Foundation. (2001). *Evaluation handbook.* Battle Creek, MI: Author. Retrieved May 1, 2001, from the World Wide Web: http://www.wkkf.org/Documents/WKKF/EvaluationHandbook/EvalHandbook.pdf.

## REFERENCES

Center for Substance Abuse Prevention. (1996). *A review of activities and alternatives in youth-oriented prevention.* Rockville, MD: U.S. Department of Health and Human Services.

Center for Substance Abuse Prevention. (n.d.). *Prevention decision support system.* Rockville, MD: U.S. Department of Health and Human Services. Retrieved January 30, 2002, from the World Wide Web: http://www.preventiondss.org.

National Center for the Advancement of Prevention. (2000). *NCAPTion Training Guide.* Rockville, MD: U.S. Department of Health and Human Services.

Western Center for the Application of Prevention Technologies. (2001). *Step 7: Evaluation.* Reno: University of Nevada, Reno. Retrieved May 15, 2001, from the World Wide Web: http://www.open.org/~westcapt/evaluate.htm.

W. K. Kellogg Foundation. (2001). *Evaluation handbook.* Battle Creek, MI: Author. Retrieved May 1, 2001, from the World Wide Web: http://www.wkkf.org/Documents/WKKF/EvaluationHandbook/EvalHandbook.pdf.

# 9 Communication Strategies

Prevention professionals need to learn to become competent communicators on a number of levels. Much prevention work relies on skills in public speaking, group facilitation, and communication with program staff. Although it may seem obvious that people need to enhance their communication skills so that ideas can be exchanged in a clear manner, the topic of communication is often ignored in the field of substance abuse prevention. This chapter brings the communication process to the forefront because skill in this area can help prevention professionals provide a good quality science-based prevention program.

This chapter will begin with a thorough discussion on a single communication model. This model breaks down the communication process into its discrete elements. A discussion on the importance of listening will follow. Active listening requires a set of skills not often explored to lead to the proper functioning of the communication process. Some tips and techniques will be discussed for a variety of communication settings, including public presentations, group **facilitation**, and **leadership** styles; however, most techniques can be used in a variety of settings.

## Communication Models

There are many models of communication that attempt to capture the unique exchange that occurs when people communicate. All these models have strengths and limitations. As the purpose of this textbook is not to provide an exhaustive review of communication models, the most commonly used classical model will be presented as a sampling of the many models on communication exchange.

The following communication model is probably considered the most common model in communication and is widely accepted as one of the main seeds out of which communication studies has grown (Fiske, 1982, p. 6). It was originally created by Shannon and Weaver (1949) and is also sometimes referred to as the process model of communication (Lucas, 1992; Beebe & Beebe, 1994; Katula, 1987; Adler & Towne, 1990). Figure 9.1 presents this communication model.

### Sender

The **sender** in the communication exchange process is the person delivering the message. It is important that the sender be as clear as she or he can when communicating so that the

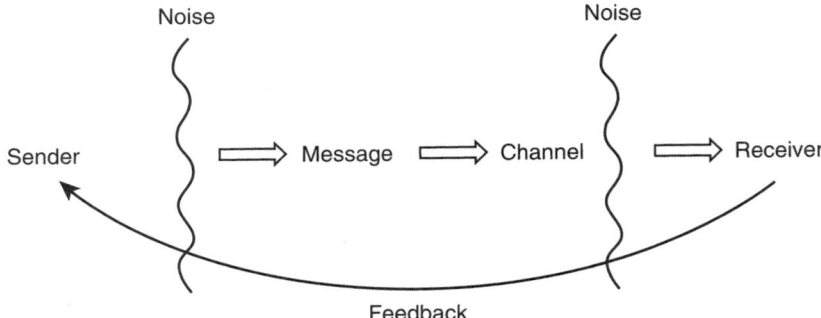

**FIGURE 9.1  Process Model of Communication**

receiver(s) can understand what is being discussed. The sender then needs to assume a lot of responsibility in making sure her or his verbal and nonverbal communication is presented concisely. In the case of a prevention coalition meeting, the chairperson of the meeting would be the sender of the message. However, if another member of the coalition decides to speak at the meeting, he or she at that instant would be the sender. Generally people take turns sending communication messages and a number of cues tell people when it is their turn to speak.

## Message

The **message** is generally the idea or theme that the sender is trying to communicate. For example, in the case of the prevention coalition meeting, the chairperson may deliver the message that "substance abuse is rising and we must implement more science-based prevention programs that work." This is a verbal message and conveys several ideas to the coalition members. Nonverbal messages always accompany verbal ones. For example, assume that the chairperson of the coalition is well-dressed, confident, and has all the relevant facts about substance abuse at her or his fingertips. Nonverbally, the message that she or he is conveying is that she or he knows what she or he is talking about, so it must be time to problem-solve this situation. On the other hand, if she or he is nervous, digs around for her or his notes, arrives at the coalition meeting late, and looks like she or he just woke up, her or his nonverbal message may communicate nervousness, disorganization, and a general loss of credibility. Messages are very important and include both verbal and nonverbal cues.

## Channel

The communication **channel** refers to the means by which a message is communicated. For example, the prevention coalition meeting is held in a medium-sized room without a lot of noise so there is no need for a microphone. If there is a microphone, that would be the channel through which the message would travel. Because there is no microphone, the channel is the space through which the message must travel to get to the receiver. If, for example, the chairperson's address is being broadcasted to the community at large, the television image and the voice could be perceived through both these channels. The most direct channel is one that does not require any electronic support.

## Receiver

The **receiver** is the person or people listening to the message from the sender that was sent through the channel. The receiver listens to the message and generally responds in some manner to others in the **communication environment**. Individual perception plays an important role in the mind of the receiver. For example, looking at the prevention coalition meeting, after the chairperson sends the message that the rate of substance abuse is up and there is need to implement some science-based prevention programs, a receiver may think that the existing program is sufficient. Instead of hearing the "call to action," this coalition member gets angry and feels threatened because he or she may fear that his or her program may lose its funding. Receiver perceptions are important considerations for prevention professionals to understand when they are in the sender role. Although people cannot control others' perceptions, they can try to communicate clearly to prevent any misunderstandings.

## Feedback

**Feedback** is the verbal and nonverbal processes that occur after the message has been sent and received. For example, if the coalition member who thinks his or her existing prevention program may be threatened looks worried, casts his or her eyes downward, and grimaces, these nonverbal cues would indicate to the sender that something is wrong. In this instance, the receiver becomes the sender and the sender becomes the receiver. Communication between the two of them has occurred without a single word being spoken. Feedback is very important and happens in every communication setting. The careful and competent communicator picks up on these cues and tries to adjust his or her message to clearly communicate the message again.

## Noise

There are a number of noises that may occur during any communication event. **Noise** is defined in this model as any interference that impedes the message. For example, there are a number of people attending the prevention coalition meeting. The meeting site is located next to a busy street. While the chairperson is speaking, a fire truck drives by with its sirens blaring. Additionally, the air-conditioning system is very noisy and when it turns on it makes a low, grinding sound. While all this is happening, a member arrives at the coalition meeting late, comes in loudly, and spills her coffee while reaching for her ringing cellular phone. Although this may sound chaotic, these are the normal disruptions that occur at many prevention meetings. The sender in these instances needs to be sensitive to all these potential communication barriers, and adjust her or his communication message accordingly. One common mistake made by speakers is to ignore the noise and proceed with the meeting. This is not advised, as people tend to stop listening to the speaker and focus on the disrupting noise. It is better to stop communicating, solve the problem, and then start again when people are ready to listen. Remember that the goal when communicating is to try to keep the attention of the receiver(s) and achieve understanding between people. This may sound easy, but in reality it can be quite challenging.

In summary, the communication model, with its many components, demonstrates how communication occurs. It is important to note that although the process model of communication is presented as a fixed, linear model, it is actually a dynamic process of events that occur simultaneously. For purposes of discussion, it has been broken down into its discrete parts.

The process of communication is both complex and simple. It is complex in that there are many variables to consider when communicating. It is also simple because humans have been communicating for years without models to enhance their understanding. Often, prevention professionals well trained in communication rapidly rise to leadership positions. It can be challenging to facilitate coalition meetings or to present a public speech on the accomplishments of a science-based prevention program. Communication is a skill that will help prevention professionals convey clear messages.

# Listening

Prevention professionals need to think about **listening** skills for a number of reasons. First, when engaged in any type of communication exchange, much time is spent listening. In fact, researchers estimate that most people spend the majority of their total communication time in the role of a listener (Katula, 1987; Beebe & Beebe, 1994; Adler & Towne, 1990). Second, prevention professionals in leadership positions need good listening skills. Listening well helps prevention professionals understand the true scope and depth of the substance abuse problems plaguing a community, helps in problem-solving staff and volunteer dilemmas, and finally conveys a sincere concern to the person doing the speaking. For example, reflect on a conversation you have had and identify signs of good and bad listening. In the bad-listening cases, you might have experienced a person who was busy looking at his or her watch, looking around the room, and seemed like they wanted to be anywhere but listening to you. This may have left you with a feeling that your opinions were not valued, that that person did not care about you, or that your perspective simply did not matter to him or her. On the contrary, cues that someone is listening to what you had to say may have included an interest in what you were saying, asking questions at an appropriate time, nodding of the head, leaning forward, and displaying other positive signals. The feelings you experienced may have been happiness, empowerment, and a sense of connection and understanding. Third, listening is important because a prevention professional who can rephrase ideas clearly and concisely serves a valuable role in any group setting, such as a coalition meeting. Listening actively takes a lot of energy and skill, but the rewards are many.

Many people do not understand the difference between hearing and listening. **Hearing** is a physiological process in which sound waves are transformed into auditory nerve impulses (Katula, 1987, p. 27). For example, while at a coalition meeting, a loud siren transmits a signal from a nearby road. Hearing this siren along with the air conditioner loudly clicking on and off and another member's cellular phone ringing are all examples of sounds being heard. These sound waves are transformed into auditory nerve impulses which are heard. In short, people hear sounds even though they have not intended to hear them. Listening, however, is quite different. Listening involves paying close attention to, and making sense of, what is heard (Lucas, 1992, p. 30). A number of different models explain what occurs when people move from hearing to listening. Regardless, all require that the listener be engaged actively in the information that is transmitted.

There are a number of barriers to effective listening (Beebe & Beebe, 1994; Lucas, 1992; Adler & Towne, 1990; Osborn & Osborn, 1988). One of the most obvious reasons why people do not listen very well is the discrepancy between human capacity to understand words and the common rate of speech. Research shows that the human brain can understand up to 400 words per minute. Human beings tend to speak at about 125 to 150 words per minute (Katula, 1987, p. 27). What the brain does with the extra time varies from person to person. Most people start thinking about something else, turning their attention away from the information being communicated by doodling or fantasizing. Although quick "breaks" of this nature are not always harmful in themselves, it can become a task to end these personal thoughts and return to the topic that is being discussed. For example, assume a prevention staff meeting is occurring. All the staff is assembled and the director begins talking about some plans to provide technical assistance to a customer in Hawaii. She eloquently describes the problem, presents a plan for implementation, and provides a budget so everyone can see how much it will cost. When she mentions "Hawaii," this acts as a **trigger word** and suddenly one of the staff members takes a quick mental "break" and recollects her honeymoon in Hawaii. Trigger words are words so intense with positive or negative connotative meaning that they can block critical listening (Osborn & Osborn, 1988, p. 69). As she reflects on the great time she had, she misses all the pertinent information. Suddenly, the director asks for her opinion and she finds herself unprepared to answer. This type of situation happens often, as it takes a lot of energy to listen carefully, especially at meetings where some of the information seems unimportant.

**Information overload** is another reason why people do not listen very well. Information overload means the overwhelming amount of messages that occur at any given point in time. For instance, when participating in prevention conferences, a lot of prevention speakers give presentations on a diverse range of topics. Prevention professionals, inexperienced in conference attendance, may decide to attend everything. Soon they may find themselves unable to listen well because they are overwhelmed by all the information they have heard and read. A better technique would be to decide which speeches are of interest versus those that would not be critical to attend. This prioritizing method is a good way to prevent information overload and ensure active listening.

Outside noise distractions, such as a passing fire engine with blaring sirens, is another reason why people do not always listen carefully. When conducting a meeting, for example, try to keep noise from occurring. When this cannot be prevented, stop speaking and deal with the problem. Too often, people will try to speak over the noise. It is better to simply stop speaking, deal with the outside distraction, and then continue the meeting when the noise level returns to normal. This has been mentioned earlier but deserves additional emphasis because outside noise is often not dealt with effectively. For example, when running a prevention program with children, if loud noise occurs while the prevention professional is giving directions about the next activity, stop communicating and wait for the noise to pass. It is important that children listen carefully before beginning a program activity so they know what the behavioral expectations are.

## Tips for Better Listening

Just as there are a number of reasons why it can be difficult to listen well, there are also a number of suggestions that can assist people with good listening habits. The following discussion highlights a few ideas that can help engage the listener in the content conveyed by the speaker, including note taking, listening for ideas, suspending judgments, and "listening" with both eyes and ears.

Taking notes is a demonstrated method to help people become better listeners. Research has shown (DiVesta & Grey, 1974) that listeners who take notes during three- to five-minute speeches are able to recall more ideas from the message than those who do not take notes. Writing down the speaker's key ideas is a good way to actively develop good listening habits.

Taking notes is valuable for a number of reasons. First, note taking helps the prevention professional listen actively for key ideas, as mentioned above. Second, notes provide a written reminder of specific tasks that need follow-up and completion. Third, notes help provide a written record of the proceedings and can keep the group on task when participants forget previous agreements and decisions. Good note-taking is a skill that serves prevention professionals well. Try to capture key themes or action items but do not try to write down everything. Attempting to capture all the details detracts from focusing on the key points made and hinders productive listening.

Listen for ideas and rather than just focusing on the specific words themselves (Katula, 1987). The prevention professional needs to focus and understand the key ideas or themes being discussed. There is a danger in focusing on specific words, because this can hinder understanding. For example, assume a coalition meeting is being conducted. A member of the committee starts speaking and is using a word that people find offensive. Because this word, sometimes called a trigger word, is used repeatedly, people are no longer listening for the ideas but are focusing on the word. Although this can be a challenging situation, try not to get so focused on the words that the bigger point is missed. Focus on the larger ideas or themes that the speaker is trying to present, and continue listening until the speech is finished.

Another listening technique involves suspending judgments until after the speaker has completed the message. Several authors (Osborn & Osborn, 1988; Katula, 1997; Lucas, 1992; Adler & Towne, 1990) all recommend that it is very important not to judge a speaker's ideas prematurely before they are completely presented. For example, reflect on a time when a public speaker presented a speech with some ideas in prevention that strongly contradicted experience and research. An immediate reaction might be to discount everything the speaker says, start critiquing what is said, and conclude that none of the ideas presented was legitimate. It can be very hard to suspend judgments and listen proactively even when disagreements with the speaker are apparent. However, when prevention professionals acknowledge that this is happening and still attempt to listen critically, the end result may produce more positive benefits than would discounting everything said.

Listening with both your eyes and ears (Katula, 1987) is another method of helping prevention professionals listen critically. The nonverbal communication style can convey stronger messages than the spoken or verbal communication of a speaker. For example, when listening to speakers, notice whether they are using hand gestures to emphasize main points. Watch for how well they handle their visual aids or props and how confident they appear. It is always a good rule of thumb to appear relaxed and confident when in public at prevention meetings. Speakers can achieve this by practicing their speech and working with props. It will also help keep listeners engaged on the important content of the message without distracting them from the issues at hand.

In summary, the art of listening is an important consideration in any communication exchange situation. Often, people misunderstand the difference between hearing and listening. Additionally, they feel that listening is a passive activity devoid of skill and meaning. Contrary to this common assumption, listening is an extremely important skill that promotes understanding and helps achieve clear communication between people. Since prevention professionals spend much time attending prevention coalition meetings, prevention staff meetings, task forces, and work groups, the importance of listening cannot go unaddressed.

# Public Speaking Skills

Although some people may secretly dread the occasion of the public speech, public speaking skills are critical in the prevention profession. Numerous surveys have been conducted on public speaking attitudes and how adults react to these occasions. One specific study (McCroskey & Richmond, 1980, p. 15) found in a national survey of adults in the United States that speaking in public was their number one fear. In fact, this study showed that more people feared public speaking than feared death, heights, or water. **Speech anxiety**, therefore, is quite common and, in some cases, normative. Because the nature of prevention work requires skill in communication, it is crucial that prevention professionals try to become more comfortable with public speaking.

## Organizational Planning

Prevention professionals are often called on to speak in public for a variety of reasons. One of the most common reasons is to inform or train people, or the public at large, about their prevention program. This type of public speech would be called an informative speech, because its purpose is to inform the public about the program. Another reason prevention professionals are asked to prepare a public speech is to advocate for more funding or for changes in public policy. This type of public speech is called a persuasive speech because its purpose is to persuade people to take a specific course of action, such as funding their program or changing a law or policy. Finally, prevention professionals are often asked to train people on a core curriculum, programmatic aspects, or other prevention topics. Facilitation skill, is this instance, is needed and will be explored in detail in a subsequent section of this chapter.

Regardless of the type of public speech given, there are a number of skills that one can incorporate to make the message meaningful for the listeners. One of the first skills needed is to organize speeches into three main points. Many public speeches are organized this way and although listeners do not always consciously know about this format, keeping a speech organized around three main points is a proven and effective oral communication technique. Numerous authors of public speaking texts have advised that the clear organization of key ideas is an important consideration for any successful speechwriter (Peterson, White, & Stephan, 1984; Osborn & Osborn, 1988; Katula, 1987; Lucas, 1992; Beebe & Beebe, 1994).

When designing a public speech, it is important to keep a time limit in mind from the very beginning. Many speakers neglect to consider this and end up talking for too long about a topic, which loses listeners. Find out how long the speech needs to last and adhere strictly to those time limits. Additionally, when organizing the speech, divide remarks into three main parts: introduction, body, and conclusion. The purpose of the introduction is to gain audience attention and provide an overview of the three main points presented in the body of the speech. The purpose of the body of the speech is to present the three main points and to provide examples and facts for each point. The purpose of the conclusion is to rephrase the three main points and to provide a "call to action" statement. A "call to action" statement is a challenge that the speaker gives to the audience, encouraging the listeners to do something useful or helpful for the cause.

## Prevention Speech Vignette

Jennifer Smith, a prevention professional located in a small rural town in Nebraska, was asked to provide some remarks on her science-based prevention program. A press conference was going to be held in reaction to a recent automobile accident where four teenagers had been hurt because of a drinking-and-driving-related automobile collision. Citizens were concerned that teenagers were drinking and driving and wanted to learn about what prevention programs existed in their community to help prevent this problem from occurring again. Jennifer had been contacted because she was the director of a program that had been funded for a number of years.

Jennifer first asked how long her remarks needed to be. The press conference contact told her she would only have about five minutes at the podium. Additionally, she asked what specific information people wanted to know about her program. The press conference contact said she needed to talk about the purpose of the program, the success rate, where funding came from, and how people could join the program. Jennifer immediately thought that this information could be easily organized into three main points and began planning her speech while still on the phone.

Jennifer also thought that one really good visual aid might help enhance her message, so she created a large picture of some youth joined hand-in-hand wearing program T-shirts and smiling. She made sure this photograph was large, poster board sized, so that everyone could see the "human" side of prevention.

Next, Jennifer wrote her remarks. She decided she would organize her speech around three points. First, she would state the mission of her organization and some of the evaluation findings from her program. Second, she would talk about the diversified funding her program received from federal and state grants and private donations. Third, she would talk about how people could enroll in her program and the fees associated with participation. Next, she created an introduction and conclusion, which were somewhat parallel, as both highlighted the three main points of her speech. During the introduction, Jennifer had a catchy attention gainer—she talked about the youth in the picture (visual aid) and how these program participants were now in college, happy, healthy, and living drug- and alcohol-free lifestyles. During the conclusion, she encouraged people to become involved in her program, either as participants or volunteers. To further prepare, Jennifer practiced her speech, timed its delivery, and tried to anticipate questions from the audience.

The day of the event, Jennifer dressed in her best suit, showed up to the press conference early, and placed her visual aid on a stand next to the podium, observed the layout of the room, tested the microphone, and tried to relax. When her time arrived to speak, Jennifer was nervous, but because she was so well prepared, everything went very well and the delivery was smooth. The time and effort spent preparing for the speech far exceeded the actual time spent speaking, but she received many compliments on her succinct and effective public speech.

## Visual Aids

Good **visual aids** can amplify most speeches. A visual aid is a prop or other article used to pictorially enhance the message being presented. There are multiple considerations to contemplate when choosing, creating, or using visual aids (Peterson, White, & Stephan, 1984; Osborn & Osborn, 1988; Katula, 1987; Lucas, 1992; Beebe & Beebe, 1994). The first is that your visual aid should look as professional as possible, as the goal of a visual aid is to enhance your message, not distract from it. Second, your visual aid should be large enough for everyone in the audience, including those in the back of the room, to see and read. Third, your visual aid should be crucial to the message you are conveying. Finally, your visual aid should be simple, not overly complicated. People have a tendency to ignore these considerations, which can result in a poor communication. More in-depth considerations will be discussed below.

Objects, models, graphs, photographs, drawings, charts, slides, PowerPoint presentations, and the speakers themselves are all commonly used visual aids. Always remember that a visual aid is used to emphasize a message that could not be communicated in the same way without an aid. Selecting and creating visual aids requires careful preparation. Like the speech-making process, the time put into the creation of the visual aid will be well worth it if it enhances the message.

There are also some tips about what to avoid when using and creating visual aids (Beebe & Beebe, 1994; Lucas, 1992; Osborn & Osborn, 1988). First, avoid using dangerous or illegal visual aids. Try to avoid using actual drugs if at all possible. Most research has shown that showing drugs is not an effective prevention strategy, so if you must show drugs, try using large photographs or slides versus the actual drug itself. Second, avoid complicated, hand-written poster boards created at the last minute. These look sloppy, are hard to read, and will detract from the credibility of the message you are trying to convey. Third, avoid using chalkboards for visual aids. The main problem with chalkboards is that if prevention professionals write on it while giving speeches, they have to turn their backs to the audience. This is something that should be avoided at all times because turning around muffles speech sounds and is not an effective strategy. Finally, avoid passing visual aids, such as photographs or handouts, to the audience before or during the speech. This distracts the audience from the speech, makes lots of noise, and generally detracts, rather than enhances, the message. If this type of visual aid must be used, pass it out after the speech has been concluded. Finally, consider color when creating visual aids. Light or pale colors, such as yellow, peach, and pink, are not easily seen from the audience and should only be used as background colors. Do not use hard-to-read colors or font styles that cannot be read from a distance. Black, red, and bright colors work well for letters on visual aids. These considerations should be followed when creating and working with visual aids.

## The Confident Speaker

Confident speakers are usually enjoyable to listen to and can be very persuasive. However, confidence is a difficult quality to fake in a public speaking situation. The following suggestions may help a prevention professional feel more confident when speaking in public. The first is to dress well. Many times, looking professional helps to project confidence to the audience. Spend some extra time before the speech grooming and dressing professionally. Second, practice the speech a number of times. Going over a well-thought-out and prepared presentation in advance naturally builds confidence. Not only will all the potential problems be worked out with the speech, but the prevention professional will be more comfortable with the material, which in turn will create more overall confidence. Third, breathe deeply and use other relaxation techniques before the presentation. A certain amount of anxiety is normal, and good, in a public speaking event. Try to channel the energy positively in a manner that helps make the speech more interesting. For example, smiling can release nervous energy naturally. Channeling nervous energy into contagious enthusiasm is another technique to help keep anxiety under control. Try not to let frazzled nerves control the situation.

Vocal variety is another important speech consideration and will help the prevention professional communicate clearly. It is crucial that vocal volume be adjusted to the size of the audience and the environment. If a prevention professional speaks too softly when working with youth in an outdoor prevention program, for example, the participants might not be able to hear the instructions. Additionally, rate, or the fastness or slowness of the spoken word, should also be slow enough that listeners can hear and process all the information conveyed. For example, when people are nervous they may tend to speak at a rapid rate. When speaking too fast, listeners often stop listening and start focusing on unrelated matters. Vocal pitch refers to the highness or lowness of a voice. Sometimes speakers have a singsongy quality to their pitch, which makes it very difficult for audience members to listen to and appreciate what they have to say. It is important to use pitch variety when emphasizing key points or words to keep the message interesting. For example, before an important point, the speaker should pause, say the word or prevention statistic in a lower pitch, and then complete the thought. This is a vocal technique that can effectively highlight an important word or point, orally, to let the listeners know that they should pay attention to the message. In summary, good use of the voice, and practice, can help increase a speaker's confidence.

## How Not to Speak at a Meeting

There are many rules and tips that guide prevention professionals to be more effective communicators. However, sometimes people learn best by talking about what not to do. The following discussion captures some common pitfalls that prevention professionals should try to avoid when communicating in a variety of settings (Peterson, White, & Stephan, 1984, pp. 30–32).

*The Moving Target.*   This describes a speaker who walks, paces, or rocks to the point of distraction. This type of communicator is so nervous that his or her nonverbal behavior becomes more interesting than the message. If this happens to you, try to stand or sit confidently. Even if you are nervous inside, people will not notice if you appear relaxed and stand still. Also, try to imagine yourself as a successful public speaker and play that role while speaking in public.

*The Musician.*   This type of speaker likes to play with keys, change, or anything that is within reach, whether in a pocket or on a table. This can become a terrible distraction to the listeners because the speaker fidgets with pens, paper, or other items instead of focusing on the message she or he is trying to convey. It soon begins to sound like a musical accompaniment to the message being communicated as pens tap, paper is jiggled, and glasses are held nervously.

*The Peacock.*   This speaker is nervous about the way he or she looks. The preening peacock messes with his tie, straightens his coat, or touches his hair over and over again. This behavior signals to others that he is nervous or simply unprepared for the remarks he is making. Spend time in advance of the speech making sure all clothing is fastened correctly so there will be no last-minute worry about physical appearance. If you cannot stop yourself from fidgeting, put your hands at your side and try to relax.

*The Great Scientist.*   This is a speaker who, although brilliant, uses such big words or jargon that no one can figure out what she or he is saying. For example, a prevention researcher who comes to a meeting may be very excited about the results of a prevention program that she has just evaluated. In her enthusiasm, she loses listeners by talking about variables, sophisticated statistical equations, and P values. Remember that the goal to communication interaction is to understand and to be understood by others. Using language with which listeners are not familiar can be both alienating for the listeners and frustrating for the speaker.

*The Clincher.*   This is a speaker who clinches onto a podium or microphone so tightly that it appears he or she is hanging on for dear life. Again, the rule of thumb is to try to be relaxed when communicating, or at least appear relaxed. Public speaking can be intimidating for prevention professionals as well as for people in other professions. Work on some relaxation techniques and try to appear confident.

*The Disorganized Artist.*    This is a speaker who is so disorganized with notes and ideas that his or her area of the meeting table or podium begins to resemble an artistic collage. It is crucial to have a clear agenda or outline when running a meeting or presenting a formal speech. Simply speaking without purpose or a clear goal in mind will confuse the listeners, the speaker, and the reason why the meeting was called in the first place. A few suggestions for keeping organized include keeping on task, on topic, and on time. These are the three "T's" for successful organization, and they will help you avoid the disorganized artist attributes described above.

## Summary

There are many considerations to follow when creating, organizing, and presenting a public speech. Prevention professionals are encouraged to take public speaking courses, join speech groups, and practice giving speeches. Over time, skill and confidence will improve as your ability to communicate a message increases. Communication with prevention programs, staff, and participants and with the general public is an important component of any science-based prevention program. Without the ability to communicate clearly and effectively, prevention professionals lose the ability to share program success with both their staff and the public.

# Group Facilitation and Leadership Skills

Prevention professionals, especially those who are powerful communicators, often find themselves in leadership positions. Leadership roles generally require some strong group facilitation skills to keep tasks moving forward and keep people interested. Much has been written on group facilitation and leadership skills; so the discussion here will highlight a few important considerations, beginning with some definitions. In this context, "facilitation" is defined as a person or people (known as cofacilitators) who have been designated by group members to be caretaker of the meeting process (Webne-Behrman, 1998, p. 1). "Leadership," refers to a process of social influence in which one person is able to enlist the aid and support of others in the accomplishment of a common task (Chemers, 1997, p. 1). In some prevention instances, leadership and facilitation occur simultaneously, and in other cases they occur distinctly. For purposes of this discussion the two will be used both interchangeably and separately.

Six facilitator roles have been highlighted by Webne-Behrman (1998, pp. 2–4). The first is that the facilitator should encourage full participation of everyone in the group. This can be challenging, but it is important to involve as many members as possible in the discussion of group agenda items. More about this will be provided below. Second, it is important to foster effective listening. Much time has been spent on the importance of listening actively and these same rules apply to the facilitator. Third, a facilitator should clarify goals and agendas. The facilitator should help members clarify the nature of the work at hand and help them solve problems, keep the group focused, and keep track of time so all items on the agenda are addressed. Fourth, the facilitator should balance individual needs with group tasks. When working in groups, it soon becomes obvious that both personal agendas and group agendas are present. As facilitator, it is important to recognize the individual needs of group participants and to try, when possible, to blend these with the agenda of the group. Additionally, it is important for the facilitator to help orient new members to the group, help them understand the group norms that have emerged, and allow individual and group tasks to develop. Fifth, the facilitator should always encourage shared leadership. It is not the job of the facilitator to take responsibility for every task generated by the group. Encouraging shared leadership is healthy, helps the members create a buy-in to the decisions made, and allows other leadership roles, responsibilities, and styles to emerge. Sixth, the facilitator should share her or his role with others. Sometimes prevention facilitators may lead a meeting process for a while and then leave the group. This is a common situation for prevention professionals who provide technical assistance. It is important, during these occasions, to encourage members to take on the role of the facilitator so the group process can continue after the first facilitator leaves.

## Creating an Agenda

Any facilitator, board chair, or leader should create an agenda well enough in advance that all members have a chance to review it beforehand. Numerous articles and books have been written on meeting preparation (Morrison, 1988; Doyle & Straus, 1976; Lawson, 1980) and all contend that agendas are crucial to meetings. Morrison (1988) states that "[T]he preparation of an agenda must be specific enough to make it truly useful to the participants. A well-conceived agenda fully prepares the group for the business at hand and assures an expedient and productive meeting" (p. 25).

The following describes tips that guide the creation of a good agenda for meetings. The first is to create an agenda with time-limited discussions. This helps keep the group on track and can always be adjusted during the meeting if the members require more discussion time. Second, try not to list two time-consuming topics next to each other. Members get anxious if they feel the agenda items are not being addressed at an acceptable rate. Third, send out the agenda in advance. This rule is often ignored. People can plan for the meeting more effectively if they know, in advance, what topics will be discussed. Fourth, indicate who will be responsible for each item. When members request that items be added to the agenda, list their name next to the item. This helps move the discussion forward and allows natural leadership from within the group to emerge. Fifth, avoid items on the agenda that are not of interest to all group members. There are, of course, other things to consider about agendas, but this list comprises some of the more important ideas to consider when creating one.

## Allowing All to Speak

Skilled facilitators allow all people to speak and share their opinions. Although this is obvious, it can be a challenge. Most groups have people who love to talk and attempt to dominate the communication occurring at a meeting. This situation can quickly become a problem. A technique often used to solve this problem is to allow the person to speak, but remind them that time is short and that others' opinions are important as well. When this technique does not work, the facilitator can encourage them to conclude their remarks and offer to stay after the meeting to discuss some of their ideas with them individually. If this technique still does not work, the facilitator can encourage other members to speak and help deal with the situation. Establishing ground rules for group behavior early in the group process can also help prevent this situation from occurring.

All kinds of personalities work in the field of prevention, including people who are quiet and reserved. Facilitators should encourage quiet people to share their ideas with the group. One way to do this is to call on them individually and ask them to share their opinions. Many times quiet people have good ideas, even when they do not feel comfortable offering them to others in a group setting.

Finally, many groups have "hecklers." A heckler is a person who has side conversations during group discussion, makes a lot of jokes on the side during the meeting, or generally disrupts the flow of the meeting. There are a number of techniques that can be employed to work with these individuals. If the facilitator is standing at the front of the room, he or she can simply move toward the heckler. This action generally stops the disruptive behavior. Calling on the heckler to answer a question posed to the group or to comment on the last thought conveyed by a member is also a good way to bring them to attention. Finally, talking with hecklers outside of the meeting about their behavior is also a good option. Ignoring the person, hoping they will just be quiet, or publicly embarrassing them are three strategies that usually do not work well and can actually harm the group process. Leadership has its challenges, and confronting unwanted participant behavior is one of them.

Sometimes a facilitator finds himself or herself in a position where everyone seems to want to talk at once. There are a number of solutions for this situation. The first is to call on people as their hands go up to request speaking time. This can be challenging for the facilitator because it is hard to keep track of who will speak next. The second way to deal with this situation is to keep a written list of hands as they go up. Between speakers, remind the group that you are keeping a list and recite who is on it. The problem with this method is that the topic may change over time with each new speaker and the comments the person may have wanted to share have passed. A third strategy is to conduct a "round robin" of sharing, where each person is called upon to comment. If a given person has no remarks, he or she simply passes his or her turn to the next person.

Facilitating meetings, trainings, and discussions is an important skill for prevention professionals. The facilitator should try to remain diplomatic and allow people to communicate as much as possible. However, the facilitator is also responsible for making sure that timelines are met and that overly talkative people do not dominate the discussion. Practice and observation of those skilled in group facilitation will help prevention professional learn how to best manage this task.

## Leadership Styles

Leadership is another substance abuse prevention consideration. Effective leadership relies on effective communication skill to convey messages and motivate behavior. Science-based prevention programs require strong leaders who can motivate team members to work together to achieve positive outcomes. Without good communication methods and strong leadership, even the best prevention programs could fail. Good leadership skills for prevention work cannot be overstated.

Leadership deserves mention because of its crucial role in the development of the substance abuse prevention profession. People generally are promoted if they are competent and suddenly find that they are in a leadership position. This leadership position may take its form as the chairperson of a community coalition, a director of a substance abuse prevention program, or a team leader in a youth substance abuse prevention program.

> Leadership is not limited to the chairman. Leaders exist at all levels of the organization. . . . Leaders are made, not born. Leadership is a mix of skills, attitude, will, and motivation. To become a leader, you must want it, work on it. It requires much effort to get there and remain there. (Hevesi, 1996, p. 11)

Although this discussion will describe prevention professionals in leadership positions and the styles they may use, the above information applies to all disciplines.

There are numerous books, articles, and workshops based on the topic of leadership. For purposes of this discussion, however, the focus will be on the Hersey-Blanchard situation leadership theory, which defines four leadership styles (Beck & Yeager, 1994). According to Beck and Yeager (1994) this theory is based upon earlier leadership models and theories, such as those developed by Lewin, Lippitt, and White (1960), Tannenbaum and Schmidt (1958), Stogdill and Coons (1959), and Likert (1961), as well as Blake and Mouton's (1964) managerial grid, Fiedler's (1967) contingency theory, and Reddin's (1967) model. Situational leadership theory has expanded and enhanced components from these earlier theories and created four leadership styles that can be used in differing situations.

Leadership styles are organized and labeled into the following four categories: director, problem solver, developer, and delegator. Prevention professionals need to determine their natural leadership style and then ascertain when to use this style or others, depending on the situation. Matching leadership styles to situations is both a desirable and effective skill to develop. Every leadership style has strengths and limitations and will be mentioned accordingly.

## The Director

The director leadership style is one that is used by people who like to make decisions on their own, prefer to give explicit instructions to team members, follow up with close supervision, and value followers who comply with their wishes. This style is especially helpful when uniform results are desired; for example, cooking hamburgers that are made the same way time and time again. Directors generally like to run everything and can be counted upon for clear direction. In substance abuse prevention, a director leadership style could be used when a task needs to be accomplished according to strict guidelines and principles. For example, this style may be helpful when teaching new staff members how to implement a prevention curriculum that allows for no deviation from what is written. Directors generally need to review many or all of the details of the operation, and everyone on the team clearly understands that the boss is in charge. The weakness with this style is that this type of leader can come across as dominating when people already know what to do or want more responsibility.

## The Problem Solver

A problem solver is a leader who involves group members in the problem-solving process. These leaders are good at listening to issues and challenges and making decisions based on their recommendations. This style is especially effective when others, besides the leader, have access to key information but are not in a position to make any decisions. The leader makes the ultimate decision but involves others in the process. In the prevention field, this leader may listen to those who are providing direct youth services and make decisions based upon their recommendations. Although this can be good, it can also distract the leader from other organizational issues, and staff can find it exhausting to inform the leader on multiple prevention program details. The limitation to this style is that the problem solver can get overinvolved in all the details and overinvolve others in processes that are not necessary and can be perceived by staff as a waste of time.

## The Developer

The developer style is one of the most common styles of leadership. The developer is a very good listener, is great at asking pertinent questions, and empowers staff to make their own decisions. This leadership style challenges staff to grow and learn how to solve their own problems. In the prevention field, a leader of this style would empower staff to solve their own problems in a program. For example, if parents were not attending a parent training program, the staff would have the ability to discover how to solve the problem. If lack of child care was keeping parents from the program, staff would provide free child care as a service to increase participation. If the leadership style matches the skill and motivation of the employee, this strategy can be very effective, and if not, it can be disastrous. The weakness to this style is that the leader can appear overaccommodating by listening too much and letting others make decisions that should be made by the leader. The employees, if empowered by this approach, may feel valued and motivated to solve problems on their own. However, if a prevention staff member is new to the job and is looking for explicit detail on the functions of the job, this approach is not advised.

## The Delegator

This type of leader delegates by giving followers meaningful responsibilities and letting them handle their assignments on their own. Decision-making occurs at the staff level and the delegator simply guides the process. In prevention, this style might be used effectively when staff are competent at implementing a science-based prevention program. However, if staff members struggle to understand the scope of their work, this style would not be the best way to manage this situation. The weakness of this style is that when people feel overwhelmed, they are likely to accuse this type of leader of abdicating her or his responsibility to someone else.

In summary, the situational leadership approach encourages leaders to match the appropriate style to any given situation. This is relevant to what occurs in prevention programs. This is more difficult than it sounds. People sometimes tend to prefer one style over another and it can be difficult to change styles as quickly as staff situations demand. A skilled leader is one who can fluctuate between the styles of director, problem solver, developer, and delegator as situations present themselves. For example, assume you are directing a group of peer leaders in a youth prevention program. One of the peer leaders, who has been with the program for a long time and is someone who is very competent and skilled in working with youth, suddenly runs into a problem. Not knowing what to do next, the peer leader asks for specific guidance. Although you have generally been a delegator with this leader, you try the developer style and ask questions, listen carefully, and try to help the leader solve his or her own problems. If this approach works, you can go back to delegation, and if not, you might try the problem solver approach.

Leadership is an important component of successful prevention programming and needs to be explored carefully. Leadership, like communication and facilitation, is a skill that is often taken for granted. Indeed, this should not be the case. Special attention should be given to the topic.

## Summary

This chapter has focused on communication, facilitation, and leadership styles. Because good communication skills are essential to any science-based prevention program, the topic was explored in detail. Communication tips and techniques can be used in all types of environments, including considerations when facilitating meetings or leading people. Too often, prevention professionals find themselves in leadership or facilitation positions without the required skills to conduct the work successfully. Although this chapter highlighted just a few of the many approaches to facilitation and leadership, prevention professionals are encouraged to read more, take classes, and learn from others about these processes.

Additionally, public speaking and listening skills are at the heart of what prevention professionals do on a daily basis. Learning how to communicate clearly and how to deal with a variety of situations will only help prevention professionals run their programs effectively. As a final thought, remember that communication competence is a topic relevant to all professions, regardless of discipline. Once these techniques are incorporated into daily life, the process will not seem so daunting. Prevention professionals who understand science-based programming and who can also communicate effectively will doubtless find themselves in leadership positions. This is an exciting development and well-trained professionals will undoubtedly begin teaching others how to climb the ladder of success.

## KEY TERMS

| | | |
|---|---|---|
| channel | information overload | receiver |
| communication environment | leadership | sender |
| facilitation | listening | speech anxiety |
| feedback | message | trigger word |
| hearing | noise | visual aid |

# DISCUSSION QUESTIONS

1. What is the process model of communication? Describe it and include all key components. What other models of communication exist and how do they differ?

2. Why are facilitation skills important? List and describe five of the six skills mentioned.

3. What are some of the roadblocks to active listening? Why are listening skills important?

4. What is the situational leadership model? What are the four main styles of leadership? List the strengths and weaknesses of each style.

# APPLICATION EXERCISES

1. Why should a prevention specialist know about communication models, listening skills, and public speaking skills? How do you feel about speaking in public and what can you do to increase your own personal speaking skills?

2. Why are facilitation skills and leadership styles important when implementing a science-based prevention program? What, hypothetically, could happen if a prevention program did not have a person with this skill set heading up the program? Visit a prevention program and determine what leadership styles are used. What recommendations can you give the program to improve leadership?

3. Conduct a literature review of other leadership styles. How do these compare and contrast to the situational leadership styles? Visit a prevention program and talk with both managers and staff about leadership to learn what occurs versus what could occur with training on leadership styles. Present your findings in a three- to five-minute speech to the class.

4. Create and present an 8- to 10-minute speech on the importance of implementing a science-based prevention program.

# SUGGESTED READINGS

Beck, J., & Yeager, N. (1994). *The leader's window: Mastering the four styles of leadership to build high-performing teams.* New York: John Wiley & Sons.

Lucas, S. E. (1992). *The art of public speaking* (4th ed.).San Francisco: McGraw-Hill.

Webne-Behrman, H. (1998). *The practice of facilitation: Managing group process and solving problems.* Westport, CT: Quorum Books.

# REFERENCES

Adler, R. B., & Towne, N. (1990). *Looking out looking in* (6th ed.). San Francisco: Holt, Rinehart, & Winston.

Beck, J., & Yeager, N. (1994). *The leader's window: Mastering the four styles of leadership to build high-performing teams.* New York: John Wiley & Sons.

Beebe, S. A., & Beebe, S. J. (1994). *Public speaking: An audience-centered approach* (2nd ed.). Englewood Cliffs, N.J.: Prentice-Hall.

Blake, R. R., & Mouton, J. S. (1964). *The managerial grid*. Houston, TX: Gulf.

Chemers, M. M. (1997). *An integrative theory of leadership*. Mahwah, NJ: Lawrence Erlbaum Associates.

DiVesta, F. J., & Grey, G. S. (1974). Listening and note-taking. In R. Huseman, C. Logue, & D. Freshley (Eds.), *Reading in interpersonal and organization communication* (2nd ed.) (pp. 558–570). Boston: Holbrook Press.

Doyle, M., & Straus, D. (1976). *How to make meetings work*. La Jolla, CA: University Associates.

Fiedler, F. E. (1967). *A theory of leadership effectiveness*. New York: McGraw-Hill.

Fiske, J. (1982). *Introduction to communication studies*. New York: Methuen & Company.

Hevesi, G. (1996). *Checklist for leaders*. Portland, OR: Productivity Press.

Hershey, P., & Blanchard, K. (1982). *Management of organizational behavior: Utilizing human resources* (4th ed.). New Jersey: Prentice-Hall.

Katula, R. A. (1987). *Principles and patterns of public speaking*. Belmont, CA: Wadsworth.

Lawson, J. D. (1980). *When you preside*. Danville, IL: Interstate Printers and Publishers.

Lewin, K., Lippitt, R., & White R. (1960). Leader behavior and member reaction in three social climates. In D. Cartwright and A. Zader (Eds.), *Group dynamics: Research and theory* (2nd ed.). Evanston, IL: Row, Peterson, and Company.

Likert, R. (1961). *New patterns of management*. New York: McGraw-Hill.

Lucas, S. E. (1992). *The art of public speaking* (4th ed.). San Francisco, CA: McGraw-Hill.

McCroskey, J. C., & Richmond, V. (1980). *The quiet ones: Communication apprehension and shyness*. Dubuque, IA: Gorsuch Scarisbrick.

Morrison, E. K. (1988). *Working with volunteers: Skills for leadership*. Tucson, AZ: Fisher Books.

Osborn, M., & Osborn, S. (1988). *Public speaking*. Boston: Houghton Mifflin.

Peterson, B. D., White, N. D., & Stephan, E. G. (1984). *Speak easy: An introduction to public speaking*. (2nd ed.). New York: West.

Reddin, W. J. (1967, April). The 3-D management style inventory. *Training and Development Journal,* 8–17.

Shannon, C., & Weaver, W. (1949). *The mathematical theory of communication*. Urbana-Champaign: University of Illinois Press.

Stogdill, R. M., & Coons, Alvin E. (1959). Leader behavior: Its description and measurement. Research monograph, 88.

Tannenbaum, R., & Schmidt, W. H. (1958, March/April). How to choose a leadership pattern. *Harvard Business Review,* 95–102.

Webne-Behrman, H. (1998). *The practice of facilitation: Managing group process and solving problems*. Westport, CT: Quorum Books.

# 10 Grant Writing

Grant writing can be intimidating for those who are new to the process. However, by using information gleaned from experienced grant writers, many of the "unknowns" around grant writing can be exposed, diminishing some of the fears that may exist. This chapter includes information about how to get started in the grant writing process, including gathering background information and identifying and contacting potential grant makers. Furthermore, writing a shorter letter proposal will be explored. Common components in letter proposals include reference to prior contact(s) with the funder, summary of the proposal, sponsor appeal, statement of need, solution to address need, capabilities of the agency, budget, measurable outcomes, conclusion, and attachments. The next section covers how to write a long proposal, including the development and drafting of the following components of a proposal: cover letter, table of contents, executive summary or abstract, introduction, statement of need, objectives, methods, evaluation, dissemination, budget, and appendices. Finally, general tips about grant writing are explored.

In this chapter, general guidelines, components, and recommendations for writing grant proposals are covered. However, if the guidelines and instructions provided by grant makers differ from those in this chapter, grant writers should always follow the information from the grant makers.

## Introduction to Grant Writing in Prevention

### Soft Money

One of the first realizations that prevention professionals have when they enter the field of substance abuse prevention is that the pursuit for funding never ends. Because nearly all of substance abuse prevention funding is **soft money**, or time-limited funding, prevention professionals often end up in the role of grant writer. Consequently, it is important for prevention professionals to have strong grant-writing skills. If they do not have those skills, professionals may find themselves writing many grant proposals, but seeing little to no results from all their efforts.

## Accessing Grant Funding

Many in the substance abuse prevention field wonder whether it is worth the time and effort to write grant proposals. In short, the answer is yes. Foundations in the United States alone gave over $150 billion in grants in 1999 (Miner & Miner, n.d.). More than 37,500 private foundations and corporate giving programs exist in the United States (YouthTree USA, n.d.). Other sources of grants include government programs, religious organizations, and individuals (Morris & Adler, 1998). Consequently, numerous opportunities exist to gain funding for all types of programs and activities. The key is to find the **grant maker**, or funder, with a mission similar to that of the prevention program. This will be discussed in detail later in the chapter.

## How Program Planning and Evaluation Tie into Grant Writing

Program planning and evaluation, as discussed in previous chapters, are a crucial part to effective grant writing. If prevention professionals have completed all of the program and evaluation planning steps prior to writing a grant, they will have much of the crucial information needed to complete grant proposals. Without the information provided by the completion of the program planning and evaluation steps, proposals will inevitably have many holes and will likely not be funded.

A mistake that prevention professionals often make is when they view program planning and grant planning as two separate, virtually unrelated entities. "Ideally, grant planning should be only one phase in the whole program development, program implementation, and evaluation cycle" (McGee, 1995, para. 1). Therefore, the likelihood of writing successful grant proposals will increase when grant writing and program planning are closely intertwined.

The following are some ways in which the seven steps of a good program can be incorporated into grant proposal writing. First, Step 1 of the program planning cycle is community readiness and community mobilization. Documentation that a community is ready for a prevention program, thus increasing the likelihood of success, can provide grant makers with evidence that their money will be well spent. Furthermore, if a community coalition has been formed through mobilization activities, grant writers can show in their proposals that key players in the community are ready and willing to take action to ensure that the program is a success.

Next, Steps 2 and 3 in the planning process, conducting a community risk assessment and translating data into priorities, provide grant writers with the factual information necessary to document need. In most cases, it is not sufficient to quote national statistics as a method of showing need. Instead, local statistics that illuminate the specific needs of the target community can provide grant makers with the confidence that the needs truly exist. This can also show how the need is not the grant writer's need, but the community's need. This is very appealing to many grant makers.

With the completion of a resource assessment, Step 4 of the planning process, the grant writer has the information to show that programs funded by the proposal will not duplicate existing efforts in the community. It will also show that the programs will address the service gaps in the community. This is important because funders typically avoid funding projects that are not in some way novel, creative, and/or greatly needed.

Step 5, selecting a target population, will provide the grant writer with key information nearly always required in proposals. Often grant makers have specific target populations that they wish to reach with their funds. So it is essential that prevention professionals understand the target population they desire to reach and then assess whether this matches the priorities of the grant makers.

If Step 6, the selection of a program/strategy to implement, has been completed, then grant writers will have the details they need to describe the objectives and methods in their proposals. This enables one to paint a clear and specific picture in the proposal of what the grant maker would be funding. Similarly, Step 7, evaluation, will provide the information needed when drafting the evaluation section of a proposal. This will show the grant makers how the programs they have funded are successful. In summary, all seven steps, when completed, provide the data and information necessary to write a comprehensive, accurate, and successful grant proposal.

## Motivations of Grant Makers

Before applying for any grants, it is essential to understand the motivations of grant makers. What motivates them to give money away? In many cases, grant makers have a sincere concern for the social problems, injustices, or inequities that exist in our society. In turn, they identify an area or areas of concern in which they are willing to invest their money to make a difference. Although they have great concerns regarding specific social problems and they have the money to address the problems, they often do not have the staff, services, expertise, and/or programs to address the problems. Consequently, they provide grants to those organizations that can do this footwork for them.

For foundations specifically, they are required to "give away five percent of their market value assets or interest income each year, whichever is greater, over a three-year period" (GrantProposal.com, 2001). If they do not give away at least five percent, they risk losing their tax-exempt status with the federal government. Consequently, besides being motivated to award funds to address a social problem, they also are mandated by federal laws to distribute a minimum amount of funds each year.

The motivation of corporations to provide funds to nonprofit organizations is often to address social problems in the community, as well as to improve their image with their employees, their clients, and/or the general public. Keep this important aspect in mind during the grant-writing process, because it will be essential to show corporations how a prevention program will improve their image if they award funds for a project.

The key is to identify the social problems, injustices, or inequalities that the grant maker wishes to address. These priorities must match the project being proposed. Then grant writers must reflect these priorities to the grant makers through their proposals. If the grant makers do not see a match in priorities, an application is often immediately rejected. The following section will focus on how prevention professionals can find a solid match between their funding needs and the grant makers' funding priorities.

# Preliminary Steps to Grant Writing

## Gather Background Information

Before beginning any writing of proposals, grant writers must pull together key background information. As identified by the Foundation Center (n.d. b), three areas of documentation are needed before writing a proposal: concept, program, and expenses. If this documentation is gathered prior to writing a proposal, it will make the writing process much easier. Fortunately, if the program and evaluation planning process has already taken place, much of this background information will exist already.

The concept area is the overarching idea of the project. This includes the philosophy and mission of the prevention agency and the needs, as identified by the community risk assessment. The grant writer will need to identify how the agency's philosophy and mission match the needs to be addressed.

Next, the program area includes the nature of the program and how it will be conducted. A timetable to carry out the program and/or activities needs to be established at this point. The evaluation plan, including measurable outcomes, is also included in the program area. Finally, the staffing needs for the project must be detailed. Will volunteers be used? Will staff working on other projects be reassigned if the grant is funded? Will new staff be hired?

Finally, the expense area is the budget associated with the project. Although the grant writer may not have the details to create a detailed budget at this stage of the proposal development process, a broad outline needs to be established. This is essential because some foundations and corporations will offer only small amounts of funding whereas others are willing to look at funding larger projects. Therefore, the amount of funding needed for the project will affect which foundations can be approached. However, if the costs seem prohibitive for the amount of work to be completed, it may be important to revise the project in order to reduce costs. Once information is gathered on the concept, program, and expense areas, it is time to turn attention to identifying potential funding entities.

## Identify Potential Grant Makers

Because such a large number of grant makers exist, it is important to conduct a methodical review of potential funders who would be interested in supporting one's proposal. Fortunately, resources abound to help potential grant writers identify grant makers. The steps to complete a thorough yet focused search for grant makers include: identify directories of grant makers, narrow down the list of potential sponsors, order the application forms and guidelines, call a past grantee, call a past reviewer, and contact the program officer. Following these steps will increase the likelihood that a proposal submitted would be funded. The next section provides details about how to complete each of these steps.

***Identify Grant Makers.*** The first step of the process, after compiling background information, is to locate potential grant makers. One way to do this is to "find out which foundations have given grants in your region similar to your planned proposal" (Lone Eagle

Consulting, n.d., para. 2). Another method is to study the many grant maker directories that exist. Three main sources provide information about public grants from the federal government. First, the *Catalog of Federal Domestic Assistance* is the "most complete federal grant reference source" (Miner & Miner, n.d., Finding Out about Public Grants section, para. 1). This publication is available from the Superintendent of Documents in Washington, D.C. It can also be accessed on the Internet at http://www.cfda.gov/. The catalog is published each spring, followed by supplements each fall.

Another source of information on federal public grants is the *Federal Register*. This is commonly referred to as the government's "daily newspaper." Because of the frequency of its publication, the *Federal Register* is a good source of current information. It is also available from the Superintendent of Documents in Washington, D.C., as well as on-line at http://www.access.gpo.gov/su_docs/aces/aces140.html.

*Commerce Business Daily* is the third source of information on public grants. It contains notices of proposed government procurement actions, contract awards, sales of government property, and other procurement information. The *Commerce Business Daily* is issued every business day and can be found on the Internet at http://cbdnet.access.gpo.gov/.

Several federal government agencies fund prevention programs through grants. The Center for Substance Abuse Prevention (CSAP) within the Substance Abuse and Mental Health Services Administration funds various substance abuse prevention initiatives through granting processes. In the past, CSAP has awarded substance abuse prevention conference grants, high-risk youth grants, and community partnership grants, among others. The National Clearinghouse for Alcohol and Drug Information (NCADI), funded by CSAP, can be a good source of information regarding funding opportunities from CSAP. NCADI can be reached either on-line (http://www.health.org) or by phone (800–729–6686).

Another federal agency that provides funds for substance abuse prevention is the Department of Education (DOE), through its Safe and Drug-free Schools Programs (http://www.ed.gov/offices/OESE/SDFS/). However, much of the funding from DOE is funneled to local schools through the state systems, such as the state department of education, the single state agency responsible for substance abuse prevention and treatment, or the governor's office. Local prevention programs should contact their state Safe and Drug-free Schools coordinator and/or their local coordinators to gather information about funding availability.

The Office of Juvenile Justice and Delinquency Prevention, or OJJDP, (http://ojjdp.ncjrs.org/) has also funded substance abuse and delinquency prevention programs. This has included the Drug-free Community grants implemented in partnership with the Office of National Drug Control Policy (http://www.whitehousedrugpolicy.org). OJJDP focuses on providing national leadership and resources to help states and local jurisdictions improve their juvenile justice systems.

Two agencies in the National Institute of Health provide funding opportunities for research projects on substance abuse prevention and treatment. The National Institute on Alcohol Abuse and Alcoholism (http://www.niaaa.nih.gov/) is a research organization that focuses on alcohol-related problems. The National Institute on Drug Abuse (http://www.nida.nih.gov/) is the lead agency for other drug abuse research.

On the private side of funding, several resources exist that can assist grant writers in identifying foundations and corporations that are potential sponsors. According to Miner and Miner (n.d.), more than 43,000 private foundations exist in the United States, awarding more than $8 billion dollars annually. At the same time, about one-third of the 2.5 million corporations in the United States make contributions to nonprofit organizations (Miner & Miner, n.d.). Consequently, identifying the foundations and/or corporations that give funding for specific types of projects can be challenging. Fortunately, resources exist that can make this process easier.

The Foundation Center (800–424–9836, http://fdncenter.org/) has five libraries across the nation to assist grant writers in identifying potential funders. It also has agreements with cooperating centers in almost every state that house their collection of information. The cooperating centers are "free funding information centers in libraries, community foundations, and other nonprofit resource centers that provide a core collection of Foundation Center publications and a variety of supplementary materials and services in areas useful to grantseekers" (Foundation Center, n.d. a). Included within these collections are CD-ROMs that contain information on 20,000 foundations. Several other organizations sell foundation databases that can be useful for grant writers. It is recommended that searches be conducted on the Internet to locate which databases are available at the time.

***Narrow Down the List of Potential Sponsors.*** Once one has identified all the directories of grant makers, it is essential to narrow down the list dramatically. Several steps can assist in this process. First, identify the grant makers that provide funding for substance abuse prevention programs or similar projects. Next, assess whether the grant makers provide funding in the geographic location where the project is to take place. Then ensure that the grant maker will award funds to the type of agency where the grant would be housed. For example, if the prevention agency were a private nonprofit organization, any grant makers that fund schools only would not be a good fit. Next, assess for what purposes the funds can be used; for example, capital improvement, technology, and direct services. In addition, the target populations must match. For example, a foundation may only provide funds for programs for older adults or for ethnic minority groups. Finally, the funding period for the grant must match the program implementation timeline. For example, if funds are needed for a school-based program that operates the entire year, a grant that will not distribute funds until December may not be a good match. Assessing all of these areas should narrow down the possibilities considerably. If a grant maker does not fit closely to your situation, do not pursue that avenue. Doing so will waste both your time and the grant maker's time. For those grant makers that look like potentially good matches, it is time to evaluate each of them more thoroughly.

## Contact Potential Prospects

The first step in contacting the remaining possible grant makers is to obtain the grant application and guidelines. More often now, these applications and guidelines are available on-line. This is, in most cases, the easiest and quickest way to obtain the information needed at this stage. If it is not available on-line, then a phone call or letter to the grant maker will be necessary.

If the grant application guidelines have been received and reviewed thoroughly and the grant maker still looks like a good fit, it is important to obtain names from the grant program officer of past grantees and reviewers. Once you have some names, contact the project director or grant writer of a past grantee. Speak with this person about the funding source. Specifically, approach the past grantee with the list of questions composed by Miner, Miner, and Griffith (1988) shown in Box 10.1.

Once information has been gathered from a past recipient, it is time to contact a past reviewer. Reviewers can provide invaluable guidance for the writing of the proposal, including the actual process that is followed when proposals are reviewed. Box 10.2 presents questions from Miner, Miner, and Griffith (1998) as guidelines to the type of information to be gathered from a past reviewer.

Finally, after reviewing the application and guidelines thoroughly, contacting a past grantee, and speaking with a past reviewer, it is time to contact the grant program officer. The purpose of this call is to see whether the project is a good match with the grant maker's

---

BOX **10.1**

## Questions for a Past Grantee

- Did you call or visit the sponsor before writing the proposal? This will give you a clue about the extent to which the grantee engaged in pre-proposal contact.
- Who did you find most helpful on the funding source staff? This will help identify an "in-house hero," the agency staff person who may be the best source of inside information.
- Did you use any special advocates on your behalf? This will indicate what role, if any, people outside of the organization played in securing the grant.
- Did the funding source review a pre-proposal or proposal draft prior to final submission? This will help identify their receptivity to pre-proposal contact. Most agencies welcome this, given sufficient lead-time. One federal program officer recently commented that "less than 1 percent of our proposals are funded 'cold' without any pre-proposal contact."
- Was there a hidden agenda to the program's guidelines? Priorities change; what was a top priority at the time the grantee's proposal was funded may have changed again as you plan to submit now.
- What materials did you find most helpful in developing your proposal? This answer will suggest which reference materials and tools the grantee found valuable in writing the proposal.
- Did you have a site visit? If one occurred, ask what took place, who attended, how long the visit lasted, to whom did you speak, and so forth.
- How close was your initial budget to the awarded amount? The interest here is to identify the extent to which budget negotiations took place. What got cut or increased? What level of documentation was required to justify budget items?
- What would you do differently next time? Invariably, people learn from the positive experience of getting a grant and have a number of suggestions about things they would do next time to strengthen a proposal.

*Source:* Miner, Miner, & Griffith, *Proposal Planning and Writing,* 2nd ed. (Oryx Press, an imprint of Greenwood Publishing Group, Westport, CT, 1998). Reprinted with permission.

**BOX 10.2**

## Questions for a Past Reviewer

- How did you get to be a reviewer? Usually you submit a resume and express an interest, showing how your background and expertise meshes with agency concerns.
- Did you review the proposal at the funding source or at another location? The difference here is between a mail and a panel review. Mail reviews are done under more relaxed conditions but often require greater documentation, whereas a panel review is apt to be done more quickly, placing a higher premium on proposal readability.
- Did you follow a particular point or scoring system? Invariably, some portions of a proposal carry greater weight than do other portions. This information will enable you to concentrate your greatest efforts on the highest-scoring portions.
- What were you told to look for? Often reviewers must assign specific points to various evaluation categories. Any special "flags" raised by the program officers should be attended to as you develop your proposal.
- How would you write a proposal differently now that you have been a reviewer? Again, people invariably learn from the positive experience of seeing the inside process of awarding grants and have a number of suggestions about things they would do next time to strengthen a proposal.
- What were the most common mistakes you saw in the proposals you read? The answers are errors that you want to be sure to avoid, such as failing to number the pages, omitting the resumés of project directors or consultants, or miscalculating budgets.
- How many proposals were you given to read? This answer will give you an idea of what your immediate competition will be like.
- How much time did you have to read them? If the reviews have essentially unlimited time to read a proposal (as in a mail review), then you will write one way, but if they are under severe time constraints, then you will write another way. One reviewer recently noted that in a panel review situation, he could spend approximately 20 seconds per page in order to finish the review process on time. Although that is not the norm for proposal review, it does suggest that you would use a certain proposal-writing strategy under such conditions, e.g., simple and short sentences, creative use of headers and sub-headers, lots of white space, boldface for emphasis, and bulleted lists.
- Was there a staff review following your peer review? This will give you a clue about what happens after the review process is over. You especially want to find out how much discretionary authority the program officers have over the peer review results.

*Source:* Miner, Miner, & Griffith, *Proposal Planning and Writing,* 2nd ed. (Oryx Press, an imprint of Greenwood Publishing Group, Westport, CT, 1998). Reprinted with permission.

priorities. Furthermore, if the project is a good fit, this is the first opportunity to begin cultivating a relationship with the program officer. Consequently, it is essential to make a good first impression. Ruskin and Achilles (1995) suggest that you fax your questions to the program officer prior to the call. They also recommend that you schedule an appointment with the program officer to get your questions answered.

At the start of the call, convey that you have reviewed the guidelines carefully and have some questions. If you did not schedule the phone call ahead of time, ask if this is a good time to ask him or her a few questions. If it is a good time to talk, identify yourself and your organization. Then share that after reviewing their guidelines and other materials, you believe your project is a good fit with their funding priorities, but you wanted some feedback as to whether this is correct. Give a *short* overview of the project for which funds are being pursued. If it appears that the program officer is interested in your project, double-check with him or her that you have the correct information regarding when and where to send the proposal. It is critical that you prepare well for this call and that you keep the length of the call to a minimum, in order to leave a favorable impression with the program officer.

The list in Box 10.3 from Miner, Miner, and Griffith (1998) gives some additional questions that can be useful in guiding a discussion with the program officer.

Once all of the above steps are completed, it is time to turn one's attention to writing the proposal. However, the type of proposal required by the grant maker determines whether a shorter letter proposal or a long proposal is to be written. Typically, public agencies require long proposals, while foundations and corporations often request that shorter letter proposals be submitted. Some foundations and corporations also require that a long proposal be submitted once a shorter proposal is accepted. Review the grant application and guidelines carefully to determine which type of proposal is being requested.

## Writing Shorter Letter Proposals

A shorter letter proposal is typically a maximum of three pages, covering the following topics: reference to prior contact with the funder, summary of proposal, sponsor appeal, statement of need, solution to address need, capabilities of agency, budget, measurable outcomes, conclusion, and attachments. These are common components of letter proposals, but it is important to review any guidelines provided by the grant maker. If the guidelines specify certain topics to be addressed in the letter, structure the letter around those topics. However, as most letters include the above information, the following will provide detail about how to address those topics.

Although it may appear that writing a three-page letter is a "breeze" compared to a 20-, 30-, or 40-page proposal, it can be very challenging. All of the background work mentioned above must be done in order to incorporate the information into the letter. And all of the topics discussed below must fit into three pages, so the necessity to be succinct is obvious. Every sentence must convey vital information to the grant maker.

### Components of Letter Proposals

***Reference of Your Prior Contact with Funder and Summary.***    If any prior contact has been made with the funder, mention this first in the letter. Specify the names of the individuals with whom contact has been made. Then state the intent to request support from the grant maker. Next, in one or two sentences, summarize the entire proposal. This summary should include the organization's name, the specific request from the grant maker, and the outcomes of your project.

B O X **10.3**

## Questions for a Grant Program Officer

- Does the project fall within your current priorities? If it doesn't, explore different objectives that might yield a better fit or ask for suggestions of other grant makers who might be interested in your project.
- Do you expect last year's award of $XXX to change this year? This answer should help you determine your project budget size.
- What is your current budget? This answer will tell you how much money is allocated to your grant program.
- How much of that money will be available for new awards as opposed to non-competing continuation awards? This answer will tell you how much money is actually available for new projects like the one you are proposing.
- Will awards be made on the basis of special criteria, e.g., geography or type of organization? This answer will help to reveal any hidden agenda. For instance, they may be especially interested in receiving proposals from small organizations in the Midwest or private hospitals in the Southeast.
- Does the program provide one-time-only support or will it permit other funding opportunities? This answer will let you know if you can go back for future funding requests or are likely to receive only one award.
- What is the anticipated application/award ratio? These funding odds will tell you your mathematical chances for success. There are no guarantees in the grant-seeking business. Funding odds are highly variable among grant programs, ranging from 5 percent to 50 percent.
- Are there any unannounced programs or unsolicited funds to support my project? Sometimes you will discover unobligated or uncommitted funds by asking this question.
- What are the most common mistakes in proposals you receive? Pay particular attention to the answers, for these are things you want to be sure to avoid.
- What would you like to see addressed in a proposal that other applicants may have overlooked? Many program officers like to feel a part of the proposal development process. This question provides them with an opportunity to articulate their "pet ideas."
- Would you review our pre-proposal (two- or three-page concept paper)? If they will (and many do), then you will have an important opportunity to better match your proposal to their priorities.
- Would you review our draft proposal if we got it to you early? Again, a favorable response will help you cast your proposal to their expectations. Be sure to give them enough response time; don't expect them to do this three weeks before the program deadline.
- Would you recommend a previously funded proposal for us to read for format and style? Sometimes a model proposal is helpful to review.
- How do you review proposals? Who does it? Outside experts? Board members? Staff? This information will help you analyze your reviewer audience.
- Should the proposal be written for reviewers with non-technical backgrounds? The level of technicality in your proposal should be geared to the background of your reviewers.
- What percentage of your awards is made in response to unsolicited proposals? If they fund few unsolicited proposals, you may be wasting your time.
- Can you have a copy of the Reviewer's Evaluation Form? Use the same headers and subheaders on your proposal.

*Source:* Miner, Miner, & Griffith, *Proposal Planning and Writing,* 2nd ed. (Oryx Press, an imprint of Greenwood Publishing Group, Westport, CT, 1998). Reprinted with permission.

***Sponsor Appeal.***    Follow the introductory information with a "sponsor appeal." Take the opportunity at the outset to illustrate how funding this grant proposal will benefit the grant maker, particularly if it is a foundation or a corporation. It will be necessary to borrow from the background information gathered earlier in the process to pinpoint what would appeal to the sponsor. Annual reports, tax records, and grants awarded in the past can provide some clues as to what the grant maker values.

***Description of Need.***    In a succinct manner, state what need exists that this project, program, or equipment would address. Document the need using statistics, case studies, testimony, quotations, and other measurable data. Do not simply say, "This is a great need." Instead state, "Forty-five percent of the youth at the community's high school reported drinking alcohol in the last month." Back up any statements of need with factual data. However, present the information in such a way that leaves the reviewers with hope that the problems can be overcome. If the problems loom too large, the reviewers may see the case as hopeless.

***Solution.***    Next, propose to address the need that was described in the previous section. Provide enough detail to gain the interest of the grant maker and to paint a picture of how the funding would actually be used. If appropriate, convey how the program or strategy has been effective in other communities. Finally, summarize the objectives of the project.

***Agency Data.***    This section provides the opportunity to illuminate the strengths of the organization. Detail what qualifications the organization has to administer the project to be funded. In particular, establish the existence of a "(1) credible organization proposing a (2) credible idea to be directed by a (3) credible project director" (Miner & Miner, n.d., Letter Proposal section, para. 7). Also, provide enough information so the grant maker gets to know your agency. You may want to include your mission statement, a brief description of programs offered by your agency, the number of people served, and staff and volunteer capacity.

***Budget.***    Indicate the total cost of the project and the amount requested of this potential grant maker. As mentioned above, be certain that the grant maker has awarded grants in the past in the amount requested. Decide how much detail on the budget will be included in the letter. A more detailed budget can be included as an attachment, if allowed by the grant maker.

***Evaluation.***    In a few sentences, explain how the organization and the grant maker will know that the project is successful. Outline measurement indicators for the project. For example, if the project to be funded is a parenting education program for high-risk parents in the community, then some measurable outcomes could be: The parents are able to demonstrate the knowledge and ability to set clear guidelines for their children, monitor their children's behavior closely, and deliver appropriate consequences. In this case, knowledge and skills might be measured through the use of pre- and post-tests and/or observation of the parents modeling appropriate behaviors and attitudes during interactions with their children.

*Conclusion.* End the letter proposal with a strong conclusion. Make a final appeal for funding for the project, including what you want to do and why it is important. Specify a person who can provide more information about the proposal, if needed. Finally, have the person of highest authority in the organization (e.g., president, director, board chair) sign the letter.

*Attachments.* Include as attachments those items that the grant maker requests. These may be verification of tax-exempt status, resumés of key staff, a list of board members, a detailed budget, a timeline, or evaluation tools. Review the grant maker's guidelines to verify what additional information will need to be submitted and whether attachments are allowed.

# Writing Long Proposals

Long proposals are usually required for publicly funded grants and for a portion of the foundation and corporation applications. Some foundations and corporations will require a long proposal to be submitted once a letter proposal has been approved. In essence, it can be the second step in an application process.

Components often seen in long proposals include: cover letter, table of contents, executive summary or abstract, introduction, statement of need, objectives, methods, evaluation, dissemination, budget, and appendices. The following provides information and ideas to consider when completing the various sections of the long proposal. However, when submitting a proposal, carefully follow the format outlined by the grant maker or the application may be rejected without a thorough review process.

## Common Components of Long Proposals

*Cover Letter.* Cover letters are typically brief, one-page documents that serve as introductions to the applicant and summaries of the proposals. The cover letter is crucial because it is often the first chance to make a good impression. You may want to reevaluate your logo and letterhead to ensure that they convey professionalism. It is important not to include any information in the cover letter that is not in the proposal. This is essential, because the cover letters are not always kept with the proposals.

Included within the cover letter should be a description of why the project is a good fit with the grant maker's priorities and values. There should also be a reference to any previous contact with the grant maker, such as the program officer, or a board member. If board members or volunteers are employees of the company, that should also be noted.

Next, a summary of the project and the amount of funding being requested should be included in the cover letter. A sentence or two conveying enthusiasm for the project should follow. Finally, a contact person and his or her phone number and e-mail address should be listed. Overall, the cover letter should be no longer than one page in length, should have correct grammar and spelling, and should concisely and clearly convey the scope of the project.

*Table of Contents.* If the proposal is more than five pages in length (including appendices), a table of contents should be included (GrantProposal.com, n.d.). The table of contents and sequence of documents should follow the format detailed in the grant application and guidelines, using the same topics that the grant maker has used in the grant guidelines. For example, if the grant maker states that a section on "Statement of Need" must be included, then use that as the title of the section. Do not name the section "Problem Statement." When listing the appendices, include the name of each appendix. For instance, if Appendix A includes the resumés of key staff, then it should be listed as "Appendix A: Resumés of Key Staff" in the table of contents.

***Executive Summary/Abstract.***   The first section of the long proposal is typically the executive summary or the abstract. This is often considered the most important paragraph in the whole proposal (Lone Eagle Consulting, n.d.). This section is normally no longer than one page in length, or 250 to 500 words. The executive summary functions as a synopsis of the entire proposal. Although it is placed as the first section in the proposal, it is best to write it last. Waiting until the end to write it makes it easier to capture all of the highlights of your proposal.

The executive summary should include a brief statement of the need, the proposed solution, objectives of the project, funding requirements to complete the project, and the capacity of your organization and staff to complete the project. When writing the executive summary, view it as the "sales document designed to convince the reader that this project should be considered for support" (Foundation Center, n.d. b, The Executive Summary section, para. 1).

***Introduction.***   The purpose of the introduction section is to establish credibility with the grant maker. This provides the opportunity to show that the organization has the experience, skills, and knowledge to complete the project successfully. Grant writers must convey in this section how the project addresses the grant maker's priorities and values. As Miner and Miner (n.d.) noted, in their Introduction section, "for novice writers, the psychological orientation is 'I-I, Me-Me' while successful writers take a 'You-You' perspective" (Proposal Writing: Introduction section, para. 2). Thus, the need to focus on "sponsor appeal" (as discussed in the shorter letter proposal) is critical in this section.

***Statement of Need.***   The statement of need contains information that the reader needs in order to learn about the issues. It includes the reason why the project needs to be funded. The Foundation Center (n.d. b) identified some points that should be followed when writing the statement of need. First, facts, statistics, case studies, testimony, and other measurable data that provide evidence of the need for the project should be included. Grant writers should ensure that all of the facts and statistics they include in their proposals are accurate and that they all pertain to the project. Second, convey a sense of hope in the statement of need. If the needs are presented in such a dramatic fashion, the grant reviewers may think that funding the project could not possibly impact the problem. Third, review the question as to whether or not to present the project as a model for others to replicate. If you do present it as a model for others to replicate, the grant maker may expect you to actually implement the replication plan. Fourth, be cautious when portraying the agency or program as superior to others. Do not be critical of the competition, as the grant reviewers will likely view this negatively. In fact, the grant maker may have funded your competition in the past.

Therefore, convey the value of collaboration, along with an eagerness and willingness to work with others to address the needs that exist in the community. However, at the same time, still communicate that the organization has the skills, knowledge, and experience to complete the project effectively. Finally, a fifth point to consider when writing the statement of need is to avoid circular reasoning. In other words, do not state the absence of your project as the problem. For example, do not state that the lack of parent education programs in your community is the problem and the solution is to implement parent education programs. Instead, provide information about the lack of parenting skills and the impact that these deficits have on children. Then you can present the parenting education program as a means to increase parenting skills in the community.

Although many points must be covered in the statement of need, strive toward a concise, logical statement of need that captures the readers' attention and leads them logically to the proposed solution. As Miner and Miner (n.d.) point out, "the reviewers should be able to anticipate your solution based upon your analysis of the problem. This important transition paragraph is frequently left out of proposals written by beginning proposal writers" (Statement of Problem or Need: Writing Tips for the Problem section, para. 1).

***Objectives.***   The objectives section identifies the intended accomplishments for the project. They include the measurable items that can indicate success, or the lack thereof. Consequently, it is essential to create realistic and measurable objectives. More specifically, objectives should indicate what outcomes would emerge from the project in the short term. These objectives should be linked logically to the ultimate goal(s) of the project.

The logic model created during Step 7 of the planning process will generate most (if not all) of the objectives. The first row (the risk or protective factors to be addressed) is typically the goal(s), while the next two rows (strategies and target group) contain information on objectives. From the sample logic model in Chapter 8 (see Table 10.1), some of the objectives that could be extracted include:

- A tutoring program will be held for three hours per week for one school year.
- A minimum of 50 students who are struggling academically in grades 1 through 3 will participate in the tutoring program.
- A minimum of 45 of the 50 participants will move to the next grade at the end of the school year.

In some cases a product may also be an objective. For example, a substance abuse prevention social marketing campaign could include objectives regarding the development of print materials, radio spots, and television spots. Or, if the proposal was for a research project comparing the effectiveness of two prevention curricula, an objective could be to document the implementation methods used and to assess the relative effectiveness of the curricula. In short, the objectives must indicate what you intend to accomplish through the project.

***Methods.***   The methods section is the *how, when,* and *why* of your proposal (Foundation Center, n.d. c). This section should provide a picture for the reader of what would actually happen if the project were funded. *How* refers to a description of what will occur from the

**TABLE 10.1  Logic Model with Designs and Methods**

|  | 1. Logic Model | 2. Evaluation Questions | 3. Designs and Methods |
|---|---|---|---|
| A. Goals | Reduce academic failure. | Was academic failure reduced in the target population? | Pre-post survey conducted with the student participants. |
| B. Strategies | Tutoring: 3 hours per week for one school year; 50 students. | How many students participated in a tutoring program for 3 hours per week for one school year? | Program records from the tutoring program coordinator. |
| C. Target group | Children in grades 1–3 at the local elementary school who are struggling academically as identified by teachers (selective population). | How many participants were in grades 1–3 and struggling academically? | Program records from the tutoring program coordinator. |
| D. If-then statement | If tutoring is offered to students having academic problems, then students will have the opportunity to improve their academic skills. If the students take the opportunity, then they will improve their academic skills. If they improve their academic skills, then they will not fail in school. If they don't fail in school, then they are less likely to abuse alcohol, tobacco, and other drugs. | How many students who were selected for the program participated? How many participants' reading skills improved? How many participants failed in school after participating in the program? How many participants abused alcohol, tobacco, and other drugs after participating in the program? | Program records from the tutoring program coordinator and pre-post test surveys of the student participants. |
| E. Short-term outcomes | Participants' grades improve; participants move to next grade level on time. | How many participants' grades improved? How many participants moved on to the next grade? | Pre-post design using the existing database at the school to examine grades of participants. |
| F. Long-term impacts | Participants do not begin using alcohol, tobacco, and other drugs within 3 years after participating in the program. | How many participants used tobacco, alcohol, and other drugs within 3 years of the end of the program? | Pre-post survey conducted with the student participants 1 year, 2 years, and 3 years after the end of the program. |

start to the end of the project. This description must be consistent with the objectives from the previous section. *When* is the timetable for the activities that will occur over the course of the project. And *why* is the reason that these methods were selected to address the problems that were identified in the statement of needs. This is particularly important if the methods to be used in this project are new or unconventional.

When writing this section, it may be useful to begin by creating a timetable of the tasks to be accomplished in the project. This in turn will provide structure and flow for the text. If allowed by the grant guidelines, it may be useful to include this timetable in the grant. It is also important to link the tasks back to the objectives listed in the previous section. Illustrate how the objectives will be accomplished by the activities of the project.

*Evaluation.*    As with the objectives section, the logic model for the project will assist in writing the evaluation section. If during the creation of your logic model it was decided that an external evaluator would be used, it is crucial to have that evaluator assist in the development of this section. The evaluation questions, designs, and methods can be extracted from the project's logic model for inclusion in this section. It should be clear to the grant reviewer how the evaluation would illuminate whether the objectives were met. Consequently, it may be beneficial to organize this section by objective. Furthermore, include, at a minimum, the following information from the evaluation plan: who will oversee the evaluation, what data collection instruments will be used, how data will be collected and analyzed, how much the evaluation will cost, and the timeline for implementing the evaluation. Overall, "be tangible and realistic in what you set out to achieve, and in how you'll know whether you've achieved it after the money is spent" (Lone Eagle Consulting, n.d., p. 18).

*Dissemination.*    Some grant makers require that a dissemination plan be included in the proposal. A dissemination plan outlines, in essence, how you will share information about the project, including the results, with others. For many grant makers this is the section that shows how publicity for them will be generated from this project. Also, it shows how the knowledge, skills, and experience gained from this project will be transferred to others.

Instead of making only general statements about dissemination, be specific about where, when, and how dissemination will occur. For example, instead of stating, "workshops will be conducted at conferences," specify the names, dates, and places that the conferences will be held. Other dissemination options include a project newsletter, seminars, site visits, interim working papers, convention papers, journal articles, pamphlets, books or manuals, speeches, press releases, and postings on computer networks or Website pages (Miner & Miner, n.d.).

*Budget.*    Depending on the guidelines of the grant proposal to which you are responding, the budget will be either a detailed, complex budget or a simple one-page budget. Regardless of the type of budget required in the grant, it must reflect the objectives, methods, and evaluation described in the sections above, and it must be realistic. Grant readers will look to see if the budget is reasonable for the proposed activities. Therefore, it is imperative to research budget needs carefully. If grant reviewers perceive that there are either too little funds to complete the project or that the budget is overinflated, they will view the budget negatively. "A major red flag for grant reviewers is the indication you've planned to accomplish more than you can realistically attain within your budget. It is better to limit your proposal to less, more assuredly attainable goals, than to promise more than you can deliver" (Lone Eagle Consulting, n.d., p. 12).

The budget should be created only after the objectives, methods, and evaluation sections are well developed. Review the proposal narrative and note all the expenses related to completing each task. "Unless you carefully develop the budget and understand the relationship between each item and the proposed plan of action, you will be unprepared to answer questions or engage in final fiscal negotiations" (Hall, 1988, p. 155). Include the **direct costs** associated with the completion of the tasks, such as supplies, personnel, logistics (site costs, food, travel), and others. Also, if required by the grant maker, include a budget match. If a match is required, then you will need to provide a specified amount of funds to match what you are requesting from the grant maker. Furthermore, estimate the **indirect costs** to the agency, such as payroll, accounting, space and equipment, and general project administration. If allowed by the grant maker, calculate the indirect cost as a percentage of your direct costs. For example, if the direct costs are $100,000 and the indirect cost rate is 15 percent, then the indirect cost would be $15,000. Be certain to keep a record of the origin of the various figures in the budget. It may be necessary to refer to your records at a later date during negotiations with the grant maker and/or for monitoring the grant during its implementation. In some cases, grant makers will require that you provide this information in a budget justification section that describes how monies are allocated by line item.

If it is anticipated that revenue will be generated from the project, it will be important to note this on the budget also. For example, if registration fees will be charged for participants, then include the expected amount of fees to be collected in the budget. Finally, if there are any unusual expenditure items, include an explanation in the budget justification.

For some grant makers, errors in the budget can be grounds for immediate rejection of the whole proposal. Consequently, always double-check your budget for errors. It is useful to have several people with calculators and/or software programs review the budget for errors.

*Appendices.*    The last section of a proposal is the appendices. These typically include information that is requested by the grant maker, and may include letters of support, assurances, resumés of key project personnel, the agency's tax exemption letter, organizational chart, and list of board members. Be certain that all attachments requested in the grant guidelines are included. At the same time, when including appendices that are not requested (if permissible by the grant makers), do not overwhelm the grant readers with volumes of information. In some cases, the grant makers do not circulate the appendices to the grant readers. Consequently, information that is essential for the proposal should be included in the narrative.

# General Grant-writing Tips

Many organizations and individuals have writing tips, guidelines, and suggestions for proposal writers. The following are some of the most frequently cited ideas to keep in mind when writing a proposal and/or shorter letter proposal. Keep in mind that if the application instructions contradict any of the tips below, always follow the instructions from the grant maker.

## Create a "Look" for the Proposal

Miner and Miner (n.d.) recommend that grant writers format their proposals in a "look" similar to one the grant maker uses. For example, review the font size and style, colors, and formatting often used in the grant maker's materials. When possible and appropriate, use the same look in the proposal. By doing this, the proposal will have a familiar look to the grant readers. And "a familiar proposal is a friendly proposal" (Miner & Miner, n.d., Proposal Appearance section, para. 1).

## Be Cognizant of Reading Styles of Reviewers

The reading style that the reviewer will be using when scoring applications is important to keep in mind when writing the proposal. The reading style the reviewers will use is greatly influenced by how the grant maker has structured the review process. For example, if the reviewers will only be skimming proposals due to a short time frame, then it is better to have a lot of white space, headings, and ragged right margins (Miner & Miner, n.d.). Yet it is important to use bold type, lists, and examples if the evaluators will be scanning the proposal using an evaluation sheet to award points for the proposals (Miner & Miner, n.d.). Finally, if an evaluator has ample time to review the proposals (e.g., the proposals are mailed to the reviewers), then focus on transitions, type style, and line spacing (Miner & Miner, n.d.). If you gathered information on the review process, as was discussed earlier, then you will have a good idea about which of these writing techniques to use in your proposal.

## Know the Funder

First and foremost, be certain that your project is a good match with the funding source (GrantProposal.com, n.d.): "Do not try to make the grantor's program fit what you want to do—your program must be in line with the funding agency's priorities" (SchoolGrants, n.d., Grant-Writing Tips section, para. 2). Do not submit a proposal without verifying that the project fits with the grant maker's priorities. Most grant makers will immediately discard applications that do not fall within their set of priorities. Do not waste your time or the funders' time by submitting proposals that are not a good match in priorities.

## Verify Available Funding

After deciding that a grant maker is potentially a good fit for your project, verify that funding is still available. If it is available, identify the timelines for grant awards by the grant maker. Double-check that the grant maker's timeline for awarding funding fits for your project. Furthermore, ask only for an amount that they say they are willing to fund. If the guidelines say that the maximum grant is $50,000, do not ask for one penny over that amount. Otherwise, the proposal may be immediately rejected.

## Read the Application Guidelines

Many grant makers provide detailed instructions regarding how and when to submit a proposal, as well as what the proposal must contain. Follow the guidelines detailed in the application to the very last detail. This is essential because many funders receive so many applications that they will simply discard those proposals that do not follow the guidelines. Check and recheck that you are following the guidelines throughout the proposal development process.

## Customize Proposals for Each Grant Maker

Preparing a unique proposal for each grant maker is essential. However, text can be "recycled" when appropriate. For example, it is considered to be inappropriate to submit the same proposal to more than one grant maker (Lone Eagle Consulting, n.d.). But, you can change the proposal slightly so that if both proposals were funded, they would work well together. When submitting a similar proposal with some "recycled" text, however, double-check and triple-check that all references to the grant maker are correct.

One way to customize proposals to each grant maker is to use the same "buzz words" that the grant maker includes in the grant application and guidelines. For example, if the grant guidelines mention "personal safety and security" several times, then craft your proposal to include those words when appropriate. At the same time, do not use words that the grant maker does not want to see. For example, if the guidelines state that funds may not be used for capital improvement, do not use the words "capital improvement" anywhere in your proposal.

## Review Successful Applications

Reviewing successful applications to generate ideas for your own proposal is useful. It is also a good learning tool. Many foundations have copies of successful proposals that they are willing to share upon request. If they do not have any proposals to share, they are often willing to give contact information for past recipients. These past recipients are usually willing to share their proposals. However, if the past recipients will be competing against you for their future funding, it is obviously not recommended that you ask for copies of their past proposals. Copies of successful proposals can also be found in the library and on the Internet. Another way to become exposed to grant applications is to become a grant reviewer. This provides you with the opportunity to read both successful and unsuccessful applications. Consequently, you learn both what mistakes to avoid in grant writing, as well as what makes an application strong.

## Pay Attention to the Format

Even if the content of your proposal is superb, if the format is lacking, it could jeopardize your chances of getting a grant. Consequently, pay careful attention to the formatting details. First, use bold type to emphasize key words, but do not overuse bold, because it can be distracting to the reader. Next, include page numbers throughout the entire proposal, including the appendices. The top right or bottom center are the locations preferred by many grant writers. It is also important to use ragged right margins. Do not use right justification, as it is more difficult to read: "It is easier for the reader's eye to track from the end of one line to the beginning of the next line when the right-hand margins are jagged" (Miner & Miner, n.d., Proposal Writing Tips section, para. 9). Finally, ensure that there is white space in your document. This makes your proposal more appealing to the reader. A document with very little white space can be very intimidating to grant reviewers. White space between paragraphs and sections also helps the reader understand which sections belong together. In summary, after creating the content for your proposal, revise the document format to ensure that it is pleasing to the reader.

## Be Clear and Concise

A clear and concise proposal is essential. Grant reviewers typically have to review a large number of proposals at a time. So the more clear and concise the proposal, the more likely the reviewer will view it favorably.

Communicate your ideas in a precise, easy-to-understand style: "Be succinct. Volumes of documentation are imposing, not impressive" (J.C. Downing, n.d., Maintain a Simple Approach section, para. 1). Do not use acronyms, jargon, or other terms specific to the prevention field that the reviewers may not understand (Carlson, 1995). Once you have completed a draft of your proposal, it is recommended that you have a colleague who is not involved in the project review your proposal (SchoolGrants, n.d.) and provide you with some honest feedback (Carlson, 1995). Have this person review the narrative for comprehensiveness of content, ease of readability, and grammar and spelling. Specifically, when reviewing the document, look at whether ideas are complete, whether the proposal has enough substance, the logical organization of the proposal, correct facts and figures, clearly expressed ideas, and visual appeal (Miner & Miner, n.d.).

## Proofread, Proofread, Proofread!

Spelling and grammar errors will draw the reviewers away from the content of your proposal. They also convey a lack of attention to detail, with the implication that your agency produces poor products. Once the proposal has been drafted, put it down for a couple of days and then review it again. Also, as mentioned above, have a colleague who is not involved with the project review your proposal. Have your colleague look for correct spelling, grammar, and punctuation.

## Convey Your Willingness to Collaborate

In your proposal, share your history of success with collaboration on past projects and your willingness to collaborate with others on the project detailed in the proposal. Demonstrate familiarity with others who have worked on similar projects and who may assist on this one. Your resource assessment completed during program planning activities will provide this information for you.

## Address Sustainability

Most reviewers will want to know how a project will be sustained once funding from the grant maker is gone (Ruskin & Achilles, 1995). Many projects cease to exist after funding from a grant maker ends. Consequently, it is important to demonstrate to the grant maker that the impact of her or his funding will continue once the funding is gone.

## Access the Internet for More Assistance on Grant Writing

Many wonderful Websites have been developed to assist grant writers in creating successful grant applications. Use these wonderful resources as much as possible. A good way to conduct a search for grant writing Websites is simply to enter "grant writing" as the topic to be searched. Also, review the Websites that are listed in the reference section for this chapter.

# What Happens Next?

Once a proposal is submitted, several things can happen. First, you can receive the dreaded letter stating that you did not receive the grant. Or the grant maker may communicate to you that she or he would like you to submit more information. For example, if you have submitted a shorter letter proposal, it may be requested that you submit a long proposal. Alternatively, you may receive the wonderful news that you received the grant. The following outlines in more detail what may happen next.

## What Happens if You Are Not Awarded the Grant?

Although a letter of rejection may be very discouraging, all of the work you have done on the proposal will not be lost. The planning, researching, and writing that you have done can be used to complete other proposal processes. Furthermore, sections of the proposal can be reused for a new proposal. Also, it is important to try to obtain feedback from the reviewer(s). Ask the grant maker if she or he will share the reviewer comments with you. The comments can provide you with useful information when writing your next proposal. You can also ask the grant maker if it would be worth submitting a revised application in the future.

## What Happens if You Are Awarded the Grant?

Sometimes what can be more frightening than getting a rejection letter is getting a letter saying that you were awarded the grant! Now you actually have to do all the things that you promised in your proposal. After receiving an award letter, the first step is to write a letter of thanks to the grant maker. Next, find out all you can about the funding and reporting requirements that the grant maker has. It is essential that you get as many details as possible about appropriate funding expenditures, data to be gathered for reports, and reporting timelines. Next, create an organized system of grants management for the length of the project. As outlined by SchoolGrants (n.d., Managing Your Grant section, para. 4), an effective grant management system includes:

- Continuously monitoring how well the project is meeting its goals and objectives;
- Verifying that all expenditures of grant funds are allowable and appropriate;
- Completing required programmatic and fiscal reports on a timely basis;
- Conducting a thorough project evaluation–including the distribution and submission of any agreed-on reports;
- Preparing for audit visits that the grantor may wish to conduct during and/or after the project; and
- Closing out the project according to the grantor's guidelines.

A well-managed grant accomplishes several objectives. First, it provides staff with the timelines for reports so they can schedule their activities accordingly. Next, it provides staff with the details necessary to collect the data required by the grant maker. It is very difficult to "create" data at the end of a project! Instead it must be collected throughout the life of the project. Finally, "how well you manage your grant will shape your reputation and may determine whether you receive future funding" (SchoolGrants, n.d., Managing Your Grant section, para. 5). Your reputation will precede you, for better or for worse, when you look to gain more funding in the future.

# Summary

Substance abuse prevention professionals must often rely on their grant-writing skills to continue funding their programs and/or to begin a new project. Consequently, it is essential that prevention professionals gain grant-writing skills so they can develop successful proposals. Conducting thorough background research on funding organizations and completing all seven steps in the planning process will prepare prevention professionals for the grant-writing process. Furthermore, following the guidelines of the grant maker, writing concisely and clearly, and proofreading the document several times are just a few of the many tips that experienced grant writers can offer prevention professionals. Once these new skills and tips are applied, the opportunities for grant awards will increase significantly.

## KEY TERMS

direct costs                    indirect costs                    soft money
grant maker

## DISCUSSION QUESTION

1. Discuss the advantages and disadvantages of completing the seven steps to prevention program planning prior to writing grant proposals.

## APPLICATION EXERCISES

1. Identify at least three directories of grant makers, with at least one providing information on public grants, and another on private grants. Review these directories and identify at least three grant makers (at least one private and one public) that appear to be a good match for substance abuse prevention projects.

2. Identify a science-based substance abuse prevention program for which you would like to obtain funding. Create a short letter proposal to a foundation requesting funding for the project.

3. Write a long proposal to obtain funding for a science-based substance abuse prevention project. Include all the components listed in the long proposal section of this chapter.

## SUGGESTED READINGS

The Foundation Center's Website has a short course on proposal writing, a form to record your review for potential funders, and a searchable database of foundations. http://fdncenter.org/.

Grant-writing tips can be found at the following Website: http://lone-eagles.com/granthelp.htm.

The following Website has information for individuals writing grants for K-12 schools. It contains grant opportunities, sample proposals, grant tips, and fund-raising opportunities. http://www.school grants.org/.

Grant Proposal.com is a Website devoted to providing free resources for both advanced grant-writing consultants and inexperienced nonprofit staff. It has many tips on grant writing. http://www.grant proposal.com/.

Oryx Press has an excellent "Guide to Proposal Planning and Writing" document on its Website: http://www.oryxpress.com/miner.htm.

A useful book on how to write a successful grant application is: Carlson, M. (1995). *Winning grants step by step.* San Francisco: Jossey-Bass.

## REFERENCES

Carlson, M. (1995). *Winning grants step by step.* San Francisco: Jossey-Bass.

Foundation Center. (n.d. a). Cooperating collections. Retrieved July 27, 2001, from http://fdncenter.org/collections/.

Foundation Center. (n.d. b). Proposal writing short course. Part one. Retrieved July 13, 2001, from http://fdncenter.org/learn/shortcourse/prop1.html.

Foundation Center. (n.d. c). Proposal writing short course: Part two. Retrieved July 13, 2001, from http://fdncenter.org/learn/shortcourse/prop2.html.

GrantProposal.com. (n.d.). Aesthetics and technicalities for grantwriters. Retrieved July 24, 2001, from http://www.grantproposal.com.

Hall, M. (1988). *Getting funded: A complete guide to proposal writing.* Portland, OR: Continuing Education Publications, Portland State University.

J.C. Downing Foundation. (n.d.). General Guidance. Retrieved July 13, 2001, from http://www.jcdowning.org/resources/generalguide.htm.

Lone Eagle Consulting. (n.d.). Grantwriting tips. Retrieved July 13, 2001, from http://lone-eagles.com/granthelp.htm.

McGee, S. (1995). Grant and program planning. Retrieved July 13, 2001, from SchoolGrants Website: http://www.schoolgrants.org/grant_tips2.htm.

Miner, L. E., Miner, J. T., & Griffith, J. (1998). *Proposal planning and writing*. Westport, CT: Oryx Press.

Miner, J. T., & Miner, L. E. (n.d.). A guide to proposal planning and writing. Retrieved July 13, 2001, from Oryx Press Website: http://www.oryxpress.com/miner.htm.

Morris, J. M., & Adler, L. (Eds.). (1998). *Grantseekers Guide* (5th rev. ed.). Wakefield, RI: Moyer Bell.

Ruskin, K. B., & Achilles, C. M. (1995). *Grantwriting, fundraising, and partnerships: Strategies that work.* Thousand Oaks, CA: Corwin Press.

SchoolGrants. (n.d.). More grant-writing tips. Retrieved July 13, 2001, from http://www.schoolgrants.org/grant_tips2.htm.

YouthTree USA. (1999). Helpful grant writing tips. Retrieved July 13, 2001, from www.youthtreeusa.com/grants.cfm.

# CHAPTER

# 11 Bringing It All Together

Throughout this textbook the reader has been introduced to a discussion on the importance of using science-based best practices to develop, implement, and evaluate prevention programming. The body of knowledge in the area of substance abuse prevention is growing and changing at a rapid rate. In many cases, what had been thought to work in the past has been shown through rigorous scientific research and evaluation processes to be ineffective. This situation is not surprising; disciplines often evolve in this manner.

An important step in understanding science-based prevention research findings is being able to apply the knowledge in the field. This chapter is aimed at helping the prevention professional apply what has been learned in this book to the "real" world. Although conceptually this may sound like an easy task, it is in fact quite challenging. If prevention professionals want to apply these principles to a prevention program that is already in existence, they may run into a number of challenges. This chapter discusses a few of these issues and also provides two hypothetical grant applications for review.

## Challenges in Applying Science-based Prevention Principles to Prevention Programs

Now that each chapter of the textbook has been explored, it is time to apply what has been learned. Suppose a prevention professional is called on to provide some technical assistance to an existing prevention program by its board of directors. This may not be an easy task because many challenges and barriers can present themselves. The first is that the existing program director and staff may like the program the way it is and be very resistant to change. A second issue is that the program staff may be willing to change, but not know what needs to be changed or how to do it. Finally, the participants in the program may not want to change and may resist any attempts to improve the program. These are just three of a long list of potential challenges that may arise when trying to implement science-based principles with an existing program.

Several strengths are also present in this scenario. First, the fact that the board of directors is supporting a change to science-based prevention programming is a positive sign that recommendation for improvement will be accepted. Second, the board has taken an additional step in trying to find some outside expert to provide technical assistance to move the program in a new direction. This is a very positive change, as the leadership has

276

made some decisions to move forward and is demonstrating an openness to innovative thinking from an outsider. Finally, most likely some staff will support this change. It will be important to identify who these "insiders" are and to work with them to convince others that this change is good.

In some cases, implementing a brand-new prevention program may be easier, although this is not always the case. The advantages to new program implementation include hiring and training new staff who are not resistant to change and are committed to a science-based approach. A second advantage is that evaluators can be engaged in the prevention program process from the beginning and can help guide the progression of the program and related staff. A third advantage is that participants can be recruited and become accustomed to the science-based program from the beginning. This said, there are also a number of potential problems that can occur when implementing a new prevention program. These can include the difficulty of finding and hiring competent staff, replicating and culturally adapting the program, recruiting participants, marketing the new program, finding money to support the new program, and engaging the community to support the program.

There are obvious strengths and limitations to changing an existing program and implementing a new science-based prevention program in a community. It is important to consider both situations and to try to move forward proactively when applying these principles to actual programs.

## Review of Book's Chapters

This textbook was divided into 11 chapters. It is very important for prevention professionals to understand each of these chapters as building blocks and to apply the information from them in their daily prevention work. Without this knowledge and skill, prevention professionals will continue to make the same mistakes that have been made by others in the past. Each chapter, then, was developed to teach these building blocks or skills to students who may choose to work as prevention professionals in the future.

**Chapter 1, Introduction,** detailed the definitions of the terms "use," "misuse," "abuse," and "addiction," and presented a discussion about the evolution of a discipline. A historical timeline was provided to demonstrate how lessons learned from the past are still sometimes repeated today. Finally, a discussion about the importance of science-based prevention in the everyday work of prevention was put forth.

**Chapter 2, Prevention Research,** provided substantial information on current prevention research. Three dominant theoretical orientations were thoroughly reviewed in this chapter, including risk and protective factor theory, resiliency, and developmental assets. This module provided in-depth information on science-based prevention research findings, Center for Substance Abuse Prevention (CSAP) strategies, and best practices. Tips were given on how to design an effective prevention program.

**Chapter 3, Prevention Program Planning,** contained information on planning, assessment, and evaluation, and highlighted the seven steps for building a successful prevention program. All the information contained in this section was science based and was designed to encourage a careful prevention planning process. This chapter also contained information on the Institute of Medicine's (IOM) classification scheme for prevention: universal, selective, and indicated.

**Chapter 4, Facts about Drugs,** provided an elementary orientation to pharmacology. It is important for all prevention professionals to understand some basic facts about tobacco, alcohol, and other drugs. Although an extensive understanding of drugs is not necessary for prevention work, understanding the effects of tobacco, alcohol, and other drugs is helpful.

**Chapter 5, The Cultural Context and Ethics of Prevention,** presented prevention information on culture and ethics. Culture is an important attribute to consider when planning and implementing prevention programs. The discussion centered on defining the term "culture," elements of culture, characteristics of culture, and how to adapt prevention programs to specific cultural groups. Identifying a code of ethics for the prevention field was also introduced. This is important because ethics guide professionals on what behavior is appropriate when encountering a variety of situations.

**Chapter 6, Incorporating Human Development Theory into Prevention,** contained information on human development models. It is important for prevention professionals to understand human development needs and desires before working with a prevention target population. Erikson's classical developmental stages were presented as one approach to understanding human development. Other approaches dealt with in this chapter included Abraham Maslow's hierarchy of needs theory, Jean Piaget's stages of development, and the Medicine Wheel model. This chapter was not meant to be an exhaustive overview of the multiple theories and perspectives in human development, but was intended to engage the prevention professional in thinking about developmental stages when designing a prevention program and working with people.

**Chapter 7, The Media and Prevention,** provided a special discussion on communication and the media. Social marketing, which is a relatively new development in the field in prevention, was discussed. One particular type of social marketing, "social norming," was explored. An overview of media advocacy was provided, with information on the skills needed to advocate for prevention policies. Additionally, media literacy, which is the ability to analyze messages critically, was discussed.

**Chapter 8, The Logic Model and Evaluation,** provided information on scientific methods that measure programmatic impact. This chapter discussed the logic model, defined key concepts used in the science of evaluation, and taught the reader how to use evaluation to enhance and improve prevention services.

**Chapter 9, Communication Strategies,** provided information for prevention professionals on the basics of communication skills. This chapter included a discussion on a classical communication model, tips for speaking in public, successful facilitation skills, and leadership styles. Numerous examples were provided that demonstrated why good communication skills are necessary for prevention professionals.

**Chapter 10, Grant Writing,** provided some pragmatic suggestions for writing, and winning, successful grants. A discussion was provided on the differences between approaching government agencies and approaching foundations to fund substance abuse prevention programs. Additionally, some resources were suggested to help prevention professionals gain knowledge in this area.

**Chapter 11, Bringing It All Together,** gives a summary of all of the book's chapters and challenges the reader to begin applying the knowledge she or he learned in each of the other chapters. Some hypothetical sample grant applications are provided that prompt students' skills and get them thinking about how to apply the core building blocks to actual grant applications. Additionally, a case study that allows students to read about the lessons learned from the Center for Substance Abuse Prevention's National Center for the Application of Prevention Technologies is provided in Appendix D.

# Grant Applications

In order to provide an actual application exercise, please review the hypothetical grant applications in Box 11.1 and Box 11.2, and the sample grant assessment in Box 11.3. Remembering all the information learned in this textbook, apply the knowledge from each chapter to these applications. Read the grant applications first, then take the assessment and rate these applications in terms of their scientific content. Finally, read the discussion comments in the following sections.

---

**BOX 11.1**

## The Hope Unlimited Grant Application

Hope Unlimited is a community-based organization serving Silver County. Its mission is to prevent alcohol, tobacco, and other drug use by youth. The agency's executive director has prepared the following draft of a grant application to the Health and Wellness Foundation and has asked for a critique. A separate checklist, entitled "The Assessment," will guide the process.

### Agency Resources and Staff

*Composition by Ethnicity*

|              | White | Hispanic | African American | Native American | Asian Pacific Islander | Other |
|--------------|-------|----------|------------------|-----------------|------------------------|-------|
| Service area | 65%   | 20%      | 10%              | 2%              | 3%                     | 0     |
| Board        | 80%   | 10%      | 5%               | 0               | 5%                     | 0     |
| Staff        | 90%   | 5%       | 0                | 0               | 0                      | 5%    |

*(continued)*

B O X   **11.1**   **Continued**

*Composition by Sex*

|  | Male | Female |
|---|---|---|
| Service area | 53% | 47% |
| Board | 10% | 90% |
| Staff | 5% | 95% |

*Qualifications of Staff.*   The agency employs 20 full-time staff. Due to low funding, most of the staff have less than five years of experience. Only one staff member, the executive director, has a graduate degree (M.S.W.). None of the staff have received formal training to be prevention professionals; their training has been informal and on the job.

*Code of Ethics.*   We have general guidelines concerning confidentiality and nonuse by staff and volunteers.

**Project Description**

This project will involve three components: an education curriculum for students, alternative activities, and a community task force to change laws and norms. The educational curriculum will involve a six-week curriculum taught at the local high school. The six-week curriculum includes videos about the effects of alcohol on the body and alcohol-related fatal traffic crashes. They will also listen to lectures from people whose lives have been affected by alcohol (victims, recovering alcoholics, and children of alcoholics). Recreational activities will include Friday night alcohol-free dances, sports, and club meetings. Community leaders will be asked to serve on the community task force. The task force will work with the city council to increase taxes on alcohol and increase enforcement of the existing laws relating to alcohol.

**Program Goals and Objectives**

*Goals.*   The program goals are to increase the participants' knowledge about the dangers of alcohol and increase alcohol taxes, thereby preventing the use of alcohol by teenagers.

*Objectives*
- 110 high school students will participate in the six-week alcohol education course.
- 110 high school students will attend the Friday night alcohol-free dances, sports events, and the club meetings.
- Alcohol excise taxes will increased by 5 percent.
- Compliance checks will be conducted at 10 alcohol retail outlets per quarter.

**Target Group and Recruitment**

We will work with the local law enforcement agency, and students that are arrested for alcohol violations will be referred to the education component of the project. Students will attend the course after school for six weeks once a week. The Friday night alcohol-free dances, sports, and club membership will be open to all students.

**Cultural Context**
- Only English versions of the curriculum materials are currently available.
- Our staff works well with a diverse population, but few youth of color participate in the recreation programs.

- Compliance checks will be conducted in all areas of the city.
- All participants share one culture.

## Strategies

Please place an "X" by the target population that the above project will include.

_X_ universal

____ selective

_X_ indicated

Please place an "X" by the specific strategies that the above project will include.

____ information dissemination

_X_ education

____ community-based process

_X_ alternatives

_X_ environmental

_X_ problem identification and referral

Please place an "X" by the risk factors and protective factors that the above project will address.

### *Community*

_X_ availability of drugs

_X_ community laws and norms favorable toward drug use

____ transitions and mobility

____ low neighborhood attachment and community disorganization

____ extreme economic deprivation

### *Family*

____ family history of the problem behavior

____ family management problems

____ family conflict

____ parental attitudes and involvement in drug use

### *School*

____ early and persistent antisocial behavior

____ academic failure beginning in elementary school

____ lack of commitment to school

### *Individual/Peer*

____ alienation/rebelliousness

____ friends who engage in the problem behavior

_X_ favorable attitudes toward the problem behavior

____ early initiation of the problem behavior

____ constitutional factors

*(continued)*

BOX **11.1**   **Continued**

*Protective Factors*
_____   individual characteristics

_____   bonding

__X__   healthy beliefs and clear standards

**Human Development**

The education course will provide an opportunity for participants to express their feelings and opinions, which is important for the developmental stage they are in. The alternative activities will allow participants to socialize with their peers, which is also important for this age group.

**Prevention Program Planning**

*Community Readiness.*   Our staff spoke to parents and teachers, who all said this is a much-needed program. We did not do a formal community readiness assessment but do talk with people about this topic occasionally.

*Needs Assessment.*   Archival data was looked at for school and community risk factors. A school survey was looked at from 4 years earlier.

*Prioritizing Risk and Protective Factors.*   The executive director informally polls key community members and they agree that we need to reduce these risk factors. People tell us what we need to know.

*Resource Assessment.*   There are no other programs like this in the community. Since we know this, there is no need to conduct a resource assessment in our community.

*Targeting the Population.*   It is important to reach kids who are experimenting with drugs and intervene so that they do not develop more severe problems. We target anyone who wants to come to our program. We are not selective about who attends.

*Implementing Best Practices.*   The six-week curriculum is based on a model program that was evaluated and shown to be promising in preventing substance abuse with middle school students. Alternative activities have been shown to be effective with high-risk youth and when used in combination with other prevention efforts. Increasing taxes has been shown to be effective in reducing consumption among youth.

*Evaluation.*   We plan to keep attendance records for the alcohol education course and the alternative activities. Pre-post tests will be administered to determine if participants increased their knowledge about the dangers of alcohol and if their attitudes against drinking changed. We will look at recidivism rates for the referred students to determine if they re-offended. We will keep track of the compliance check rates to determine if sales to minors decreased. We will assess whether taxes on alcohol were increased.

*Source:* Reprinted with permission from the Rocky Mountain Center for Health Promotion and Education, *Prevention Generalist Manual.* Copyright © 1991, Alcohol and Drug Abuse Division, Colorado Department of Health and Human Services.

**BOX 11.2**

# The Ponca Prevention Program Grant Application

The Ponca Prevention Program is a community-based organization serving Dixon County in Ponca, Nebraska. Its mission is to prevent alcohol, tobacco, and other drug use by youth. The agency's executive director has prepared the following draft of a grant application to the Health and Wellness Foundation and has asked for a critique. A separate checklist, entitled "The Assessment," will guide the process.

## Agency Resources and Staff

*Composition by Ethnicity*

|  | White | Hispanic | African American | Native American | Asian Pacific Islander | Other |
|---|---|---|---|---|---|---|
| Service area | 60% | 15% | 10% | 15% | 0 | 0 |
| Board | 60% | 10% | 10% | 20% | 0 | 0 |
| Staff | 60% | 10% | 10% | 20% | 0 | 0 |

*Composition by Sex*

|  | Male | Female |
|---|---|---|
| Service area | 53% | 47% |
| Board | 50% | 50% |
| Staff | 50% | 50% |

*Qualifications of Staff.*   The agency employs 10 full-time staff. All the staff members are certified prevention specialists and have taken college courses in substance abuse prevention. Most of the staff have more than five years of experience. Three staff members, including the executive director, have graduate degrees.

*Code of Ethics.*   The Ponca Prevention Program has adopted a code of ethics. All staff have read and received training on the organization's code of ethics and have signed an agreement to adhere to them. The executive director holds quarterly in-service trainings where questions and ethical concerns are discussed with the staff.

## Project Description

This project will focus on replicating a proven, science-based prevention program, entitled the Best Way Prevention Program. This science-based program involves a 12-week curriculum with yearly booster sessions initially targeting 5th-grade students. The curriculum will be implemented

*(continued)*

as designed and no revisions or adaptations will be made, so that program fidelity can be maintained. The Best Way Prevention Program was originally developed using a similar population in a rural community. The original program results showed a 25 percent decrease in substance use by youth tested three years after program completion compared to a control group that did not receive the program. An evaluator will be hired to replicate the study to determine if the program effects are the same with students in Ponca, Nebraska.

### Program Goals and Objectives

*Goal.*    The program goal is to decrease substance use by 25 percent over a three-year period.

### *Objectives*
- Thirty 5th-grade school students will participate in the 12-week curriculum.
- Annual booster sessions will be provided to the students for a total of three years in grades 6, 7, and 8.
- Compliance checks will be conducted at 10 alcohol retail outlets per quarter.

### Target Group and Recruitment
The target group will be a universal population, as all 5th-grade students will be invited to participate in the Best Way prevention program. Active consent parental permission slips will be sent home with the students before program implementation. All students who have returned the parental slips will participate in the program, follow-up booster session, and the related evaluation study.

### Cultural Context
- English and Spanish versions of the curriculum materials are currently available. A Native American version is currently under development and it is anticipated that this will be available before the program begins.
- The Ponca Prevention Progam employs a diverse staff who work effectively with a diverse population. Many youth of color participate in other Ponca Prevention Program activities, so anticipation of similar success is likely to occur.
- Because participants share multiple cultures, the Ponca Prevention Program honors and values cultural differences. The school principal awarded the Ponca Prevention Program executive director, who is Native American, a diversity excellence award last spring.

### Strategies
Please place an "X" by the target population that the above project will include.

        **X**    universal

        ____    selective

        ____    indicated

Please place an "X" by the specific strategies that the above project will include.

        ____    information dissemination

        **X**    education

        ____    community-based process

        ____    alternatives

_____ environmental

_____ problem identification and referral

Please place an "**X**" by the risk factors and protective factors that the above project will address.

## *Community*

_____ availability of drugs

_____ community laws and norms favorable toward drug use

_____ transitions and mobility

_____ low neighborhood attachment and community disorganization

_____ extreme economic deprivation

## *Family*

_____ family history of the problem behavior

_____ family management problems

_____ family conflict

_____ parental attitudes and involvement in drug use

## *School*

_____ early and persistent antisocial behavior

_____ academic failure beginning in elementary school

_____ lack of commitment to school

## *Individual/Peer*

_____ alienation/rebelliousness

__X__ friends who engage in the problem behavior

__X__ favorable attitudes toward the problem behavior

_____ early initiation of the problem behavior

_____ constitutional factors

## *Protective Factors*

__X__ individual characteristics

_____ bonding

__X__ healthy beliefs and clear standards

## Human Development

The Best Way Prevention Program was created based on the developmental needs of 5th-grade boys and girls. The curriculum accounts for the developmental stage of the youth and encourages a wide variety of learning opportunities, including information sharing, group projects, individual and group activities, and hands-on creativity sessions.

*(continued)*

BOX **11.2**    **Continued**

**Prevention Program Planning**

*Community Readiness.*    A formal community readiness assessment was conducted six months ago. An outside researcher was hired to conduct the community readiness and needs assessment (see below) so that the Ponca Prevention Program could scientifically understand the level of readiness that existed in the community. The assessment revealed that most citizens acknowledge substance abuse as a problem and are ready to support a program to address this problem.

*Needs Assessment.*    The outside researcher reviewed archival data from a variety of sources, including the school district, police department, and one local church. Additionally, a validated risk and protective factor survey was administered with the residents of Ponca. The response rate was 42 percent and the data that was collected informed the selection of the Best Way prevention.

*Prioritizing Risk and Protective Factors.*    After the archival and survey data were collected, the risk and protective factors were prioritized. In this case, the two risk factors documented above were identified as priorities in both the archival data and the survey results.

*Resource Assessment.*    A resource assessment was conducted in Ponca, Nebraska. We gained valuable information about the amount of programs and activities available to 5th- though 8th-graders. There was a gap in programming for 5th-graders in the school system. This is why the Best Way program was selected.

*Targeting the Population.*    It is very important to target program participants carefully. We will use a universal targeted prevention program as we are targeting 5th-grade students.

*Implementing Best Practices.*    The 12-week curriculum is based on a model program that was evaluated and shown to reduce substance abuse with middle school students by 25 percent.

*Evaluation.*    A qualified outside evaluator will be hired to implement the program evaluation. As this is a model program, the evaluation tools have already been developed. The evaluator will use these same tools to measure the programmatic impact. Additionally, a longitudinal study will be conducted to determine the long-term effects of the Best Way program. Finally, the program staff will work closely with the program developers to make sure that all tools and evaluation processes are followed as closely as possible to the original design. The outside evaluator will also meet periodically with program staff to ensure that program fidelity is preserved and to address any problems with program delivery.

**BOX 11.3**

## The Assessment

**The Assessment**
Complete this sheet based on the grant application.

**1.** Assess the adequacy of agency resources and staff

| Area | Adequate | Inadequate | Comments |
|---|---|---|---|
| Composition | | | |
| Qualifications | | | |
| Ethics | | | |

**2.** Assess the adequacy of how the agency addresses cultural diversity:

_____

_____

_____

_____

_____

**3.** Assess the strategies employed:

_____ Are the strategies related to the program objectives?

_____ Would other strategies be more appropriate?

_____ Are the risk factors and protective factors adequately addressed?

**4.** Assess the developmental appropriateness of the approach:

_____

_____

_____

_____

*(continued)*

B O X   **11.3**    **Continued**

5.  Assess the adequacy of the agency in the following areas by checking either the "adequate" or "inadequate" box

| Area | Adequate | Inadequate | Comments |
|---|---|---|---|
| Assessing community readiness | | | |
| Prioritizing risk and protective factors | | | |
| Conducting a resource assessment | | | |
| Targeting the population | | | |
| Implementing best practices | | | |
| Evaluation | | | |

6.  *Recommendations:*  For each of the deficiencies noted in your analysis, make a recommendation for improvement.
7.  *Redesign:*  Review the research and the approaches we've discussed and suggest ways that this program can be more effective.

*Sources:* Adapted with permission from the Rocky Mountain Center for Health Promotion and Education, *Prevention Generalist Training.* Copyright © 1991, Alcohol and Drug Abuse Division, Colorado Department of Health and Human Services.

## Hope Unlimited Discussion

This grant application presents an interesting challenge to prevention professionals. Obviously, it presents some strengths and some limitations. Remembering the preceding chapters and the lessons found in each, a few comments are in order. In terms of strengths, this grant application demonstrates that Hope Unlimited wants to do something for youth in the community to prevent the use of alcohol, tobacco, and other drugs. The application presents a cursory understanding of risk and protective factor theory as the applicant is asked to "check off" those factors that seem to correlate to the program they are advancing. Finally, Hope Unlimited has an evaluation component, which is better than not having one at all.

Turn to Box 11.3, "The Assessment." The following discussion will assess the limitations of the application in the same order as the assessment sheet guided the review.

## Assess the Adequacy of Agency Resources and Staff

The grant application is inadequate with regard to composition, as staff does not represent several ethnic groups within the service area. The qualifications are also inadequate because there is no formal training for staff. The ethics of Hope Unlimited are inadequate, as well, as the agency must have a written policy addressing nondiscrimination, competence, integrity, nature of services, confidentiality, and other related issues.

## Assess the Adequacy of How the Agency Addresses Cultural Diversity

A number of facts were noted in the application. First, the group only offers English-speaking materials; yet material in other languages may be needed. Second, it is not clear how the organization assesses its ability to work with diverse populations. This is not mentioned at all in the grant application. Third, when reviewing the demographic information, it is noted that although 20 percent of the service area is comprised of Hispanics and 10 percent are African American, the staff is primarily White. Staffing patterns should more closely resemble the target population to ensure cultural competency. Although this does not guarantee that cultural competency will be advanced, it begins the process of staff diversification. All staff should be trained for cultural competency to help ensure adequate program delivery. Finally, the applicant states that the participants share only one culture. People belong to multiple cultures, such as cultures of gender, race, occupation, and so on. Therefore, this statement does not make much sense.

## Assess the Strategies Employed

The first question in the assessment asks if the strategies are related to the program's objectives. Hope Unlimited uses scare tactics, information about alcohol, and recovering alcoholics' testimonies to reduce youth alcohol use. Yet research from the preceding chapters indicates that using scare tactics is ineffective in preventing the use of alcohol, tobacco, and other drugs. Scare tactics, information on alcohol, and recovering alcoholics' testimonies all constitute the strategy of information dissemination. This strategy, when used in isolation from other strategies, is also ineffective in preventing the use of alcohol, tobacco, and other drugs. It appears that Hope Unlimited's objective is to reduce drunk-driving arrests and alcohol-related accidents, though this is not clearly stated. The group states that it is targeting youth (most of whom are not yet driving). Consequently, these objectives and strategies do not seem related, at least in the short term.

The second question in point number 3 of the assessment asks if other strategies would be more appropriate. Environmental strategies to reduce youth access might be a good choice combined with a social norms marketing campaign to change the notion that everyone is drinking (which, in turn, could change the social norms regarding use). Additionally, Hope Unlimited could offer more realistic information about the consequences of alcohol consumption.

The third question in point number 3 asks about whether the risk factors and protective factors are adequately addressed. They address favorable attitudes toward the problem behavior, but with unproven tactics. The Hope Unlimited grant application does not adequately address healthy beliefs and clear standards.

## Assess the Developmental Appropriateness of the Approach

Hope Unlimited describes using lectures for their prevention sessions. Yet a lecture style is not always adequate for children. Multiple methods of training are preferable to accommodate a variety of learning styles among participants, including use of peer leaders, interactive techniques, and providing positive recognition for desirable behavior. Additionally, developmental theorists were not cited and were probably not used in program development. Finally, the curriculum they are using was developed for middle school students, but Hope Unlimited is using it with high school students. Again, because it was not designed for this developmental age group, it would most likely be inappropriate.

## Assess the Adequacy of the Agency

The first row in point number 5 asks for an assessment of the adequacy of community readiness. This agency is inadequate in accessing community readiness because its methods are too informal and lack sophistication. Because only selected parents and teachers were talked to, the information collected could be biased and inaccurate. The second row asks for an adequacy assessment on prioritizing risk and protective factors. This agency's discussion is also inadequate and does not demonstrate that a formal process was conducted to prioritize which risk and protective factors need to be addressed by the program. The executive director informally polls people he or she knows, which is a biased method of collecting information. The third row, "Conducting a resource assessment," is also assessed as inadequate. Hope Unlimited does not state whether there are other programs that address alcohol use and/or abuse or related issues in the community that will either complement or contradict efforts. They assume they are the only resource in the community. The fourth row, "Targeting the population," is also assessed as inadequate because it appears that only youth involved in the summer youth program will receive training. Additionally, it is stated that Hope Unlimited targets whoever wants to attend the program. Prevention programs need to target specific populations and be very clear about whom they are trying to reach. Program strategies differ by target population. The fifth row, "Implementing best practices," is assessed as inadequate because the response is not based on research. Several types of prevention programs and strategies are mixed together without carefully linking the assumptions to program outcome. The sixth row is "Evaluation." The rating is assessed as inadequate because although pre- and post-tests may be effective, not enough information is given regarding the instrument used in evaluating program effects. There is no way, with the information provided, to determine whether behavioral changes are a result of the program.

## Recommendations and Redesign

Overall, the Hope Unlimited grant application needs to be expanded, using science-based prevention information. A more complete understanding of risk and protective factor theory, coupled with the seven steps for building a successful prevention program, are in order. The seven steps for building a successful prevention program need to be understood and followed in order to keep the information that is collected unbiased and useful. This process is much more scientific and is not merely based on someone's personal opinion. The evaluation component, cultural competency section, and the developmental appropriateness approach needs greater development and expansion to reflect the information found in this textbook. Additionally, environmental and social marketing strategies would enhance the program significantly but need to be linked to the target population. The media could also be used to advocate for changed policies in the area of tobacco, alcohol, and other drugs. Finally, training existing staff and hiring trained and culturally diverse prevention professionals would greatly improve the quality of the prevention program being implemented (Rocky Mountain Center for Health Promotion and Education, 1986).

## The Ponca Prevention Program Discussion

The Ponca Prevention Program grant application is an example of a proposal that shows some sophistication and displays multiple strengths. It is obvious that the applicant has a good working knowledge of prevention, the seven steps to building a successful prevention program, risk and protective factors, the value of educated staff, human development, and cultural understanding. This applicant proposes replicating a proven substance abuse prevention model program to all fifth-grade students. Additionally, this applicant does not "skip" steps in the application process but explains how their organization has addressed multiple programmatic components with its prevention project. Notice that the staff is well trained and educated, and has credentials in substance abuse prevention. Additionally, the program has in-service training on key prevention topics, such as prevention program ethics. Overall, this application is a substantial improvement over the application created by Hope Unlimited.

### CASE STUDY

A case study for prevention is provided in Appendix D. It is a description of six centers that provide technical assistance in the area of science-based prevention. The Center for Substance Abuse Prevention funds six regional Centers for the Application of Prevention Technology. This case study presents a paper published about the first three years of the project. It discusses the project and presents many of the challenges and successes that occurred during this first funding cycle.

## Summary

This is an exciting time in the evolution of substance abuse prevention. Science has much to offer both new prevention professionals and those who have been working in the field for years. This textbook has oriented the reader to science-based prevention practices and strategies that are important for the development of the field. Additionally, much discussion was provided on the importance of applying these key lessons gleaned from research. In the end, this book is only as successful as the reader's ability to apply what has been presented in an actual substance abuse prevention program. Only then can prevention praxis be achieved. It is important to try the techniques and strategies promoted in this book and to teach others about the importance of doing the same. Only then can the field evolve to the next stage of development.

## DISCUSSION QUESTIONS

1. What did you learn from the grant applications?

2. What is prevention praxis and why is this an important concept when discussing the evolution of prevention? How does the term apply to the grant applications provided in this chapter?

3. What are the three most critical things that you learned from this textbook? How will you apply this in your work?

## APPLICATION EXERCISES

1. Make copies of the assessment worksheet shown in Box 11.3 and fill it out as you read the grant applications. Spend at least 30 to 40 minutes critiquing these sample applications.

2. How realistic do you think these two grant applications are? Do you think that you could prepare a better application? What changes would you make to improve these applications?

3. Read the case study presented in Appendix D. What are three lessons that CSAP's National CAPT System identifies as important when conducting technical assistance on science-based prevention programs? What barriers are cited? What recommendations can you give to these centers as they continue their work?

## REFERENCE

Rocky Mountain Center for Health Promotion and Education. (1986). *Prevention generalist training.* Denver: Alcohol and Drug Abuse Division, Colorado Department of Health and Human Services.

# Community Readiness Survey

The following tool was included in the National Institute on Drug Abuse's Community Readiness for Drug Abuse Prevention: Issues, Tips, and Tools, Exhibit 3 (1997). The survey was designed to assist you in determining where your community is in terms of readiness for prevention. This survey, developed by Goodman and Wandersman at the University of South Carolina, uses key leaders to look at three areas: awareness, concern, and action across community levels. Key leaders respond to questions in these three areas, both on a personal level and on a perceptual level of their organization's responses.

No scoring sheet is available for this survey, because the authors did not create one. They recommend that communities average the responses for each question and then interpret the results in the context of their own community.

**TABLE A.1   Community Readiness Survey**

| | Not at all true | Slightly true | Moderately true | Very true |
|---|---|---|---|---|
| **1.** I am aware of programs in my community that address alcohol and other drug abuse prevention. | 1 | 2 | 3 | 4 |
| **2.** I spend time collaborating with others concerning the prevention of alcohol and other drug abuse in my community. | 1 | 2 | 3 | 4 |
| **3.** I don't know why preventing alcohol and other drug use is so important for communities to address. | 1 | 2 | 3 | 4 |
| **4.** I am interested in learning more about community-related alcohol and other drug abuse prevention programs. | 1 | 2 | 3 | 4 |
| **5.** I believe preventing alcohol and other drug abuse among youth is important. | 1 | 2 | 2 | 4 |
| **6.** I am not certain why some individuals consider alcohol and other drug abuse prevention important. | 1 | 2 | 3 | 4 |
| **7.** I am not interested in becoming actively involved in improving alcohol and other drug abuse prevention programs in my community. | 1 | 2 | 3 | 4 |
| **8.** I don't know what programs in my community address alcohol and other drug abuse. | 1 | 2 | 3 | 4 |
| **9.** I am interested in more information on the time and energy commitments that a community-related alcohol and other drug abuse prevention program would require. | 1 | 2 | 3 | 4 |

*(continued)*

**TABLE A.1  Community Readiness Survey** (*continued*)

|  | Not at all true | Slightly true | Moderately true | Very true |
|---|---|---|---|---|
| 10. I know which alcohol and other drug abuse prevention programs serve my community. | 1 | 2 | 3 | 4 |
| 11. I can distinguish the type of services offered by the different alcohol and other drug abuse programs in my community. | 1 | 2 | 3 | 4 |
| 12. I am concerned about whether my community has sufficient alcohol and other drug abuse prevention programs. | 1 | 2 | 3 | 4 |
| 13. I am not involved with the alcohol and other drug abuse community prevention programs in my community. | 1 | 2 | 3 | 4 |

*Directions:* For the following questions, circle the number of the response that *best fits your answer.*

|  | Decreased a lot | Decreased a little | Not changed | Increased a little | Increased a lot |
|---|---|---|---|---|---|
| 14. In the last 12 months, my personal concern for preventing alcohol and other drug abuse in my community has: | 1 | 2 | 3 | 4 | 5 |
| 15. In the last 12 months, my personal knowledge of the risk factors that contribute to alcohol and other drug abuse has: | 1 | 2 | 3 | 4 | 5 |
| 16. In the last 12 months, my personal knowledge of community programs that address alcohol and drug abuse has: | 1 | 2 | 3 | 4 | 5 |
| 17. In the past 12 months, my personal involvement in organized activities for the prevention of alcohol and other drug abuse has: | 1 | 2 | 3 | 4 | 5 |

*Directions:* For the following questions, circle the number of the response that *describes your organization.*

|  | Not at all true | Slightly true | Moderately true | Very true | Don't know enough to judge |
|---|---|---|---|---|---|
| 18. My organization is involved with alcohol and other drug abuse prevention programs in our community. | 1 | 2 | 3 | 4 | 5 |
| 19. Members of my organization are currently learning that alcohol and other drug abuse community prevention programs exist in our community. | 1 | 2 | 3 | 4 | 5 |

| | Not at all true | Slightly true | Moderately true | Very true | Don't know enough to judge |
|---|---|---|---|---|---|
| **20.** My organization has a written policy concerning the use of alcohol or other drugs by employees. | 1 | 2 | 3 | 4 | 5 |
| **21.** In general, staff in my organization know which alcohol and other drug abuse programs serve our community. | 1 | 2 | 3 | 4 | 5 |
| **22.** As part of its mission, my organization is concerned with preventing alcohol and other drug abuse among youth. | 1 | 2 | 3 | 4 | 5 |
| **23.** Members of my organization are assigned to collaborate with others concerning the prevention of alcohol and other drug abuse in our community. | 1 | 2 | 3 | 4 | 5 |
| **24.** My organization is interested in information on the time and energy commitments that a community related alcohol and other drug abuse prevention program would require. | 1 | 2 | 3 | 4 | 5 |
| **25.** In general, staff in my organization can distinguish the types of services offered by different alcohol and other drug prevention programs in our community. | 1 | 2 | 3 | 4 | 5 |
| **26.** In general, staff in my organization are aware of community programs that address alcohol and other drug abuse prevention. | 1 | 2 | 3 | 4 | 5 |

*Directions:* For the following questions, circle the number of the response that *best fits your answer*.

| | Decreased a lot | Decreased a little | Not changed | Increased a little | Increased a lot | Don't know enough to judge |
|---|---|---|---|---|---|---|
| **27.** In the past 12 months, our organization's involvement in our community for addressing alcohol and other drug abuse has: | 1 | 2 | 3 | 4 | 5 | 6 |
| **28.** In the last 12 months, our organization's exchange of information with other organizations concerning the prevention of alcohol and other drug abuse has: | 1 | 2 | 3 | 4 | 5 | 6 |

*(continued)*

**TABLE A.1 Community Readiness Survey** (*continued*)

| | Decreased a lot | Decreased a little | Not changed | Increased a little | Increased a lot | Don't know enough to judge |
|---|---|---|---|---|---|---|
| **29.** In the last 12 months, our organization's referrals to or from other organizations concerning the prevention of alcohol and other drug abuse has: | 1 | 2 | 3 | 4 | 5 | 6 |
| **30.** In the last 12 months, our organization's sharing of resources (e.g., equipment, supplies) with other organizations concerning the prevention of alcohol and other drug abuse has: | 1 | 2 | 3 | 4 | 5 | 6 |
| **31.** In the last 12 months, our organization's cosponsoring events with other organizations concerning the prevention of alcohol and other drug abuse has: | 1 | 2 | 3 | 4 | 5 | 6 |
| **32.** In the last 12 months, our organization's coordinating services with other organizations concerning the prevention of alcohol and other drug abuse has: | 1 | 2 | 3 | 4 | 5 | 6 |
| **33.** In the last 12 months, our organization's undertaking joint projects with other organizations concerning the prevention of alcohol and other drug abuse has: | 1 | 2 | 3 | 4 | 5 | 6 |
| **34.** In the last 12 months, our organization's participation in media coverage concerning the prevention of alcohol and other drug abuse has: | 1 | 2 | 3 | 4 | 5 | 6 |

*Directions:* For the following questions, circle the number of the response that best fits *your personal opinion.*

|  | Not at all true | Slightly true | Moderately true | Very true |
|---|---|---|---|---|
| **35.** I am aware of specific programs offered to employees and their families in the workplace that address alcohol and other drug abuse prevention. | 1 | 2 | 3 | 4 |
| **36.** I am aware of specific programs offered to employees and their families in the workplace that address child and spouse abuse prevention. | 1 | 2 | 3 | 4 |
| **37.** It is very effective to offer alcohol and other drug abuse prevention resources to employees and their families at their workplace. | 1 | 2 | 3 | 4 |
| **38.** It is very effective to offer child and spouse abuse prevention resources to employees and their families at their workplace. | 1 | 2 | 3 | 4 |
| **39.** My organization would be quite willing to make available alcohol and other drug abuse prevention resources to employees and their families. | 1 | 2 | 3 | 4 |
| **40.** My organization would be quite willing to make available child and spouse abuse prevention resources to employees and their families. | 1 | 2 | 3 | 4 |

*Directions:* Please take a moment to circle the answer to the following questions about yourself.

**41.** GENDER—Which one describes your gender?

1. Male
2. Female

**42.** AGE—Which of the following categories include your age?

1. Under 20 years old
2. 20 to 29 years old
3. 30 to 39 years old
4. 40 to 49 years old
5. 50 to 59 years old
6. 60 to 69 years old
7. Over 70 years old

**43.** RACE—Which of the following describes your race?

1. African American (Black)
2. American Indian
3. Asian
4. Caucasian (White)
5. Hispanic
6. Other (please specify)_____

*(continued)*

**TABLE A.1   Community Readiness Survey** (*continued*)

**44.** EDUCATION—What is the highest level of education that you completed?

1. Eighth grade or less
2. Some high school
3. High school graduate
4. Vocational school beyond high school
5. Some college
6. College graduate
7. Some graduate education
8. Graduate degree

**45.** OCCUPATION—Which of the following categories describes your occupation?
(Circle the *best one choice*)

1. Executive, director, or services manager
2. Professional
3. Technical
4. Sales
5. Administrative support (e.g., clerical, secretarial)
6. Service
7. Industrial
8. Homemaker
9. Unemployed
10. Other (please specify) _____

**46.** TYPE OF ORGANIZATION—Which of the following categories describes your organization? (Circle the *best one choice*)

1. Private business (for profit)
2. Government agency
3. Nonprofit private social agency
4. Religious organization
5. School
6. Other (please specify) _____

**47.** LENGTH OF TIME IN CURRENT POSITION—Which of the following categories describes the length of time you've been in your current position?
(Circle the *best one choice*)

1. Less than 1 year
2. 1–2 years
3. 3–5 years
4. 5–10 years
5. More than 10 years

Thank you for your time and effort. Please place survey in return envelope. No postage is necessary. All responses are treated with confidentiality.

# APPENDIX B

# Validated Archival Indicators

The following are the archival indicators that have been validated through research by the Social Development Research Group (n.d.) to assist you in determining the level of risk in your communities. The indicators are listed by risk factor. For risk factors that do not have any validated indicators, suggested indicators are included.

**TABLE B.1**

**Availability**

| | |
|---|---|
| Alcohol sales outlets | The average yearly number of retail alcohol sales outlets on record in relationship to the total population. |
| Tobacco sales outlets | The average yearly number of retail tobacco sales outlets on record in relationship to the total population. |

**Community Laws/Norms (Not Validated)**

| | |
|---|---|
| | Possible indicators: attitudes favoring gun control; average length of prison sentence; disposition of juveniles arrested; sentencing below federal guidelines; school polices regarding alcohol, tobacco, and drugs, by region. |

**Transitions and Mobility**

| | |
|---|---|
| New home construction | The number of new building permits issued for single and multifamily dwellings. |
| Households in rental properties | The percentage of households in rental housing. (Calculated as [Renter Occupied Units/Total Occupied Housing Units] × 100.) |
| Net migration | Reported as the number of new residents moved into an area minus number of residents moved out of an area, per 1,000 population. Does not include numbers of births and deaths within the area. |

**Low Neighborhood Attachment/Community Disorganization**

| | |
|---|---|
| Population voting in elections | Reported as the percentage of the population registered to vote that vote in the November elections. |
| Prisoners in state and local correctional systems | Reported as the duplicated number of new admissions to state and local prisons, by prisoner's county of residence, per 100,000 population. |

*(continued)*

**TABLE B.1** (*continued*)

| | |
|---|---|
| **Extreme Economic and Social Deprivation** | |
| Unemployment | The percentage of labor force not employed, reported on an average annual basis as a percentage of the total workforce. |
| Free and reduced lunch program | The percentage of students in public schools (K–12) whose applications have been approved for Free and Reduced Lunch Programs. |
| Aid to families with dependent children (AFDC) | The rate of persons (all ages) participating in AFDC programs, per 1,000 population. |
| Food stamp recipients | The average monthly number of food stamp recipients, per 1,000 population. |
| Adults without high school diploma | The percentage of total population age 25 and older, completing 9th–12th grades, without obtaining a diploma. |
| Single-parent family households | Reported as the percentage of family households with spouse absent. Calculated as {Other family (male and female, no spouse present)/(Married couple family + Other family)} × 100. |
| Family history of substance abuse | |
| Adults in alcohol and other drug (AOD) treatment programs | The unduplicated number of adults (18 and older) in state-supported AOD programs, per 1,000 adults (18 and older). |
| **Family Management Problems** | |
| Children living away from parents | Reported as the rate of children (age 0–17) living in home situations other than with one or both parents or guardians, per 1,000 children (age 0–17). Calculated as: {(Householder or Spouse + Other Relatives + Nonrelatives + In Group Quarters)/Children age 0–17} × 1,000. |
| Children living in foster care | The duplicated average daily rate of children (age 0–17) in state-supervised, family-based foster care; regardless of parental rights termination or length of care; per 1,000 children (age 0–17) per year. |
| **Family Conflict** | |
| Divorce | The rate of divorce (dissolutions and annulments), per 1,000 population. |
| Domestic violence arrests | The rate of domestic violence arrests of partners (including spouses, former spouses, and lovers), per 1,000 adults (age 18 and older). Does not include child abuse. |
| **Favorable Parental Attitudes and Involvement** | |
| | Possible indicators: adult alcohol-related arrests; adult property crime arrests; adult violent crime arrests; alcohol and tobacco use during pregnancy; babies born affected by alcohol or other drugs. |
| **Low Commitment to School** | |
| Event dropouts | The percentage of students (grades 9–12) who drop out of school in a single year without completing high school. |

Status dropouts

The percentage of adolescents (age 16–19) who have not completed high school and are not enrolled in school, regardless of when they dropped out. Calculated as: {(Armed Forces: Not enrolled in school, not high school graduate + Civilian: Not enrolled in school, not high school graduate)/Population age 16–19)} × 100.

**Early and Persistent Antisocial Behavior**

Possible indicators: elementary school special education classes—emotional disturbance; elementary school special education classes—learning disabilities; elementary school students with behavioral disorders.

**Academic Failure Beginning in Late Elementary School**

Possible indicators: ACT test scores; G.E.D. diplomas issued; math proficiency; reading proficiency; SAT test scores; science proficiency; writing proficiency.

**Alienation and Rebelliousness**

Possible indicators: reported gang involvement; suicide death rates by age; suicide thoughts, planning, and attempts, by gender and grade; vandalism and graffiti damage.

**Friends Who Engage in the Problem Behavior**

Possible indicators: adolescents diagnosed with sexually transmitted diseases—gonorrhea and syphilis; reported use by friends—alcoholic beverages, reported by 12th-graders; reported use by friends—binge drinking; reported use by friends—cigarettes; reported use by friends—cocaine; reported use by friends—drinking alcoholic beverages; reported use by friends—marijuana.

**Favorable Attitudes toward the Problem Behavior**

Possible indicators: attitudes regarding marijuana laws; disapproval of drug use for: binge drinking, cigarettes, cocaine, marijuana; perceived harmfulness of use of: alcohol, binge drinking, cigarettes, cocaine, marijuana.

**Early Initiation of Problem Behavior**

Dropouts prior to ninth grade

The number of students (grades 7–8) dropping out of school prior to ninth grade, per 1,000 students (grades 7–8).

Vandalism arrests, age 10–14

The rate of adolescents (age 10–14) arrested for vandalism (including residence, nonresidence, vehicle-venerated objects, police cars, or other), per 1,000 adolescents (age 10–14).

Alcohol-related arrests, age 10–14

The rate of adolescents (age 10–14) arrested for alcohol-law (DUI, drunkenness, liquor law violations) violations, per 1,000 adolescents (age 10–14).

(*continued*)

**TABLE B.1** (*continued*)

| Personal and property crime arrests, age 10–14 | The rate of adolescents (age 10–14) arrested for personal (criminal homicide, aggravated assault, robbery, rape) and property (burglary, larceny theft, arson, motor vehicle theft) crimes, per 1,000 adolescents (age 10–14). |
|---|---|

*Source:* Social Development Research Group. (n.d.) Validated archival indicators. Unpublished manuscript, University of Washington, Seattle.

# APPENDIX C

# Three Case Studies in the Ethics of Prevention

The following case studies, reprinted and adapted from *Prevention Generalist Training* Colorado Alcohol and Drug Abuse Division (1986), can help to guide group discussion concerning ethical issues in prevention.

## CASE STUDY 1

Mr. [Martin] Matthews, known as "Marty" by the students in Founders' Valley Middle School, is a popular English teacher and the girls' basketball coach. Because Martin is fairly new to teaching, energetic, and youthful, the principal thought him the perfect candidate to lead the school's new prevention program. Martin first formed the "Stay Clean" committee with his top six academic achievers, all female students aged 11 to 14 years, to serve as youth role models for the rest of the student body. To orient the new committee to the prevention project's goals, Martin proposed a weekend training camp at his remote beach home.

When Debi, one of the chosen committee members, brought home her permission slip, her mother was somewhat hesitant. After Debi's insistence, however, she permitted Debi to go. After all, Mr. Matthews was a professional person. When Debi returned home from the training, she was very excited. She told her mom about how special she felt to be picked to participate on the committee and that Marty mentioned to her that she was the prettiest and most special of all "his" girls. Debi's mom called Marty to ask about this preferential treatment. Marty insisted that he did not do or say anything wrong and that she should not worry about Debi's affection for him. "Such affection," he stated, "is natural at that age. Besides, all that matters is keeping Debi away from drugs."

1. Has Martin violated any ethical standards? If so, what are they?
2. Should Debi's mom be concerned?

## CASE STUDY 2

The Safe Communities Coalition, like many other coalitions, is a struggling nonprofit organization. Within the next year, a significant funding source will no longer be available as the grant nears completion. Ms. Applebee, the coalition's director, is contemplating layoffs and significant reductions in prevention services as a result of the impending lack of funding.

The president of Sierra Golden, a local microbrewery, publicly denounced prevention efforts in the past as ineffective and unnecessary. He then contacted Ms. Applebee, suggesting that they coapply for grant funding from a national brewing company, Bottle Time Inc., that historically markets alcohol through the use of gimmicks that appeal to youth.

1. Should Ms. Applebee consider the collaboration with the local microbrewery?
2. Should Ms. Applebee consider accepting funds from the national brewery?
3. What ethical conditions might be involved with either Sierra Golden or Bottle Time Inc. that would make it impossible to continue collaboration or to accept the funding?

## CASE STUDY 3

For the past ten years, Custom County teachers have enthusiastically implemented the "Don't You Dare" curriculum in every junior high school to prevent youth drug use. Recently, the state university funded an evaluation study of the beloved program. The research demonstrated that not only did implementing the curriculum fail to prevent drug use; in many cases, an increase in drug use followed program implementation.

The county's substance abuse coordinator knows that the process of finding or developing a new curriculum will require significant time and effort. To notify program funding agencies, teachers, and parents about the results of the study and to abandon the "Don't You Dare" curriculum would devastate the credibility of the county's program and therefore jeopardize funding sources. The advisory board has suggested that the county coordinator keep the evaluation information secret until a suitable replacement curriculum is ready for implementation.

1. Should the coordinator keep the evaluation information secret from teachers? From funding agencies? From parents?
2. Should the coordinator continue to implement "Don't You Dare"?
3. What are some possible alternatives to continuing the "Don't You Dare" program?

## REFERENCE

Rocky Mountain Center for Health Promotion and Education. (1986). *Prevention generalist training.* Denver: Alcohol and Drug Abuse Division, Colorado Department of Health and Human Services.

# APPENDIX D

# Case Study in Prevention

## Closing the Gap between Research and Practice—Lessons of the First Three Years of CSAP's National CAPT System, 1997–2000

## Abstract

This paper presents the lessons learned by CSAP's National CAPT program in supporting CSAP's mission to reduce substance use and abuse by bringing science-based prevention to every community. As a key CSAP training and technical assistance mechanism, CSAP's CAPTs [Centers for the Application of Prevention Technologies] have faced a myriad of challenges and developed unique solutions to helping states and communities to increase the application of science-based approaches to prevention. The core lessons learned by CSAP's CAPTs address issues related to:

- Motivating the field to embrace a science-based approach to prevention planning, implementation, and evaluation.
- Promoting application of these approaches.
- Supporting the ongoing implementation of these approaches in day-to-day prevention practice.

305

This paper is intended to stimulate further discussions within the field about how to further advance the application of science-based approaches to prevention.

# Introduction

The Center for Substance Abuse Prevention (CSAP), Substance Abuse and Mental Health Services Administration (SAMHSA), provides national leadership in the development of policies, programs, and services to prevent the onset of illegal drug use, to prevent under-age alcohol and tobacco use, and to reduce the negative consequences of using substances. Its mission is to decrease substance use and abuse by bringing effective prevention to every community. CSAP develops science-based prevention knowledge, makes this knowledge available, and builds the capacity of states, communities, and other groups to apply this knowledge effectively. CSAP also seeks to facilitate the adoption of science-based prevention through education, publications, technical assistance, and training.

CSAP's Centers for the Application of Prevention Technologies (CSAP's CAPTs) system are major mechanisms by which CSAP brings research to practice. Established in 1997, these six regional centers provide materials, training, technical assistance to:

- *Motivate* the field to embrace a science-based approach to prevention planning, implementation, and evaluation
- *Promote* the application of science-based strategies
- *Support* the implementation of science in day-to-day prevention practice

The primary target audiences for CSAP's CAPT services include CSAP's State Incentive and Border Incentive Grantees, Single State Agencies for alcohol, tobacco, and drug issues, prevention providers within communities including Drug-Free Community grantees, and providers and funders within state, territorial, and tribal governments.

This paper will capture, amplify, and synthesize the lessons learned by CSAP's CAPTs and the CSAP staff with whom we have worked so closely in the first three years of the National CAPT program. We will discuss the issues we have faced, the solutions we have developed, and the work that still needs to be done to increase the application of science-based approaches to prevention. Our goal is to inform Congress, policy makers at CSAP, SAMHSA, and the states and territories, practitioners in the field, and the research community about the work of CSAP's National CAPT program and the lessons we have learned from it. Perhaps more important, we wish to stimulate thought and discussion about how best to apply these lessons to advance our common goal of preventing the negative health and social consequences of alcohol, tobacco, and drug use.[1]

## Our Continuing Challenge

We have made tremendous strides in our understanding of the causes of alcohol, tobacco, and drug use and related problems. And we have developed and tested a wide variety of prevention approaches that reduce use and problems. But we have had challenges promoting the use of these scientific advances by the policy makers, practitioners, and concerned citizens that are responsible for the vast majority of prevention planning and implementation.

In some American communities, lack of awareness of scientific progress leads to continued implementation of strategies that are less effective than are alternative approaches of similar complexity and cost. In other communities, strategies that have been shown to be ineffective are used year after year owing to longstanding and entrenched beliefs about what constitutes prevention or because they are easy to implement. And in many communities, effective approaches go unused not because policy makers and citizens are unaware of them, but because of a lack of expertise and the organizational infrastructure to implement them. Overall, our scientific knowledge is much more advanced than is evident in the day-to-day practice of prevention.

In discussing the application of scientific knowledge to practice, Haynes (1993) concludes that our national enthusiasm for research studies often neglects the fact that "most of the evidence generated from such studies is going to waste because we do not know how to overcome the problems of dissemination and application" (p. 221).

It will surprise some readers to learn that Haynes is referring not to substance abuse prevention, but to healthcare practice. We do not make this comparison to science-based healthcare simply because misery loves company. Rather, we wish to emphasize that problems of promoting science-based practice are endemic in the health field. They are by no means limited to substance abuse prevention. And they are not easily solved in any area of health policy and health services.

## Expectations for the Promotion of Science-based Prevention

Research on the promotion and adoption of science-based prevention is sparse. Available reviews tend to address problems of implementation (Toomey at al., 1996; Giesbrecht et al., 1993; Moskowitz, 1989). A handful of papers have directly examined the factors that facilitate or impede the adoption of specific science-based substance abuse prevention practices (see, for example, Wagenaar, 2000). These papers focus primarily on alcohol policy and the difficulties encountered in attempting to stimulate needed legislation or enforcement activities.

Conceptually, promoting science-based prevention practice fits within the more general arena of diffusion of innovation in healthcare. The healthcare literature, in turn, fits within the extensive literature on the diffusion of innovation—a problem that has been studied by social scientists for over a century (see Rogers, 1995 for a historical review and Klitzner, 1999 for a comprehensive review of the health area). A consideration of this larger literature provides a useful context for the current discussion.

The literature suggests that the diffusion process can be divided into five stages (strategy planning, awareness, conversion, adoption, and ongoing implementation). Each of these stages, in turn, subsumes multiple empirically derived factors that increase or decrease the probability that an innovation will be adopted (Klitzner, 1999). So, for example, the *conversion phase* includes factors such as (1) the belief by targets[2] that promoters understand their needs (disciplinary/sectorial cultural competence), (2) the availability of concrete evidence of results, and (3) endorsement of the innovation by credible sources and by people like the targets. Similarly, the implementation phase includes factors such as (1) the availability of organizational support and adequate resources, and (2) ongoing technical assistance and boosters.

The nomenclature in the area of diffusion science is widely variable and deserves comment. Some use the term "dissemination" interchangeably with the term "diffusion." Others assign distinct meanings to these two terms to distinguish proactive dissemination processes from more spontaneous diffusion processes—analogous to the diffusion of molecules in chemistry. Still others, including CSAP, reserve the term "dissemination" for the distribution of materials and ideas only. In this paper, we will use the term "diffusion" to refer to the entire process of motivating, catalyzing, and supporting the use of science-based prevention and the terms "dissemination," "distribution," or "promotion" to refer to activities concerned with packaging and distribution information. We note, however, that, CSAP's mandate to its CAPTs is unequivocally proactive.

As already noted, there are few studies of strategies specifically designed to catalyze diffusion of science-based prevention. Thus, direct empirical support for many of our recommendations is lacking. However, the broader literature to which we have referred allows us to make logical inferences concerning the potential of generic diffusion strategies when they are applied to prevention science and practice. The guiding principles and major findings of diffusion science differ little by substantive area. Accordingly, to the extent that our efforts in prevention mirror those that have been shown to be effective in healthcare generally and/or in the wide variety of areas in which diffusion has been studied over the last century (agriculture, education, computer and other technology, economic development, community planning, etc.) we can infer their applicability in the current context.

The literature of the diffusion of healthcare innovations supports four important generalizations:

1. *The number of factors that must be successfully addressed increases at each successive stage of the diffusion process*—Roughly speaking, this means that as one moves from strategy planning to implementation, the challenges increase and the probability of success decreases. Not surprisingly, the number of diffusion efforts in the health field that lead to ongoing implementation of an innovation (the final stage) is small (Walker et al., 1994).

2. *Person-to-person contact is a factor at each stage*—Among the most successful attempts to introduce science-based practice into healthcare are those that rely on face-to-face contact in all components of the diffusion process (see Nardella et al., 1995). Like other diffusion strategies, however, face-to-face contact will only succeed when the target believes that the communicator understands his or her needs, working context, and constraints.[3]

3. *The majority of factors are target-oriented rather than program/strategy/policy-oriented*—An understanding of targets' needs, perceptions, values, and readiness for change is a primary determinant of the success of diffusion efforts.

4. *Adoption and implementation are heavily dependent on fitting the innovation to the context in which it is implemented*—No matter how committed people are to an inno-

vation, it will fail to take hold if the necessary organizational supports are not in place. Capacity building must precede implementation. Moreover, innovations that are inconsistent with community values will not generally survive even if they have positive effects.

The diffusion of innovation literature provides important guidance about the levels of success we may expect in promoting the application of science-based prevention. As suggested above, the diffusion process is complex and dependent on a large number of factors. For this reason alone, our expectations about the success of our diffusion efforts should be conservative.

Our expectations for promoting science-based prevention often seem to derive from Ralph Waldo Emerson: "Make a better mousetrap, and the world will beat a path to your door." In other words, we seem to believe that science-based prevention should be readily adopted because it is *better*. However, the diffusion literature suggests that science-based prevention strategies will not necessarily be embraced by policy makers, practitioners, and citizens based solely on scientific evidence of better results. In practice, there is often little relationship between the evidence supporting an intervention and its adoption by the field (Grube and Nygaard, in press; La Fond et al., 2000; Wagenaar, 2000; Gorman, 1995, 1996).

This is not to suggest, as does some conventional wisdom, that policy makers, practitioners, and citizens are resistant to new ideas or unable to understand the importance of a scientific approach. This conventional wisdom ignores important differences between the role of the researcher and the role of the practitioner. As Greer reminds us, "just as science is not practice, practice is not merely applied science." The products produced by prevention scientists must be fit into the day-to-day realities of the practitioner. Attempts to force fit policies or programs into new contexts will almost always fail. And the practitioner is the only reliable expert concerning what can and cannot be implemented in his or her community or setting.

We must also be realistic about the resources required to advance science-based prevention. The need for resources is well recognized by the U.S. Department of Agriculture (USDA), whose knowledge diffusion program is arguably the most successful in the world (Rogers, 1995). One major reason for the USDA's success is that for every dollar spent on knowledge production, one dollar is spent on knowledge diffusion. Consider the extremely ambitious diffusion effort that accompanied the publication of the landmark *Guide to Clinical Preventive Services* (United States Preventive Services Task Force, 1989). As reported by Woolf et al. (1996), the release of the guide was heavily covered in the medical press and large-circulation medical journals. More than 64,000 copies have been sold and translations have been distributed in Japan, Spain, Italy, Argentina, and Russia. The entire guide is accessible on-line through the National Library of Medicine, and *American Family Physician* and *JAMA* have reprinted major sections. Despite this massive diffusion effort, which far exceeds what is commonly done in prevention, rates of awareness of the guide (let alone use of its recommendations) were as low as 20 percent for some relevant specialty areas.

In prevention, we often set up high expectations for our efforts. The use of phrases such as "alcohol free" and "drug-free communities" in describing prevention program goals, although intended to inspire community action and buy-in, may lead to expectations

BOX 1

## Marketing Prevention

As is the case in the marketing of consumer products and services, social marketing seeks the optimal mix of product, price, promotion, and place.

The *product* in a social marketing campaign is the specific behavior we wish to catalyze. In the current case, the product is science-based prevention—as a framework for planning, as a guide to the selection of strategies, as the criterion against which success is measured, and so on.

The *price* may be measured in a psychological, social, personal resource, or economic metric. For example, adopting a science-based approach in a community may involve anxiety over abandoning traditional assumptions, conflict with providers of current services, substantial additional work for professionals and volunteers, or the need for new resources.

*Promotion* refers to the way the target behavior is packaged and presented. That is, what benefits are targets to be told they will enjoy as a result of "buying" the product? Clearly, safe, healthy communities are valued by all Americans, but a promotion may also appeal to self-esteem, enlightened self-interest, the promise of an improved business climate, etc. Promotion also refers to the specific communication strategies to be used—e.g., how the message is to be structured and delivered, by whom it is to be delivered, what the tone will be, and so on.

*Place* refers to the availability of the product (i.e., science-based prevention information and technology). As Wallack (1990a) notes, no one has ever bought a product they could not find. Just as manufacturers and distributors compete for the best shelf space in retail outlets, new prevention approaches compete for priority and resources in any community. Once communities become interested in science-based prevention, they must have ready access to additional information, training, and technical assistance. Otherwise, our promotion efforts will fail to catalyze utilization of science-based prevention.

(The above discussion is adapted from the social marketing plan for NIAAA's Leadership to Keep Children Alcohol Free initiative.)

---

that are unlikely to be attained. Even when goals are more attainable, expectations of rapid change are contrary to all that is known about the diffusion of innovation.

In summary, the literature on diffusion of innovations in healthcare suggests that the infusion of science-based programs and strategies into the day-to-day practice of prevention is a complex and dicey undertaking. Examples of successful diffusion in any area of healthcare are rare. Perhaps the most important lesson from this literature is that practitioners are unlikely to adopt science-based prevention simply because it is "better." Rather, the factors that facilitate and impede adoption are focused largely on the extent to which the needs of targets and the constraints in the contexts in which they operate are addressed. The literature also dictates modest expectations concerning the success of diffusion efforts. The evidence is clear that changes in practitioner behavior are not easily realized and protracted time frames are the rule. We may set ourselves up for failure when we promise to accomplish too much in too short a time.

## The Social Marketing Approach

A major challenge for CSAP's CAPTs is to package and market science-based prevention in ways that will compete successfully with all the other appeals that reach prevention professionals. The challenge is not unlike those we face in packaging health promotion messages to compete with the flood of commercials that encourage Americans to drink, smoke cigarettes, eat fatty foods, and so on. Social marketing (Wallack 1990a, 1990b; Atkin and Arkin, 1990) has provided CSAP's CAPTs with a set of strategies that can assist in meeting this challenge.

Social marketing uses a framework borrowed from the promotion of consumer goods and services, but combines these with concepts from social influence theories and other social scientific formulations related to health behavior. The marketing concepts of product, price, promotion, and place are reinterpreted within the context of specific health or social objectives and are then used as the basis for campaign planning.

The fundamental goal of social marketing is to make it easy for targets to act in compliance with the message (see Boxes 1 and 2). Social marketing theorists also point out the utility of the concept of exchange. That is, strategies must be designed cognizant of the fact that targets are being asked to exchange some resource for the product we are promoting (science-based prevention). The terms of this exchange (price vs. payoff) must be favorable to the targets—otherwise, there is little reason for them to adopt science-based practices.

---

BOX **2**

## Porque Si Importa

In Minnesota the Central CAPT helped organize and support an English and Spanish version of a social marketing initiative, entitled "Because It Matters" or "Porque Si Importa," targeting adults about providing alcohol to youth. Based on the research that many youth get alcohol from their own homes, messages were tested and communicated about adult providers, social host liability, and guidelines/standards within the family. Concurrently, other groups collaborated with CAPT assistance in public policy change, eventually increasing public support for state leadership that significantly contributed to new laws passed stiffening penalties for adult providers of alcohol, including not only parents and adult friends, but liquor retailers as well.

In marketing terms, the *Product* was the behavior change sought, specifically, to reduce and prevent alcohol giving or selling to youth by adults. The *Price* was commitment to confront adult providers, even friends, and to change the environment that tolerated giving/selling of alcohol to youth. The *Place* was parent education classes, Parent-Teacher-Community meetings, faith communities, local employers. The *Promotion* included a "Because it Matters" logo and a campaign kit that contained press releases, free print ad copy, background articles, radio scripts, outdoor board specs, a campaign Use Agreement (to guidelines), a "20 Things You Can Do" reprintable direct mail piece, and a website. The logo was reproducible, and was often applied to all local activities that fit the theme and goal of youth alcohol access prevention. The widespread use of the logo was intended to gain the power-in-numbers force, much like the Nike Swoosh, which fits all forms of physical activity.

# Lessons Learned

Over the last three years, we have amassed a rich body of experience in motivating, catalyzing, and supporting the application of science-based approaches to prevention. As regional centers, each of CSAP's CAPTs faces different challenges related to target population needs, geographic and sociodemographic factors, and attitudes, beliefs, values, and priorities regarding alcohol and drug problems. This diversity provides a varied tapestry of experience from which to derive lessons to share with the field.

Data on CSAP's CAPTs activities are available from a variety of sources. Each CAPT maintains process-oriented databases on (1) the provision of technical assistance (contact database), (2) sponsorship of or participation in events such as conferences, trainings, workshops, and meetings (event database), and (3) products that have been developed (product database). Data on the immediate or short-term outcomes of selected CAPT events are collected by pretests and/or posttest questionnaires. The dimensions assessed differ across CSAP's CAPTs and by event, but some common measures of satisfaction are used. Data on long-term outcomes—changes in the way the business of prevention is conducted at the state or local or other levels—is recorded in the contact database. Recently, a separate outcome database was designed to collect more detailed information. An array of additional methods is used by the individual CAPTs: face-to-face interviews, phone interviews, focus groups, and facilitated discussions.

Overall, the data collected by CSAP's CAPTs to date are largely descriptive. Accordingly, synoptic analyses have been used to extract lessons learned for this paper. There are a number of inferential problems that arise in drawing conclusions about outcomes from the data collected by CSAP's CAPTs. We will discuss these in more detail below. Despite these inferential problems, a number of useful lessons can be extracted from first three years of CAPT operation. We will present these lessons under four main headings:

- Motivating the field to embrace a science-based approach to prevention planning, implementation, and evaluation.
- Promoting application of these approaches.
- Supporting the ongoing implementation of these approaches in day-to-day prevention practice.
- Other lessons.

## Motivating the Field

As noted earlier, the social marketing perspective teaches that successful packaging and marketing of science-based prevention requires gaining the attention of target audiences and capturing their interest—positioning the innovation so that it will stand out from all the other programs and strategies that are marketed to prevention policy makers and practitioners. The social marketing perspective also teaches that successful diffusion of innovations in the health field requires a nuanced understanding of targets' aspirations, needs, preferences, values, and budgets.

***Lesson 1: Diffusion Activities Must Stand Out from the Surrounding Noise.*** We have taken several steps to make CSAP's CAPTs' diffusion activities stand out from the "noise" created by all these competing materials. First, we have amplified our message by using the terms "science-based," "effective prevention," and "best practices" as often as possible when communicating with our constituents (over a third of the products available on the CAPTUS.ORG Website contains one or more of these phrases in the title). As commercial advertisers well know, repetition is the single most important determinant of message memorability. Second, we have taken a narrow focus in many of our sponsored activities. For example, the regional summits that constituted a major activity of the first contract year focused on science-based environmental strategies. Such focus allows participants an immersion experience in a specific topic rather than the usual roster of speakers and workshops on different topics.

Most important, we have emphasized face-to-face contact as a major vehicle for disseminating information to states, U.S. territories, and community-based organizations. This diffusion strategy is further discussed under *Promoting Application.*

***Lesson 2: Regionalization Facilitates Effective Packaging and Marketing of Science-based Prevention.***      Aspirations, needs, perceptions, values, and budgets for prevention vary immensely in the U.S. and its territories. For example, local attitudes towards alcohol control policies are generally more favorable in politically conservative areas (Wagenaar, 2000) and less favorable in resort areas, areas whose economies are dependent on alcohol production, or areas where alcohol use is a part of ethnic heritage or local tradition. Similarly, neighborhood watch programs may be easier to introduce into communities where police-community relations are historically positive than in areas where these relations are strained. Thus, packaging and marketing strategies for science-based prevention must also be diverse.

Regionalization of CSAP's CAPT system has facilitated specific responses to regional challenges—e.g., independent attitudes in many Western states and underage individuals

---

BOX 3

## You Can't Teleconference without Telephones

Teleconferencing, videoconferencing, and other distance learning technologies have become a popular and effective method for disseminating science-based prevention. For example, a "Moving Research to Practice" interactive videoconference was developed and implemented by Central CAPT for the Iowa Single State Agency. Evaluations indicated this training built strong capacity among the Iowa prevention training network.

Applying the same technology in the Pacific Jurisdictions would have been difficult, if not impossible. Phone lines are unpredictable and service is far from universal. In addition, our experience taught us that Pacific Islanders expect and value face-to-face contact. Accordingly, the Western CAPT staff flew to Guam and facilitated a training of trainers event. Evaluations of the training were overwhelmingly positive.

Here, two very different dissemination methods were dictated by the needs and practical constraints of the recipients. Both were successful because the CAPTs understood these needs and constraints and responded to them.

crossing the U.S./Mexican border to drink. Despite these important regional issues, the regions themselves are also highly diverse. For example, the Southeast CAPT includes the high-tech corridor of northern Virginia, the dry counties of Kentucky, the offshore islands of the Carolinas, and the Caribbean/Latino culture of Puerto Rico. The Central CAPT includes the cosmopolitan Twin Cities, the coal-mining towns of West Virginia, Big Ten towns such as Madison, Ann Arbor, and Bloomington, and the Red Lake Nation. However, this diversity is much more manageable than is the diversity of the entire nation. Thus, CSAP's CAPTs have succeeded in addressing diversity to an extent not possible for a national technical assistance and training system. Just as commercial marketers segment consumer groups, CSAP's CAPTs have been able to segment the prevention "market" and develop specific appeals for specific audiences.

***Lesson 3: CSAP's CAPTs Should Serve as Consumer's Reports of Prevention.***    Prevention is a growth industry with a variety of products competing for the attention of policy makers and practitioners. Some of these products are aggressively marketed even though they lack scientific evidence of effectiveness.

   CSAP's CAPTs have served as a "Consumer Reports" for prevention policy makers and practitioners. That is, we strive to educate our constituents to make them more savvy consumers of prevention products, to assist them in identifying misleading claims, and to direct them to programs and strategies that are worthy of further investigation. CAPT publications, such as *Science-Based Prevention Primer*, *What Is Scientifically Defensible Prevention?*, *Selecting and Implementing Appropriate Prevention Programs*, and *Using Science-Based Prevention*, reflect this orientation.

***Lesson 4: Science Should Not Be "Oversimplified" for States and Communities.***
An enduring American myth holds that science is too complex and arcane to be understood by anyone but scientists. Thus, there is a common expectation that practitioners must be provided overly simplified versions of scientific findings to ensure easy understanding. However, as Greer (1987) reminds us, there is little to be gained by the belief that "practitioners are merely slow scientists." In fact, the result of such an orientation is to lend credence to the belief among many practitioners that scientists are disconnected from the realities of agencies and communities.

   In our experience, practitioners want science and understand science. When failures to understand occur, we believe that the fault is usually not with the subject matter or the audience. It is with the way the materials are presented. Most prevention science articles in journals are written by scientists for scientists. By contrast, we have found it possible to package complex arguments (e.g., the scientific rationale for environmental prevention strategies) in ways that assume no particular science background. Rather, we try to adopt the perspective of the audience and anchor scientific concepts to everyday experience, define terms as we go along, and present numerous familiar examples. In other words, we follow the long-standing tradition of packaging science education for the interested lay person as reflected in the Smithsonian Institution's Associate Program, the PBS *Nova* television series, and the many best-selling books for general audiences written by eminent scientists. Our experience suggests that policy makers, practitioners, and concerned scientists expect CSAP's CAPTs to provide science-based prevention information in accessible formats, which can be used easily by states and communities as they work to integrate this information into their prevention efforts.

***Lesson 5: Computer Technology Is Promising, but Has Limitations.***    The prevention field has done an excellent job of putting computer technology to work. From PREVLINE (www.health.org) to PreventionDSS (*www.preventiondss.org*) to e-mail newsletters and distance mentoring, computer technology has been used to expand the reach, scope, speed, and interactivity of information diffusion. The Northeast CAPT, for instance, has completed state-level interviews and local level surveys, in preparation for developing an online course for practitioners; the findings suggest a high level of interest in using a Web environment for learning and for an exchange of ideas.

In our enthusiasm for these new technologies, CSAP's CAPTs remain mindful of the digital divide, not only among private citizens, but among providers as well. While taking advantage of the unique benefits of electronic information transfer, CSAP's CAPTs strive to utilize a variety of other communication channels to reach the small but significant segment of our colleagues who do not have electronic access.

Moreover, it is not yet clear the extent to which electronic information dissemination is successful. A 1996 study by Wallingford and colleagues (Wallingford et al., 1996) of 300 National Institute of Medicine computer-based outreach programs found marginal rates of penetration into the healthcare provider community. Kanouse et al. (1995) studied the use of various health databases by providers. Most users relied on the databases to answer specific questions. Browsing or other searching to gather new information or to stay current was rare, reducing the probability of encountering any information for which users were not specifically looking. Allowing that comfort with and acceptability of on-line databases has increased in recent years, these two studies and others like them suggest that the power of computer technology as a dissemination tool should not be assumed.

It also must be recognized, however, that, in some areas, telecommunications technology is the *only practical method* by which ongoing information transfer and technical assistance can occur. These areas include remote Native Alaskan villages, numerous frontiers in the Territories, continental U.S. towns isolated by geography or weather, and so on. Ironically, of course, these are the areas that may be least likely to have access to modern communications and computer technologies.

The same issues have been faced in providing such areas with specialty medical care. Telemedicine practitioners have developed numerous technologies to bring telecommunications to the remote areas they serve. These same technologies could be explored to open paths of ongoing communication between CSAP's CAPTs and communities with limited communications access.

## Promoting Application

Promoting application of science-based prevention involves two interdependent processes. First, targets must conclude that a given program, policy, or strategy is a good idea and superior to current practices. Second, they must decide to try the new approach. As is the case for packaging and marketing, the chances of adoption are increased when targets believe that the disseminators understand their specific circumstances (cultural, disciplinary, sectorial) and when the innovation is consistent with the current operation of the systems into which it will be introduced. The dissemination literature also suggests the importance of local reinvention, allowing targets to customize strategies and their implementation to meet local needs and constraints.

*Lesson 1: Face-to-Face Contact Is One Important Avenue for Promoting Application.* Face-to-face contact is one extremely effective way to get a message across. A brochure, article, or booklet can be thrown out, a videotape can be ignored, and a Website can be skimmed and exited. By contrast, a person sitting across the desk or table is hard to ignore. In addition, there is no substitute for the give and take that occurs in a face-to-face meeting—questions can be answered, concerns addressed, and the process of tailoring interventions to local needs can be initiated. Face-to-face contact is also labor-intensive and expensive, and may not be an efficient strategy with some communities.

As noted earlier, the success of person-to-person contact relies heavily on the relationship between the change agent and the target. The change agent must demonstrate a nuanced understanding of the circumstances and culture of the community, its values and beliefs, its readiness for change, and its concerns and anxieties.

Equally important, the change agent must understand the sectorial concerns of the practitioners and professionals who are being asked to adopt new strategies. If a family-based early intervention strategy is to be implemented, the change agent must fully understand the philosophy and operational characteristics of the agencies that will participate. Similarly, if a new school policy is recommended, the change agent must be thoroughly familiar with existing policies and discipline procedures.

*Lesson 2: Use Networking as a Vehicle for Promoting Application.* Social support can be a key factor in facilitating application. Such support assists individuals in addressing the concerns and anxieties that often exist when trying something new, different, and potentially risky (Backer 1991a, 1991b). Several of CSAP's CAPTs have established "learning communities" to facilitate networking among communities and practitioners who are working to adopt science-based prevention. For example, CSAP's Southeast CAPT sponsors attendance at national prevention events for four or five individuals from different parts of the Southeast region. The CAPT then supports conference calls that allow these individuals to continue to exchange ideas, offer mutual support, and so on. CSAP's Southwest CAPT works with the various sectors in its region through one-day learning community meetings attended by representatives from demand reduction funding streams (e.g., juvenile justice, public/highway safety, single state agency, National Prevention Network, governor's office, and education). Often these representatives also serve on the Southwest CAPT's regional coordinating council, which meets following the learning community sessions. These sessions help to build long-term, one-to-one linkages between various state offices as well as linkages between similar offices across states.

*Lesson 3: Proceed Incrementally.* For many states, agencies, and communities, adopting science-based approaches is a complex challenge because of factors such as organizational capacity, resistance to changes in prevailing practice, and funding constraints. If our message is understood as, "give up everything you are currently doing and substitute a wholly different approach," the message is likely to be rejected. We have found it very important to allow policy makers, practitioners, and concerned citizens to "get their feet wet" by beginning with a science-based strategy that is nonthreatening, easy to implement, and low in cost. In some cases, the first step may be to provide materials or technical assistance to introduce science-based components into existing efforts. Several CSAP CAPT products can facilitate such initial steps (e.g., the Western CAPT's *Seven Steps to Building an Effective Prevention Program,* the Central CAPT's *Effective Prevention Programs Database,* and the Northeast CAPT's *Science-Based Prevention Strategies*).

In other cases, initial steps may focus on assisting policy makers, practitioners, or concerned citizens in entering a new prevention area (e.g., social policy). For example, citizen action groups can begin to address social norms by surveying the "pro-alcohol" messages in their communities that appear to be directed at people under age 21 (e.g., point of sale advertising, industry sponsorship of community events, promotions on college campuses). Such an activity is very low cost, serves as an awareness-raising function, and can function as a needs assessment for action planning. Similarly, a community wishing to implement a program to strengthen families can begin by establishing a multisectorial work group to review available model programs for consistency with community norms, cultural appropriateness, and feasibility with available resources. Such a program review can assist in establishing a common understanding of prevention goals, team building across sectors, and the development of broad ownership of the program initiative.

***Lesson 4: Address Systems Issues.***   The dissemination literature speaks clearly on the need to address systems issues. Several studies have described dissemination failures in healthcare even when policy makers and practitioners are strongly committed to adopting an innovation. Here the source of resistance is the system into which the innovation is introduced (see, for example, Cook et al., 1997).

We have perhaps learned more about dealing with system issues than about any other area. These lessons include the need to:

- *Establish Communication Linkages Among System Actors*—Science-based prevention strategies are typically multisectorial—that is, they require participation from multiple state and community agencies and organizations. For many policy makers and practitioners, communication, cooperation, and coordination across sectorial boundaries will be a new experience. One important function of the coalitions that now exist in many communities is to facilitate intersectorial communication and to provide an opportunity for system actors to learn about one another's goals, priorities, methods of operation, and constraints.
- *Prepare the System before Change Is Introduced*—Most science-based prevention strategies attempt to change systems—families, schools, enforcement, and whole communities. Any weekend gardener knows that even carefully tended seeds will fail to grow if we do not prepare the soil before we plant. Similarly, innovations fail when the system is not prepared to adapt to them. Characteristically, change in any part of a system affects all components of the system, so all components need to be considered in preparing to introduce an innovation. This means that all affected agencies, organizations, and individuals must be on board. For example, it is counterproductive to

BOX 4

## Nothing Succeeds Like Success

As a result of the Illinois SIG effort to improve the state prevention system and put evidence-based practices at the foundation of that system, the state's Bureau of Substance Abuse Prevention redirected block funding toward evidence-based prevention. Providers receiving block grant funds are required "to spend 40% of their time implementing research-based prevention models." Providers also choose from a menu of outcomes to measure their prevention efforts. Research-based model programs have been incorporated into the training plan of state-supported training and resource center.

establish student assistance programs if community agencies have not been prepared to handle increased caseloads. Equally important, any conflicts between the innovation and the goals and priorities of affected agencies, organizations, and individuals must be addressed, as must any required changes in the system's structure.

- *Establish the Availability of Needed Resources*—Some science-based prevention efforts require new resources to be implemented. These resources may be needed to acquire equipment (e.g., cell phones for neighborhood watch programs), for personnel (e.g., youth workers for an after-school supervised recreation program), or for training (e.g., to assist coaches and other school personnel in preventing steroid use among student athletes). Sometimes, needed resources can be acquired through donations (e.g., cell phones from a local provider). In other cases, however, the resources must be developed or leveraged in order to support the new approach. However they are obtained, these resources are an absolute necessity for successful adoption. The best intentions will not substitute for needed personnel, equipment, and training.

To deal with systems issues, CSAP's Northeast CAPT conducted a regional summit in which they employed a series of activities and tools specifically designed to enable state teams to design action plans that allowed them to focus on science-based prevention strategies overall and collaboration as a strategy in particular.

## Supporting Ongoing Application

The ultimate goal of our dissemination efforts is, of course, to foster ongoing implementation of science-based prevention strategies in the states and territories we serve. The early history of prevention witnessed a procession of passing fads and changing priorities as practitioners and policy makers searched for workable solutions to a seemingly intractable problem. Now that science-based solutions are becoming available, our challenge is to encourage, nurture, and support their application over time.

As noted by Holder (1999), those science-based strategies that rely on changes in policies may be the easiest to sustain over time. Establishment of policies requires a one-time effort (albeit an intensive effort in many cases) rather than the year-to-year effort needed to sustain, for example, a media campaign. Even with decaying compliance and enforcement over time, some policies (e.g., the minimum legal drinking age) have demonstrated residual effects.

Most new initiatives first take hold tenuously. People committed to trying the initiative may not be committed to its continued implementation, continued funding may be contingent on the success of a "pilot program," and naysayers may be watching for the first indication of problems. For all these reasons, we believe that significant attention must be given to fostering and supporting ongoing implementation and to building sustainability into the initiatives we catalyze or support. We are beginning to learn how to meet this challenge.

CSAP's Southeast CAPT is developing a highly detailed logic model for sustaining prevention initiatives. This model directs attention to the importance of addressing sustainability issues at multiple levels—the strategy itself, the organization that houses or sponsors the strategy, the community, and the state. The model includes strategy-specific issues (e.g., appropriateness to target population needs, fidelity of implementation, and person power development), institutional issues (e.g., creating an institutional "home" for prevention, creating institutional support for the specific strategy), resource issues (e.g., ensuring multiple funding streams), and communications/advocacy issues (e.g., developing prevention "champions" at the organizational, community, and state levels). Here, we present some specific lessons derived from the work of the Southeast and other of CSAP's CAPTs in the area of sustainability.

***Lesson 1: Help Policy Makers, Practitioners, and Concerned Citizens Anticipate Barriers.***   One important component of supporting ongoing implementation is helping policy makers, practitioners, and concerned citizens anticipate barriers. We now have enough experience with implementing science-based prevention that we can anticipate some of the obstacles that are likely to arise as specific strategies take hold in states and communities. These obstacles include difficulties in recruiting and sustaining the interest of participants in parenting programs, peer educator programs, neighborhood initiatives, and community coalitions; resistance from retail alcohol and tobacco outlets who may feel "blamed" for what they perceive as a problem with individual users; competition from other pressing problems in the community, state, or territorial agenda; difficulty in achieving the policy or regulatory changes needed to support many environmental strategies; and problems sustaining enforcement. Obstacles may also be encountered from individuals with a vested interest in traditional ways of doing things and from those concerned that the community's image will suffer if substance-related problems are discussed openly. Useful introductions to these and other barriers are found in CSAP's *Environmental Strategies: Putting Theory into Practice* (a video and CD-ROM resource package), in CSAP's Border CAPT's *Selecting and Adapting Programs: Does It Fit* guide addressing cultural issues, and in CSAP's Southwest CAPT's *Planning for Change: A Systems Model for Communities and Organizations,* addressing change theories and methods.

We have found that the most effective way to deal with barriers is to assist policy makers, practitioners, and concerned citizens in considering what these might be and how they can be addressed. In other words, an analysis of potential barriers should be a part of strategic planning. CSAP's Northeast CAPT's video on enforcement provides one relevant example. Considering barriers in strategic planning allows some barriers to be addressed proactively—e.g., those from whom resistance is anticipated can be brought into the planning process to air their concerns and negotiate ways to address them. Other barriers can be anticipated and strategies can be developed to deal with them—e.g., resources can be set aside for stepped-up outreach to parents in the later years of a parenting initiative. This sort of planning helps avoid the usual "damage control" approach that is required when problems arise.

As elsewhere, face-to-face discussions have been helpful in facilitating strategic planning to address barriers. Thus, technical assistance has been one vehicle of choice for this activity. A related strategy has been to link new adopters with communities that have successfully implemented a particular science-based prevention strategy.

***Lesson 2: Help Policy Makers, Practitioners, and Concerned Citizens Anticipate "Spin-off" Effects.*** Precisely because most science-based prevention strategies affect systems, they can have unintended spin-off effects. For example, effective parenting education or early intervention programs may increase demand for assessment and counseling services. Similarly, zero blood-alcohol content (BAC) tolerance laws for underage drivers may increase the burden on prosecutors, courts, and corrections. These spin-off effects complicate the task of sustaining science-based prevention—effective efforts may fall victim to their own successes.

As is the case with barriers, these unintended spin-off effects can be anticipated as part of strategic planning. Policy makers, practitioners, and concerned citizens should be encouraged to make a systemwide analysis of the potential spin-off effects of any new initiative. This analysis should examine possible effects on individuals, agencies, and organizations beyond those that are directly and immediately involved or affected. Community coalitions are an excellent vehicle for this assessment, as representatives of most relevant systems actors should be members.

***Lesson 3: Provide Ongoing Technical Assistance Tailored to Changing Needs.*** At one time, prevention technical assistance (TA) was commonly viewed as a one-shot activity aimed at solving specific problems. Although there is still a need for such TA, today's science-based prevention strategies tend to develop over time in phases and stages (see, for example, CSAP's *Decision Support System*). Thus, we believe that technical assistance should be a planned and ongoing collaboration between CSAP's CAPTs, the State TA contract, as well as the Model Programs Dissemination Initiative and the states, territories, and organizations we serve. In particular, our experience suggests that a portion of technical assistance resources should be reserved for the implementation phase when additional support can mean the difference between a sustainable innovation and one that decays or disappears.

## Other Lessons

We have learned a number of other lessons that do not fit comfortably into any given category. We offer them here.

BOX 5

# What Comes Around Goes Around

Scientists did not develop many science-based prevention innovations. Rather, the innovations originated with policy makers, practitioners, and concerned citizens in the field. From the earliest alternative programs to the currently ubiquitous community coalition movement, the "science-to-practice bridge" has really been a bridge from practice to science.

We are an "experimenting society," endlessly creative in our search for solutions to social problems. As Donald Campbell (1975) pointed out a quarter century ago, trying out solutions is not enough—we must also "retain, imitate, modify, or discard them on the basis of apparent effectiveness on the multiple imperfect criteria available" (p. 71). A bridge from practice to science will help ensure that the myriad promising innovations developed in states and communities come to the attention of those with the training and resources to evaluate and disseminate them.

*Lesson 1: The Bridge between Science and Practice Is a Two-way Street.* As disseminators of science-based prevention, CSAP's CAPTs demonstrate the feasibility of creating a bridge between science and practice. Although the bridge metaphor is apt (there is, after all, a sometimes impassable divide between the world of the researcher and the world of the practitioner), we are struck by the consistency with which the bridge in this metaphor is assumed to carry one-way traffic only. That is, innovation flows from scientist to practitioner. Greer (1987) and Ferguson (1995) have noted a similar belief in healthcare generally—i.e., that science and practice form a hierarchy, with practitioners taking directives from researchers.

Our experience suggests that the bridge between science and practice is and must be a two-way street—that is, new knowledge must flow from practitioners to scientists as well as the reverse. First, policy makers, practitioners, and concerned citizens can supply invaluable information about the changing needs of communities. For example, NIDA's Community Epidemiology Work Group uses local informants in metropolitan areas to gather current descriptive information regarding the nature and patterns of drug abuse, emerging trends, characteristics of vulnerable populations, and social and health consequences. Second, policy makers, practitioners, and concerned citizens can alert researchers to indigenous innovations that warrant scientific assessment of effectiveness. Finally, closing the loop between researchers and practitioners can speed the process of refining innovations and developing alternative versions that fit the needs, values, and resources of the diverse communities we serve.

*Lesson 2: CSAP's CAPTs Can Increase Their Value to the Field through Developing Areas of Emphasis.* CSAP's CAPTs were designed to fulfill the role of well-qualified generalists. However, because CAPT services respond to the needs of their regions, and because these needs differ, each CAPT has developed selected areas of emphasis. For example, CSAP's Western CAPT has developed expertise in workforce development,

CSAP's Central and Northeast CAPTs in social marketing, CSAP's Southeast CAPT in sustainability, CSAP's Southwest CAPT in program planning and evaluation, and CSAP's Border CAPT in adaptation and cultural issues. The evolution of different areas of emphasis is value added for CSAP, its CAPT system, and for the field. The knowledge resources of any given CAPT are resources that can be brokered for the target population of any other CAPT. Such sharing, in turn, increases the efficiency and effectiveness of all CSAP's CAPTs in meeting the needs of their regions.

### Lesson 3: CSAP's CAPTs Must Remain Flexible to Meet the Needs of the Field.

The speed with which our field has changed and evolved is clear to all who have been involved in prevention for any length of time. Today, we have a sophisticated and established system of prevention epidemiology, service development, and delivery with national coordination and regional and state support. Undergraduates can take courses and even major in prevention, and masters and doctoral dissertations on prevention topics are commonplace. Today, rich epidemiologic information is available from a variety of sources, etiologic studies number in the hundreds, and theoreticians engage in productive debates concerning the best models to synthesize and explain the data. Prevention scientists have their own journals, conferences, and professional societies. And many of today's policy makers, practitioners, and concerned citizens are effectively promoting the scientific rationales for the strategies they adopt.

The rate of evolution in prevention shows no signs of slowing. Indeed, recent infusions of resources by both federal agencies and private foundations will likely catalyze even greater development and stimulate even more change. Accordingly, CSAP's CAPTs cannot be static if we are to keep up with the field we serve. Rather, we must remain flexible to meet changing needs and to support the many new innovations and initiatives that will doubtless emerge. This flexibility will require our own willingness and preparedness to adapt. It will also require CSAP to promote and support the development of mechanisms that will allow CSAP's CAPTs as well as the CSAP State Technical Assistance contract and the Model Programs Dissemination Initiative to make course corrections as dictated by the emerging needs of the field.

### Lesson 4: Outcome Evaluation of CSAP's CAPTs Presents Significant Challenges.

We clearly recognize the need for outcome evaluation of CSAP's CAPTs' activities. We expect of ourselves no less accountability than we expect from state or local programs. We have learned, however, that attempting an outcome evaluation of an initiative like CSAP's CAPTs is a challenging enterprise with many pitfalls.

Some of these challenges are conceptual. The dissemination literature makes clear that the adoption and implementation of a given science-based prevention strategy will result from a complex interaction among factors associated with the intervention itself, the way the intervention is packaged and disseminated, the target audience, and the context in which the target audience operates. Such multicomponent systems are not studied easily with traditional experimental approaches and appropriate alternatives are only now being explored. In addition, CSAP's CAPTs are one of numerous change agents that are currently promoting science-based prevention. From a dissemination perspective, these multiple message channels are highly desirable. However, they significantly increase the difficulty of making causal inferences about the isolated effects of CSAP's CAPT activities.

For all these reasons, we believe that expectations for outcome evaluation of CSAP's CAPTs should be modest. Again, this is not to say that such studies are not needed. Rather, we wish to highlight the need for a tight focus in any study (or series of studies) we undertake.

## Summary of Lessons Learned

Perhaps the most succinct summary of the lessons we have learned in the first three years of operating CSAP's CAPTs is this:

> Science-based strategies are the beginning, but only the beginning, of increasing the effectiveness of prevention efforts in states, territories, and communities. In order for these strategies to realize their potential, CSAP's CAPTs and other similar initiatives must develop solutions to a variety of problems in dissemination, implementation, and sustainability.

Building a better mousetrap is not enough. Considerable effort, ingenuity, and persistence are necessary in order to catalyze and sustain its use.

# The Future

Much remains to be done in developing approaches to the promotion of science-based prevention. We have a considerable body of research and experience to guide our efforts. But we must continue the task of applying this knowledge to the specific circumstances of our field. There are considerable gaps in our knowledge of:

- Current levels of adoption of science-based prevention.
- The most important factors that promote adoption in different kinds of state and community settings.
- The extent to which various strategies can be reinvented locally while still maintaining their integrity and effectiveness.
- The most effective ways to package and market prevention innovations.
- The best ways to support long-term implementation.

The diffusion literature suggests that progress in these areas will occur not only through research, but also through the accretion and compilation of practical experience. The current paper provides one such compilation. Many others should be published and we invite other SAMHSA, NIDA, and NIAAA grantees and contractors to follow our lead in sharing their experiences.

There are still gaps in our knowledge of workable strategies for conducting the kinds of outcome evaluations that will assist in answering specific diffusion-related questions. These gaps are endemic in social science, and solutions are being explored in a variety of disciplines. For the moment, systematic descriptive studies and highly focused outcome studies (e.g., comparisons of various adaptations of the same intervention) seem most likely to yield usable information.

Considerable professionalization has occurred in prevention, and today's prevention professionals are much more sophisticated than they were decades ago. But, a more highly skilled prevention workforce is needed to implement the increasingly sophisticated innovations that are becoming available. One mechanism for accomplishing this goal is a national Substance Abuse Prevention Specialist Training adapted by CSAP's National CAPT System from the curriculum originally developed by its Western CAPT and modified from the Prevention Generalist Training curriculum developed by the State of Colorado. Another is the on-line course offered by CSAP's Northeast CAPT. Other mechanisms include the summer schools and institutes sponsored in several states, emphasis on training at national meetings and conferences, Web-based instruction, and the development of prevention curriculum content for undergraduates and for graduate programs in the health professions, social work, clinical psychology, public administration, and related areas.

Finally, there are emerging national trends that present both opportunities and challenges. Perhaps first among these is the new White House Office of Faith-Based and Community Initiatives. The new office and the regulations that accompany it remove barriers in terms of the funding and level of involvement of faith-based organizations in human services. CSAP has long understood the need to involve the faith community in prevention and many faith-based organizations and spirituality-based approaches may be found in CSAP's portfolio. Thus, CSAP's CAPTs are well positioned to assist in ensuring that new prevention initiatives of faith-based organizations are also science-based.

The nation is also in the middle of major decisions concerning how tobacco settlement money will be spent. Wide-ranging and legitimate arguments have been forwarded for using this money for long-term care of chronic disease sufferers, for smoking cessation, for prevention, or simply to reimburse general state coffers for past smoking-related costs. We believe that CSAP's CAPTs can inform this debate by offering evidence that prevention works and by demonstrating the cost-effectiveness of prevention when compared to other possible uses of new revenues.

Finally, CSAP's CAPTs can assist prevention practitioners in adapting to a changing healthcare system. CSAP has made major contributions to establishing the role of prevention in new forms of delivery such as managed care and workplace health programs. Yet much remains to be done, in part, because the medical marketplace continues to change in ways that contradict even the recent predictions of soothsayers and pundits. As proponents of science-based prevention, we are also proponents of evidence-based practice, accountability, results orientation, and cost-consciousness. Thus, the approach of CSAP's CAPTs matches that of all responsible health-reform and cost-containment models, and thus provides a resource for prevention practitioners who wish to compete successfully in the new medical marketplace.

Overall, we have come very far and still have far to go. Our discipline is developing, growing, and maturing at a rapid rate. We believe that CSAP's CAPTs and other similar initiatives have both stimulated and focused this growth. We will continue to share our lessons learned as the years pass, and we encourage other knowledge development and application programs to share their experiences also. Our shared understanding of the dissemination of prevention innovations is, itself, an important component of science-based prevention.

# NOTES

1. This paper is a work in progress. Future revisions are planned that will further refine and expand the discussions presented in this version.
2. Some may find the term "target" a bit dehumanizing as a gloss for CSAP's CAPTs' various target audiences. We mean no disrespect, but rather use "target" as an efficiency and as a term of art in diffusion and marketing science.
3. One prototype for face-to-face diffusion—academic detailing—uses physicians as face-to-face communicators to other physicians. This approach facilitates the development of a trusting relationship between the change agent and the target.

# REFERENCES

Atkin, C., and Arkin, E. Issues and initiative in communication health information. In: Atkin, C., & Wallack, L., eds. *Mass Communication and Public Health.* Newbury Park, NJ: Sage Publication, 1990. pp. 13–40.

Backer, T.E. Drug Abuse Technology Transfer. (DHHS Publication No. (ADM91-1764). Rockville, MD: National Institute on Drug Abuse, 1991a.

Backer, T.E. Knowledge utilization: The third wave. Knowledge: Creation, Diffusion, Utilization 1991b; 12:225–240.

Cambell, D.T. Reforms as experiments. In E. Struning and M. Guttentag, Eds., Handbook of Evaluation Research. Beverly Hill, CA: Sage Publications, 1975.

Cook, D.J., Greengold, N.L., Ellrodt, A.G., and Weingarten, S.R. The relation between systematic reviews and practice guidelines. *Ann Intern Med* 1997; 127:210–216.

Ferguson, J.H. The NIH consensus development program. *Jt Comm J Qual Improv* 1995; 21:332–336.

Giesbrecht, N., et al. Community-based prevention research to reduce alcohol-related problems. *Alcohol Health and Research World* 17(1):84–88, 1993.

Gorman, D.M. Do school-based social skills training programs prevent alcohol use among young people? *Addiction Research* 4(2):191–210, 1996.

Gorman, D.M. Irrelevance of evidence in the development of school-based drug prevention policy, 1986–1996. *Evaluation Review* 22(1):118–146, 1998.

Greer, A. The two cultures of biomedicine: Can there be consensus? *JAMA* 1987; 258(1):2739–2740.

Grube, J., and Nygaard, P. Adolescent drinking and alcohol policy. *Contemporary Drug Programs,* in press.

Haynes, R.B. Some problems in applying evidence in clinical practice. *Ann N Y Acad Sci* 1993; 703:210–224.

Holder, H.D. Prevention aimed at the environment. In: McCrady, B.S. & Epstein, E.E., eds. *Addictions: A Comprehensive Guidebook.* New York, NY: Oxford University Press, 1999. pp. 573–594.

Kanouse, D., Kallich, J., and Kahan, J. Dissemination of effectiveness and outcomes research. *Health Policy* 1995; 34:167–192.

Klitzner M. The Diffusion of Clinical Guidelines and Practice Innovations. Working paper, The CDM Group, Inc., 1999.

La Fond, C., Toomey, T., Manning, W., and Wagenaar, A., Policy evaluation research: Measuring the independent variables. *Evaluation Review* 24(1), 2000, 92–101.

Moskowitz, J.M. Primary prevention of alcohol problems: A critical review of the research literature. *Journal of Studies on Alcohol* 50(1):54–88, 1989.

Nardella, A., Pechet, L., and Snyder, L.M. Continuous improvement, quality control, and cost containment in clinical laboratory testing. Effects of establishing and implementing guidelines for preoperative tests. *Arch Pathol Lab Med* 1995; 119(6):518–522.

Rogers, E.M. Diffusion of Innovations (4th ed.) New York: Free Press, 1995.

Toomey, T.L., and Wagenaar, A.C. Policy options for prevention: The case of alcohol. *Journal of Public Health Policy* 20(2):192–213, 1999.

United States Preventive Services Task Force. Guide to Clinical Preventive Service: An Assessment of the Effectiveness of 169 Interventions. Baltimore, MD: Williams & Wilkins, 1989.

Wagenaar, A.C. Alcohol policies in the United States: Highlights from the 50 states. Cambridge, MA: Alcohol Epidemiology Program: November, 2000.

Walker, R.D., Howard, M.O., Lambert, M.D., and Suchinsky, R. Medical practice guidelines. *West J Med* 1994; 161:39–44.

Wallack, L. Mass media and health promotion: Promise, problem, and challenge. In: Atkin, C., and Wallack, L., eds. *Mass Communication and Public Health.* Newbury Park, NJ: Sage Publication, 1990a. pp. 41–51.

Wallack, L. Media advocacy and social marketing approaches. In: Atkin, C., and Wallack, L., eds. *Mass Communication and Public Health.* Newbury Park, NJ: Sage Publication, 1990b. pp. 147–163.

Wallingford, K.T., Ruffin, A., Ginter, K.A., Spann, M.L., Johnson, F.E., Dutcher, G.A., Mehnert, R., Nash, D.L., Bridgers, J.W., Lyon, B.J., Siegel, E.R., and Roderer, N.K. Outreach activities of the National Library of Medicine: A five-year review. *Bull Med Libr Assoc* 1996; 84(Suppl. 2):1–60.

Woolf, S.H., DiGuiseppi, C.G., Atkins, D., and Kamerow, D.B. Developing evidence-based clinical practice guidelines: Lessons learned by the US Preventive Services Task Force. *Annu Rev Public Health* 1996; 17:511–538.

# GLOSSARY

**ATOD**  acronym for alcohol, tobacco, and other drugs.

**abstract thought**  Maslow describes this as thinking that involves categorizing, classifying, and schematizing objects of thought in order to fit information about them into one's existing system of thought. This also involves screening out information that is incompatible with existing beliefs, not useful, frightening, or that does not fit within the confines of language.

**accommodation**  Piaget's term to describe the process of changing some thinking in order to cope with a new problem effectively. Accommodation occurs when new information cannot be assimilated because there are no existing schemata that match the new information. In other words, a conflict occurs between two beliefs, causing a need for a change in thinking.

**acculturation**  the transfer of culture from one ethnic group (typically to the dominant culture) to other groups that are newly arrived.

**addiction**  compulsion and a craving to use alcohol or other drugs regardless of negative or adverse consequences. Addiction is characterized by psychological dependence, and often (depending on the drug or drugs) physical dependence. An inability to set or maintain limits, resulting in loss of control, is also a characteristic of addiction. See also "Dependence."

**affective development**  Jean Piaget uses this to depict the development of feelings, interests, desires, tendencies, values, and emotions.

**alternative activities**  provides for the participation of target populations in activities that exclude drug use. The assumption is that because constructive and healthy activities offset the attraction to drugs, or otherwise meet the needs usually filled by drugs, they help the population to avoid using drugs.

**anabolic-androgenic steroid**  a steroid pharmacologically similar to testosterone that builds muscle and strength. It also induces male sexual characteristics.

**analgesic**  a drug that kills pain by changing the perception of pain rather than by deadening the nerves of an anesthetic wound.

**anxiolytics**  drugs used to treat anxiety disorders.

**archival data**  data that already exists.

**assimilation**  Piaget's term for the cognitive process of classifying and placing new information into existing schemata (a mental filing system for information).

**B-cognition**  Maslow's term for healthy, growth-based cognition. This is characterized by the urge to grow and learn, to risk failure and even ridicule in order to become more oneself.

**B-love**  Maslow's term for an unselfish love for the total being of another.

**basic needs**  in Maslow's terms, the needs one must meet before progressing to "growth" needs. Basic needs include safety, a sense of belonging to others, love, respect, and esteem. These are sometimes referred to as "deficiency" needs.

**best practices**  prevention strategies, activities, or approaches, which have been shown through research and evaluation to be effective in the prevention and/or delay of substance use or abuse.

**cannabinols**  the psychoactive cannabinoids of the cannabis plant.

**central nervous system depressants**  a psychoactive drug, such as alcohol or an opiate, that decreases the actions in the brain, resulting in depressed respiration, heart rate, muscle strength, and other functions.

**central nervous system stimulant**  any substance that forces the release of epinephrine and norepinephrine, the body's stimulants. They increase the electrical and chemical activity of the brain.

**channel**  the means by which a message is communicated.

**chemical dependence**  a term used to describe addiction to alcohol and/or other drugs and to differentiate this type of addiction from nonchemical addiction (e.g., gambling).

**club drugs**  a certain group of drugs that are most commonly used in "raves" or clubs.

**communication environment**  the time and place where communication occurs.

**community assessment**  a systematic process for examining the current conditions of a situation (such as substance abuse) and for identifying the level of risk and protection in the community.

**community-based processes**  aim to enhance the ability of the community to provide more effective prevention and treatment services for drug abuse disorders. Activities in this strategy include organizing, planning, enhancing the efficiency and effectiveness of service implementation, building coalitions, and networking.

**community norms** the attitudes toward and policies about drug use and crime that a community holds, which are communicated in a variety of ways: through laws and written policies, through informal social practices, and through the expectations that parents and other members of the community have of young people.

**community readiness** the extent to which a community is adequately prepared to implement a substance abuse prevention program.

**concrete operations** in Piaget's theory of development, this stage typically lasts from about age 7 to about age 11. Children in this stage are able to apply logical thought to concrete problems occurring in the present.

**concrete thought** Maslow describes this as thought that involves perceiving all aspects of an object as unique and completely disconnected from any other system of ideas. In this way, the object is perceived as whole, unique, and as more than "the sum of its parts."

**cultural competence** the ability to serve individuals and communities in ways that demonstrate understanding, caring, and valuing of the unique characteristics of those served, including the cultural differences and similarities within, among, and between groups.

**culture** the knowledge, experience, values, ideas, attitudes, skills, tastes, and techniques that are passed on from more experienced members of a community to new members.

**D-cognition** Maslow's term for cognition that is organized by basic needs. This is characterized by a fear of knowing and exploring.

**D-love** Maslow's term for selfish, unhealthy love.

**deep culture** characteristics that are invisible by simply seeing someone.

**delinquency** crimes committed by juveniles under 18.

**dependence** a recurrent or ongoing need to use alcohol, tobacco, or other drugs. Psychological dependence is the need to use alcohol, tobacco, or other drugs to think, feel, or function normally. Physical dependence exists when tissues of the body require the presence of alcohol, tobacco, or other drugs to function normally.

**designer drugs** drugs, formulated by street chemists, which are similar to controlled drugs.

**direct costs** those costs associated with the completion of the tasks, such as supplies, personnel, logistics (site costs, food, travel), and others.

**disequilibrium** Piaget's term describing an imbalance between assimilation and accommodation. This occurs when a new situation involves information that is incompatible with existing beliefs.

**downers** see "Central nervous system depressants."

**environmental strategy** this strategy establishes or changes written and unwritten community standards, codes, and attitudes, thereby influencing incidence and prevalence of substance abuse in the general population. This strategy is divided into two subcategories to permit distinction between activities that center on legal and regulatory initiatives and those that relate to the service and action-oriented initiatives.

**equilibration** Piaget's term denoting the process of moving from disequilibrium, when new information is incompatible with existing beliefs, to a balanced state of equilibrium.

**equilibrium** Piaget's term depicting assimilation and accommodation in balance, meaning that an individual can both draw on past experience and respond to changed circumstances with new ways of thinking.

**ethics** the rules and standards governing professional conduct.

**evaluation** systematic collection and use of program information for multiple purposes, including monitoring, program improvement, outcome assessment, planning, and policy making.

**evaluation method** the way that the evaluation information (data) is collected.

**external assets** factors that surround young people with the support, empowerment, boundaries, expectations, and opportunities that guide them to behave in healthy ways and to make wise choices.

**external evaluation** evaluation done by consultants or researchers not working for the same organization as the program.

**facilitator** person(s) who have been designated by group members to be the caretaker of the meeting process.

**feedback** verbal and nonverbal communication that occurs during and after a message has been sent.

**formal operations** Piaget's term to describe the stage beginning at about age 11 to 15 for many but not all people. Those with formal operations can apply logical reasoning to all classes of problems existing in the past, present, and future.

**framing the issue**   the way in which a story is presented has implications for the solution, by influencing the terms of the debate to reflect a policy change instead of an individual behavior.

**gateway drugs**   any drug that is believed to lead to the use of stronger psychoactive drugs, such as alcohol, tobacco, and marijuana.

**generativity**   a term Erikson created to describe the interest of those in middle age to establish and guide the next generation or to become creative and productive in other ways.

**grant maker**   those individuals, organizations, corporations, or governmental agencies that make a grant or contribution to others.

**growth needs**   Maslow's term for needs that involve motivation to obtain one's unique potential. This is done by developing talents that are unique to one's own destiny and by pursuing greater knowledge of the world and of one's own unique nature.

**guiding principles**   findings about effective prevention programs as identified through research.

**hallucinogens**   substances that produce hallucinations, often used interchangeably with the terms psychedelic, psychotomimetic, and psychotogenic.

**hearing**   the physiological process in which sound waves are transformed into auditory nerve impulses.

**hypnotics**   drugs that induce sleep.

**IOM**   acronym for Institute of Medicine.

**identity diffusion**   Erikson's concept exploring adolescents' experiences of doubt in their identity, specifically regarding ethnicity and sexuality.

**impacts**   usually used to refer to long-term impacts, these are the long-term or ultimate effects from a program.

**indicated**   those programs and strategies designed to target individuals at risk.

**indirect costs**   costs to the agency not directly related to completing tasks, such as payroll, accounting, space, equipment, and general project administration.

**information   dissemination**   provides information about the nature and extent of drug use, abuse, and addiction, and their effects on individuals, families, and communities. It also provides information on available prevention programs and services. The dissemination of information is characterized by one-way communication from the source to the audience, with limited contact between the two.

**information overload**   an overwhelming amount of information.

**inhalants**   any substance that is vaporized, misted, or gaseous that is inhaled and absorbed through the capillaries in the alveoli of the lungs.

**internal assets**   the commitments, values, competencies, and self-perceptions that must be nurtured within young people to provide them with "internal compasses" to guide their behaviors and choices.

**internal evaluation**   evaluation done by staff within the same organizational structure as a given program.

**intoxication**   state of being under the influence of alcohol, tobacco, or other drugs so that thinking, feeling, and/or behavior are affected ("high" is a slang word for intoxication).

**leadership**   the social influence in which one person is able to enlist the aid and support of others in the accomplishment of a common task.

**listening**   the process of paying close attention to, and making sense of, what is heard.

**logical-mathematical   knowledge**   Piaget's term to describe knowledge that derives from thinking about objects and events. This form of knowledge comes from the child and is not inherent in the objects themselves.

**logic model**   a flowchart or graphic display representing the logical connections between program activities and program goals.

**media access**   making contact with the media through press releases, press conferences, letters to the editor, guest editorials, telephone calls, or other means.

**media advocacy**   the strategic use of media to advance a social or public policy initiative.

**media analysis**   questions that consumers can ask in order to find the underlying message of alcohol and tobacco advertisements. These focus on separating into elements the persuasion techniques that are used in advertisements in order to understand media messages.

**media literacy**   the ability to access, analyze, and produce information for specific outcomes. The ability to "read" and produce media messages.

**Medicine Wheel**   a valuable teaching tool used in many Native American traditions. Stories are used to help others see and understand things that are difficult to understand because they are ideas or abstract concepts instead of physical objects. Often, stories of concrete, observable events in nature are used symbolically to represent the inner development of human beings and communities.

**message**   the general idea or theme that the sender is trying to communicate.

**minor tranquilizer**   a drug used to treat anxiety, an antianxiety medication.

**model programs**   prevention programs that have been rigorously evaluated and have repeatedly demonstrated positive outcomes.

**NIAAA**   acronym for the National Institute of Alcohol Abuse and Alcoholism.

**NIDA**   acronym for National Institute of Drug Abuse.

**noise**   any interference that impedes a message.

**ONDCP**   acronym for the Office of National Drug Control Policy.

**outcome**   usually referred to as short-term outcomes, ways in which the participants of a prevention program could be expected to change at the conclusion of the program (e.g., increases in knowledge, changes in attitudes or behavior, etc.).

**output**   the immediate products or activities of a program (e.g., the number of participants, number of hours of service).

**overdose**   the accidental or deliberate use of more of a drug than the body can handle, resulting in severe medical consequences including possible coma and death.

**participatory evaluation**   evaluation that involves key stakeholders in the design, data collection, and interpretation of evaluation methods.

**peak experience**   Maslow's term for a mystical or transcendental experience in which the individual feels valuable, sincere, expressive, good, intelligent, stronger, spontaneous, worthwhile, unself-conscious, creative, unique, and free of doubt and fears.

**physical knowledge**   Piaget's term for the knowledge of physical properties of objects and events, including size, shape, texture, and weight. The child learns about these properties by physically manipulating the object and taking in information through various senses.

**place**   the communication channel for a social marketing campaign.

**praxis**   the combination of both theory and practice.

**predictive theory**   a theory that empirically states that if certain conditions are present, a probable outcome may result.

**prevention**   although there is no single definition of prevention, there is general agreement among prevention professionals on the overall goal of prevention. It is to foster a climate in which

- Alcohol use is acceptable only for those of legal age and only when the risk of adverse consequences is minimal.

- Prescription and over-the-counter drugs are used only for the purposes for which they were intended.

- Other substances that can be abused (e.g., gasoline or aerosols) are used only for their intended purposes.

- Illegal drugs and tobacco are not used at all.

**prevention education**   involves two-way communication and is distinguished from merely disseminating information by the fact that it is based on an interaction between the educator and the participants. Activities under this strategy aim to affect critical life and social skills, including decision making, refusal skills, and critical analysis (e.g., of media messages).

**price**   what the consumer has to give up in order to achieve the benefits being offered in a social marketing campaign.

**problem identification and referral**   aims to identify those who have indulged in the illegal use of drugs in order to assess whether their behavior can be reversed through education. It should be noted, however, that this strategy does not include any activity designed to determine whether an individual is in need of treatment.

**process evaluation**   evaluation that is designed to document what programs actually do, detailing program activities, participants, resources, and other outputs.

**product**   a healthy behavior or a change in attitude that is being "sold" in a social marketing campaign.

**profession**   a vocation or occupation requiring advanced education and training, and involving intellectual skills, such as medicine, law, or teaching.

**promising approaches**   programs for which the level of certainty from available evidence is too low to support generalized conclusions, but for which there is some empirical basis for predicting that further research could support such conclusions.

**promotion**   the overall strategy or message that is used to persuade the target audience of a social marketing campaign.

**protective factors**   protective factors, identified by Hawkins and Catalano, counter risks; the more protective factors are present, the less is the risk. Protective factors fall into three basic categories: individual characteristics, bonding, and healthy beliefs and clear standards.

**psychedelic**   any drug that can induce illusions or hallucinations.

**psychoactive**   any substance that directly alters the normal functioning of the central nervous system when it is injected, ingested, smoked, snorted, or absorbed into the body.

**qualitative data** information that is reported in narrative form or which is based on narrative information, such as written descriptions of programs, testimonials, open-ended responses to questions, and so forth.

**quantitative data** information that is reported in numerical form, such as test scores, number of people attending, dropout rates, and so on.

**rave** a dance party where certain drugs are available that is usually held in warehouses, the desert, nightclubs, or outdoors.

**receiver** the person or people listening to the message from the sender sent through the channel.

**resiliency factors** Werner et al. contend that these are factors that protect or buffer people against social problems or risk factors.

**resource assessment** a systematic process for examining which community resources are already in place that addresses those risk and protective factors identified as priorities during the community assessment.

**risk factors** factors shown to increase the likelihood of adolescent substance abuse, teenage pregnancy, school drop-out, youth violence, and delinquency.

**SAMHSA** acronym for Substance Abuse and Mental Health Services Administration.

**schemata** (the plural of schema) Piaget's term for cognitive structures that allow individuals to organize the environment intellectually. Schemata provide a sort of invisible, intellectual filing system within the brain that can adapt and change as an individual develops cognitively.

**scientific rigor** the process of applying scientific principles to programs to prove overall effectiveness.

**sedatives** drugs that reduce anxiety and relax the body and mind.

**selective** those programs and strategies designed to target groups at risk.

**self-actualization** Maslow's term to describe the ultimate goal of his developmental theory, when one discovers self-fulfillment and realizes one's own unique potential.

**sender** the person delivering a message.

**sensory-motor stage** in Piaget's theory, this stage lasts from birth to approximately two years. During this period, infants "think" with their bodies, through action in which they attempt to affect their surroundings, such as sucking on various objects.

**social knowledge** Piaget's term describing knowledge that is agreed on by social groups in the environment regarding rules, laws, morals, values, ethics, and language systems. This knowledge evolves through children's social interactions with people and is necessary for developing concepts that are arbitrary, not concrete, such as "honesty" and "integrity."

**social marketing** the design, implementation, and control of programs calculated to influence the acceptability of social ideas, and involving considerations of product, planning, pricing, communication, distribution, and marketing research.

**social norms marketing** a strategy used to educate or communicate the healthy behaviors practiced by the majority of the public or a selected group.

**soft money** funds that exist for a limited period of time.

**speech anxiety** overwhelming nervousness about public-speaking situations.

**stakeholders** those people with an interest in the program and its evaluation (e.g., participants, funders, managers, people not served by the program community members).

**steroids** see "Anabolic-androgenic steroid."

**substance abuse** the continued use of alcohol, tobacco, and/or other drugs in spite of adverse consequences in one or more areas of an individual's life.

**substance misuse** the ingestion of alcohol or other drugs with the experience of negative consequences or any use of an illegal substance.

**substance use** the ingestion of alcohol or other drugs without the experience of any negative consequences.

**surface culture** characteristics that we can tell about someone by looking at them.

**survey data** data that is created.

**theory** a formulation of apparent relationships or underlying principles of certain observed phenomena, which has been verified to some degree.

**tolerance** requirements for increasing doses or quantities of alcohol, tobacco, or other drugs in order to create the same effects that were obtained from the original dose. Tolerance results from physical or psychological adaptations of the individual. "Cross-tolerance" refers to accompanying tolerance to other drugs from the same pharmacological group. For example, tolerance to alcohol results in tolerance to minor tranquilizers such as Xanax, even when the individual has never used Xanax. "Reverse tolerance" refers to a condition in which smaller quantities of a drug produce the same effects as did previous large doses.

**trigger word** intense words with positive or negative connotative meaning.

**universal** those programs and strategies designed to target the entire population of a community.

**unproven program/strategies**   programs and strategies that have been shown through research to be ineffective at preventing substance abuse.

**violence**   acts against a person or people that involve physical harm or the threat of physical harm.

**visual aid**   a model, poster, or other article used to enhance a speech pictorially.

**withdrawal**   physical and psychological effects that occur when drug-dependent individuals discontinue using alcohol, tobacco, or other drugs.

# INDEX